Judith Terstriep, Stefan Gärtner (eds.)
Wealth and the Ecological Transformation

New Economies | 7

Editorial

Our current economic systems are not geared towards the satisfaction of needs and the care for our environment and our fellow human beings, but solely towards growth and profit. The consequences of this are a constant reproduction of social inequalities along the axes of class, *race* and gender as well as the isolation of individuals and the destruction of nature.

The **New Economy** book series provides explanations for these multiple crises of our time and opens up possibilities for a sustainable, solidarity-based economy. It provides an editorial space for heterodox empirical research, paving the way for pluralistic, interdisciplinary and self-reflexive economics.

Judith Terstriep (Dr. rer. pol.) is Head of the Research Department 'Innovation, Space & Culture' at the Institute for Work and Technology at Westfälische Hochschule Gelsenkirchen and a lecturer at Ruhr-Universität Bochum. She has extensive experience in innovation research. Her primary research interests focus on the interplay of innovation, social relations, and knowledge from the perspectives of innovation studies, management, and spatial theory, contributing to just transitions and societal change.

Stefan Gärtner (Prof. Dr.) is managing director of the Institute for Work and Technology at Westfälische Hochschule Gelsenkirchen. There, he is responsible for the research focus Spatial Capital. His academic work concentrates on urban and regional economies as well as on forms of urban production. He completed both his studies and his doctorate at Technische Universität Dortmund.

Judith Terstriep, Stefan Gärtner (eds.)

Wealth and the Ecological Transformation

Interdisciplinary Perspectives on Reciprocal Dynamics

[transcript]

This project was financed with help of the Volkswagen-Foundation.

VolkswagenStiftung

Bibliographic information published by the Deutsche Nationalbibliothek
The Deutsche Nationalbibliothek lists this publication in the Deutsche Nationalbibliografie; detailed bibliographic data are available online at https://dnb.dnb.de

transcript Verlag | Hermannstraße 26 | D-33602 Bielefeld | live@transcript-verlag.de

Cover design: Maria Arndt
Printing: Elanders Waiblingen GmbH, Waiblingen
https://doi.org/10.14361/9783839424506
Print-ISBN: 978-3-8376-7534-4 | PDF-ISBN: 978-3-8394-2450-6
ISSN of series: 2942-1489 | eISSN of series: 2942-1497

Printed on permanent acid-free text paper.

Contents

Introduction—Navigating the Wealth-Ecology Nexus

Benedikt Pühmeyer, Inga Seiffert, Judith Terstriep & Stefan Gärtner

In public debate, the ecological transformation is often cast as a purely technological or regulatory undertaking; yet mounting evidence shows that its trajectory is inseparable from the distribution and composition of wealth (Chancel & Rehm, 2025; Chancel et al., 2024; Drupp et al., 2024; Markkanen & Anger-Kraavi, 2019). In this volume, wealth is understood as a multidimensional construct encompassing material assets (income, property, infrastructure), social and cultural capital (networks, skills, norms), institutional entitlements (legal protections, political voice), and spatial endowments (locational advantages and ecosystem services). These resources shape household carbon footprints, exposure to climate risks, and, crucially, the capacity of social groups, ventures, and regions to influence transition pathways. The interrelationship is reciprocal: decarbonization policies revalue certain assets, create new rent streams, and reorder labor demand, thereby reorganizing the very structure of wealth. If these redistributive effects remain unacknowledged, climate policy could entrench existing inequalities under a "green" veneer, undermining both legitimacy and effectiveness. Contemporary ecological emergencies are tightly interwoven with patterns of social inequality; yet dominant techno-economic paradigms in climate research and policy still frame these challenges mainly as issues of technological efficiency, thereby obscuring their inherently distributional dimensions (Bärnthaler, 2024; Sovacool et al., 2025).

To orient the discussion, the volume is organized around three guiding research questions:

a) How do wealth and ecological transformation co-evolve?
b) Which mechanisms perpetuate or mitigate the outcomes that emerge from this co-evolution?

c) Which policy instruments, ownership arrangements, and social practices can foster a just ecological transition that is both scientifically sound and sensitive to diverse local contexts?

The chapters that follow illustrate these reciprocal dynamics empirically, identify where current debates oversimplify them, and outline the research questions that structure this volume.

Amid the mutually reinforcing dynamics of wealth accumulation and ecological change, a critical question is how—and to what extent—wealth inequalities interact with several aspects of a just transition[1] toward a sustainable future (Bocksch, 2022; Chancel et al., 2023). This analysis proceeds from the assumption that ownership confers decision-making power and that high incomes accelerate carbon emissions through elevated consumption (Chancel et al., 2025; de Arce & Mahia, 2023). Moreover, it is assumed that transformative measures designed to mitigate or adapt to climate change can themselves reconfigure socioeconomic structures, including patterns of wealth distribution (Gazzotti et al., 2021). In this regard Chancel et al. (2025, 4) observe:

> "The remaining carbon budget for 1.5°C is nearly exhausted, with disastrous consequences for ecosystems and human livelihoods. At the same time, the world is marked by extreme wealth inequality, with the wealthiest 10% of the global population owning three quarters of all assets."

Building on this stark observation, while the global inequality estimates by Chancel et al. (2025) are indispensable for framing the debate, they can be critiqued for relying on incomplete or 'patchy' data—particularly because the wealth of the wealthiest households can only be approximated through model-specific assumptions. Sensitivity analyses show that alternative model assumptions (e.g., different Pareto parameters) can lead to substantially divergent results, highlighting the considerable uncertainty in widely cited statistics such as "the top 10% own X% of global wealth". Reliable microdata are exceptionally scarce in many countries, especially in the Global South (Davies et al., 2017), and historical as well as regionally comparative studies confirm that wealth distributions are highly context-dependent (Biewen et al., 2025).

1 Following Stark et al. (2023), "just transition", as employed here, refers to a decarbonization process that fairly shares benefits and burdens through inclusive participation of affected workers, communities, and regions.

Even where data exists, significant cross-country welfare gaps persist. While some studies indicate that partial global convergence in disposable income (Oxford University, 2016), the globally weighted Gini coefficient falls only when economic growth in poorer countries outpaces that of richer ones and wage convergence occurs; at the same time, within-country inequality continues to rise in many nations (Chrisendo et al., 2024). This pattern suggests that globalization may have enabled more people to participate meaningfully in consumption, even if the overall inequality remains pronounced, thereby contributing to increased CO_2 emissions. To illustrate the point, from a global perspective, a large share of the German population would fall within the top 10% of global income distribution.

Importantly, economic status is not the sole axis along which climate responsibility and vulnerability are distributed. Gender, race, age, and indigeneity intersect with wealth to shape exposure to environmental hazards, access to adaptation resources, and political voice. Accounting for these intersectional inequalities is therefore essential for designing climate policies that are both effective and socially legitimate.

The picture is therefore less straightforward than it might appear: A common sentiment when social dynamics in tackling climate change are reflected critically can be summarized as follows: If most of the carbon emissions are generated by the richest of the rich people, why would the rest of society invest so much effort in lowering the remaining emissions? Should policy not instead focus on reducing the luxury emissions of the wealthiest decile? Though this perspective appears reasonable at first glance, it risks oversimplification and neglects key mechanisms. It fails to adequately capture the reciprocal relationship between the forces driving transformation and the systems being transformed. Recognizing this limitation underscores the urgent need for a more nuanced understanding of how the process of ecological transformation interacts with society's socio-economic structure.

Public understandings of these intertwined issues are not formed in a vacuum. Instead, discourse on ecological transformation and just transition crystallizes through the dynamic interaction among technological affordances (e.g., social media, algorithms), legal-institutional constraints (e.g., speech and competition law), market incentives (e.g., advertising revenue, green finance), and prevailing social norms. This co-productive process determines which voices are amplified, whose interests prevail, and how distributive questions are framed—gaps the present anthology sets out to address.

In so doing, this volume transcends simplistic dichotomies. It delves into the complexities of a society in transition, facing the uncertainty of a changing climate, struggling with unequal consumption patterns, and possessing disparate capacities to bear environmental harm. To discuss these pressing issues, the authors convened in Gelsenkirchen in September 2024 for a summer school on "Ecological transformation, space and the (re-)production of wealth" funded by the Volkswagen Stiftung. Pooling their disciplinary expertise, the participants facilitated interdisciplinary discourse, formulated new research questions, and pinpointed critical knowledge gaps within organized civil society. Through a series of transdisciplinary workshops with civil society representatives and dialogues among junior and senior researchers, the guiding questions outlined above were refined and operationalized.

Charting the Journey Toward a Just Ecological Transition

Acknowledging the complexities inherent in achieving a just transition, the summer school convened researchers who presented the multifaceted challenges associated with the reciprocal dynamics of wealth and ecological transformation.[2] Participants discussed introducing a consumption ceiling to delineate a "sustainable consumption corridor" that simultaneously acknowledges a lower threshold for minimum provision (Bärnthaler, 2024; Gough, 2020). However, the proposal raises the question of who qualifies as "rich"—in other words, how should the ceiling be defined (Niehues, 2020). Moreover, it is necessary to strike a balance between the imperative of improving the economic position of many and the obligation to limit overall climate impact. This is particularly difficult as the so-called "Great Acceleration" of human activity, and its impact on Earth's systems is increasingly driven by the global effort to raise income and quality of life for the masses (Oswald et al., 2020; Steffen et al., 2015). This includes expanding essential infrastructure, housing, and healthcare worldwide to levels comparable to those in industrialized societies.

2 During a summer-school workshop, researchers met with civil-society representatives to hear their questions and knowledge gaps on wealth and ecological transformation. We thank Veronika Nickl (Ernährungsrat Bochum), Mark Rosendahl (DGB Emscher-Lippe), Simon Rahn (Attac Essen), Peter Köddermann (Umbaulabor Gelsenkirchen), and Heike Rößler (Quartiersmanagement Bochum) for their candid insights and productive dialogue. Their input grounded our theoretical debates in practical realities and highlighted new research avenues.

Taken together, these dynamics underscore the need for a holistic approach to ecological transformation that integrates the complex interplay of multiple scientific disciplines to effectively address the socio-ecological challenges of our time.

The participants of the summer school addressed these pressing questions, which inevitably entailed a critical reexamination of long-standing assumptions. For instance, because human dominance over the natural environment has long been considered a hallmark of progress, the task is to reconceptualize this notion into a more resilient, equitable, and climate-responsive—hence ecologically grounded—framework. Furthermore, the entrenched separation between economics and the social sciences warrants deeper scrutiny. Interrogating—and, where necessary, dismantling—the methodological barriers that insulate mainstream economics could reveal novel insights.

Addressing the consequences of climate change thus means addressing the structures that condition, accelerate, and are themselves affected by it. On an individual level, this includes psychological processes associated with climate (mis)information. On a structural level, it involves assessing both the relevance and ownership of infrastructures, as these factors shape political decisions on ecological policy. Finally, the summer school turned to the practical realm: Which local and regional policy instruments have proven effective, and what lessons can be drawn from existing examples?

The Contributions

This anthology provides a nuanced understanding of a just transition toward a sustainable future by pooling diverse expertise to identify critical knowledge gaps. Drawing on interdisciplinary insights from economics, political science, sociology, philosophy, and psychology, it aims to improve the effectiveness of climate-related policy decisions. Further the book addresses the substantial gap between theoretical expectations and empirical evidence in the implementation of climate-related policy measures by proposing that a more comprehensive understanding of social, local and behavioral factors is essential for designing policies that are ecologically effective and socially acceptable. The ten chapters are each written to answer the questions that were formed during the summer school.

The volume targets scholars, policymakers, and civil society practitioners interested in the distributive dimension of ecological transformation. Organized in three parts—Diagnosis & Challenges, Challenging the Status Quo, and Reimaging Transformation—it combines conceptual clarifications, empirical analyses, and methodological reflections. Each chapter's disciplinary perspective differs, yet all contribute to the overarching research agenda introduced above, thereby ensuring thematic coherence.

In the following, the chapters are summarized.

Part I—Diagnosis & Context

The opening section asks what conceptual and empirical baselines are required to understand the reciprocal dynamics between wealth and ecological transformation. Bringing together perspectives from political economy, environmental philosophy, and socio-metabolic research, the three chapters lay the definitional and normative groundwork for the remainder of the volume.

Stefan Gärtner and Judith Terstriep inaugurate the discussion by highlighting the definitional ambiguities that hamper research and policy on green transition. In Chapter 1, they disentangle four often conflated concepts in scholarly and public discourse: *structural change*, *transformative change*, *just transition*, and *transformative regional development*, and situate them in a cascading logic that connects each concept to specific measurement challenges, governance mechanisms, and demonstration projects. They conclude by proposing avenues for future research designed to capture the complexity of ecological transformation while remaining actionable for policymakers.

Marlen Reinschke then critically examines the Enlightenment's linear concept of progress, which emphasizes human mastery over nature, arguing for a necessary reconceptualization that effectively responds to current ecological realities and ethical imperatives (Chapter 2). Drawing on the complementary frameworks of Hans Jonas's ethics of responsibility and Bruno Latour's actor-network theory, she elaborates an ecologically informed concept of progress. She foregrounds an ethic of care and stewardship, promoting mutual entanglement and collaborative survival instead of traditional exploitative paradigms.

Taking a political science perspective, in Chapter 3, **Philipp Schepelmann** complements these discourses by interrogating the entrenched "rich versus poor country" dichotomy that underpins many debates on resource distribution. Using comparative resource-use data, he shows that the expansion of decent living conditions in middle-income countries has become a significant driver of global environmental change. Recognizing this overlooked source of resource demand alters the equity calculus.

Part II—Challenging the Status Quo

Where Part I sets the stage conceptually, Part II asks which structural and behavioral lock-ins impede a just ecological transition and how interdisciplinary perspectives can uncover "blind spots" in widely used policy instruments. The contributions draw on infrastructure studies, heterodox economics, political sociology, and environmental psychology to identify mechanisms that reproduce both carbon intensity and socio-economic inequality.

Christian Hein begins by demonstrating the relevance of infrastructures for an ecological transformation, as well as their role in shaping the social sphere (Chapter 4): Not only do they form the backbone of transportation and commerce, but they also encode societal priorities and lock in emission trajectories for decades. Because planning horizons are long and sunk costs enormous, he argues that infrastructures must be subjected to critical, anticipatory evaluation if they are to serve as levers of decarbonization rather than obstacles.

Economic analyses of carbon pricing are presented in the Chapters 5 and 6 **Michelle Alfers** and **Elias-Johannes Schmitt** show, through a detailed case comparison, that economics can benefit from insights from political science and sociology when evaluating real-world carbon pricing schemes. By exposing disciplinary blind spots—most notably regarding power relations, behavioral rebound effects, and administrative feasibility—they arrive at a more realistic appraisal of the instrument's effectiveness.

Michelle Alfers widens the lens yet further, arguing that policies promoting sustainability must integrate concerns about economic equality. She synthesizes three streams ofliterature to explicate that inequality (i) reinforces unsustainable consumption patterns, (ii) erodes social cohesion and institutional trust, and (iii) concentrates political power in constituencies least vulnerable to climate impacts. Without explicit redistributive design features, she concludes, green policy may inadvertently worsen both environmental and social outcomes.

Marvin Fendt, Fabian Reinwarth and Peter Adriaan Edelsbrunner's close Part II by investigating the individual-level drivers of credibility judgments regarding climate change information, specifically focusing on manipulative content (Chapter 7). Drawing on a survey of 675 participants, they distinguish *mis*information (false or inaccurate content) from *dis*information (deliberately deceptive content), exploring how various factors influence discernment and sharing behavior. Their findings—conspiracy thinking undermines, while persuasion knowledge strengthens, credibility assessment—have direct implications for science communication and counter-disinformation strategies in climate policy.

Part III—Reimagining Transformation

If Part II uncovers barriers, Part III explores how ownership models, governance arrangements, and forward-looking methodologies can be redesigned to realign wealth, power, and ecological imperatives. The chapters engage critical infrastructure studies, scenario planning, and commons theory to put forward actionable pathways for transformational change.

Carlotta Terhorst opens with an empirical analysis of the European Union's strategic turn toward hydrogen (Chapter 8). Treating infrastructures as socio-political objects, Terhorst shows how incumbent gas-pipeline owners leveraged their positional power—through lobbying, standard-setting, and control of technical knowledge—to shape policy, often prioritizing their assets over scientific consensus and delaying genuine transformation. This ownership-based carbon inequality leads her to the provocative question: "Who owns the present, owns the future?"

Acknowledging that climate change and digitalization pose challenges, especially for public administration, **Elias-Johannes Schmitt** then examines qualitative scenario planning as a governance tool in this context (Chapter 9). Using two cases from the city of Bochum—one conducted with local government, the other with the Smart City Innovation Unit—he illustrates how scenario workshops can integrate multiple stakeholders under conditions of deep uncertainty. The chapter notes both the method's capacity to open imaginative space and its limitations, including participation fatigue and the tendency to reproduce existing power hierarchies if facilitation is weak.

In Chapter 10, **Hannah Müller** concludes the volume with an integrative literature review of local energy commoning practices. She develops an analytical framework that links community activities, governance structures, and collective negotiation processes to broader outcomes of the energy transition. Synthesizing cases from Europe and the Global South, Müller argues that energy commons can contribute simultaneously to decarbonization and social cohesion, but that their effectiveness depends on legal recognition, access to finance, and compatibility with municipal planning regimes.

Together, the three parts move the discussion from conceptual clarification to critical interrogation of existing structures to empirically grounded proposals for transformative change. Although many issues inevitably remain unresolved, the three parts collectively answer the summer school's guiding questions and offer empirically grounded pathways for a just ecological transition.

The book also highlights the need for further research to clarify how expanding wealth participation in the Global South can proceed without exacerbating climate change. Specifically, it calls for policy instruments—particularly in the Global North—that can preserve a high level of human well-being while simultaneously achieving climate targets. For example, higher energy prices or other climate policy measures must be calibrated so that particularly affected, lower-income groups receive compensation proportional to their income, thereby avoiding the emergence of new severe climate-damaging consumption patterns. Concurrently, research should identify which social and physical infrastructures can simultaneously enhance quality of life and mitigate climate impacts, and clarify how these measures can be utilized at local and regional scales.

By identifying established insights and illuminating the research frontiers that remain, the volume positions itself as a springboard for future interdisciplinary collaboration. Accordingly, it serves scholars, policymakers, and civil-society practitioners seeking to realign prosperity with planetary boundaries while attending to distributive justice.

References

Bärnthaler, R. (2024). When enough is enough: Introducing sufficiency corridors to put techno-economism in its place. Ambio. 53, 960–969. https://doi.org/10.1007/s13280-024-02027-2.

Biewen, M., Glaisner, S., & Kleimann, R. (2025). The shape of the wealth distribution and differences in wealth inequality across Euro area countries. The Journal of Economic Inequality, 23(1), 1–25. https://doi.org/10.1007/s10888-024-09630-z

Bocksch, R. (2022). Der riesige CO2-Fußabdruck der Reichen. Retrieved November 27, 2025, from https://de.statista.com/infografik/26885/anteil-der-einkommensschichten-an-den-globalen-co2-emissionen/

Chancel, L., & Rehm, Y. (2025). Accounting for the carbon footprint of capital ownership advances the understanding of emission inequality. Climatic Change, 178(11). https://doi.org/10.1007/s10584-025-04044-w

Chancel, L., Bothe, P., Voituriez, T. (2023). Climate Inequality Report 2023, World Inequality Lab Study 2023/1. Retrieved November 29, 2025, from https://wid.world/document/climate-inequality-report-2023/

Chancel, L., Mohnen, C., Bothe, P., & Semieniuk, G. (2024). Climate Change and Wealth Inequality: A Literature Review and Numerical Insights. World Inequality Lab, Working Paper, 2024/27. Retrieved Novermber 29, 2025, from https://wid.world/document/climate-change-and-wealth-inequality-a-literature-review-and-numerical-insights-world-inequality-lab-working-paper-2024-27/

Chancel, L., Mohren, C., Bothe, P., Muti, S., & Villaverde, P. (2025). Climate Inequality Report 2025. Climate Change: A Capital Challenge. Why Climate Policy Must Tackle Ownership. World Inequality Lab Key Report 2025. Retrieved Novermber 29, 2025, from https://wid.world/www-site/uploads/2025/10/Climate_Inequality_Report_2025_Final.pdf

Chrisendo, D., Niva, V., Hoffmann, R., Masoumzadeh Sayyar, S., Rocha, J. C., Sandström, V., Solt, F., & Kummu, M. (2024). Income inequality has increased for over two-thirds of the global population. Research Square. https://doi.org/10.21203/rs.3.rs-5548291/v1

De Arce, R. & Mahía, R. (2023). Unbiasing the estimate of the role of income in carbon footprint of households: Analysis of the Spanish case as a a pilot study. Heliyon, 9(6), e16394. https://doi.org/10.1016/j.heliyon.2023.e16394

Drupp, M. A., Kornek, U., Meya, J. N., & Sager, N. (2024). The Economics of Inequality and the Environment. cesinfo Working Papers, 11036. Retrieved Novermber 29, 2025, from https://www.ifo.de/DocDL/cesifo1_wp11036.pdf

Gazzotti, P., Emmerling, J., Marangoni, G., Castelletti, A., Van der Wijst, K., Hof, A. & Tavoni, M. (2021). Persistent inequality in economically optimal climate policies. Nature Communications, 12(1), 3421. https://doi.org/10.1038/s41467-021-23613-y

Gough, I. (2020). Defining floors and ceilings: the contribution of human needs theory. Sustainability: Science, Practice and Policy, 16(1), 208–219. https://doi.org/10.1080/15487733.2020.1814033

Davies, J. B., Lluberas, R., & Shorrocks, A. F. (2017). Estimating the Level and Distribution of Global Wealth, 2000–2014. Review of Income and

Wealth, International Association for Research in Income and Wealth, 63(4), 731–759. https://doi.org/10.1111/roiw.12318

Markkanen, S., & Anger-Kraavi, A. (2019). Social impacts of climate change mitigation policies and their implications for inequality. Climate Policy, 19(7), 827–844. https://doi.org/10.1080/14693062.2019.1596873

Niehues, J., Stockhausen, M. (2020) Vermögensgrenzen: große gruppenspezifische Unterschiede, IW-Kurzbericht, Nr. 105, Köln

Oswald, Y., Owen, A. & Steinberger, J.K. (2020). Large inequality in international and intranational energy footprints between income groups and across consumption categories. Nature Energy 5, 231–239. https://doi.org/10.1038/s41560-020-0579-8

Oxford University (2016). Global income inequality down in relative terms, up in absolute sums. Retrieved November 30, 2025 from https://www.ox.ac.uk/news/2016-08-25-global-income-inequality-down-relative-terms-absolute-sums

Sovacool, B. K., Devine-Wright, P., Mander, S., Rowley, J., & Ryder, S. (2025). Realising a locally-embedded just transition: Sense of place, lived experience, and social perceptions of industrial decarbonisation in the United Kingdom. Global Environmental Change, 94. https://doi.org/10.1016/j.gloenvcha.2025.103051

Steffen, W., Broadgate, W., Deutsch, L., Gaffney, O., & Ludwig, C. (2015). The trajectory of the Anthropocene: The Great Acceleration. The Anthropocene Review, 2(1), 81–98. https://doi.org/10.1177/2053019614564785

Part I—Diagnosis & Context

From Regional Cohesion and Structural Policy to Just Transition and Transformative Change?

A growing Lack of Conceptual Clarity

Stefan Gärtner & Judith Terstriep

Abstract: *This chapter aims to clarify the conceptual and policy ambiguities that hamper governance of the green transition by disentangling four often conflated notions—structural change, transformative change, just transition, and transformative regional development—and showing how they interlock. Centering on Germany within the European Union's cohesion framework, it combines a historical-institutional account of regional structural policy, rooted in the Basic Law's mandate for equivalent living conditions, with a conceptual synthesis and a critical appraisal of ongoing reforms such as the 'greening' of the 'Joint Task for the Improvement of Regional Economic Structures' (GRW [Gemeinschaftsaufgabe Verbesserung der regionalen Wirtschaftsstruktur]) in Germany and the EU's pivot from ecological modernization towards green reindustrialization.*

A cascading logic is proposed: structural change reveals where regions stand; transformative change, where they must go; just transition, under what terms of fairness; and transformative regional development, how to deliver on the ground through mission-oriented coalitions. The chapter urges a shift in regional structural and Cohesion Policy from a compensatory, growth-led paradigm to a preventive, adaptive, and justice-by-design approach aligned with planetary boundaries and territorial specificity.

Two governance risks are highlighted—centralized fund management that weakens regional voice, and the concentration of flagship green investments in already advantaged regions widening spatial inequalities—and remedies proposed: binding carbon and justice conditionalities across funds, systemic capacity building, cross-fund coherence, and a revised indicator dashboard. The chapter concludes with a forward research agenda on evaluation, governance experimentation, and metrics, offering a roadmap to recast regional structural and Cohesion Policy as a driver of climate-neutral, socially equitable, and territorially sensitive transformation.

Keywords: *structural change; just transition; regional structural policy; cohesion policy; transformative regional development*

1 Introduction

The transition to a climate-neutral economy ('green transition') represents one of the most profound challenges of our time, demanding not only technological innovation but also far-reaching structural, societal, and territorial adjustments (Grillitsch et al., 2025; Tödtling et al., 2022). As discussions on directing this transformation intensify, a growing lack of conceptual clarity becomes evident, particularly regarding the relationships among structural change, transformative change, just transition, transformative regional development, and the role of structural policy. These terms, although partly used interchangeably in public and academic discourse, embody distinct logics, dynamics, interrelations, and policy implications.

Structural change is an inherent feature of economic development, reflecting the continuous adaptation of sectors, labor markets, and regional economies to technological progress, global competition, and societal preferences (Dahlbeck et al., 2022; van Neuss, 2019). However, this dynamic is not frictionless. External shocks, such as geopolitical conflicts or environmental disasters, as well as gradually unfolding changes, such as digitalization or demographic shifts, can cause disruptions that undermine economic resilience and social cohesion. In such cases, the state intervenes through structural policy, which comprises institutional and legal instruments to mitigate regional disparities and support lagging sectors. This policy domain is typically divided into sectoral and regional structural policy, with the latter gaining increased relevance in light of spatially uneven impacts of transformative change (Gärtner, 2019; Liargovas & Papageorgiou, 2024). This normative framework is grounded in Germany's constitution, which mandates equivalent living conditions nationwide. At the supranational level, the European Union pursues similar objectives under its Cohesion Policy (Li, 2025).

By contrast, *transformation* refers to a more fundamental, systemic change, often politically initiated and normatively driven (Letmathe et al., 2024; Loorbach, 2022). Transformative processes, such as the transition from a planned to a market economy in Eastern Germany or the commitments set by the Paris Agreement, entail not just adaptation but an intentional re-orientation of societal and economic systems. While structural change and transformation intersect, conflating these concepts risks analytical imprecision and, more importantly, weakens governance capacity to address the root causes of climate change and its socio-economic implications.

Within this landscape, the concept of a *just transition* (McCauley & Heffron, 2018; Wang & Lo, 2021) has gained prominence, stressing the need to ensure that the burdens and benefits of ecological transformation are shared fairly across different social groups and territories. A just transition emphasizes social inclusion, equity, and participation, particularly for those communities, regions, employees, and other citizens most affected by decarbonization and structural change (Stark et al., 2023). Thus, justice concerns must be embedded not only in climate and energy policy but also in the design and implementation of structural policy itself. So doing necessitates a redefinition of policy goals, shifting from narrowly defined economic growth to broader indicators of well-being and sustainability. As one of the EU's main investment frameworks, *Cohesion Policy* aims to reduce disparities between regions, strengthen economic, social, and territorial cohesion, and increasingly support climate-related goals (Demeterova, 2024; European Commission, 2024). In this context, it serves as both a financial instrument and a governance tool, aligning regional development with the imperatives of a just and ecological transition.

This chapter argues that regional structural and Cohesion Policy stand at a critical juncture. First, ecological transformation will inevitably trigger new forms of structural change, necessitating policy responses that embed environmental goals within economic, social, and cultural frameworks. Second, structural policy itself must evolve, moving from a compensatory instrument that reacts to the side effects of transformation to a preventive, transformative, and justice-oriented tool aligned with sustainability and inclusion objectives. Third, as ecological transformation unfolds in territorially differentiated ways, regional structural policy becomes the pivotal arena for governance. Furthermore, the re-orientation of instruments, such as Germany's 'Joint Task for the Improvement of Regional Economic Structures' (GRW [Gemeinschaftsaufgabe Verbesserung der regionalen Wirtschaftsstruktur]), already signals a soft shift toward a structurally embedded ecological logic. Fourth, the reform of the EU Cohesion Policy is currently being debated, with the emphasis on directing resources towards strategic priorities such as climate action, digitalization, and social cohesion (Filippetti & Spallone, 2025). Although the bulk of the funding will likely be channeled through Member States rather than allocated directly to regions, this centralized approach—intended to enhance oversight and administrative efficiency—has prompted concerns that specific regional needs may be overlooked (Fratesi, 2025; Rodríguez-Pose, 2025). Against this backdrop, the analysis is guided by two research questions:

How can a policy instrument originally designed to offset the side effects of market-driven structural change be repurposed to steer a deliberately accelerated, socially fair, and territorially differentiated climate transition?

How can clarifying the concepts of structural change, transformative change, just transition, and transformative regional development help re-orient Germany's regional structural policy—within the EU cohesion framework—from a compensatory, growth-led tool to a preventive, place-based, and justice-oriented driver of climate-neutral, socially equitable transformation?

This chapter explores these questions by tracing the conceptual evolution, policy realignments, and spatial implications of transformative regional structural policy in the context of ecological transformation and the emerging just transition agenda. Although the focus is on Germany's structural and regional policies, the discussion is embedded within the EU's Cohesion Policy framework and informed by the wider international academic debate on regional transformation.

Section 2 charts the historical evolution of Germany's regional structural policy, situating it within both the constitutional mandate for equivalent living conditions and the broader trajectory of EU Cohesion Policy. Section 3 disentangles the four key concepts at the heart of the debate—structural change, transformative change, just transition, and transformative regional development—pinpointing their respective logics, temporalities, and justice dimensions. Section 4 combines the critical appraisal of current policy realignments with the synthesis of principal tensions and the derivation of operational lessons: it contrasts the EU's shift from ecological modernization to green reindustrialization with Germany's 'greening' of the GRW. It assesses the attendant risks and opportunities for spatial justice, and distills implications for policymakers while laying out a forward-looking research agenda.

2 Structural Change: Dynamics and Policy Legacies

Before we can assess what a preventive, justice-oriented structural policy might look like, we must first understand how structural change has been conceived and governed to date. Accordingly, this section re-examines the economic dynamics of structural change. It traces the policy legacies, constitutional, national, multilevel, and European, that have emerged to manage its consequences in Germany. By clarifying this historical and governance context, the analysis highlights the path dependencies and conceptual blind spots that any future, climate-compatible and socially equitable reframing of regional structural policy will have to confront.

2.1 Conceptual and Constitutional Foundations

Economic structural change is generally understood as a change in the structural composition of an aggregate value, such as gross domestic product (GDP) or the workforce (van Neuss, 2019). From a sectoral perspective, it encompasses changes in the structure of economic sectors, while from a regional perspective, it refers to shifts between individual regions. In Germany, securing equivalent living conditions in the federal territory is enshrined in the constitution, making it a legal requirement. Article 72(2) of the Basic Law formulates a statement on spatial equilibrium, thereby conferring on the federal level the authority to act or legislate

> "[...] if and to the extent that the establishment of equivalent living conditions throughout the federal territory or the preservation of legal or economic unity in the national interest requires regulation by the federal law."

Article 106 of the Basic Law, which determines financial equalization among the federal states in the event of imbalanced development, also affects regions. Germany's Regional Planning Act also takes a position in Section 1(2) by requiring the establishment of *"similar standards of living in all regions"*.

Historically, regional structural policy has sought to foster balanced territorial development, driven either by socio-political considerations or economic growth objectives. Accordingly, the rationale for such a policy can be articulated on both economic and socio-political grounds. From a socio-political standpoint, regional policy seeks to guarantee citizens across Germany equivalent living conditions. When the emphasis shifts to economic growth, however, the principal question becomes where interventions will yield the highest aggregate returns. Neoclassical theory predicts that regional disparities will decline endogenously: capital and labor migrate towards lagging areas, where diminishing marginal productivity ensures relatively higher growth rates (Fingleton & Fischer, 2010). Public investment in these structurally weak regions is therefore expected to generate the greatest economy-wide benefits, as it accelerates the natural convergence process (Frey & Zimmermann, 2005; Gärtner, 2019). In this sense, a spatially equalizing structural policy is also growth-oriented, because the full utilization of resources in all territories maximizes national output.

A key pillar of Germany's regional structural policy is the GRW. Established in 1969, the GRW was conceived to harmonize and coordinate structural policy interventions across national (Bund) and state (Länder) levels of government. Instrumentally, the GRW works with incentives to direct investments into specific areas (Dettmann et al., 2025). Until the end of 2022, only structural projects were funded within the framework of the GRW that involved so-called 'distance selling', meaning they brought export income into the region (Alcaide Manthey, 2025). However, since January 1, 2023, the GRW has undergone reform, demonstrating its adaptability, and has notably incorporated many long-standing criticisms raised by regional and spatial sciences, showing its responsiveness to feedback (Suedekum, 2023). Thus, independent regional development and regional value creation are now being promoted more strongly.

Nevertheless, regional structural policy has yet to converge on approaches that prioritize quality of life and the strengthening of civil society, even though such orientations are demonstrably better suited to structurally weaker, peripheral regions. Instead, there has been a long-standing debate over the optimal degree of spatial concentration of investments in regions with growth potential (Wardenburg & Brenner, 2020). Proponents of this approach contend that weak and peripheral regions will eventually benefit from a growth-pole- or metropolis-oriented policy through spatial spillover and trickle-down effects; however, the empirical basis for this claim remains contested. Conversely, far less attention is paid to policy options for regions that lack growth potential (MacKinnon et al., 2022; Pike et al., 2024).

Implementing an unconstrained growth-pole strategy while simultaneously restricting development options elsewhere is unlikely to be efficacious, particularly in a highly decentralized country such as Germany. Such an approach risks cumulative advantages that widen spatial disparities, leaving unsupported regions increasingly marginalized and imposing welfare costs on society as a whole (Alcaide Manthey, 2025). A further, often overlooked, consequence is that peripheral areas with comparatively strong infrastructures, especially in the education sector, cultivate human capital that subsequently migrates to the growth centers, thereby reinforcing the very inequalities regional policy seeks to mitigate.

2.2 From Peripheral Regions to Old Industrial Agglomerations

Regional structural policy traditionally focused on the urban-rural divide, a goal deemed essential for both economic growth and social equality. However, the catching-up paradigm, which presumes that development deficits are confined to peripheral regions, no longer holds. Similar shortcomings are now evident in several urban agglomerations, particularly in the former West German federal states (Flögel & Gärtner, 2019). The structural development of old industrial agglomerations was therefore traditionally not the focus of regional structural policy.

Traditionally, regional structural policy was introduced to support rural, agricultural, and remote areas. The decline of the coal industry since the 1960s was the first time that an industrial agglomeration was affected by economic weakness. In the Ruhr region, for example, the contraction of employment in hard coal mining was managed in a socially responsible manner, primarily through early retirement schemes, thereby largely preserving regional social stability. For the affected miners, early retirement entailed only minimal income losses. The gradual, heavily subsidized phase-out of hard coal therefore averted major 'structural upheaval'.

However, inevitable trade-offs arise when a dominant industry, and by extension, the region whose economy it underpins, begins to decline. In such circumstances, regional policymakers often prioritize regional development through instruments such as subsidies for firms and compensation payments to workers (OECD, 2023). It is, above all, about preserving the interests of shareholders and employees in the predominant industries, because established sectors typically provide relatively high wages and attractive returns. This understanding is to be seen in the context of regional structural policy operating within a multilevel governance framework that extends from the EU, federal, and state levels down to the municipal tier (Benz, 2021). In Germany, access to lower spatial levels (e.g., federal states or municipalities) is limited by the constitutionally guaranteed local self-government. This issue has become particularly evident in Germany's 'Energiewende' (energy transition), notably in the efforts to install new high-voltage transmission lines to convey wind-generated electricity from the north to the south. For large-scale infrastructure projects of this kind, it is therefore essential to secure the active participation of the diverse stakeholders within the affected regions.

Figure 1: Levels of Regional Structural Policy

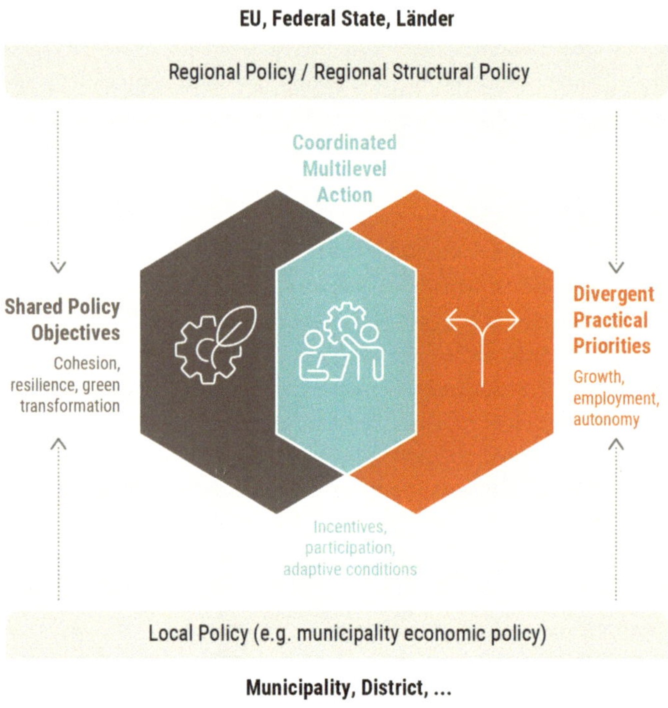

Source: Own compilation

Local economic policy—a policy that focuses on the city, county, or region—is pursued independently of the structural policy objectives of higher governance levels, as illustrated in Figure 1. Often, the aims of the different tiers complement one another; for example, structurally weak regions may draw on targeted EU or federal state programs to support balanced regional development. The distinction between regional and local economic policy, however, is far from trivial, as municipal economic initiatives can pursue egocentric goals irrespective of broader regional objectives. Thus, alongside consensus-oriented strategies, conflictual local economic policies may arise, creating situations in which not everyone benefits, for example, when many regions court the same sectors, which increases the competition. Even ostensibly balance-oriented regional strategies can inadvertently exacerbate disparities if already prosperous regions leverage 'smart' economic policies to capture a disproportionate share of the resulting benefits, thereby widening the regional welfare gap.

2.3 EU Regional and Cohesion Policy

The EU's regional and Cohesion Policy aims to reduce economic and social disparities between territories and to promote balanced development across all areas (Medeiros et al., 2024; Rodríguez-Pose, 2025). In practice, this is achieved through the provision of financial resources, for example, via the European Structural Funds (e.g., the European Regional Development Fund) and the Cohesion Fund, as well as the new Just Transition Fund, which is invested in projects at the regional or national level.

In the forthcoming programming periods, EU policy must continue to reconcile a persistent dual tension: on the one hand, it seeks to uphold a liberal economic order and an efficient, competitive single market; on the other hand, it is obliged to reduce economic, social and territorial disparities among Member States and regions—a commitment set out in Article 174 TFEU and reinforced by Article 175, which places a corresponding duty on the Member States (Cappellano et al., 2024; European Commission, 2024; Li, 2025).

Already in the 2000s, the Lisbon Strategy led to a more economically oriented approach to regional policy: funding was increasingly concentrated on growth poles, while the needs of less developed regions were considered only to a limited extent (Bachtler & McMaster, 2007; Bruijn & Lagendijk, 2005; Farole et al., 2011). The Europe 2020 strategy incorporated social and environmental goals without compromising the focus on growth. In the current funding period (2021–2027), in addition to traditional cohesion objectives, digitalization, the green transition, and crisis resilience are central priorities. Funding allocation is increasingly linked to strategic investment and reform objectives, with regional needs still taken into account, although often secondary to growth- and innovation-oriented criteria.

From 2028, a comprehensive reform of the funding architecture is planned: regional and agricultural funds could be merged into a single fund, from which resources will be disbursed to Member States—rather than directly to regions—once they submit investment and reform plans in line with the political requirements of the European Commission (Filippetti & Spallone, 2025; Rodríguez-Pose, 2025). This reform will tie funding more closely to national strategies, following a model similar to the NextGenerationEU Fund.

Schwab & Resende Carvalho (2023) point out that the digital and green transitions may further widen the gap between economically strong and weak regions in Europe. Regions with high innovation capacity, well-educated workforces, and modern infrastructure—typically urban centers such as Stuttgart or Upper Bavaria—are likely to benefit from digitalization and the green transition, enhancing their growth potential. Weaker regions, particularly rural areas or those with carbon-intensive industries, face significant adjustment costs, for instance, due to necessary investments in climate-friendly technologies or the thermal renovation of buildings.

If implemented as planned, the funding period from 2028 onwards will be characterized by a stronger linkage between national reform plans and strategic investments, leading to a nationalization of EU regional policy, as resources will primarily be managed through the Member States.

2.4 From Reactive to Anticipatory Structural Policy

Debates on precautionary, rather than merely reactive, structural policy date back to the 1970s (Rembser 1977). Trade-union proposals in the early 1980s called for the promotion of science and technology to be linked to regional aid and for crises to be pre-empted rather than compensated ex post (Bömer & Noisser, 1981; Pfeiffer, 1982). The trade union concept envisaged an anticipatory "structural policy that does not attempt to correct sectoral or regional mis-developments retrospectively but intends to avoid them from the outset" (Pfeiffer, 1982, 623).

In their study "Information Bases for Anticipatory Structural Policy", Thoss and Ritzmann (1984) sought to advance qualitative growth, fully utilize existing production factors, and secure a balanced relationship between supply and demand at the regional scale. Their proposal entailed the proactive promotion of expanding sectors, accompanied by an early and orderly withdrawal from those in decline. Crucially, they argued that such an anticipatory approach creates an extensive demand for information, necessitating detailed analyses, forecasts, and projections (Thoss & Ritzmann, 1984).

These proposals were never implemented, primarily because of the inherent difficulties in reliable forecasting. Furthermore, the recommendations remained mainly at the level of conceptual exhortation. While they highlighted the need for a stronger regional focus, this was articulated only implicitly and from an essentially macroeconomic perspective.

Subsequent historical events (like the fall of the Berlin Wall and the reunification, or the Tequila and Asian financial crises) further undermined the feasibility of long-range anticipatory policy as they demonstrated how swiftly macroeconomic and geopolitical shocks, alongside global crises, can overturn existing trajectories, necessitating ad hoc measures that leave little room for long-term planning. In the context of political transformations in Eastern Europe and Russia, and amid the ascendancy of a global market-oriented order, policymakers were also reluctant to embrace frameworks perceived as overly directive or reminiscent of central planning.

Moreover, structural policy has traditionally been justified on the basis of a regional status quo in which structurally weak regions are primarily supported (Alcaide Manthey, 2025; Weingarten, 2010). A preventive approach, however, would require policymakers to finance structural change even in regions that are currently structurally strong. Structural weakness would arise only if earlier preventive measures had failed ('the prevention paradox'). Consequently, when preventive structural policy coincides with gradual or 'silent' structural change, the political dividends are inherently limited. Preventive structural policy also poses a challenge for spatial planning, as economically obsolete land uses often persist, thereby constraining regional capacity for new development. This problem is particularly evident in regions of the automotive industry that remain prosperous, such as the Stuttgart region (Hemberger & Kiwitt, 2020). Given ecological imperatives that call for the prudent use of land resources, suitable sites for emerging sectors are scarce.

Preventive structural policy often fails because it is impossible to predict with confidence which sectors will prove competitive in the future. Nevertheless, the imperative to mitigate climate change will inevitably drive substantial economic restructuring. Beyond the intrinsic value of ecological transition for economic transformation, fostering so-called 'green' industries is expected to generate enduring, sustainable economic structures. Preventive intervention, therefore, possesses intrinsic ecological value, as it prompts early trajectory shifts and avoids unnecessary resource consumption.

The considerable challenge of identifying, at a sufficiently fine-grained level, which regions ought to be prioritized for support in the context of ecological transformation, and of calibrating funding instruments accordingly, is largely undisputed (Rodríguez-Pose, 2025; Südekum & Rademacher, 2024). Trade unions have grappled with this problem since the 1980s and continue to engage with it today. Within the German Trade Union Confederation's 'Revierwende' initiative, financed through the Coal Regions Structural Strengthening Act, union representatives emphasize that EU state-aid regulations restrict direct corporate subsidies to disadvantaged regions, thereby limiting the scope for proactive, anticipatory intervention in ostensibly stronger territories.

Having traced past attempts at anticipatory policy, we now turn to the new strategic pressures that will shape regional policy in the second half of the 2020s.

2.5 Current Policy Pressures and Emerging Fault Lines

Both Germany's regional-structural policy and the EU's cohesion architecture were designed in an era when accelerated growth and inter-regional convergence were assumed to be mutually reinforcing.

Recent strategy documents at the EU and federal levels imply a trajectory from ecological modernization—retrofitting existing industries with cleaner technologies—towards green reindustrialization, which seeks to establish entirely new value chains in renewable energy, hydrogen, battery production, and the circular economy. Reindustrialization is cast simultaneously as a decarbonization pathway and as a lever for restoring strategic autonomy in the wake of geo-economic disruptions. As a result, spatial targeting is becoming more differentiated: coal regions receive transition aid, while advanced manufacturing hubs compete for 'green-lead' projects. Yet, this putative dual solution risks reproducing established core–periphery dynamics if flagship projects become concentrated in already advantaged regions. Coal-dependent areas may receive transition aid, whereas advanced manufacturing hubs are likely to capture the lion's share of research funding, skilled labor, and venture capital, thereby potentially exacerbating spatial inequalities beneath a "green" veneer.

Although the exact design of EU regional policy for the 2027+ funding period remains uncertain and is unlikely to be implemented precisely as currently envisioned, preliminary drafts of the Multiannual Financial Framework suggest that funding for regional development and Cohesion Policy will shrink (see Section 2.3). Because the strong regionalization of EU funds is largely a German peculiarity, a partial renationalization of program management is anticipated, potentially reducing the Länder's influence. This prospect appears counter-productive to the long-standing ideal of a 'Europe of the Regions', especially given the consensus-oriented governance structures many German states have built around Cohesion Policy. As Rodríguez-Pose (2025, 1) warns, "Cohesion Policy [is] at its defining moment". Such recentralization would replace the policy's place-based partnership tenet with a compliance-and-control logic, further eroding regional voice and risking a loss of public trust in the EU—precisely the pattern already observed with National Recovery and Resilience Plans.

Even so, a more centralized framework could create new opportunities: bypassing Länder might allow local authorities to access funds directly for clearly defined objectives. Such a re-orientation could enable the federal government to strengthen equalization principles or to enhance local implementation capacity for the green transition as a routine responsibility, rather than through transient project funding. Moreover, in selected policy areas—particularly those linked to 'green transition'—the Commission could disburse funds directly to regions below federal states, subject to strict criteria such as demonstrable reductions in consumption-based CO_2-equivalent emissions.

3 Transformation, Transformative Change and Just Transition: Linking Social Justice and Ecological Goals

Building on the preceding discussion of structural change, the literature on sustainability transitions can be organized into four interconnected theoretical discourses: structural change (SC), transformative change (TC), the just transition (JT), and transformative regional development (TRD). Each layer answers a different analytical question—where we stand, where we need to go, under what terms of justice, and how to deliver in place—and must therefore be examined both separately and in concert.

3.1 Structural vs Transformative Change

While both structural change and transformative change have in common that they are umbrella terms whose meaning varies by discipline, historical period, and policy area, transformative change denotes a more profound, value-laden, and purposive re-ordering of socio-technical and socio-ecological systems (Loorbach, 2022; Schot & Steinmueller, 2018; Scoones et al., 2020). Structural change is typically viewed as being incremental, adaptive, and mainly intentional. In contrast, transformative change is systemic, normative, and deliberate, setting out to reconfigure not only production structures but also the institutional logics, cultural norms, and power relations that underpin them.

While such a heuristic helps highlight why conventional structural policies may fall short in the face of the climate emergency, it should be treated as an ideal type rather than a 'hard' dichotomy. Episodes of structural change can be both rapid and state-orchestrated—as evidenced by China's post-1978 sectoral re-allocation (Brandt & Rawski, 2022) or the accelerated contraction of coal and steel industries that continues to shape 'left-behind' areas of the United Kingdom (Kaizuka, 2024; While & Eadson, 2022). Building on these observations, contemporary transition theory frames change processes as a continuum in which incremental and radical dynamics co-evolve and may even trigger one another (Geels, 2018; Grillitsch & Sotarauta, 2020). Acknowledging this ambiguity guards against overly rigid policy prescriptions and better captures the diverse pathways through which socio-ecological transitions unfold in practice.

Transformative change is further complicated by three interacting forms of complexity (Letmathe et al., 2024). *System complexity* emerges from the tight coupling of technological, economic, ecological, and social subsystems, whose staggered and opaque causal pathways impede the timely identification of harmful trends. *Backward complexity* reflects path dependencies created by sunk investments, institutional routines, and entrenched cultural norms; these inflate the costs of deviation from established trajectories and demand convincingly articulated alternatives, inclusive stakeholder engagement, and, where appropriate, compensatory mechanisms. *Forward complexity,* finally, refers to outcome uncertainty: because the ultimate efficacy and side effects of interventions can seldom be forecast with precision, opponents may mobilize this indeterminacy to contest transformative action, thereby reinforcing existing lock-ins and underscoring the need for continual pathway analysis, adaptive governance, and reflexive control instruments (Geels & Turnheim, 2022; Huntjens & Kemp, 2022). Recognizing these complexities helps justify adaptive and reflexive forms of governance.

3.2 Just Transition Lens

Against this backdrop, the notion of a just transition adds a justice lens to the debate on transformation. First articulated in late-1970s North American labor-union circles, most notably by the Oil, Chemical and Atomic Workers Union, and subsequently broadened by environmental-justice movements, the idea of a 'just transition' has since been taken up by global institutions (Cigna et al., 2023). It is embedded in the ILO's 2015 Guidelines, referenced in the Paris Agreement and successive COP decisions (e.g., the 2018 Silesia Declaration and the 2021 Glasgow Climate Pact), and operationalized in policy frameworks such as the EU Green Deal and its Just Transition Mechanism (McCauley & Heffron, 2018; Wang & Lo, 2021). It posits that decarbonization should be evaluated not only by tons of CO_2 reduction but also by how fairly equitably costs and benefits are distributed, how inclusive decision-making processes are, and whose identities and capabilities are recognized. Equally important is how affected groups perceive this fairness; subjective judgements of (in)justice often condition public acceptance and the political durability of transition measures (Sovacool et al., 2025).

Investigated from diverse disciplinary perspectives—e.g., climate science, human and economic geography, sociology, energy economics, social policy, ethics, and law—the notion of a 'just transition' has yet to coalesce into a single, universally accepted definition. Although interpreted in multiple ways, the concept of a just transition unequivocally refers to a complex, multifaceted process that integrates climate, environmental, and energy objectives with the restorative, distributive, procedural, and intergenerational dimensions of justice (Galanis et al., 2025; McCauley & Heffron, 2018).

The term 'just' in just transition draws on classical theories of social justice articulated by philosophers such as Locke, Rousseau, Kant, and, more recently, Rawls (1971). It denotes fairness in both the distribution of benefits and burdens and in the procedures by which decisions are made (Moodie, 2025). Building on this foundation, climate justice further refines the notion of justice by stressing historical responsibility for greenhouse gas emissions, inter- and intra-generational equity, and the differentiated capacities of societies to mitigate and adapt to climate change (Newell et al., 2021; Porter et al., 2020; Rice et al., 2023). Accordingly, and distinct from 'transition', just transition processes require multiple actors and communities to actively engage in pursuing purposive change, aiming for a "better future for individuals, communities and the environment" (Kaizuka, 2024, 156). Avelino et al. (2024, 520) encapsulate this philosophy, defining transformative change as processes

> "[...] that aim to enable present and future generations, both human and nonhuman, to survive and flourish and eliminate and prevent injustices that are produced and exacerbated by unsustainability and its underlying causes."

It follows that justice concerns inevitably have a spatial dimension, as the burdens and opportunities of decarbonization are unevenly distributed across space (Binz et al., 2025; Jenkins et al., 2018; Moodie et al., 2021). Coal-dependent regions, peri-urban logistics belts facing land-use conflicts, and emerging green-tech clusters all experience the transition in markedly different ways (Coenen et al., 2024; Kaizuka, 2024; Oei et al., 2020). Crucially, the sense of place attached to these territories' shapes how citizens and other stakeholders experience change, ascribe meaning to it, and act in response, thereby influencing which transition pathways gain or lose legitimacy. If left unaddressed, such asymmetries risk widening existing spatial inequalities; if addressed proactively, they could open a window for place-based strategies that fuse ecological ambition with social inclusion, thereby creating 'new' opportunities (Barca et al., 2012; Rodríguez-Pose & Bartalucci, 2024; Weck et al., 2022).

This perspective positions regional structural, cohesion, and innovation policy as pivotal governance arenas (Li, 2025; Tödtling et al., 2022; Trippl & Tödtling, 2025). The task is to transition from an essentially compensatory logic of repairing ex-post damage to a forward-looking, preventive, and reflexive mode that aligns with planetary boundaries and justice principles. Here, the notion of socio-ecological transition comes into play (Sabato & Mandelli, 2024).

3.3 Transformative Regional Development

Transformative regional development (TRD) constitutes the fourth theoretical discourse. Whereas transformative change articulates *why* systems must change, TRD specifies *how* this change can be enacted within distinct regional contexts (Chlebna et al., 2023; Terstriep & Angstmann, 2025). Ideally, it translates high-level sustainability and justice missions into place-based strategies that mobilize local assets, address regional lock-ins and open new development paths (Grillitsch & Sotarauta, 2020; Tödtling et al., 2022). TRD is therefore neither a mere subset of regional policy nor a straightforward extension of innovation policy; rather, it is a hybrid paradigm that draws concurrently on (i) evolutionary economic geography, particularly concepts of path creation and related variety (Grashof & Basilico, 2025; Karlsen et al., 2025); (ii) socio-technical transition studies and their emphasis on multilevel dynamics and niche–regime interactions (Bos-de Vos et al., 2025; Geels, 2024); (iii) and on the place-based development scholarship around smart specialization and entrepreneurial discovery (Kruse, 2025; Moraes et al., 2025; Schaltegger et al., 2023). Three features set TRD apart from the preceding discourses:

It elevates the *region*—rather than a sector, technology, or nation-state—to the focal unit of transformation. Acknowledging the context-sensitivity of TRD, enduring industrial legacies, institutional thickness, landscape values, and social capital are viewed not as passive backdrops but as levers or constraints that shape feasible decarbonization trajectories (Binz et al., 2025; Binz et al., 2020). Consequently, identical national climate targets can yield divergent regional pathways, from green reindustrialization in former coalfields to bio-circular diversification in peripheral forest regions.

It relies on *multi-actor mission-oriented governance.* TRD relies on the orchestration of regionally embedded coalitions that span firms, universities, public authorities, trade unions, and civil society organizations (Chlebna & Suitner, 2025; Rabadjieva & Terstriep, 2021; Terstriep & Angstmann, 2025). Mission-oriented portfolios, which combine research funding, skills programs, procurement, land-use regulation, and societal innovation measures, are deployed to align entrepreneurial discovery processes with sustainability and justice goals (Mazzucato, 2018; OECD, 2024; Uyarra et al., 2025). These portfolios must remain adaptive, incorporating iterative monitoring and reflexive learning to cope with forward complexity and outcome uncertainty.

Territorial 'Just Transition Plans' under the EU's Just Transition Fund, or the ecological re-orientation of Germany's GRW, exemplify attempts to fuse decarbonization with inclusive labor-market upgrading and community participation. Success can therefore be judged not only by carbon metrics but also by indicators such as quality employment, reductions in energy poverty, ecosystem regeneration, and improvements in subjective well-being. TRD therefore requires adaptive, reflexive governance architectures with built-in monitoring and course-correction mechanisms.

Forasmuch, far from being an optional add-on, TRD can be the locus where abstract sustainability ambitions confront the realities of uneven development—where the promise of a truly just transition will ultimately be realized or forfeited.

3.4 Interrelatedness of Theoretical Discourses

Structural change (SC) discourse provides the analytical point of departure, explicating how economic activities relocate across sectors, technologies, and territories in response to long-term trends and sudden shocks (Dahlbeck et al., 2022; van Neuss, 2019). Transformative change (TC) adds a normative vector by specifying why a deep re-ordering of socio-technical and socio-ecological systems is required to keep development within planetary boundaries while enhancing social equity, as set out in the 2030 Agenda and the SDGs (Loorbach, 2022; Schot & Steinmueller, 2018; Scoones et al., 2020). The just-transition lens (JT) further sharpens this orientation, interrogating the conditions of fairness under which re-ordering should proceed—how costs and benefits are shared, whose voices count, and how historically marginalized groups and places are recognized (McCauley & Heffron, 2018; Wang & Lo, 2021). Finally, transformative regional development (TRD) operationalizes these imperatives in place, mobilizing regional assets, confronting locally embedded lock-ins, and crafting context-specific pathways to low-carbon prosperity (Grillitsch & Sotarauta, 2020; Tödtling et al., 2022). In shorthand: SC tells us where we stand; TC where we must go; JT under what terms of justice; and TRD how to get there in concrete territories.

Working together, the discourses form a cascading logic. SC diagnostics expose the sectoral structures, institutional routines, and social vulnerabilities that any transition strategy must address. TC defines directional targets—net-zero, circularity, inclusive prosperity—while JT embeds distributional and procedural guardrails. TRD then 'anchors' the composite agenda through smart specialization strategies, territorial just transition plans, and mission-oriented portfolios; successful regional experiments can be fed back to refine national or EU-level TC and JT discourses, creating an iterative learning loop across scales (Geels, 2018).

Because the geography of burdens and opportunities is uneven, JT concerns crystallize most sharply within TRD. Coalfields in Saxony, petro-chemical corridors in Zeeland, or peri-urban logistics belts around Milan face very different transition risks and potentials; without territorially sensitive justice safeguards, such asymmetries risk widening existing spatial inequalities (While & Eadson, 2022). Conversely, where TRD integrates JT principles from the outset, decarbonization can become a vehicle for social inclusion and regional renewal.

The integration of SC, TC, JT, and TRD is complicated by three interacting forms of complexity (Letmathe et al., 2024). *System complexity* stems from tightly coupled technological, economic, ecological, and social subsystems whose opaque, staggered causal chains hinder timely intervention. *Backward complexity* arises from sunk investments, institutional routines, and cultural norms that lock places into carbon-intensive paths; overcoming it demands credible alternatives, broad participation, and, where appropriate, compensation. *Forward complexity* reflects outcome uncertainty: the side effects of interventions are challenging to foresee, inviting contestation and reinforcing lock-ins.

Table 1 contrasts the four discourses, disentangling the justice lens (a normative benchmark) from TRD (the territorial delivery vehicle) and mapping their complementary contributions to a sustainability transition.

Table 1: From Structural Change to Transformative Regional Development – Distinguishing Features

Dimension	**Structural change**	**Transformative change**	**Just transition**	**Transformative regional development**
Ontological focus	Re-allocation within existing architecture	Re-configuration of the architecture itself	Re-configuration plus explicit re-distribution of burdens & benefits	Region as locus of change; creation of new place-based development paths
Normative orientation	Descriptive	Systemic & value-laden	Justice-centred (distributional, procedural, recognitional)	Place-based sustainability missions integrating justice goals

Dimension	Structural change	Transformative change	Just transition	Transformative regional development
Depth & pace	Often gradual, path-dependent	Deep & time-critical	Deep & rapid but paced to protect vulnerable groups	Deep but calibrated to regional capacities & assets
Agency & politics	Impersonal macro-drivers	Explicit contestation	Contestation + burden-sharing negotiations	Regional coalitions of firms, state, academia & civil society; place leadership
Policy connotation	Technocratic adjustment, compensation funds	Mission-oriented steering	Mission steering with justice safeguards	Smart-specialization, territorial JT plans, adaptive regional-aid schemes
Territorial focus	Generic regional disparities	Acknowledges uneven capacities	Targets adversely affected territories	Tails pathways to regional endowments, institutions & socio-ecological niches

Source: Own compilation

4 Conclusion: Toward a Transformative, Just, and Ecologically Responsible Regional Structural Policy

This chapter has sought to dispel the conceptual 'fog' that too often surrounds current debates on regional transformation. By differentiating between structural change, transformative change, just transition, and transformative regional development, we have shown that regional structural and Cohesion Policies are not merely a financial redistribution mechanism, but a multi-layered governance arena in which distinct logics, temporalities, and justice claims intersect. Structural change provides a descriptive baseline, transformative change furnishes a normative direction, the just-transition lens specifies the conditions of fairness, and transformative regional development translates these imperatives into place-specific action. Making these distinctions explicit is the indispensable first step towards policy coherence.

The notion of a place-based, just, and green transformation is gaining traction. Nonetheless, unresolved contradictions between competitiveness and cohesion, central oversight and local agency, and early-advantage and left-behind territories cast doubt on its real-world traction. As detailed in Section 2, Germany's GRW and the EU Structural Funds were grounded in precisely this growth-and-convergence rationale. Unless these tensions are confronted head-on—by embedding binding carbon and justice criteria in every funding regulations, by systematically strengthening the governance capacity of weaker regions, and by reinforcing cross-fund coherence rules that prevent contradictory investments—regional structural and cohesion policies will yield only incremental greening rather than the transformative, equitable transition they promise.

Three structural fault lines make this risk concrete. *First,* although mission-oriented and transformative innovation policies claim to address societal challenges, Cohesion Fund allocations still hinge primarily on GDP per capita (see Section 2 and Frey & Zimmermann, 2005 for the neoclassical convergence logic that originally justified this metric), thereby entrenching the growth paradigm they purport to transcend. *Second,* institutional inertia preserves legacy procedures, cost–benefit methodologies, and evaluation metrics that favor quick-payback projects, thereby crowding out longer-term system-shifting investments. *Third,* compressed decarbonization timelines magnify cross-scalar frictions, as EU thematic targets, federal energy directives, Länder spatial plans, and municipal zoning regulations frequently pull in different directions.

Together these forces create a political economy that produces clear winners and losers: regions with diversified economies, strong R&D ecosystems, and high governance capacity are positioned to capture the bulk of green opportunities, whereas mono-sectoral or peripheral areas risk relegation to subordinate roles in logistics or waste management—thereby hollowing out the "just" in just transition.

These contradictions raise strategic dilemma: how can policymakers reconcile efficiency-oriented investment in leading regions with solidarity-based support for lagging or carbon-intensive territories. It also poses the question of the costs—including economic and social dimensions—associated with transitioning from ecological modernization to green reindustrialization.

It remains to be decided how a regional Cohesion Policy should be designed. One approach is to introduce incentives that channel investment toward structurally weak regions, thereby promoting balanced economic development. A second is to scale up businesses already operating in those areas and use their expansion as a catalyst for reindustrialization. A third option would provide ongoing financial support to residents of lagging regions and subsidize essential infrastructure and public services such as retail, education, and health care. Historically, incentive schemes have dominated, in part because a growth-oriented compensation model cannot justify permanent transfer payments. Yet if full balanced regional development ultimately fails to maximize national growth, a cost-benefit assessment could demonstrate that focusing investments in the most competitive regions while subsidizing the others offers greater economic and environmental returns.

Beyond targeted subsidies, policymakers can strengthen regional economies by expanding local value chains, thereby closing supply gaps and capturing more value added within the region. Possible measures include mobilizing civil society, supporting cooperative business models, and piloting community-wealth building strategies. All of these measures reflect a broader shift toward bottom-up development that empowers local stakeholders rather than relying on top-down directives. Maintaining global connectivity remains essential; the goal is to anchor activities that can compete both regionally and internationally. Where local competitive potential is limited, external stimuli—such as relocating anchor industries or investing in high-quality digital and transport infrastructure—may still be required to jump-start sustainable growth.

Ultimately, the capacity of cities and regions most exposed to structural disruption and decarbonization imperatives to navigate the transition successfully hinges on several interlocking factors. Chief among these are the breadth of their economic base, their demographic and spatial scale, and the opportunities or constraints imposed by their geographic position and the broader regional context. Equally decisive is timing: territories that embark on change proactively and cultivate supportive coalitions are far more likely to establish resilient development paths than those in which entrenched interests delay or resist the necessary restructuring.

4.1 Policy Implications

Conceptual clarity, however, is only a precondition; regional structural policy must now shift from compensating yesterday's market failures to actively steering a rapid, fair, and territorially differentiated climate transition. The prevailing compensatory model—designed to mop up the social costs of market-driven change—must give way to a genuinely transformative mode of governance. Such a shift entails anticipating ecological disruptions through early-warning intelligence, guiding industrial and innovation systems towards territorially grounded transition missions, and cultivating resilient, inclusive development pathways rather than offering temporary subsidies to declining sectors. In short, regional structural policy must move from 'fire-fighting' to 'fire-proofing', i.e., from a reactive, to a preventive, anticipatory, justice-oriented approach. Three design principles are core:

Justice considerations have to be hard-wired into this new architecture. Distributional, procedural, and recognitional equity should condition access to both EU and national funds. Binding 'justice safeguards'—ranging from territorial needs assessments to participatory budgeting—can prevent well-resourced regions from capturing a disproportionate share of the benefits. Without such safeguards, the green agenda risks becoming a fresh engine of spatial inequality, undermining its own political legitimacy.

Environmental integrity must likewise become a cross-cutting principle rather than an afterthought. Aligning regional policy with planetary boundaries requires embedding science-based ecological criteria—such as carbon intensity, land take, biodiversity impacts, etc.—into every discretionary decision. It also means phasing out support for carbon-intensive activities through sunset clauses and just transition compacts, while mainstreaming circular economy, ecosystem restoration, and climate resilience goals across all funding lines. Only by making environmental screening a default gateway can regional action remain compatible with the broader goal of climate neutrality.

In a *multilevel governance* context, regional structural and cohesion policies must operate as nested, mutually reinforcing regimes that couple vertical coordination with horizontal, participatory mechanisms. At the EU level, framework regulations should impose binding environmental and justice conditionalities while granting national and regional authorities sufficient flexibility to tailor place-based transition missions to local industrial legacies and ecological assets. Member States should then translate these conditionalities into mission contracts with sub-national tiers, underpinned by predictable multi-annual finance, technical assistance, and shared data infrastructures. Länder and metropolitan authorities would co-design territorial roadmaps with municipalities, civil society organizations, and groups most exposed to the green and digital transitions—such as coal workers, carers, small manufacturers, and creative communities—so that the economic, social, ecological, and cultural dimensions receive equal weight. Finally, municipalities can institutionalize participatory budgeting, community-benefit agreements, and living lab instruments, embedding experimental projects within broader regional value-chain strategies. Such a polycentric architecture, reinforced by common metrics and iterative feedback loops, would enable both advanced and lagging territories to pursue ecologically sound, socially just, and culturally resonant development trajectories while maintaining pan-European coherence.

These shifts cannot be governed through the GDP-centered indicators that have long guided cohesion spending. A revised dashboard is needed—one that couples territorial carbon budgets, inclusive-employment metrics, ecosystem-service indicators, and measures of subjective well-being. Funding allocations can then be tied to multi-dimensional mission contracts rather than to historical expenditure patterns, thereby rewarding genuine progress towards low-carbon prosperity and social inclusion.

Delivering on this policy vision will demand more than political will and revised regulations; it also calls for fresh evidence, new analytical tools, and experimental arenas capable of steering and tracking change in real time—needs that set the agenda for the research priorities outlined in the next subsection.

4.2 Future Research Avenues

Achieving the transformative, justice-oriented agenda outlined in this chapter will require a research effort commensurate with the scale of the policy challenge. Five priority avenues, each conducive to systematic experimentation, stand out.

First, an EU-wide panel that couples project-level data from ERDF, the Just Transition Fund, and national funds such as Germany's GRW with annual indicators of employment, patenting, and carbon intensity at NUTS-3 scale would permit matched difference-in-difference or synthetic-control estimation of whether, when, and under what conditions green investments alter regional development trajectories (Grillitsch et al., 2025). Embedding 'rolling baselines', i.e., updating the reference year so that each new funding wave is measured against the most recent pre-intervention conditions rather than a distant historical benchmark, into successive programming periods would convert each funding round into a quasi-experimental cohort for the next.

Second, the governance dimension itself should become an object of experimentation. Building on mission-oriented innovation principles (Mazzucato, 2018) and recent work on place leadership (Grillitsch & Sotarauta, 2020), a set of trans regional 'transformative mission labs' could be established—for example, in a coalfield, an automotive cluster and a peripheral bio-economy region. Alternative constellations—such as central steering versus place-based coalitions, procurement mandates versus challenge prizes, and citizen assemblies versus expert panels—could be trialed under adaptive-management protocols, with adjustments made every 12–18 months based on predefined performance metrics (Geels, 2018). Such measures would also align with the call of Haldar et al. (2024) for human-centric energy just transitions that account for agency and capabilities.

Third, operational templates for justice-by-design that also satisfy EU state-aid rules remain surprisingly absent (McCauley & Heffron, 2018). Modular appraisal tools combining distributional microsimulation with ex-ante state-aid compliance checks could be piloted in two or three German Länder and a matched non-German region. The ambition is to reduce administrative friction while increasing the transparency—and contestability—of compensation measures aimed at workers and communities (Kaizuka, 2024).

Fourth, a new generation of metrics is required to capture both avoided emissions and social co-benefits at the regional scale. Integrating high-resolution satellite CO_2 readings with facility-level life-cycle analysis and regional input–output tables would enable researchers to track both direct and embodied emissions. Coupling these environmental accounts with dashboards on energy-poverty reduction, health outcomes, and gender-inclusive employment would provide the multi-criteria perspective needed for robust ex-post evaluation of transition interventions (Sovacool et al., 2025). 'Data sandboxes' in volunteer regions could validate the methodology before it is mainstreamed into regional structural and Cohesion Policy reporting.

To complement this advanced quantitative toolkit, a systematic qualitative strand should be embedded in the evaluation design. Longitudinal interviews, focus groups, and participatory mapping exercises can surface how workers, residents, and local leaders perceive the fairness, cultural fit, and everyday impacts of transition projects—dimensions that escape purely numerical dashboards. Such evidence helps explain why regions with comparable emission cuts or employment gains may diverge in public acceptance or institutional learning, and it can feed back into the indicator set by highlighting locally salient variables (e.g., trust in institutions, gendered care burdens, sense of place). A mixed-methods protocol that triangulates satellite-based carbon estimates and input–output models with these experiential accounts would therefore yield a far richer and more legitimate assessment of regional transition performance.

Finally, comparative transition corridors and distributed living labs could generate transferable lessons across borders. Bi- or tri-national demonstration zones, such as a German-Polish coal corridor or a Franco-Spanish hydrogen valley, would pool regulatory sandboxes, joint funding calls, and shared monitoring frameworks, thereby accelerating mutual learning and exposing context-specific pitfalls (Rodríguez-Pose, 2025). Within each corridor, school retrofit schemes, community energy cooperatives, or circular industry parks could serve as micro-level laboratories whose findings can scale up to corridor-level governance.

By combining natural experiments with deliberately designed pilot schemes, the proposed research agenda can deliver the causal evidence, governance blueprints, and high-resolution metrics required to translate rhetoric into practice. Only by embracing these conceptual, procedural, and ecological re-orientations can regional policy evolve from incremental greening to genuinely transformative, just, and future-proof regional structural development.

References

Alcaide Manthey, N. (2025). Challenging Growing Regional Inequality: Area-Based Policies in Germany as a Path to Equivalent Living Standards? *Politische Vierteljahresschrift.* Advance online publication. https://doi.org/10.1007/s11615-025-00636-4

Avelino, F., Wijsman, K., Van Steenbergen, F., Jhagroe, S., Wittmayer, J., Akerboom, S., Bogner, K., Jansen, E. F., Frantzeskaki, N., & Kalfagianni, A. (2024). Just Sustainability Transitions: Politics, Power, and Prefiguration in Transformative Change Toward Justice and Sustainability. *Annual Review of Environment and Resources,* 49, 519–547. https://doi.org/10.1146/annurev-environ-112321-081722

Bachtler, J., & McMaster, I. (2007). Sustainable growth, competitiveness and employment: Will EU cohesion policy deliver on the lisbon strategy? *Raumforschung Und Raumordnung | Spatial Research and Planning*, *65*(4). https://doi.org/10.1007/BF03183015

Barca, F., McCann, P., & Rodríguez-Pose, A. (2012). The Case for Regional Development Intervention: Place-based versus Place-neutral Approaches. *Journal of Regional Science*, *52*(1), 134–152. https://doi.org/10.1111/j.1467-9787.2011.00756.x

Benz, A. (2021). *Policy Change and Innovation in Multilevel Governance*. Edward Elgar Publishing. https://doi.org/10.4337/9781788119177

Binz, C., Coenen, L., Frenken, K., Murphy, J. T., Strambach, S., Trippl, M., & Truffer, B. (2025). Exploring the Economic Geographies of Sustainability Transitions: Commentary and Agenda. *Economic Geography*, *101*(1), 1–27. https://doi.org/10.1080/00130095.2024.2445530

Binz, C., Coenen, L., Murphy, J. T., & Truffer, B. (2020). Geographies of transition—From topical concerns to theoretical engagement: A comment on the transitions research agenda. *Environmental Innovation and Societal Transitions*, *34*, 1–3. https://doi.org/10.1016/j.eist.2019.11.002

Bömer, H., & Noisser, N. H. (1981). Zum Konzept dieses Sammelbandes und Stand der Arbeit des Arbeitskreises. In Arbeitskreis Arbeitsorientierte Regionalwissenschaft (Ed.), *Regionale Krisen und Arbeitnehmerinteressen: Materialien zur arbeitnehmerorientierten Raumordnungs- und Regionalpolitik; eine Zwischenbilanz* (pp. 7–25). Pahl-Rugenstein.

Bos-de Vos, M., Martinsuo, M., & Loots, E. (2025). Projecting to promote sustainability transitions through joint value creation. International *Journal of Project Management*, *43*(2), 102692. https://doi.org/10.1016/j.ijproman.2025.102692

Brandt, L., & Rawski, T. G. (2022). China's Great Boom as a Historical Process. In D. Ma & R. von Glahn (Eds.), *The Cambridge Economic History of China* (pp. 775–828). Cambridge University Press. https://doi.org/10.1017/9781108348485.022

Bruijn, P. de, & Lagendijk, A. (2005). Regional Innovation Systems in the Lisbon strategy. *European Planning Studies*, *13*(8), 1153–1172. https://doi.org/10.1080/09654310500336519

Cappellano, F., Molica, F., & Makkonen, T. (2024). Missions and Cohesion Policy: Is there a match? *Science and Public Policy*, *51*(3), 360–374. https://doi.org/10.1093/scipol/scad076

Chlebna, C., Martin, H., & Mattes, J. (2023). Grasping transformative regional development – Exploring intersections between industrial paths and sustainability transitions. *Environment and Planning a: Economy and Space, 55*(1), 222–234. https://doi.org/10.1177/0308518X221137346

Chlebna, C., & Suitner, J. (2025). The transition development nexus. disentangling growth and transformation agendas in regional sustainability transitions. *Review of Regional Research*. Advance online publication. https://doi.org/10.1007/s10037-025-00231-5

Cigna, L., Fischer, T., Hasanagic Abuannab, E., Heins, E., & Rathgeb, P. (2023). Varieties of Just Transition? Eco-Social Policy Approaches at the International Level. *Social Policy and Society, 22*(4), 730–746. https://doi.org/10.1017/S1474746423000192

Coenen, L., Binz, C., Murphy, J., & Truffer, B. (2024). Place and Scale in Sustainability Transitions. In J. Wesche & A. Hendriks (Eds.), *Introduction to Sustainable Transition Research* (preprint). Cambridge University Press. https://doi.org/10.33774/coe-2024-tk5mm

Dahlbeck, E., Gärtner, S., Best, B., Kurwan, J., Wehnert, T., & Beutel, J. (2022). *Analysis of the historical structural change in the German hard coal mining Ruhr area*. German Environment Agency.

Demeterova, B. (2024). Assessing regional capabilities-oriented approaches for European just and sustainable transitions. *Regional Studies, 58*(8), 1530–1542. https://doi.org/10.1080/00343404.2023.2242894

Dettmann, E., Weyh, A., & Titze, M. (2025). Employment effects of investment grants and firm heterogeneity. *Regional Studies, 59*(1), Article 2549799. https://doi.org/10.1080/00343404.2025.2549799

European Commission. (2024). Forging a sustainable future together: Cohesion for a competitive and inclusive Europe: Report of the High-Level Group on the Future of Cohesion Policy, February 2024. Publications Office of the European Commission. https://doi.org/10.2776/143512

Farole, T., Rodríguez-Pose, A., & Storper, M. (2011). Cohesion Policy in the European Union: Growth, Geography, Institutions. *Journal of Common Market Studies, 49*(5), 1089–1111. https://doi.org/10.1111/j.1468-5965.2010.02161.x

Filippetti, A., & Spallone, R. (2025). The evolution of Cohesion Policy in 40 years of economic policy agenda. *European Planning Studies, 33*(9), 1423–1442. https://doi.org/10.1080/09654313.2025.2520891

Fingleton, B., & Fischer, M. M. (2010). Neoclassical theory versus new economic geography: competing explanations of cross-regional variation in

economic development. *The Annals of Regional Science*, 44(3), 467–491. https://doi.org/10.1007/s00168-008-0278-z
Flögel, F. & Gärtner, S. (2019). Können Unternehmen zur Stabilisierung strukturschwacher Räume beitragen? SPOTLIGHT "Wirtschaft und Region" (4). Gütersloh: Bertelsmann Stiftung.
Fratesi, U. (2025). The four waves of regional policy: towards an era of trade-offs? *Regional Studies*, 59(1), Article 2436538. https://doi.org/10.1080/00343404.2024.2436538
Frey, R. L., & Zimmermann, H. (2005). Neue Rahmenbedingungen für die Raumordnung als Chance für marktwirtschaftliche Instrumente. *DisP – the Planning Review*, 41(161), 5–18. https://doi.org/10.1080/02513625.2005.10556920
Galanis, G., Napoletano, M., Popoyan, L., Sapio, A., & Vardakoulias, O. (2025). Defining just transition. *Ecological Economics*, 227, 108370. https://doi.org/10.1016/j.ecolecon.2024.108370
Gärtner, S. (2019). An attempt at preventive action in the transformation of coal-mining regions in Germany. In B. Galgóczi (Ed.), *Towards a just transition: coal, cars and the world of work* (135–154). etui.
Geels, F. W. (2018). Socio-Technical Transitions to Sustainability. In H. H. Shugart (Ed.), *Oxford Research Encyclopedia of Environmental Science* Oxford University Press. https://doi.org/10.1093/acrefore/9780199389414.013.587
Geels, F. W. (2024). *The Multi-Level Perspective on Sustainability Transitions: Background, overview, and current research topics.* https://doi.org/10.33774/coe-2024-c15gb
Geels, F. W., & Turnheim, B. (2022). *The Great Reconfiguration.* Cambridge University Press. https://doi.org/10.1017/9781009198233
Grashof, N., & Basilico, S. (2025). Divergent paths for green transition: regional disparities in technology diversification. *Regional Studies*, 59(1), Article 2363327. https://doi.org/10.1080/00343404.2024.2363327
Grillitsch, M., Coenen, L., & Morgan, K. (2025). Directionality and subsidiarity: sustainability challenges in regional development policy. *Regional Studies.* Advance online publication. https://doi.org/10.1080/00343404.2025.2492171
Grillitsch, M., & Sotarauta, M. (2020). Trinity of change agency, regional development paths and opportunity spaces. *Progress in Human Geography*, 44(4), 704–723. https://doi.org/10.1177/0309132519853870
Haldar, S., Grillitsch, M., & Bazaz, A. (2024). A human-centric approach to energy justice: Embedding agency and capabilities in transitions discourse.

EconPapers, 2024/7, 1–38. https://wp.circle.lu.se/upload/CIRCLE/workingpapers/202407_haldar.pdf

Hemberger, C., & Kiwitt, T. (2020). Glückssache oder konsequente Strategie? RaumPlanung. *RaumPlanung Fachzeitschrift Für Räumliche Planung Und Forschung*, 4-2020, 36–41.

Huntjens, P., & Kemp, R. (2022). The Importance of a Natural Social Contract and Co-Evolutionary Governance for Sustainability Transitions. *Sustainability*, *14*(5), 2976. https://doi.org/10.3390/su14052976

Jenkins, K., Sovacool, B. K., & McCauley, D. (2018). Humanizing sociotechnical transitions through energy justice: An ethical framework for global transformative change. *Energy Policy*, *117*, 66–74. https://doi.org/10.1016/j.enpol.2018.02.036

Kaizuka, S. (2024). Politics of a Just Transition: lessons from the UK coal mines. *Contemporary Social Science*, *19*(1–3), 154–177. https://doi.org/10.1080/21582041.2024.2337672

Karlsen, J., Rypestøl, J. O., & Trippl, M. (2025). Sustainable Regional Restructuring: an introduction. In J. Karlsen, J. O. Rypestøl, & M. Trippl (Eds.), *New horizons in regional science series. Sustainable regional restructuring: Insights from economic geography and regional innovation studies* (pp. 1–10). Edward Elgar Publishing. https://doi.org/10.4337/9781035330799.00008

Kruse, M. (2025). On sustainability in regional innovation studies and smart specialisation. *Innovation: The European Journal of Social Science Research*, *38*(2), 961–982. https://doi.org/10.1080/13511610.2023.2208294

Letmathe, P., Paegert, M., Roll, C., Balleer, A., Böschen, S., Breuer, W., Förster, A., Gramelsberger, G., Greiff, K., Häußling, R., Lemme, M., Leuchner, M., Piller, F., Seefried, E., & Wahlbrink, T. (2024). Societal Transformation: Transformation Research, Transformational Research, Research Transformation: A Novel Framework from RWTH Aachen University. In P. Letmathe, C. Roll, A. Balleer, S. Böschen, W. Breuer, A. Förster, G. Gramelsberger, K. Greiff, R. Häußling, M. Lemme, M. Leuchner, M. Paegert, F. T. Piller, E. Seefried, & T. Wahlbrink (Eds.), *Transformation Towards Sustainability* (pp. 3–38). Springer.

Li, H. (2025). Ensuring a Fair Development? The Role of Cohesion Policy and Just Transition Mechanism in the EU Green Initiative. *Review of European and Comparative Law*. Advance online publication. https://doi.org/10.31743/recl.18601

Liargovas, P., & Papageorgiou, C. (2024). Regional Policy: Disparities, Development and Future Direction. In P. Liargovas & C. Papageorgiou (Eds.),

The European Integration, Vol. 2 (pp. 253–286). Springer. https://doi.org/10.1007/978-3-031-47176-6_7

Loorbach, D. A. (2022). Designing radical transitions: a plea for a new governance culture to empower deep transformative change. *City, Territory and Architecture*, 9(1). https://doi.org/10.1186/s40410-022-00176-z

MacKinnon, D., Kempton, L., O'Brien, P., Ormerod, E., Pike, A., & Tomaney, J. (2022). Reframing urban and regional 'development' for 'left behind' places. *Cambridge Journal of Regions, Economy and Society*, *15*(1), 39–56. https://doi.org/10.1093/cjres/rsab034

Mazzucato, M. (2018). Mission-oriented innovation policies: challenges and opportunities. *Industrial and Corporate Change*, 27(5), 803–815. https://doi.org/10.1093/icc/dty034

McCauley, D., & Heffron, R. (2018). Just transition: Integrating climate, energy and environmental justice. *Energy Policy*, *119*, 1–7. https://doi.org/10.1016/j.enpol.2018.04.014

Medeiros, E., Potluka, O., Demeterova, B., & Musiałkowska, I. (2024). EU Cohesion Policy towards territorial cohesion? *Regional Studies*, *58*(8), 1513–1517. https://doi.org/10.1080/00343404.2024.2349736

Moodie, J. (2025). The Key Dimensions of Just Transitions – From Concept to Policy Practice. *Journal of Sustainability*, *1*(2). https://doi.org/10.55845/jos-2025-1248

Moodie, J., Tapia, C., Löfving, L., Gassen, N. S., & Cedergren, E. (2021). Towards a Territorially Just Climate Transition—Assessing the Swedish EU Territorial Just Transition Plan Development Process. *Sustainability*, *13*(13), 7505. https://doi.org/10.3390/su13137505

Moraes, M. A. de, Moraes, G. H. S. M. de, do Prado, N. B., & Fischer, B. B. (2025). Triggering Sustainable Transitions in Entrepreneurial Ecosystems: Key Enabling Conditions and Outcomes. *Sustainable Development*, Article sd.70005. Advance online publication. https://doi.org/10.1002/sd.70005

Newell, P., Srivastava, S., Naess, L. O., Torres Contreras, G. A., & Price, R. (2021). Toward transformative climate justice: An emerging research agenda. *WIREs Climate Change*, *12*(6), Article e733. https://doi.org/10.1002/wcc.733

OECD. (2023). *Regions in Industrial Transition 2023: New Approaches to Persistent Problems*. OECD Publishing. https://doi.org/10.1787/5604c2ab-en

OECD. (2024). *Mission-Oriented Innovation Policies for Net Zero*. OECD. https://doi.org/10.1787/5efdbc5c-en

Oei, P.-Y., Brauers, H., & Herpich, P. (2020). Lessons from Germany's hard coal mining phase-out: policies and transition from 1950 to 2018. *Climate Policy*, *20*(8), 963–979. https://doi.org/10.1080/14693062.2019.1688636

Pfeiffer, A. (1982). Vorausschauende Strukturpolitik durch gesamtwirtschaftliche Mitbestimmung. *Gewerkschaftliche Monatshefte*, *10*, 617–626.

Pike, A., Béal, V., Cauchi-Duval, N., Franklin, R., Kinossian, N., Lang, T., Leibert, T., MacKinnon, D., Rousseau, M., Royer, J., Servillo, L., Tomaney, J., & Velthuis, S. (2024). 'Left behind places': a geographical etymology. *Regional Studies*, *58*(6), 1167–1179. https://doi.org/10.1080/00343404.2023.2167972

Porter, L., Rickards, L., Verlie, B., Bosomworth, K., Moloney, S., Lay, B., Latham, B., Anguelovski, I., & Pellow, D. (2020). Climate Justice in a Climate Changed World. *Planning Theory & Practice*, *21*(2), 293–321. https://doi.org/10.1080/14649357.2020.1748959

Rabadjieva, M., & Terstriep, J. (2021). Ambition Meets Reality: Mission-Oriented Innovation Policy as a Driver for Participative Governance. *Sustainability*, *13*(1), 231. https://doi.org/10.3390/su13010231

Rawls, J. (1971). *A Theory of Justice*. Harvard University Press. https://doi.org/10.2307/j.ctvjf9z6v

Rembser, J. Die Förderung des wirtschaftlichen und sozialen Wandels durch die Forschungs- und Entwicklungspolitik als präventive Strukturpolitik. Rhein-Ruhr Druck Sander.

Rice, J. L., Long, J., & Levenda, A. M. (Eds.). (2023). *Urban climate justice: Theory, Praxis, Resistance*. The University of Georgia Press.

Rodríguez-Pose, A. (2025). Forging a sustainable future together: Cohesion Policy at its defining moment. *Regional Studies*, *59*(1), Article 2552869. https://doi.org/10.1080/00343404.2025.2552869

Rodríguez-Pose, A., & Bartalucci, F. (2024). The green transition and its potential territorial discontents. *Cambridge Journal of Regions, Economy and Society*, *17*(2), 339–358. https://doi.org/10.1093/cjres/rsad039

Sabato, S., & Mandelli, M. (2024). Towards an EU framework for a just transition: welfare policies and politics for the socio-ecological transition. *European Political Science*, *23*(1), 14–26. https://doi.org/10.1057/s41304-023-00458-1

Schaltegger, S., Loorbach, D., & Hörisch, J. (2023). Managing entrepreneurial and corporate contributions to sustainability transitions. *Business Strategy and the Environment*, *32*(2), 891–902. https://doi.org/10.1002/bse.3080

Schot, J., & Steinmueller, W. E. (2018). Three frames for innovation policy: R&D, systems of innovation and transformative change. *Research Policy*, 47(9), 1554–1567. https://doi.org/10.1016/j.respol.2018.08.011

Scoones, I., Stirling, A., Abrol, D., Atela, J., Charli-Joseph, L., Eakin, H., Ely, A., Olsson, P., Pereira, L., Priya, R., van Zwanenberg, P., & Yang, L. (2020). Transformations to sustainability: combining structural, systemic and enabling approaches. *Current Opinion in Environmental Sustainability*, 42, 65–75. https://doi.org/10.1016/j.cosust.2019.12.004

Sovacool, B. K., Devine-Wright, P., Mander, S., Rowley, J., & Ryder, S. (2025). Realising a locally-embedded just transition: Sense of place, lived experience, and social perceptions of industrial decarbonisation in the United Kingdom. *Global Environmental Change*, *94*, 103051. https://doi.org/10.1016/j.gloenvcha.2025.103051

Stark, A., Gale, F., & Murphy-Gregory, H. (2023). Just Transitions' Meanings: A Systematic Review. *Society & Natural Resources*, *36*(10), 1277–1297. https://doi.org/10.1080/08941920.2023.2207166

Südekum, J., & Rademacher, P. (2024). *Regionale Disparitäten in der Transformation*. https://doi.org/10.11586/2024023

Suedekum, J. (2023). The broadening of place-based policies – from reactive cohesion towards proactive support for all regions: Background paper for the OECD-EC High-Level Expert Workshop Series on "Place-Based Policies for the Future", Workshop 1, 14 April 2023. https://www.oecd.org/cfe/regionaldevelopment/place-based-policies-for-the-future.htm

Terstriep, J., & Angstmann, M. (2025). Harnessing societal innovativeness for transformative regional development. *IAT Discuss Papers*, *25*(02). https://doi.org/10.53190/dp/202502

Thoss, R., & Ritzmann, P. (1984). *Informationsgrundlagen für die vorausschauende Strukturpolitik*. Deutsche Akademie für Städtebau und Landesplanung.

Tödtling, F., Trippl, M., & Desch, V. (2022). New directions for RIS studies and policies in the face of grand societal challenges. *European Planning Studies*, *30*(11), 2139–2156. https://doi.org/10.1080/09654313.2021.1951177

Trippl, M., & Tödtling, F. (2025). Place-based transformative innovation policies. In J. Karlsen, J. O. Rypestøl, & M. Trippl (Eds.), *Sustainable Regional Restructuring* (pp. 11–26). Edward Elgar Publishing. https://doi.org/10.4337/9781035330799.00009

Uyarra, E., Bugge, M. M., Coenen, L., Flanagan, K., & Wanzenböck, I. (2025). Geographies of mission-oriented innovation policy. *Environmental Innova-*

tion and Societal Transitions, *56*, 100970. https://doi.org/10.1016/j.eist.2025.100970

van Neuss, L. (2019). The Drivers of Structural Change. *Journal of Economic Surveys*, *33*(1), 309–349. https://doi.org/10.1111/joes.12266

Wang, X., & Lo, K. (2021). Just transition: A conceptual review. *Energy Research & Social Science*, *82*, 102291. https://doi.org/10.1016/j.erss.2021.102291

Wardenburg, S., & Brenner, T. (2020). How to improve the quality of life in peripheral and lagging regions by policy measures? Examining the effects of two different policies in Germany. *Journal of Regional Science*, *60*(5), 1047–1073. https://doi.org/10.1111/jors.12500

Weck, S., Madanipour, A., & Schmitt, P. (2022). Place-based development and spatial justice. *European Planning Studies*, *30*(5), 791–806. https://doi.org/10.1080/09654313.2021.1928038

Weingarten, J. (2010). Antizipation des Wandels. Herausforderungen und Handlungsansätze für Kommunen, Unternehmen und Beschäftigte im Rahmen der kohlepolitischen Vereinbarungen in NRW [Dissertation]. Ruhr-Universität Bochum.

While, A., & Eadson, W. (2022). Zero carbon as economic restructuring: spatial divisions of labour and just transition. *New Political Economy*, *27*(3), 385–402. https://doi.org/10.1080/13563467.2021.1967909

Ecologizing the Concept of Progress

Toward a Terrestrial Ethics and Ontology through Jonas and Latour

Marlen Reinschke

> "Humans have changed the way the world works. Now they have to change the way they think about it, too."
> *(Economist, 26/05/2011)*

Abstract: *This paper reconsiders the modern concept of progress in light of ecological crisis by proposing its ecologization—an ethical and ontological reorientation grounded in terrestrial thinking. Traditionally associated with linear temporality, technological development, and anthropocentric mastery, the idea of progress is shown to be complicit in environmental degradation and systemic planetary imbalance. Drawing on Bruno Latour's political ecology and Hans Jonas's ethics of responsibility, the paper critiques this dominant paradigm and explores alternative frameworks for understanding progress in a more-than-human context. While Jonas emphasizes foresight and moral obligation rooted in human responsibility, Latour decouples agency from human exclusivity, advancing a relational ontology that includes nonhuman actors and the Earth (Gaia) itself as participants in political and ethical life. Despite their differences, both thinkers converge in their critique of techno-scientific hubris and their call for a reorientation of human agency. The paper argues that integrating Jonas's normative ethical vision with Latour's ontological pluralism enables a reframing of progress as situated, relational, and co-responsible. Such a reconfiguration, the paper concludes, is essential for developing a viable ecological ethic and navigating the demands of terrestrial life in the wake of the modernist project.*

1. Introduction

The modern concept of progress, long tethered to linear time, technological mastery, and human exceptionalism, is increasingly called into question in the face of ecological collapse and planetary destabilization. What once functioned as a secular promise of improvement now reveals its complicity in the degradation of the very conditions that make life possible. This paper argues for an ecologization of the concept of progress—an attempt to rethink its foundations through an ethical and ontological reorientation toward the terrestrial. Drawing on Bruno Latour's political ecology and Hans Jonas's ethics of responsibility, the essay explores how progress might be reconceived not as domination over nature, but as a situated, relational, and co-responsible engagement with a more-than-human world. Where Jonas articulates a moral imperative grounded in the foresight of human action, Latour offers a political and ontological framework in which nonhuman actors, entanglements, and Earth itself become part of the ethical field. Together, their thought helps outline a paradigm of progress that complicates anthropocentrism: while Jonas maintains a human-centered ethical imperative, Latour calls for a broader ecology of agency and co-responsibility. Their convergence opens space for reimagining progress in light of ecological realities.

The following chapters begin by tracing the historical development of the modern concept of progress, emphasizing its entanglement with anthropocentrism, technological optimism, and the modernist project. This is followed by a critical examination of Hans Jonas's and Bruno Latour's respective contributions to rethinking human agency and responsibility in ecological terms. Particular attention is given to the tensions and complementarities between Jonas's anthropocentric ethics of responsibility and Latour's relational ontology and political ecology. The final section synthesizes these perspectives to outline the contours of an ecologically informed concept of progress—one that resists the logic of domination and is responsive to the complex, entangled realities of life on a shared and vulnerable planet.

2. The Modern Paradigm of Progress: Origins and Critiques

The concept of progress, which emerged during the Enlightenment and solidified through modernity, has been foundational to Western thought and political practice. Rooted in the belief in linear advancement, human mastery over nature, and the perfectibility of society through science and technology, this paradigm has shaped dominant narratives of development and improvement for centuries. Progress was traditionally understood as an unequivocally positive force—a forward-moving trajectory promising greater knowledge, prosperity, and control over the environment. However, this modern paradigm is increasingly subject to criticism due to its anthropocentrism, its assumptions of limitless growth, and its role in driving ecological crises. Critics from ecological, political, and philosophical perspectives question the coherence and desirability of this linear, human-centered model. This section traces the historical development of the progress paradigm in brief and examines key critiques, forming the basis for alternative conceptions that respond to ecological realities and ethical imperatives.

Since the Enlightenment, progress has been conceived as a linear, continuous process through which human society advances via scientific discovery, technological innovation, and socio-political reform. This teleological vision implies inherent improvement over time: the future is better than the past, and the present is a steppingstone toward ever-greater mastery over nature and social conditions (Kant, 1784/1997; Condorcet, 1795/1994). The roots of this concept lie in the Enlightenment's faith in reason and human perfectibility, along with the rise of scientific naturalism and industrial capitalism. Philosophers such as Kant and Condorcet envisioned history as a rational process of emancipation and progress culminating in an era of universal enlightenment and freedom. Progress thus became a metanarrative legitimizing the expansion of knowledge, technology, and economic growth. Already in the 19th and early 20th centuries, fundamental objections to the paradigm of progress were being formulated. Romanticism, for instance, countered the rationalization of the world with a mode of thinking grounded in organic interconnectedness and a deep affinity with nature. With the onset of the "Age of Extremes" (Hobsbawm, 1998), criticism intensified: the two world wars, the Holocaust, colonialism, and the destruction of ecological systems through industrial expansion led to a deep questioning of the idea of linear moral progress.

Critical Theory, especially in the works of Horkheimer and Adorno, analyzed the idea of progress as part of a dialectical movement in which Enlightenment transforms into new forms of domination. In their *Dialectic of Enlightenment*, they argue that the same processes of rationalization that contributed to human liberation simultaneously fostered an instrumental reason that objectified both nature and the subject (Horkheimer & Adorno, 1969). Here, progress no longer appears as a guarantor of humanity, but as an ambivalent moment in an ongoing process of alienation. Postcolonial and feminist approaches also critique the implicit universalization of Western development models, which often conceal cultural hegemony and epistemic violence under the guise of progress. Progress is thus not seen as a neutral process but deconstructed as an expression of particular power relations (Spivak, 1988). Particularly in the context of climate change, the modern narrative of progress is inadequate, as it fails to take into account humanity's new role as a geological force beyond historical categories (Chakrabarty, 2009). Finally, from an ecological perspective, the destructive flip side of classical progress becomes increasingly apparent. The expansive logic inherent to the idea of "ever more" conflicts with the finitude of natural resources. The concept of progress increasingly appears as an ideological engine of ecological exploitation as a metaphysical justification for a process of planetary destabilization. Most urgently, ecological critiques emphasize that Earth's planetary boundaries (climate, biodiversity, biogeochemical cycles) are being exceeded due to the dominant, growth-oriented paradigm of progress (Rockström et al., 2009). The assumed compatibility of infinite growth with a finite planet is thereby called into question, exposing the classical ideal of progress not only as inadequate but also as dangerous. Consequently, a critical rethinking of the concept of progress is imperative—one that incorporates ecological realities and challenges the anthropocentric, linear assumptions of modernity's dominant narrative.

This growing body of critique reveals the limitations of the traditional progress narrative, particularly its failure to account for ecological constraints and the interdependence of all life on Earth. The escalating environmental crises demand a fundamental reassessment of progress—one that transcends human-centered and growth-driven assumptions. Of particular relevance are the ecological challenges confronting the modern paradigm, which demonstrate how environmental realities require a reconceptualization of progress in line with planetary boundaries and sustainable coexistence. The Anthropocene, defined as the current geological epoch marked by significant human impact on Earth's systems, underscores the urgent need to rethink progress. This epoch highlights the profound entanglement of human and nonhuman forces and exposes the limits of traditional frameworks that separate society from nature. Ecological thinking introduces key concepts such as interdependence, limits, resilience, and vulnerability, thereby destabilizing the foundations of the classical narrative of progress. It reveals that what was once considered "nature" to be conquered is, in fact, a complex, dynamic, and sensitive web of life within which humanity is inextricably embedded (Latour, 1993; 2017). The systemic risks and uncertainties characteristic of the Anthropocene render linear and growth-oriented visions of progress untenable. Furthermore, the ecological crisis introduces a temporal dimension often obscured by classical progress narratives. Environmental degradation and climate change produce long-term, often irreversible consequences, requiring a shift from short-term maximization to an ethic of future-oriented responsibility (Jonas, 1984). This challenges the dominant temporal paradigm of progress as endless forward motion, and instead suggests the necessity of precaution, care, and sustainability. Accordingly, the ecological challenge demands an "ecologization" of the concept of progress—a fundamental revision that reconfigures progress as a notion inherently entangled with planetary boundaries, ethical responsibility, and the relationality between human and nonhuman actors.

3. From Nature as Resource to Ecological Interconnectedness

A fundamental reconfiguration in the ecologization of progress involves a profound transformation in the conceptualization of nature itself. Historically, particularly within the dominant frameworks of modernity and historical materialism, nature has been conceived primarily as a resource—a vast, external stockpile of raw materials to be appropriated, exploited, and controlled for human advancement and economic growth. Karl Marx's analysis of capitalism famously emphasizes the extraction and transformation of natural resources as a driver of production and social development (Marx, 1867/1976). While foundational for industrial and technological progress, this instrumentalist view tacitly assumes nature's disposability, subordinating ecological concerns to economic imperatives. However, the environmental crises of the late twentieth and early twenty-first centuries have exposed the limitations—and dangers—of this resource-based ontology. Contemporary ecological thought increasingly rejects the objectification and commodification of nature, emphasizing instead interdependence, relationality, and the agency of the more-than-human world. Bruno Latour (among other philosophers and new materialist thinkers) critiques the modernist dualisms that separate humans from nature, arguing that such binaries facilitate domination and ecological destruction. This ontological shift carries profound ethical and political consequences. Indigenous worldviews, for instance, often conceive of humans as embedded within relational networks that include animals, plants and landscapes—networks grounded not in control or exploitation, but in reciprocity and responsibility (Whyte, 2017). Donna Haraway similarly calls for rethinking human-nonhuman relations through the concept of sympoiesis—a mode of "making-with" that emphasizes mutual entanglement and collaborative survival in the ruins of modern progress (Haraway, 2016). Such perspectives foster an ethic of care and stewardship that stands in stark contrast to the exploitative paradigms of modernity. Moreover, this reconceptualization influences policy and action. The emergence of ecosystem services frameworks and rights of nature laws in some jurisdictions reflects attempts to institutionalize the idea that nature is not merely a resource but a rights-bearing entity with intrinsic value and agency (Stone, 2010; Cullinan, 2011). These shifts challenge legal and economic systems to move beyond anthropocentric valuation and incorporate ecological interdependence into decision-making. In relation to the concept of progress, this epistemic transformation entails a move from viewing progress as technological mastery over an external nature toward progress as the cultivation and maintenance of sustainable relationships between humans and the more-than-human world. Hans Jonas's ethics of responsibility explicitly ground moral obligation in the recognition of the natural world's vulnerability and intrinsic worth, compelling humanity to safeguard ecological conditions for future generations (Jonas, 1984). Similarly, Bruno Latour's relational ontology rejects nature/society dualisms, proposing instead that humans are enmeshed in networks of heterogeneous actors, and that progress must involve the composition of new, hybrid collectives where nonhuman agencies are accounted for (Latour, 1993). Together, these perspectives suggest that a crucial prerequisite for ecologically informed progress lies in transforming the way nature is seen and valued—from a passive resource base toward a dynamic, interconnected participant in shared futures. This paradigm shift not only challenges the epistemological foundations of classical progress narratives but also opens up possibilities for ethical engagement and political innovation compatible with ecological limits. The reconceptualization of nature as relational, interconnected, and agentic not only challenges the ontological foundations of modernity but also demands a rethinking of ethical and political responsibility. If progress is no longer defined by domination over nature but by the capacity to live within ecological limits and relational networks, then the question arises: how should human agency be redefined in this transformed landscape? This question lies at the heart of both Hans Jonas's ethics of responsibility and Bruno Latour's political ecology. Although they approach the issue from distinct philosophical traditions—Jonas from existential ethics and Latour from science and technology studies—both thinkers grapple with the urgency of ecological crisis and the need to reorient human action accordingly. The following section examines their respective contributions to an ecologically grounded notion of progress, highlighting points of convergence and productive tension between their frameworks.

4. Hans Jonas and the Ethics of Responsibility

> "Act so that the effects of your action are not destructive of the future possibility of (...) life."
> *(Jonas, 1984, 11)*

Hans Jonas's philosophical intervention is pivotal for rethinking the concept of progress in light of ecological crisis. Writing in response to the rapidly advancing technological power of the mid-20th century, Jonas identified a deep ethical void at the heart of modern moral philosophy: its failure to account for humanity's unprecedented capacity to alter the planet and endanger future generations in irreversible ways (Jonas, 1984). His work responds directly to the crisis of modernity's unrestrained technological expansion, which, under the banner of progress, threatened the very conditions of life on Earth. Central to Jonas's thought is the imperative of responsibility. Unlike classical ethical theories, which focus primarily on interpersonal duties among contemporaries, Jonas extends the ethical horizon toward the long-term future and the more-than-human world. His "Imperative of Responsibility" demands that human action be evaluated according to its impact on the "permanence of genuine human life on Earth" (Jonas, 1984, 11). This is not merely a pragmatic or instrumental concern; it constitutes a new foundation for ethics—one grounded in the vulnerability of life and the irreversible scope of technological intervention. Jonas's ethical thinking introduces a new temporal dimension to moral reflection, in which the future is recognized as a distinct domain of ethical concern. Responsibility is no longer limited to the immediate or the visible but extends to future generations, whose well-being depends on the foresight and restraint of those living today (Jonas, 1984, 13). For Jonas, the modern concept of progress—rooted in Enlightenment optimism, technological confidence, and anthropocentric rationalism—is ethically obsolete. Traditional notions of progress celebrate the idea of linear advancement, the continual mastery of nature, and the limitless expansion of human capabilities. Jonas critiques this as a dangerous illusion. In his view, such faith in progress neglects the destructive potential of modern technology and assumes that innovation will always be redemptive. In response, Jonas proposes a reversal of the burden of proof: in situations where technological action could result in ecological catastrophe, the onus lies not on the critics to demonstrate harm, but on the proponents to prove safety. This precautionary principle is central to his ecological ethics. It marks a clear departure from the dominant ethos of growth and acceleration, instead advocating for restraint, humility, and moral foresight (Jonas, 1984, 13). Although Jonas remains committed to the central role of the human as a moral subject, his philosophy nonetheless challenges anthropocentrism by emphasizing the intrinsic value of life itself. He argues that the unprecedented power humans now wield over the biosphere necessitates a new form of stewardship—one grounded not in domination but in care (Jonas, 1984, 8). Life, in its vulnerability and irreplaceability, becomes the ground of moral obligation (Jonas, 1984, 10). This ontological shift, though not yet a full break with the modern subject/object divide, pushes toward a broader view of ethical relevance. Jonas does not fully dissolve the divide between humans and nature, but he demands that human agency recognize its embeddedness in and responsibility toward a larger web of life (Jonas, 1984, 7). In this sense, his work anticipates more relational and decentered ontologies without fully embracing them. Jonas offers a powerful ethical critique of modern progress and a compelling normative vision for ecological responsibility. He situates human action within a widened moral and temporal field, emphasizing care, sustainability, and the preservation of life (Jonas, 1984, 12). His imperative of responsibility remains a crucial resource for grounding ecological thought in ethical terms. Yet Jonas's framework, while ethically expansive, still operates within a modern metaphysical architecture that privileges the human as the central moral actor. Agency remains largely human, and nature, while valued, is not politicized or ontologically equal. The categories of "nature" and "humanity" remain distinct, and the conditions under which responsibility is exercised are not redefined at the ontological level. To move beyond this limitation, and to fully ecologize the concept of progress, it becomes necessary to question the very constitution of the modern subject and its separation from the nonhuman world. This is the project undertaken by Bruno Latour, whose political ecology seeks not only to expand ethical responsibility but to redistribute agency, dissolve dualisms, and recompose the world in terms of entangled, more-than-human collectives. Where Jonas offers an ethical compass, Latour provides the ontological and political tools necessary to rethink progress as situated, relational, and co-constructed by human and nonhuman actors alike. While Hans Jonas's ethics of responsibility powerfully expands the moral horizon by emphasizing human foresight, care, and restraint in the face of ecological vulnerability, it remains rooted in a fundamentally anthropocentric framework. His normative vision centers on human agency as the bearer of ethical obligation and conceptualizes nature primarily as an object of human stewardship. However, as ecological challenges intensify and the limitations of human-centered ethics become increasingly evident, a further rethinking is required—one that not only broadens ethical responsibility but also reconfigures the very ontological categories of agency, subjectivity, and the nature-society divide. Bruno Latour's political ecology offers this next step by decentering the human subject and advocating for a relational, more-than-human conception of progress. Latour challenges the modern dualisms that Jonas retains and proposes a framework in which humans and nonhumans co-constitute political and ethical collectives. In doing so, Latour provides a complementary but ontologically radical approach to ecologizing progress—one that reconceives agency, responsibility, and the composition of shared worlds beyond traditional boundaries.

The following section will thus explore Latour's thought as a critical extension and transformation of the ethical groundwork laid by Jonas, focusing on the implications of Latour's relational ontology for redefining progress in the Anthropocene.

5. Bruno Latour's political ecology

Building on Hans Jonas's foundational ethics of responsibility, Bruno Latour's political ecology offers a vital ontological and political reconfiguration necessary to fully ecologize the concept of progress. While Jonas expands the ethical horizon by emphasizing human foresight and moral obligation toward future life and ecological vulnerability, Latour pushes further by challenging the very categories through which modernity has understood agency, nature, and society. He argues that rethinking progress requires not only a normative recalibration but also a profound revision of the conceptual and political frameworks that sustain the dominant human-centered worldview.

Latour's relational ontology dissolves the rigid nature-society divide, presenting humans and nonhumans as interconnected actors within dynamic networks. Central to his thought is the concept of "composition," which denotes the ongoing collective assembling of heterogeneous beings and forces into new political and ecological configurations. This framework opens the way for a politics of the terrestrial—anchored in the figure of Gaia as a political-ecological actor—where progress is no longer about human mastery but about coexisting and composing sustainable worlds. Moreover, Latour critiques the limitations of traditional critique and envisions the emergence of an ecological class—new political subjects whose identities and interests are inseparable from the terrestrial. This perspective highlights how ecological challenges necessitate political innovation and collective responsibility that transcends old dichotomies and power structures. In what follows, this chapter will explore these dimensions of Latour's thought, showing how his political ecology not only complements but crucially extends the ethical insights of Jonas. Together, they provide a robust conceptual and normative foundation for an ecological reconceptualization of progress suited to the complexities of the Anthropocene.

The ecological crisis presents not only urgent practical challenges but also deep conceptual questions for the categories underpinning political and ethical modernity. The concept of progress, rooted in Enlightenment and industrial modernity, proves inadequate when confronted with planetary limits. It remains bound to a profound anthropocentrism that reduces nature to a mere resource for human ends, and to a linear temporality demanding constant innovation and forward momentum—often at the cost of present ecological destruction (Latour, 2018; Jonas, 1984). Consequently, a thorough revision of progress is imperative—an ecologization that redefines it not as the mere extension of technological mastery but as a relational, responsibility-infused coexistence with nonhuman entities. The philosophical approaches Bruno Latour's political ecology and Hans Jonas's ethics of responsibility prove especially fruitful in this regard. Latour critiques the modern concept of progress as embedded within a dualistic framework that artificially separates nature and society—a foundational gesture of modernity. In *We Have Never Been Modern* (1993), he argues that the modern constitution rests on two simultaneous but contradictory operations: the purification of conceptual domains (i.e., drawing clear distinctions between nature and culture, facts and values), and the proliferation of hybrids, meaning the ongoing creation of entities that mix natural and social elements—such as climate models, genetically modified organisms, or technological infrastructures (Latour, 1993, 10–12). These hybrids are ubiquitous in modern life, yet modern discourse systematically represses their entangled nature by maintaining the illusion of pure categories. This paradox reveals what Latour calls the "modern constitution": a hidden rule that organizes knowledge and power by separating what is considered objective (nature) from what is considered subjective or constructed (culture or society), while in practice continuously entangling them (Latour, 1993, 13–15). According to Latour, this dichotomy is not an empirical reality but an ideological framework that legitimizes a certain regime of politics, science, and progress. It allows nature to be rendered as a passive, external realm governed by immutable laws, while society is imagined as the active domain of values, decisions, and history. Latour argues that this artificial division has contributed directly to ecological degradation. By excluding nature from the political sphere—treating it as a background to human action rather than a participant in it—modernity has obscured the fact that "natural" systems are deeply enmeshed in social, economic, and technological networks. The ecological crisis, in this light, is not merely the unintended consequence of technological development, but a crisis of representation and ontology: we lack the categories and institutions to adequately represent the more-than-human world in political terms (Latour, 1993, 25–30; 96–99). By exposing this contradiction, Latour fundamentally challenges anthropocentrism. If there is no ontological divide between nature and society, then agency and significance cannot be reserved for humans alone. What modernity treated as "natural" and inert is, in fact, already imbued with political and epistemic agency. The very idea of human exceptionalism collapses, revealing a world composed of actor-networks-assemblages of human and nonhuman agents that co-construct reality (Latour, 1993, 105–117). From this vantage point, the ecological crisis is not simply a failure of environmental management, but a failure of the modern epistemological order. Progress, as traditionally conceived, relies on the very dualisms (nature/culture, subject/object, human/nonhuman) that now appear untenable. Latour's call is not to abandon the concept of progress altogether, but to recompose it on a different ontological foundation: one that recognizes the hybrid, relational, and co-constitutive nature of the world we inhabit.

In *Down to Earth* (2018), Latour lays out what can be read as a terrestrial manifesto—a constructive political ecology that builds directly on his earlier critique of modernity. He argues that the modern project of progress, conceived as liberation from material constraints through science, economics, and globalization, has reached its limits. Faced with ecological breakdown, it is no longer viable to imagine the future as a space of boundless expansion or technological transcendence. Instead, Latour insists that we must "land"—to come back down to Earth and recognize our material and ecological dependencies (Latour, 2018, 11). What modernity framed as a triumphant ascent—toward reason, mastery, and universalism—has become a dangerous detachment from the very conditions that sustain life. Latour provocatively argues that the ideal of a shared, global horizon—the so-called "Global"—is dissolving before our eyes, giving rise to new forms of denialism, nationalism, and ecological isolationism (Latour, 2018, 11–18). In response, he introduces the figure of the Terrestrial, a mode of existence defined not by abstract universals or national identities, but by attachment to specific material conditions, territories, and networks of interdependence. Progress, from this perspective, must be redefined as a project of re-orientation: no longer a forward flight, but a turning back—*not backward*, but *downward*—toward the Earth as the shared condition of survival. Crucially, Latour does not treat the Earth as a passive background or inert resource. Drawing on James Lovelock's Gaia hypothesis (Lovelock, 1979), he reinterprets Gaia not as a harmonious superorganism but as a reactive, dynamic, and unstable system of feedback loops—an Earth that responds, resists, and acts (Latour, 2017, 95–101). Gaia, in Latour's reading, is not a metaphysical being but a political actor: a force that disrupts human plans, withdraws stability, and demands recognition. The ecological crisis thus becomes not merely an environmental issue, but a crisis of representation—of who or what counts as a participant in the political field (Latour, 2017, 102–108). Through this lens, the idea of progress must be radically transformed. Rather than measuring advancement by technological innovation or economic growth, Latour urges us to evaluate it in terms of our ability to compose livable worlds with others—human and nonhuman alike (Latour, 2018, 81–89). Progress becomes a question of inhabitation: of learning to stick to the soil, and to reframe politics not around sovereignty or abstraction, but around shared vulnerability and entangled agency. Latour's critique of the modern constitution and his call for a terrestrial reorientation reveal the depth of the conceptual revision required in response to the ecological crisis. By dismantling the nature-culture divide and challenging the narrative of unbounded progress, he exposes the ontological and political blind spots of modernity. Yet his project is not merely deconstructive. Latour's political ecology aims to reassemble the world on new terms—through concepts like Gaia, composition, and the proliferation of nonhuman agency. These ideas signal a profound shift: progress must no longer be conceived as transcendence or mastery, but as situated, collective and ecologically embedded world-making. The following sections develop this shift in more detail, unpacking the ontological, ethical, and political dimensions of Latour's terrestrial thought.

5.1 Latour's Relational Ontology: Rethinking Agency Beyond the Human

Bruno Latour's work offers a radical ontological reconfiguration that undercuts the modernist dualisms shaping Western thought—especially the foundational separations between nature and society, subject and object, fact and value. In *We Have Never Been Modern* (1993), Latour identifies these binaries as the pillars of what he terms the "modern constitution": an epistemic-political order that claims to purify domains (separating Nature from Culture) while simultaneously generating hybrids—complex entanglements of human and nonhuman forces (Latour, 1993, 10–13). The central paradox of modernity, according to Latour, is that it denies the existence of these hybrids even as it depends on them. Latour's relational ontology begins by rejecting the idea that agency belongs exclusively to human subjects. Instead, drawing from Actor-Network Theory (ANT), he proposes that agency is distributed among heterogeneous assemblages of actors—including people, machines, institutions, microbes, and landscapes—each contributing to the stabilization or transformation of reality (Latour, 2005, 71–72). Agency, in this view, is not a property but an effect: it emerges from the capacity of an entity to make a difference within a network. This challenges the anthropocentric bias of classical political and ethical frameworks, opening the way for a more-than-human politics. This rethinking of agency is tied to Latour's "critique of critique." In his influential essay *Why Has Critique Run out of Steam?* (2004), Latour criticizes traditional critical theory for its tendency to debunk and deconstruct, often without offering constructive alternatives. He observes that critique has become too detached, too skeptical, and increasingly ineffective in mobilizing political action—especially in the context of ecological crises and climate denial (Latour, 2004, 227–229). Instead, he calls for a shift from critical subtraction to "composition," an epistemic and political practice concerned with assembling and maintaining fragile, contested collectives of humans and nonhumans. This proposal is developed in his later writings as compositionism, an approach that aims not to purify or unmask, but to carefully compose worlds—through science, politics, ethics, and art—without denying their multiplicity and entanglement (Latour, 2010). Compositionism, as Latour puts it, takes up the task of building, maintaining, and caring for collectives of humans and nonhumans, rather than seeking to destroy, demystify, or disqualify them (Latour, 2010, 474). Progress, in this framework, is no longer understood as linear advancement or control over nature, but as the iterative, negotiated process of composing livable worlds in response to ecological and political attachments. This ontological shift is inseparable from a political one. Latour famously imagines a "Parliament of Things"—a provocative metaphor for the inclusion of nonhuman actors in deliberative and representative processes (Latour, 1993, 142–145). While nonhumans cannot speak for themselves, they speak through instruments, measurements, symptoms and proxies. What is required, then, is not simply extending rights to nature but reorganizing the institutions of political life to account for the agency and effects of nonhumans. The "parliament" metaphor signals the need for a new ecology of representation—one capable of articulating the entangled interests of all Earthbound actors. This compositionist vision of collectivity directly challenges the classical notion of progress. Rather than valorizing control, speed, or innovation, Latour's relational ontology redefines progress as the cultivation of situated attachments and responsive alliances—fragile, ongoing, and materially embedded. In this sense, Latour resonates with Hans Jonas's ethics of responsibility, particularly in his insistence on care, precaution, and future-orientation. Yet Latour moves beyond Jonas by refusing to center the human as the exclusive bearer of ethical weight. His project instead seeks to decenter human agency, placing it within wider assemblages of ecological actors and planetary interdependencies. Progress, then, becomes a matter of collective world-making: not a transcendence of limits, but a negotiation with them; not an assertion of mastery, but an act of composition. This shift not only critiques modernity's ontological assumptions—it provides tools for constructing alternatives grounded in relationality, vulnerability, and the shared task of inhabiting a threatened planet. Latour's relational ontology lays the groundwork for a redefinition of progress—one that no longer centers on human mastery or technological acceleration, but on the fragile, situated work of composing livable collectives across the human—nonhuman divide. By displacing the nature/society binary and redistributing agency, Latour invites us to reimagine politics as a more inclusive and responsive enterprise. Yet this ontological shift does not remain abstract. It culminates in a powerful cosmopolitical vision grounded in the figure of Gaia—a non-metaphysical, politically charged conception of the Earth as an active and reactive presence. In the following section, we turn to this concept to examine how Latour expands the ethical and political implications of ecological entanglement, and how Gaia compels a profound reorientation of the idea of progress itself.

5.2 Latour's Gaia: A Political-Ecological Actor Beyond Metaphysics

A central development in Latour's ecological thought is his reinterpretation of "Gaia, a (finally secular) figure for nature" (Latour, 2017, 75). Drawing inspiration from the Gaia hypothesis but decisively distancing himself from metaphysical or spiritualized readings, Latour frames Gaia as an emergent political-ecological actor—a complex collective of human and nonhuman agencies that constitute the Earth system (Latour, 2017). While the original Gaia hypothesis suggested Earth as a self-regulating organism, Latour rejects viewing Gaia as a mystical or supernatural entity. Instead, he emphasizes that Gaia should be understood as a complex network of real, material interactions—geological, atmospheric, biological, and technological—that together shape the conditions for life on the planet. Gaia is not a spirit, a god, or an essence, but a contingent, fragile, and active collective whose existence depends on the political recognition and care by human and nonhuman actors. This political-ecological framing grounds Gaia firmly in empirical realities and political stakes rather than abstract metaphysical speculation. This reconceptualization of Gaia has significant consequences for the idea of progress. It demands acknowledging that human societies are fundamentally enmeshed in these entangled networks and that the notion of progress as linear technological or economic advancement is no longer viable. Instead, progress must be rethought as a process of coexistence, negotiation, and mutual adjustment within the Earth system. Gaia functions as a political actor insofar as it compels humans to engage collectively and responsibly with nonhuman agencies, challenging anthropocentric assumptions of control (Latour, 2015). This emphasis on collective responsibility and political composition resonates with Hans Jonas's ethical demand for responsibility toward future generations, though Latour extends this to include the more-than-human world as an active participant. By positioning Gaia as a political-ecological entity rather than a metaphysical force, Latour avoids spiritual metaphysics or animism while providing a powerful conceptual tool for ecological politics. Integrating Latour's Gaia into the ecologization of progress enriches the discourse by foregrounding the systemic, relational conditions that enable and constrain human action. It calls for new political formations and ethical sensibilities that recognize Earth's agency, thereby expanding the horizon for an ecological concept of progress that is both pragmatic and normatively compelling.

This chapter's exploration of Latour's reinterpretation of Gaia underscores a pivotal shift in ecological thought—from viewing Earth as a passive backdrop or mystical entity to recognizing it as a politically active, relational collective. By reframing Gaia as an emergent actor within a network of human and nonhuman agencies, Latour challenges anthropocentric and metaphysical assumptions that have historically underpinned modern notions of progress. This shift opens up new pathways for political engagement and ethical responsibility that are grounded in ecological realities and the interconnectedness of life. Building on this reconfigured political ecology, the next section will delve deeper into Latour's broader critique of critique itself and his concept of composition. This will further illuminate how progress can be reimagined as a collective process of assembling heterogeneous entities, transcending the limitations of traditional modernist dichotomies and opening up innovative possibilities for ecological coexistence.

5.3 Latour's Critique of Critique and the Concept of Composition

Bruno Latour's ecological thought fundamentally interrogates not only the ontological assumptions of modernity but also the intellectual tools traditionally employed to challenge them. In his influential essay "*Why Has Critique Run Out of Steam?*" (2004), Latour argues that the longstanding tradition of critique—rooted in exposing illusions, deceptions, and ideological constructions—has reached a limit, particularly within ecological debates. This critique, while historically essential for revealing the blind spots and power relations of modernity, increasingly falters when confronting the complexity and urgency of the Anthropocene. Latour observes that critique often relies on a skeptical posture: its primary mode is to debunk and deconstruct existing knowledge claims and institutional arrangements, especially those related to science and politics (Latour, 2004, 230). Yet, this mode tends to reproduce the very dichotomies it seeks to dismantle—most notably the nature/culture and human/nonhuman divides. By relentlessly pointing out that hybrids or entanglements are "false" or "constructed," critique paradoxically reinforces the modernist idea that pure, uncontaminated categories should exist. In *We Have Never Been Modern*, Latour diagnoses modernity as a "constitutional" order based on strict bifurcations that separate society from nature, and humans from nonhumans, while in reality these hybrids have always existed, yet remain repressed (Latour, 1993, 7–9). This dilemma is acutely felt in ecological discourse, where the stakes are existential. The negative logic of critique breeds skepticism and distrust but rarely offers a constructive path forward. Latour suggests that it risks immobilizing political and ecological action by fostering cynicism and paralysis rather than transformation. This is especially evident in the persistence of climate change denial and science skepticism, phenomena that undermine collective efforts to address ecological crises by casting doubt on scientific consensus and delegitimizing environmental concerns. In response, Latour calls for a new approach he terms *compositionism*—a mode of thinking that moves beyond tearing down to actively assembling new configurations of humans, nonhumans, technologies, and environments (Latour, 2010). Compositionism acknowledges the irreducible hybridity of the world and embraces the task of creating new collective forms that respect and incorporate ecological entanglements. Instead of focusing on exposing illusions, compositionism aims at building workable political ecologies and durable alliances capable of addressing complex environmental challenges. In *An Inquiry into Modes of Existence*, Latour elaborates on this epistemological and political shift, emphasizing the necessity to compose "common worlds" through the active negotiation and assemblage of heterogeneous actors (Latour, 2013). This approach aligns closely with the demands of the ecological crises, where progress depends not on dominating nature but on negotiating ongoing relationships and dependencies among diverse actors. Moreover, Latour's idea of a *parliament of things* exemplifies compositionist politics by advocating for the inclusion of nonhuman entities as political subjects. Such political reconfiguration expands responsibility and agency beyond the human sphere, resonating with but also extending Hans Jonas's ethics of responsibility to a pluralistic and distributed model of ecological governance. By advocating for composition over critique, Latour provides a vital conceptual and political tool to overcome the impasse of ecological skepticism and nihilism. This transition from a deconstructive to a constructive logic reinvigorates the concept of progress, situating it within an active and relational politics of care, negotiation, and cohabitation on a fragile planet. Latour's diagnosis of critique's exhaustion does not call for its abandonment, but for its transformation. In the face of ecological urgency, critique as debunking is no longer sufficient—what is needed is a mode of thought capable of assembling and sustaining the fragile attachments that constitute our shared world. Compositionism, as Latour proposes, offers a more generative framework: it resists the impulse to stand above or outside of entanglements, and instead urges us to take part in their careful reweaving. This shift is not merely methodological; it bears directly on how we understand progress itself. If critique once aimed to liberate us from illusions, composition insists we take responsibility for what we build together. Progress, in this light, is no longer a linear trajectory of technological mastery or ideological purification, but the pragmatic, plural, and situated work of composing a livable world.

Having examined the ontological and political implications of Latour's compositionism, we now turn to his vision of *terrestrial politics*—a vision in which the idea of progress is fundamentally reoriented. In *Down to Earth*, Latour calls not for acceleration or escape, but for a return: to Earth, to locality, to the shared material conditions that bind all earthly beings together. The next section explores how this "landing" challenges modernist notions of futurity, mobility, and emancipation, and offers an alternative model of ecological progress grounded in situated responsibility and planetary entanglement.

5.4 Progress as a Return to Earth: Latour's Terrestrial Politics

In *Down to Earth* (2018), Bruno Latour presents one of his most pointed political interventions, urging a redefinition of progress not as expansion or transcendence but as "landing"—a return to the Earth. This return is not nostalgic or regressive; rather, it is a deliberate reorientation of political imagination and ethical responsibility toward the material and relational conditions of earthly life. Against the backdrop of climate change, ecological destabilization, and political fragmentation, Latour argues that the modern trajectory of "progress" has come to mean escape: escape from nature, from limits, from locality, and ultimately from responsibility. This imagined upward trajectory—toward globalization, technological transcendence, or even space colonization—is, for Latour, a dangerous illusion. It reflects what he calls the "Out-of-This-World" orientation, the dream of detachment from terrestrial entanglements and planetary constraints (Latour, 2018, 33). In contrast, Latour proposes the *Terrestrial* as a new attractor—a mode of being politically and ecologically situated (Latour, 2018, 39). The Terrestrial demands attachment, belonging, soil, and localized responsibility; it cannot be abstracted or globalized without dissolving the very conditions of life. Progress, then, is redefined as a process of *relocalizing* our political and ethical commitments. Rather than aiming for mastery, growth, or escape velocity, progress involves reattaching ourselves to the networks—ecological, social, and technological—that support life. This includes a recognition that no single actor, whether state, corporation, or individual, can act alone. The political challenge of the Terrestrial is the composition of a new collective that includes human and nonhuman agents alike. Latour connects this planetary reorientation to the urgency of climate politics. The refusal to confront ecological reality—seen in climate denial, reactionary nationalism, and techno-utopianism—is, in his view, a symptom of modernity's crisis. The promise of endless growth without territorial or ecological responsibility failed and let some elites chose to cut themselves off from the rest of the world, protecting their own survival while denying planetary limits (Latour, 2018, 20). The result is not only ecological devastation but political disintegration: a retreat from shared futures and democratic institutions. The return to Earth, by contrast, demands a politics of inhabitation. It requires that progress be conceived not as forward motion into an abstract future, but as the careful work of making a shared world livable, considering the material and relational conditions of life. In this sense, progress becomes inseparable from care, maintenance, and situated responsibility. It is no longer about moving forward on a universal track, but about the imperative to protect the habitability of the Earth (Latour & Schultz, 2022). Latour's terrestrial politics thus resonate deeply with the ecological reframing of progress explored throughout this paper. Like Jonas, he foregrounds responsibility; but where Jonas grounds this in human foresight and moral imperative, Latour embeds it in a networked ontology and a pluralist political vision. His call to "return to Earth" is not a rejection of progress, but its radical transformation—a move from vertical conquest to horizontal composition, from abstraction to situated entanglement. Latour's vision of progress as a return to Earth or the Terrestrial radically shifts the trajectory of modern politics. Rather than pursuing emancipation through detachment or abstraction, it demands new forms of attachment—grounded, situated, and ecologically responsive. This terrestrial reorientation reframes the political landscape: no longer structured by traditional left-right or global-local dichotomies, it calls for entirely new axes of alignment. But who, then, can speak for the Earth? Who composes the collective capable of inhabiting the Terrestrial? These questions bring us to a pivotal point in Latour's political ecology: the emergence of an *ecological class*. As the climate crisis redraws the boundaries of political conflict, Latour suggests that a new form of political subjectivity is forming—one no longer defined primarily by economic interest, but by the shared struggle to defend the conditions of life on a vulnerable planet. The next section explores this proposal and its implications for ecological progress in the Anthropocene.

6. On the Emergence of an Ecological Class: Political Reorientation in the Anthropocene

> "Being a materialist today means not only reproducing the material conditions that are favorable to humans, but also taking into account the conditions necessary for the Earth to be habitable. These conditions force us to consider not only what the political economy of traditional parties has sought to simplify under the name of 'resources,' but also a new material reality of the planet."[1]
> *(Latour & Schultz, 2022, 21)*

The preceding chapters have shown that the classical idea of progress—understood as linear development, technological mastery, and emancipation from natural constraints—is fundamentally inadequate in the face of the ecological crises of the Anthropocene. In response, this chapter outlines the key dimensions of an alternative understanding: an ecologized concept of progress. Drawing together insights from Hans Jonas's ethics of responsibility and Bruno Latour's Earthbound relational ontology, this reconfigured concept emphasizes interdependence, restraint, and cohabitation. First, ecological progress must be viewed as situated, not universal. Classical modern progress narratives often assume a singular trajectory, applicable to all societies and measured by abstract metrics such as GDP or technological capacity. In contrast, ecological progress is context-sensitive and plural, rooted in specific ecological, cultural, and material conditions. It rejects the notion of a single human destiny and instead affirms the diversity of ways of living well within ecological limits. Second, progress must be redefined in terms of responsibility and foresight. Here, Hans Jonas's ethics offers a crucial orientation. The imperative to act in ways that safeguard the future of life remains essential, particularly in light of human technological power. Jonas reminds us that without a strong normative orientation, ecological thought risks lapsing into relativism or passivity. His anthropocentric ethics, though limited in scope, provides an indispensable moral compass (Jonas, 1984). Third, ecological progress requires a non-anthropocentric ontology, as articulated by Bruno Latour. Progress is no longer defined as human separation from or control over nature, but as participation in a dense web of human–nonhuman relations.

---

1 Translation by author from: Latour, Bruno; Schultz, Nikolaj (2022): Zur Entstehung einer ökologischen Klasse. Ein Memorandum. Berlin: Suhrkamp.

Latour's "parliament of things" and his emphasis on relationality and agency expand the ethical and political community to include nonhuman actors. This ontological shift demands new forms of representation, governance, and care.

Latour introduced this rethinking already in *Politics of Nature* (2004), where he interprets the ecological crisis as an uprising of things—that is, of all nonhuman entities. These entities, Latour suggests, demand to be taken as matters of concern (Latour, 2004, 66). He proposes to replace the modern division between nature and society with a political ecology that acknowledges and foregrounds hybrids—entities that are neither purely natural nor purely social. The term "hybrid" serves to avoid the dualism of subject and object, since for Latour, both co-constitute each other through networks of influence. As he elaborates in *Pandora's Hope* (1999), the relation between humans and artifacts is not one of unilateral agency. Rather, both are propositions that shape and transform one another. Translated to the relationship between nature and society, this means that nature can no longer be conceived as a passive realm acted upon by autonomous human subjects. Instead, nature and society are deeply entangled and continuously co-producing one another. Within this framework, Latour grants actantial agency to all entities, human and nonhuman alike. Crucially, Latour's network theory does not deny that humans are a decisive force in ecological destabilization. On the contrary, his calls for a materialist politics rely on repositioning existing conceptual categories. While he builds on the Marxist insight that societies must be understood in relation to their material conditions, he insists that "it is no longer the same materiality"[2] (Latour & Schultz, 2022, 19). The vision of an "ecological class" is therefore not a continuation of socialist traditions, but a conceptual shift grounded in the new planetary condition—the New Climatic Regime. The ecological question, Latour insists, can no longer be treated as secondary to social or economic ones. On the contrary, the livability of the Earth must be placed at the center of political analysis. Thus, Jonas and Latour, despite their differences, can be read as complementary. Jonas provides the ethical foundation for responsibility toward future life; Latour redefines the ontological terrain in which such responsibility must be enacted. An ecologized concept of progress entails both normative commitment and ontological humility: it requires human responsibility, but within an expanded field of actors and relations. Finally, ecological progress must be po-

2 Translation by author from: Latour, Bruno; Schultz, Nikolaj (2022): Zur Entstehung einer ökologischen Klasse. Ein Memorandum. Berlin: Suhrkamp.

litically organized. In *On the Emergence of an Ecological Class*[3] (Latour & Schultz, 2022), the authors argue that ecological transformation will not occur solely through individual ethical insight or philosophical realignment. It demands the formation of new social alliances—an "ecological class" capable of challenging dominant modes of production, consumption, and governance. Importantly, Latour and Schultz deliberately reframe the notion of "class" beyond its traditional Marxist roots. Unlike classical classes defined primarily by economic relations to capital and production, the ecological class is a political formation united by a shared interest in preserving the habitability of the Earth. For Latour, this redefinition is necessary because social questions, such as the distribution of production and wealth, depend entirely on the prior question of planetary habitability. Therefore, the ecological must be addressed before and as the condition of possibility for any meaningful social politics. The demand for environmental protection is no longer a marginal concern but the core of a new political order. While questions of production and economic justice remain crucial, they must now be embedded within ecological realities. This repositioning of the class concept also implies a decoupling of progress from prosperity. The societal orientation can no longer be guided by narratives of emancipation or autonomy that ignore interdependence. Instead, the full entanglement of humans and nonhumans must be acknowledged and addressed with regard to sustaining a livable planet. On this basis, Latour proposes the formation of an ecological class—a collective subject that articulates political demands from the standpoint of Earth's habitability and evaluates political programs accordingly. This perspective reframes progress as a collective political project: not the utopian unfolding of reason, but the contingent and contested composition of livable futures on a damaged planet. From that perspective, an ecological concept of progress does not reject the aspiration to move forward. Rather, it redefines what "forward" means: not acceleration, expansion, or abstraction, but deceleration, reattachment, and repair. It is a form of progress that begins with the Earth and orients itself toward preserving its habitability—materially, ethically, and politically.

---

3 Translation by author; the German edition was used here: Latour, Bruno; Schultz, Nikolaj (2022): Zur Entstehung einer ökologischen Klasse. Ein Memorandum. Berlin: Suhrkamp.

7. Between Foresight and Entanglement: Jonas and Latour in Dialogue

Hans Jonas and Bruno Latour approach the ecological crisis from distinct philosophical traditions—Jonas through existential ethics, Latour through posthumanist ontology—but their works converge in important ways when rethinking the idea of progress under planetary conditions. Examining their positions side-by-side reveals both tensions and complementarities that enrich an ecological reconceptualization of progress. Jonas's ethics centers on the uniquely human capacity for foresight and the imperative of responsibility that arises from it (Jonas, 1984). His moral framework emerges from the unprecedented scale and impact of modern technological power, obliging humanity to act on behalf of future generations and the broader web of life. This responsibility is rooted in an asymmetry: humans possess the power to alter the conditions of life irreversibly, while future beings are vulnerable and voiceless. Although Jonas's approach remains anthropocentric—grounded in human moral agency—it is deeply ecological in its emphasis on fragility, temporality, and care. Latour, in contrast, challenges the ontological dualism underpinning such anthropocentrism. In e.g. *We Have Never Been Modern* (1993) and *Facing Gaia* (2017), he argues that the strict nature-culture divide is a historical artifact that obscures the hybridity and entanglement of humans, nonhumans, and technologies. Responsibility, for Latour, is distributed across a network of heterogeneous actors rather than vested in a singular, sovereign human subject. This shift from a human-centered ethics to an ecology of collective agencies reframes progress as the careful composition of shared worlds, emphasizing relationality and political inclusion of the more-than-human (Latour, 1993; 2017). Despite these differing ontological starting points, Jonas and Latour share a profound critique of modern techno-scientific hubris and the myth of progress as human liberation from nature. Both insist on limits: Jonas on moral responsibility toward future life, Latour on the political recognition of Earth's agency and the dissolution of the nature–culture binary. Progress, in their combined view, must be reimagined as embeddedness, restraint, and cohabitation rather than mastery, acceleration, or domination. Importantly, these frameworks are not mutually exclusive but complementary. Jonas's ethics of foresight offers a crucial normative anchor for the more expansive, non-anthropocentric ontology Latour proposes. Conversely, Latour's distributed politics and ontological humility enrich Jonas's anthropocentric stance by expanding the moral field to include nonhuman agencies. Together, their insights invite a radical shift from progress as conquest toward progress as composition—a collective care for a fragile Earth, oriented not toward transcendence but attentiveness. This dialogical tension between foresight and entanglement thus lays the conceptual foundation for ecologizing progress. By bridging ethics and ontology, normative responsibility and political composition, Jonas and Latour provide a robust philosophical basis for rethinking progress as a relational and responsible practice attuned to planetary limits. Drawing on the complementary frameworks of Hans Jonas's ethics of responsibility and Bruno Latour's relational ontology, the paper now moves from critical reflection to constructive reconfiguration. The next chapter will develop an ecologized concept of progress—one that is inherently situated, attentive to the plurality of life forms and anchored in a profound sense of responsibility toward both present and future earthly communities. This reconceptualization addresses the urgent need to rethink progress beyond linear, anthropocentric paradigms, as Jonas and Latour have laid the groundwork for such a transformation (Jonas, 1984; Latour, 1993). By grounding progress in ecological relationality and ethical foresight, the ensuing discussion aims to translate philosophical insights into practical orientations for sustaining life on a finite planet.

8. Ecologizing Progress: Toward a Situated, Responsible and Relational Concept

The preceding chapters have demonstrated that classical notions of progress—rooted in linear development, technological mastery, and human exceptionalism—are fundamentally inadequate in the context of the Anthropocene and its attendant ecological crises. Both Hans Jonas's ethics of responsibility and Bruno Latour's political ecology call for a profound rethinking of progress, one that moves beyond the illusions of modernity's dualisms and the myth of unbounded growth. Building on these foundations, this section outlines a reconfigured concept of progress defined by three interrelated dimensions: situatedness, responsibility, and relationality, each essential for an ecologically viable and politically relevant understanding of progress.

Situated Progress. As Latour argues in *Down to Earth* (2018), humans are "Terrestrials" whose futures are inseparable from the specific earthly conditions they inhabit. The Earth is no longer the inert backdrop to human history; it is an active, troubled participant in the collective we must now compose (Latour, 2018, 40). This insight challenges universalistic progress narratives that assume a singular path of development applicable across diverse contexts. Instead, ecological progress must be rooted in the multiplicity of local ecosystems, cultures, and material histories. Progress thus becomes a pluralistic and context-sensitive endeavor—attuned to the diversity of life-worlds and ecological limits. Such situatedness rejects abstract, one-size-fits-all visions of progress and affirms the necessity of place-based knowledge and practices.

Responsible Progress. Hans Jonas's *Imperative of Responsibility* (1984) remains pivotal in articulating the ethical core of ecological progress. Jonas emphasizes the necessity of foresight and moral accountability for the long-term consequences of human technological power—a capacity that demands restraint rather than unreflective expansion. He cautions: "Act so that the effects of your action are compatible with the permanence of genuine human life" (Jonas, 1984, 11). This ethical orientation insists that progress is not merely an expansion of power or capability, but an exercise in preserving the conditions necessary for life's continuation. Jonas's focus on responsibility toward future generations grounds progress in a temporal horizon that disrupts modernity's emphasis on immediate gain and short-term planning (Jonas, 1984).

Relational Progress. Latour's critique of the nature-culture dichotomy and his relational ontology provide a further critical reorientation. In *We Have Never Been Modern* (1993), Latour reveals how the modernist separation of humans and nature creates ecological blind spots, rendering nonhuman actors invisible within political and ethical considerations. He shows that the modern constitution consists in assembling a coherent fiction: nature is one, society is another; their hybrids are disavowed. Latour's concept of compositionism, developed further in *An Inquiry into Modes of Existence* (2013) and *Facing Gaia* (2017), reimagines progress as the ongoing assembling of heterogeneous entities, human and nonhuman, into collective worlds. His *parliament of things* metaphor envisions political communities that include nonhuman agencies and challenge anthropocentric governance. It aims at us to learn to compose with new actors who are neither human nor society but agents in the making of our common world. This relational dimension expands the moral and political community, demanding new forms of representation and coexistence that are attuned to ecological entanglements.

8.1 Synthesis and Political Implications

Together, these dimensions crystallize into an ecologized concept of progress that both critiques and transcends the legacy of modernity's hubris. This concept demands a pluralistic politics attentive to ecological diversity and the emergence of new social alliances, as articulated by Latour and Schultz's notion of an "ecological class" (2022). An ecologized concept of progress thus needs a redefinition what it means to move ´forward': Not a linear acceleration or abstract expansion, but a project of repair, care, and composition rooted in the finitude and fragility of the Earth system. In sum, ecologizing progress entails a paradigmatic shift—from domination and infinite growth toward humility, attentiveness and a deep commitment to the flourishing of both human and nonhuman futures. This redefinition opens the way for an ethical and political practice capable of navigating the complexities of the Anthropocene, grounded firmly in the situatedness, responsibility and relationality that Jonas and Latour have articulated. This ecologized concept of progress does not abandon the notion of advancement but radically redefines its direction and meaning. Rather than aspiring toward transcendence, control, and abstraction, it invites a turn toward groundedness, care, and composition. By drawing together Jonas's call for responsibility with Latour's ontological pluralism, we gain a conceptual framework that is ethically robust, politically resonant, and responsive to the ecological urgencies of our time.

9. Conclusion: Toward an Ecological Concept of Progress

This paper has traced the need for a fundamental rethinking of the concept of progress in light of the ecological disruptions that define the Anthropocene. The modern ideal of progress—anchored in notions of linear development, technological domination over nature, and the promise of perpetual improvement—has proven increasingly untenable in the face of planetary limits, climate instability, and ecological degradation. Rather than offering solutions, this inherited paradigm often blinds us to the entangled vulnerabilities of human and nonhuman life. By engaging the philosophical frameworks of Hans Jonas and Bruno Latour, we have reconstructed an alternative conceptual foundation for understanding progress—one that is both ethically grounded and ontologically expanded. Jonas calls for a radical extension of moral responsibility in response to the unprecedented scale and permanence of human technological power. His imperative to act in ways that preserve the conditions for future life provides a normative anchor in a time of existential ecological risk. At the same time, Latour dismantles the modernist dualism of nature and culture, inviting us to recognize the Earth as an active political actor and to compose new collectives that include nonhuman agencies. His concept of *compositionism* shifts progress from a logic of extraction and transcendence to one of attachment, repair, and coexistence. Throughout this paper, we have shown that an ecological concept of progress must incorporate three core dimensions:

1) Situatedness: Progress is no longer universal or abstract but rooted in diverse ecological, cultural, and material conditions. It is place-based, relational, and attuned to the specificities of life-worlds and ecosystems.
2) Responsibility: Ethical foresight becomes central. Drawing on Jonas, ecological progress demands moral accountability toward future generations and the biosphere, prioritizing precaution over unchecked expansion.
3) Relationality: Inspired by Latour, progress is understood not as control over nature but as entanglement with a more-than-human world. It calls for a redefinition of agency, community, and care beyond the boundaries of the human.

Together, these dimensions form the contours of a revised, ecologized concept of progress—not as acceleration, growth, or conquest, but as the ongoing composition of livable worlds within planetary limits. Such a concept refuses the hubris of modernity and instead embraces humility, interdependence, and collective responsibility. It challenges us to envision futures that are not built on domination, but on the care for fragile entanglements that sustain life. A reorientation of the course of progress in ecological terms is required, with a shift from the concepts of escape to return, abstraction to situatedness, and sovereignty to responsibility. This concept suggests a halt to questioning how to quicken our progress or expand our reach. Instead, it highlights the imperative to cultivate coexistence with other entities and all forms of life on our shared, finite planet. Consequently, the extent of progress would be measured by the degree to which we succeed in acting responsible in a terrestrial sense to preserve the Earth's habitability.

References

Chakrabarty, D. (2009). The climate of history: Four theses. *Critical Inquiry, 35*(2), 197–222.

Condorcet, J.-A.-N. de C. de. (1994). *Sketch for a historical picture of the progress of the human mind.* Noonday Press. (Original work published 1795)

Cullinan, C. (2011). *Wild law: A manifesto for Earth justice* (2nd ed.). Chelsea Green Publishing.

Haraway, D. J. (2016). *Staying with the trouble: Making kin in the Chthulucene.* Duke University Press.

Horkheimer, M., & Adorno, T. W. (1969). *Dialektik der Aufklärung: Philosophische Fragmente.* Fischer.

Jonas, H. (1984). *The imperative of responsibility: In search of an ethics for the technological age.* University of Chicago Press. (Original work published 1979)

Kant, I. (1784). Idee zu einer allgemeinen Geschichte in weltbürgerlicher Absicht. *Berlinische Monatsschrift*, November 1784, 385–411.

Latour, B. (1993). *We have never been modern.* Harvard University Press.

Latour, B. (1999). *Pandora's hope: Essays on the reality of science studies.* Harvard University Press.

Latour, B. (2004). *Politics of nature: How to bring the sciences into democracy.* Harvard University Press.

Latour, B. (2005). *Reassembling the social: An introduction to actor-network-theory.* Oxford University Press.

Latour, B. (2010). An attempt at a "compositionist manifesto." *New Literary History, 41*(3), 471–490.

Latour, B. (2013). *An inquiry into modes of existence: An anthropology of the moderns.* Harvard University Press.

Latour, B. (2017). *Facing Gaia: Eight lectures on the new climatic regime.* Polity Press.

Latour, B. (2018). *Down to Earth: Politics in the new climatic regime.* Polity Press. https://www.are.na/block/22813640

Latour, B., & Schultz, N. (2022). *Zur Entstehung einer ökologischen Klasse: Ein Memorandum.* Suhrkamp.

Lovelock, J. (1979). *Gaia: A new look at life on Earth.* Oxford University Press.

Marx, K. (1976). *Capital: A critique of political economy* (Vol. 1; B. Fowkes, Trans.). Penguin Classics. (Original work published 1867)

Rockström, J., et al. (2009). A safe operating space for humanity. *Nature, 461*(7263), 472–475. https://doi.org/10.1038/461472a

Said, E. W. (1978). *Orientalism.* Pantheon Books.

Spivak, G. C. (1988). Can the subaltern speak? In C. Nelson & L. Grossberg (Eds.), *Marxism and the interpretation of culture* (pp. 271–313). University of Illinois Press.

Stone, C. D. (2010). *Should trees have standing? Law, morality, and the environment* (3rd ed.). Oxford University Press.

The Economist. (2011, May 26). Europe's new crisis. https://www.economist.com/leaders/2011/05/26/welcome-to-the-anthropocene

Whyte, K. P. (2017). Indigenous climate change studies: Indigenizing futures, decolonizing the Anthropocene. *English Language Notes*, 55(1–2), 153–162. https://doi.org/10.1215/00138282-55.1-2.153

Affluence and consumption of natural resources

Lessons from the Global Resources Outlook 2024 about the drivers behind the Great Acceleration

Philipp Schepelmann

Abstract: *A predominant focus on "rich" and "poor" tends to distort the perception of the link between affluence and the consumption of natural resources. Based on the findings of the Global Resources Outlook 2024, the author argues that global material consumption is no longer dominated by high-income economies; instead, middle-income countries now account for the largest share. This underlines the relevance of the IPAT equation as a heuristic tool for analyzing the driving forces behind the Great Acceleration of the Anthropocene. The article discusses the political and communicative challenges arising from the shift in focus from the rich-poor dichotomy towards a complementing consideration of growing populations and affluence of middle-income economies.*

1. Introduction

The connection between affluence, consumption of natural resources, and global environmental change is strongly supported by a substantial body of literature (Constanza et al., 1997, Herwich, 2005, Jackson & Michaelis, 2003, Sattherwaite et al., 2010). Globally, the growth in affluence over the past half-century has consistently driven an increase in resource use and pollutant emissions at a rate that far outpaces reductions achieved through technological advancements. High production and consumption rates require large inputs of materials and energy which has physical consequences. The high-input industrialization of production and consumption patterns is a primary determinant and accelerator of global environmental change. A significant and direct relationship exists between per capita impacts on the environment and economic growth (Hertwich, 2010). Generally, increased affluence leads to greater resource consumption due to enhanced purchasing power and a higher demand for a wider array of goods and services. Affluent societies produce and consume goods and services that require more resources for their production, infrastructure as well as for their operations. Around 70% of the environmental impacts from high-income industrialized societies primarily occur in housing, transport, and the food sectors (Tukker et al., 2006). Specific resource-intensive consumption patterns are linked to affluence. For instance, in the food sector the increased demand for meat exerts significant pressure on limited water resources and international grain supplies (Myers & Kent, 2003). An integrated assessment of environmental and socio-economic effects arising from final consumption of food products by European households have shown that even when technological developments and changes in the mix of consumed food products result in reductions in environmental pressures, positive effects are offset by an overall growing volume of consumption (Schepelmann et al., 2020). Wiedmann et al. (2015) showed that for every 10% increase in a nation's Gross Domestic Product (GDP), its average material footprint expands by 6%.

Due to the strong connection between affluence and resource consumption literature often contrasts the stark differences in resource consumption between high-income countries, often referred to as the "Global North" and low-income countries, in the so-called "Global South". The disparity in per capita resource consumption between affluent and less affluent nations is often perceived as inequitable. For example, the per capita resource consumption in North America is substantially higher than that of an individual residing in Africa. Consequently, high-income countries, despite having smaller populations, account for disproportionately large material footprints putting higher environmental pressure on the planet than low-income economies. The United Nations Environment Programme (UNEP) confirms this view in the headline of its press release of 1st of March 2024 in which it announces the publication of the Global Resources Outlook 2024:

> "Rich countries use six times more resources, generate 10 times the climate impacts than low-income ones."[1]

1 https://www.unep.org/news-and-stories/press-release/rich-countries-use-six-times-more-resources-generate-10-times

This article will show that this headline is misleading. One would expect that a press release for an important UN report such as the Global Resources Outlook would indicate its most important news. We will show that this is not the case. It is rather confirming a popular shared belief on the expense of important but inconvenient findings of the report. The headline is an expression and promotion of what Rosling et al. (2018) refer to as the "gap-instinct". This phenomenon is not an instinct in a biological sense, but rather a widespread bias or a popular misconception leading to the preference of dividing the peoples of the world into rich and poor, with a gap between the two groups. However, as we will show, most people and the largest share of resource consumption are in the middle. Rosling explains:

> "The gap instinct is very strong. The first time I lectured to the staff of the World Bank was in 1999. I told them the labels "developing" and "developed" were no longer valid (...). It took the World Bank 17 years and 14 more of my lectures before it finally announced publicly that it was dropping the terms "developing" and "developed" and would from now on divide the world into four income groups. The UN and most other global organizations have still not made this change. So why is the misconception of a gap between the rich and the poor so hard to change? I think this is because human beings have a strong dramatic instinct toward binary thinking, a basic urge to divide things into two distinct groups, with nothing but an empty gap in between. We love to dichotomize. Good versus bad. Heroes versus villains. My country versus the rest. Dividing the world into two distinct sides is simple and intuitive, and also dramatic because it implies conflict, and we do it without thinking, all the time. Journalists know this. They set up their narratives as conflicts between two opposing people, views, or groups. They prefer stories of extreme poverty and billionaires to stories about the vast majority of people slowly dragging themselves toward better lives. Journalists are storytellers. So are people who produce documentaries and movies" (Rosling et al, 2018, 52).

The quotation shows that for overcoming the "gap-instinct" Rosling recommends dropping the binary distinction between "developing" and "developed" countries in favor of a more granular classification system with four income groups. As Rosling indicated, the World Bank already implemented such a system. Further information on the World Bank income groups can be found in the following chapter. They are further explained in the book "factfulness" (Rosling et al., 2018) from where the quotation above is taken as well as the online tool "Dollar Street", which can be visited at the portal of the Gapminder Foundation[2]. "Dollar Street" helps to understand the implications of the four income groups by means of visual exemplification showing what different incomes in the four categories mean for the lifestyle and everyday consumption of the people in each group. Factfulness and Dollar Street make a convincing case that four income groups are a considerable progress compared to a binary distinction.

The research question that this article would like to answer is: What changes if analysis shifts from a binary North-South/rich-poor perspective towards a view on four income groups as promoted by Rosling and the Gapminder Foundation? Does this reveal any relevant information on affluence and resource consumption that would not be considered from a binary perspective and if so, what could be the consequences for evidence-based policymaking as well as research and teaching on global environmental change?

For this purpose, we will use data from the Global Resources Outlook 2024 (GRO 2024) by the United Nations Environment Program (UNEP), accompanied by the press release quoted above. So ironically, we will set into contrast on one hand the binary view expressed by the headline of the UNEP press release and the more differentiated view of at least parts of the International Resource Panel (IRP) by analyzing and comparing resource consumption and its drivers in four different income categories as implemented in the Global Resources Outlook 2024.

Over the past decade, Rosling and the Gapminder Foundation have discovered widespread and persistent misconceptions about population dynamics, the development of affluence and quality of life in a series of so-called misconception studies including the Gapminder Misconception Study (2017), the Global Misconception Study (2019), the European Health Misconception Study (2019), the Sustainable Development Misconception Study (2020), and the Refugee Misconception Study (2023). The studies revealed considerable misconceptions and biases including the so-called "gap-instinct". The Gapminder research raises the question whether the discussion surrounding affluence, resource consumption, and global environmental change may also be biased and affected by misconceptions, potentially leading to misguided discourses and policies. This article aims to uncover what the headline of the press release is concealing. By doing so, it will be possible to understand how

2 https://www.gapminder.org/dollar-street

common misconceptions, such as the gap instinct, impede the recognition of recent trends in global affluence and resource consumption. Furthermore, the acknowledgement of the dramatic shifts in global resource consumption described in the Global Resources Outlook (GRO) is key for comprehending one of the most significant ecological phenomena of our time: the Great Acceleration of the Anthropocene, which we will discuss in the concluding chapter of this article.

2. The quantification of resource consumption in four income groups

The International Resource Panel (IRP) covers in the Global Resources Outlook 2024 (GRO 2024) over 180 countries which are grouped into seven world regions and four country income groups. The seven world regions are:

1. Africa
2. Asia and the Pacific
3. Europe
4. Latin America and the Caribbean
5. North America
6. West Asia (Middle East), and
7. Eastern Europe, Caucasus and Central Asia (EECCA).

The World Bank annually classifies the world's economies into four primary income groups. This classification, which is updated annually, is based on the gross national income (GNI) per capita. The classification serves primarily statistical and analytical purposes. However, it also has far-reaching implications for development research, the international perception of countries, and the definition of development strategies.

The annual gross national income (GNI) per capita is a measure of the total income earned by a country's citizens, regardless of where the income is earned. It includes not only domestic income but also income earned by citizens abroad.

The World Bank uses GNI per capita because it is available for most countries and is considered a reliable indicator of a country's economic capacity and level of development. Although it is not a perfect measure, it typically correlates strongly with other key development indicators, such as child mortality, life expectancy, and access to basic services.

Despite its widespread use and usefulness, GNI per capita has significant limitations as a measure of development. As an average, it cannot indicate inequalities in income distribution within a country. A high GNI per capita does not imply that the entire population enjoys a high standard of living and resource consumption.

For 2020 the World Bank classifies countries according to the following ranges of annual Gross National Income (GNI) per capita:

1. low income, $1,045 or less
   Economies in this category are typically characterized by high levels of poverty, heavy dependence on agriculture, limited infrastructure, and often political instability
   Examples: Afghanistan, Burundi, Democratic Republic of Congo, Malawi, Niger, Sierra Leone, Syria, Yemen
2. lower middle-income, between $1,046 and $4,095
   This category is extremely heterogeneous and includes countries that are in transition from predominantly rural to urban societies and from an agricultural to an industrial base.
   Examples: Egypt, El Salvador, Honduras, India, Kenya, Nigeria, Pakistan, Philippines, Ukraine, Vietnam
3. upper middle income, between $4,096 and $12,695
   These are emerging economies that play an increasing role in global production and consumption.
   Examples: Argentina, Brazil, China, Colombia, Costa Rica, Indonesia, Iraq, Mexico, Russia, South Africa, Turkey.
4. high-income, $12,696 or more
   These countries are generally characterized by advanced service and industrial sectors and high per capita GDP.
   Examples: Australia, Canada, Chile, France, Germany, Japan, Qatar, Saudi Arabia, Singapore, South Korea, United Kingdom, United States.

3. Material Flow Analysis

For quantifying resource consumption, the International Resource Panel uses different material flow indicators based on material flow analysis (UNEP, 2021). Material flow analysis (MFA) comprises a group of methods to analyze the physical flows of materials into, through and out of a given system. This can be applied at different levels of scale including products, firms, sectors, regions and whole economies. The analysis may focus on individual substances or materials, or aggregated flows such as resource groups (e.g. fossil fuels, metals or minerals). In the following we will focus on economy-wide MFA (ewMFA). EwMFA offers a comprehensive overview of the material inputs and outputs of an entire economy. It provides the basis for producing indicators on the metabolism of countries in terms of material inputs such as raw materials and products, consumption and output, such as products, waste and emissions. By analyzing all material flows, ewMFA can help in assessing the overall environmental impacts associated with the extraction, use, and disposal of materials. Therefore, it can serve as a general proxy of an economy's environmental impacts, not just climate change.

For global governance, economy-wide Material Flow Analysis is used for monitoring progress towards two related United Nations Sustainable Development Goals:

- SDG 12.2 on the sustainable management and efficient use of natural resources. The MFA indicator used for this goal is Domestic Material Consumption (DMC).
- SDG 8.4 on improving resource efficiency in consumption and production. The indicator used for this goal is Material Footprint (MF).

In the following we will concentrate on the results of the GRO 2024 related to these two UN SDG indicators. Therefore, we will briefly introduce DMC and MF.

3.1 Domestic Material Consumption

Domestic Material Consumption (DMC) is a key indicator used to measure the total amount of materials directly used within an economy. This includes various material categories, such as metals, non-metallic minerals, biomass, or fossil energy carriers. It represents the annual quantity of raw materials extracted from a country's territory, plus all material imports, minus all material exports. Essentially, it shows the direct consumption of materials within a country. Thus, it provides insight into the absolute level of resource use of an economy distinguishing resource requirements driven by domestic demand and the resources needed for exports. In national policymaking it helps to identify areas of excessive domestic material use where strategies for resource efficiency could be required. High DMC values can indicate significant environmental impacts, such as resource depletion, pollution, and habitat destruction, but it does not account for "hidden" flows, meaning the upstream materials used in the production of imported goods and their impact on the environment.

3.2 Material Footprint

Over the past ten years significant progress in material accounting has enabled science to go beyond the domestic use of material by tracking the materials used throughout entire supply chains, including those materials extracted in other countries for imported goods. This input-output-based accounting is referred to as footprinting (Giljum et al., 2015). Thus, the ewMFA-indicator "material footprint" (MF) indicates the total amount of raw materials extracted globally to satisfy an economy's demand for final consumption of households and the public sector. In essence, it complements assessments of resource use within a territory by including "hidden" non-domestic material flows required to support the affluence of the people living in that territory. It complements the territorial perspective of the DMC indicator with a consumption-based perspective, highlighting domestic demand as reason for non-domestic material flows in various categories, including biomass, fossil fuels, metal ores, and non-metallic minerals.

4. Affluence and the IPAT equation

Economic wealth of a given population can be expressed as affluence with the indicator Gross National Income (GNI). In plain language affluence means that the population of a country can afford a certain volume of products and services which is expressed by the size of its GNI. The frugal heuristics behind this indicator are that a population can afford less products and services is less affluent than a population which can afford a larger volume of products and services. Consequently, affluence as ratio between GNI and population depends on the size of the GNI (the numerator) and the size of the population (the denominator). A country with a larger GNI in relation to the size of its population is more affluent than a country with a smaller GNI. If a given GNI volume is divided among more people, the population is considered less affluent, because the per capita availability of goods and services is smaller. Thus, the affluence of a country increases either by a growing GNI or by a receding population. An important limitation of this frugal heuristic is that it ignores the quality and distribution of goods and services within an economy. Especially in countries with unequal income distribution it is likely that resource use is also unevenly distributed. Nevertheless, for macro comparisons between countries the GNI is widely accepted.

How does affluence impact on the environment?

The impact of an affluent economy on the environment is highly contingent. There have been several attempts to understand this relationship and competing frugal heuristics exist. For example, proponents of the environmental Kuznets curve (EKC) assume that there is a dynamic relationship between economic development and environmental protection depending on the stage of per capita income and development (Suri & Chapman, 1998). According to this hypothesis, as an economy grows and income levels increase, environmental degradation initially worsens, but after reaching a certain level of income per capita, the trend reverses, and environmental quality begins to improve. The EKC is based on the idea that in the early stages of economic development, industrialization and urbanization lead to increased pollution and resource depletion. As incomes rise, affluent societies invest in cleaner technologies, enforce environmental regulations, and adopt sustainable practices, reducing environmental degradation.

The simple heuristics that could be derived from the EKC could be caricatured as "get rich and clean up later!". It neglects the causal relation between affluence in high-income economies and domestic as well as "hidden" material flows of production and consumption and overrates the positive impact of clean technology. The simple heuristics that global environmental change can be reduced primarily by deploying the right technology is too simple. However, it is still very popular, even though it was already contested by Ehrlich and Holdren more than half a century ago. In the late 1960ies Commoner argued similar to the EKC proponents that the environmental crisis was primarily due to faulty technologies used in post-World War II industrial societies, rather than population growth or rising affluence (Commoner et al., 1971/2010). He claimed that 95% of environmental problems were attributable to these ecologically inept choices of productive technologies. Commoner emphasized that changes in productive technology had a far more powerful effect on pollution levels than population or affluence. He believed that the pattern of economic growth and the technological transformation of the United States economy were the major reasons for the environmental crisis. Ehrlich and Holdren disagreed with Commoner's claim that environmental degradation was primarily caused by inappropriate technology. They argued that environmental problems are caused by the interaction of multiple factors, including population, affluence, and technology. They emphasized that neglecting any of these factors, or their interactions, is dangerous. In their paper "Impact of Population Growth" they introduced the IPAT equation (Impact = Population x Affluence x Technology) to illustrate the importance of considering three contributing factors simultaneously. They believed that addressing overpopulation, excessive affluence, and faulty technology together is essential for finding effective solutions to environmental crises.

Based on this understanding, IPAT heuristics have typically been utilized in quantitative research. There are various versions of the formula. IPAT heuristics are frequently applied through the Kaya identity to model greenhouse gas emissions in climate science. In material flow analysis, it is essential for modeling natural resource consumption. In the GRO 2024, the IRP has used Herendeen's (1998) logarithmic version of the IPAT formula to assess the significance of overarching drivers of material demand at an economywide level and to estimate associations between changes in impacts and drivers. It is important to note that in this context, the T in IPAT does not specifically refer to technology but encompasses all drivers other than population and per capita income.

5. Results of the Resources Outlook 2024

According to the UNEP press release quoted above:

> "Extraction of the Earth's natural resources tripled in the past five decades, related to the massive build-up of infrastructure in many parts of the world and the high levels of material consumption, especially in upper-middle and high-income countries. Material extraction is expected to rise by 60 per cent by 2060 and could derail efforts to achieve not only global climate, biodi-

> versity, and pollution targets but also economic prosperity and human well-being".

Outstanding is the increase in total domestic material consumption in Asia over the past fifty years. In absolute terms the Asia Pacific region increased resource consumption almost by a factor of seven from about 8 (1970) to almost 54 billion tons. In the West Asia region, the increase in DMC has been tenfold.

The Asian growth in domestic resource consumption is most remarkable not only in absolute terms, but also in relation to the established industrialized world in Europe and North America. In 1970, Europe and North America each consumed about a quarter of the global DMC. These shares were equal to the DMC share of Asia and the Pacific. Over the past fifty years Europe and North America's share decreased to 10%, while the share of Asia and the Pacific rose to 60% of the global domestic material consumption. The IRP points out that Europe's and North America's contributions to the global DMC are now equal to Latin America and the Caribbean, where the share has remained stable since the 1970s.

The analysis of the IRP reflects a dramatic change in the distribution of regional natural resource consumption over the past fifty years:

> "In 1970, Asia and the Pacific had the lowest per capita DMC of all world regions (3.75 tons), which was even below Africa and West Asia (which both posted about 5 tons per capita in 1970) (...). In 2020 Asia and the Pacific posted per capita DMC of 12 tons, which was around the world average but slightly lower than in Latin America and the Caribbean and Europe, and around half that of North America." (UNEP, 2024, 33)

The increase of Domestic Material Consumption in Asia and Pacific over the past fifty years has a considerable impact on the distribution of contributions of countries to natural resource consumption in relation to their income. In 1970 more than half of the global DMC had occurred in high-income countries. In 2020 their share has halved to about a quarter of the global DMC. In the same period while the contribution of high-income countries decreased the upper middle-income countries increased their share from about a third to more than half of the global DMC. In other words, instead of high-income countries the upper middle-income countries now dominate global material consumption. The importance of domestic resource consumption of middle-income countries is even more pronounced, if the increased share of lower middle-income countries is additionally considered.

In contrast to the rise of domestic resource consumption in middle income countries, the DMC in low-income countries has over the past fifty years remained at 3% of global DMC.

In relation to their material footprint overall trends are similar to domestic resource consumption. The Asia and Pacific region accounted for almost 60% of the material footprint in 2020. The shares of Europe and North America dropped to about 10%. Corresponding to the DMC assessments, the demand of middle-income countries creates the largest material footprint, while the share of high-income countries has been reduced to about a third:

> "In 2000, high-income countries accounted for 51% of the global footprint and upper middle-income countries for 34%. By 2020, these numbers had practically reversed." (UNEP, 2024, 33)

In summary, over the past fifty years the global extraction of natural resources tripled resulting in an absolute increase in environmental pressure. Dramatic changes of global resource consumption occurred not only in terms of quantity but also in terms of its geographical expansion and distribution among income groups. The contribution of domestic resource consumption of high-income economies to global resource consumption has halved in favor of the share of middle-income economies, which now dominate global resource consumption with more than half of the global resource demand. Roughly speaking, North America, Europe as well as Latin-America and Caribbean countries each contribute about 10% of global domestic resource consumption, while Asia and the Pacific contribute 60%.

Globally, rising population and affluence drive material demand. While affluence is the key driver in Europe, North America, and Asia-Pacific regions, population growth is more significant in Africa, West Asia, Latin America and the Caribbean.

Over the past fifty years per capita resource demand (DMC) increased worldwide by 50% from 8 to 12 tons per capita. According to the IRP assessment there are only two exceptions:

- Between 2000 and 2020 the per capita DMC of North America decreased by 20% (from 32 to 26 tons per capita). Yet, this is still more than twice the global average (12 tons per capita).

- Eastern Europe, Caucasus and Central Asia (EECCA) are a unique case where a decline in economic prosperity as consequence of the post-Soviet transition during the 1990ies resulted in a substantial and prolonged reduction in per capita resource consumption at regional level.

6. Discussion of results

The International Resource Panel's analysis of the Domestic Material Consumption of 1970 and 2020 reveals dramatic dynamics of global resource consumption (Table 1):

a) **Global resource consumption has increased at a faster rate than world population.** While the world population has doubled over the past fifty years, the consumption of natural resources has tripled. If we assumed constant per capita resource consumption by simply multiplying the total resource consumption of 1970 by the population growth rate (factor 2.1) this would explain two thirds of the delta between 1970 and 2020. Consequently, one third of the additional growth would be attributable to the increased per capita consumption of a more affluent world population.

b) Population and economic dynamics have resulted in major shifts in global resource consumption over the past fifty years:

1. **Dominance of resource consumption in middle-income countries**
   In absolute terms, the population of high-income economies has slightly increased as well as their per capita resource consumption. However, in relative terms their contribution to global resource consumption has halved in favour of the share of middle-income economies. Between 1970 and 2020 the population of lower and upper middle-income economies increased from 2.4 to 5.8 billion people, which is more than the total world population of 1970 (3.6 billion). The increased demand of populations with a middle-income has not only been driven by high birth rates but is also a consequence of increasing affluence coupled with growing per capita resource demand, which has most significantly increased. In upper middle-income economies per capita resource consumption in 2020 is even higher than in high-income economies. Thus, population growth coupled with an increasing per capita demand has resulted in global resource exploitation, which is now dominated by the demand of middle-income economies.

2. **Marginalization of North America and Europe—rising importance of Asia**
North America, Europe as well as Latin-America and Caribbean countries each contribute about 10% of global domestic resource consumption, while Asian and Pacific countries contribute 60%. Its share of global resource consumption now corresponds to its share of the world population. In absolute terms domestic resource consumption in Asia and the Pacific increased by a factor of 7 from 7.7 to 53.5 billion tons, which is more than 170% of the total resource consumption of humanity in 1970.
3. **Continuous low resource consumption in low-income countries**
Over the past fifty years the total population of low-income countries increased by a factor of three, their relative share in the total world population has increased from 4 to 7%. At the same time their per capita resource demand has remained the same which resulted in a continuously small contribution of low-income countries to global resource consumption of less than 4%.

Table 1: Population and DMC per capita in 4 income groups

	Population 1970	DMC per capita 1970	Population 2020	DMC per capita 2020
high-income	1.0	17	1.4	19
upper middle-income	1.4	8	2.8	20
lower middle-income	1.0	3	3.0	5
low income	0.2	5	0.6	5
World	**3.6**	**8**	**7.7**	**12**

Source: UNEP, 2024, https://fred.stlouisfed.org/[3]

3 The methodological annex of the GRO 2024 does not contain data on the population of the four income groups of countries. Therefore, the FRED has been chosen as a source of Worldbank statistics easily at hand. Consequently, the absolute numbers deviate from the GRO 2024, which is also due to rounding, however the proportions remain similar.

Table 2: Domestic Material Consumption (DMC) in four income groups

	DMC in billion tons 1970	DMC in billion tons 2020
high-income	17.2	26.5
upper middle income	11.5	55.7
lower middle-income	3.1	14.8
low income	0.7	2.8
World total	**32.5**	**99.8**

Source: UNEP, 2024, https://fred.stlouisfed.org/7

Figure 1: DMC 1970 and 2020 in high/low and middle-income countries

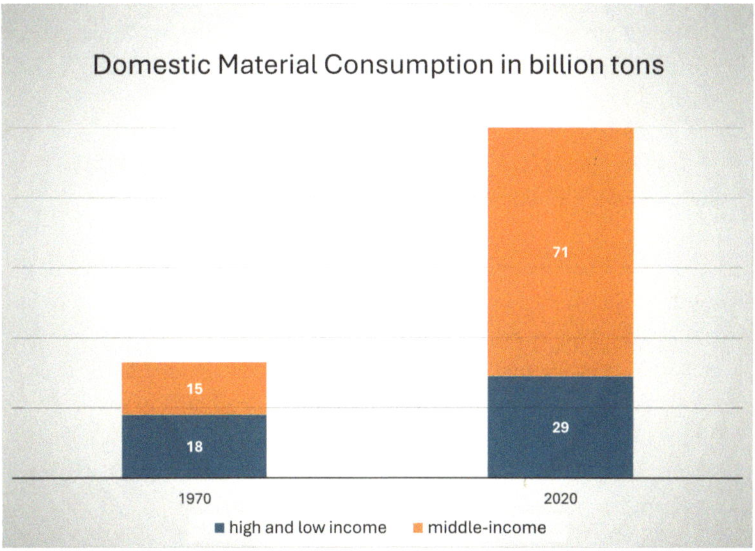

Source: IRP, https://fred.stlouisfed.org/[7]

What makes the difference between a binary North-South/rich-poor perspective towards a fourfold view on different income groups?

In 1970 the population of high- and low-income economies had been 1.2 billion people in 2020 this number has increased to 2.1 billion, which would be roughly one third of the population. In terms of the world's natural resource consumption (1970) it would have covered more than half (Figure 1). A focus on the high resource consumption of the rich in contrast to the poor could be justified, because most of the resource consumption would be addressed and the large differences in per capita resource consumption of more than a factor 3 could be highlighted, with meaning for the rest of the population living in middle-income countries with comparable low per capita resource use. Today, with a view on the 2020 data, the situation has completely changed. A focus on 27% of the population living in rich and poor countries would address less than one third of the world's natural resource consumption (Figure 1). Therefore, a binary perspective North-South/rich-poor has two major disadvantages:

- It neglects 70% of the world's natural resource consumption by more than 70% of the world population living in middle-income economies.
- It addresses a factor four inequality in per capita resource consumption between high-income and low-income economies, but it would neglect the same difference in per capita resource consumption between higher and lower middle-income countries (Table 1).

7. Conclusions and outlook

This article has started referring to the research of Hans Rosling and the Gapminder Foundation about significant misconceptions regarding the development of global affluence and its worldwide distribution. We may conclude that the bias which Rosling referred to as the "gap instinct" also affects the associated ecological debate and risks to contaminate related discourses. The concluding chapter of this article takes up more space than usual, because it aims at outlining implications and possible solutions for overcoming widespread misconceptions.

7.1 The established dichotomy

Framing the discussion about affluence and resource consumption primarily as antagonism between a rich Global North and a poor Global South offers several advantages. It allows analysis to be embedded in established historical and geopolitical contexts. It connects to existing discourses on colonialism, inequality, and global justice, making the discussion more accessible and relevant to a wider audience. According to Rosling et al (2018) binary views appeal to people's preference to divide populations into two opposing groups. This makes dichotomies more intuitive and emotionally engaging, which can increase public attention and appeal. The Global North-South framing is widespread and well-established. It is frequently used by media, political decision-makers, and civil society, which facilitates its acceptance and the dissemination of matching narratives. Therefore, we may conclude that the decision of UNEP to use a headline which appeals to the gap-instinct for introducing the Global Resources Outlook in its press release of March 1st 2024 is understandable to improve acceptance and dissemination.

However, taking a binary perspective also has disadvantages. The focus on 30% of the population living in high and low-income economies neglects 70% of the world's population using 70% of the world's natural resources. The headline of the press release with a focus on "rich countries" and "low-income ones" distracts from the real news of the GRO 2024 which are that global material consumption is now dominated not by high-income but middle-income economies (Figure 1). Furthermore, it does not offer an explanation why the difference between per capita resource consumption in high-income and low-income economies is worth a headline, while a similar difference between upper middle-income and lower middle-income countries[4] is not (Table 1).

7.2 The World Bank income groups

The more nuanced classification of countries into four income groups, as applied by the International Resource Panel, enhances the understanding of natural resource consumption and leads to a more accurate and comprehensive analysis of the dynamics of resource demand than established rich-versus-poor dichotomies. This offers the chance to develop more realistic assessments of global resource challenges as precondition for evidence-based policies. However, categorizing countries into four income groups might complicate the understanding and communication of the dynamics of global resource demand. So far, there seems to be a lack of appealing narratives

4 This refers to DMC for the year 2020: the difference between high-income (19 t per capita) and low-income economies (5 t per capita) – for upper middle-income (20 t per capita) and lower middle-income (5t per capita). If the consumption-oriented Material Footprint is considered the difference among the two middle-income group is slightly less pronounced: high income (24t per capita) and low-income (4 t per capita) – upper middle-income (19t per capita) lower middle-income (5t per capita).

and frugal heuristics which could replace the North-South dichotomy. While blaming the luxury and overconsumption of a rich elite in the "Global North" is tempting, it is harder to problematize the rising consumption of a growing volume of middle-income households ("the vast majority of people slowly dragging themselves toward better lives", see quote by Rosling above). It is socially acceptable to condemn private jets or large mansions for their resource-intensity and high emissions, while material and energy-intensive development of decent housing and infrastructure is considered to be an expression of social progress, e.g. for reaching the so-called Sustainable Development Goals. However, not only the waste of resources for rich elites deserves public attention but also waste of resources for the masses such as the Evergrande incident in China's building sector, which resulted in a massive loss of energy, materials and land. This raises general questions about resource-efficiency, governance, and corruption in real estate and infrastructure development in emerging economies which could deserve further research and analysis.

7.3 Between rich and poor: a new world order

The focus on the North-South divide obscures the view of new political, economic and ecological realities which are increasingly shaped by the rise of middle-income economies. As a result, research and discourses about environment and development are often deficient.

The GRO data clearly indicates that the tripling of resource demand over the past twenty years is more due to increasing affluence of highly populated middle-income economies, while the physical marginalization of the established high-income world formally known as "the Global North" proceeds. On the one hand income distribution and resource intensive lifestyle of the rich elites, and on the other hand the growing affluence of the total population in middle-income economies is increasingly relevant. The data suggests that they are the largest drivers of global environmental change of our time and future generations. Not only the luxury yachts for leisure of the rich, but also the container shipping giants providing goods for the masses would be an appropriate symbol of accelerating global resource demand.

The rise of the BRICS expresses the ambiguity of current resource trends which are insufficiently reflected by theory, research and media. The BRICS alliance has been established by middle-income countries as a consequence of their growing economic and political importance. Initially it comprised Brazil, Russia, India, China, and South Africa. The group has expanded to include Egypt, Ethiopia, Iran, and the United Arab Emirates, with the latter being the only high-income member. Additionally, Indonesia joined the group in 2025. As of early 2025 around 3.64 billion people live in BRICS member countries. This accounts for approximately 45% of the world population. In line with Rosling's critique the BRICS are insufficiently reflected in scientific and popular literature as well as public media which tends to focus on the rich versus poor dichotomy. However, the BRICS alliance does not fully align with established binary narratives, given the differing historical backgrounds and economic, cultural, and social diversity of its member countries. A possible approach to address the limitations of existing theories would be to supplement them with frugal heuristics like the IPAT equation and develop new evidence-based narratives (Schepelmann et al, 2021).

7.4 Relevance of the IPAT equation

The GRO 2024 demonstrates the explanatory potential of the IPAT equation not only for quantitative analysis of past developments but also for forward-looking agenda-setting, analysis and policy formulation.

As demonstrated in the GRO 2024 the decomposition analysis of population, affluence and technology is a rich source of data and insight. Quantifying and comparing drivers and their manifestation in specific production and consumption patterns, both in absolute and relative terms, enables evidence-based assessments of proportions. This approach allows for prioritization and the deduction of targeted strategies tailored to the distinct social, ecological, and economic realities of low-, medium-, and high-income countries.

However, the International Resource Panel exhibits in the GRO 2024 some inconsistencies in the application of IPAT. Particularly, the evaluation of population and affluence presents mixed conclusions. On one hand, the IRP asserts that "globally, population and affluence growth had a similar impact on material demand" (UNEP, 2024, 39). On the other hand, it claims that "affluence is the main global driver of environmental impacts" (UNEP, 2024, 63).

The examples given in the GRO illustrate the difficulties of separating population and affluence. "For instance, in China, the rise in material footprint is predominantly attributed to affluence. In contrast, Africa's impacts are largely influenced by its growing population". However, it needs to be considered for both Africa and China, that it is always the product of the factors population, affluence and technology that eventually determines the contribution to global resource extraction. For instance, assuming a similar technological level a significant increase in affluence in Luxembourg has minimal impact in absolute terms due to its small population. In contrast, a slight rise in affluence in China substantially affects global material flows. The projected doubling of the population in Africa from 1.5 to 3 billion people by 2070 will have a considerable ecological impact, particularly if coupled by socially desirable increases in affluence, including the development of housing, infrastructure and industrialization resulting in higher per capita resource consumption.

7.5 Factor P

While the GRO 2024 clearly identifies population as a major driver of global material flows, it fails to treat it as a manageable factor. Even though the IRP considers population to be less important than affluence, the GRO 2024 offers no explanation as to why population is not addressed as an area for target setting, policy formulation, or implementation. This seems representative of the current resource policy debate. However, with regards to population dynamics synergies of SDGs such as poverty reduction, education as well as sexual and reproductive health and rights (SRHR) offer opportunities for social policies (Rosling, 2018). In the domain of SDG 3 on "Good Health and Well-being" target 3.7 specifically aims to "ensure universal access to sexual and reproductive health-care services, including for family planning, information and education, and the integration of reproductive health into national strategies and programmes". Furthermore, SDG 5 on "Gender Equality" seeks to "achieve gender equality and empower all women and girls". Sexual and reproductive health and rights are a key aspect of women's and girls' empowerment, allowing them to control their bodies, make their own choices about their sexuality and reproduction, and live free from violence and discrimination. Target 5.6 emphasizes "universal access to sexual and reproductive health and reproductive rights".

Since population is an important driver of resource consumption in Africa, West Asia, Latin America and the Caribbean there is a discrepancy between its empirical significance and its treatment in the public resource debate, for which the GRO 2024 is a prominent example. It shows that beyond its importance for regional and country-specific design of evidence-based policies, the IPAT-equation is relevant for a more general reflection of values and human development. This concerns not only population, but also affluence and technology.

7.6 Factor T and A

It is largely accepted that global environmental change is a technological challenge, for example, renewable energy sources such as solar and wind power can reduce reliance on fossil fuels and decrease greenhouse gas emissions. Electric vehicles can replace traditional gasoline-powered cars, reducing air pollution and greenhouse gas emissions (Muratori, 2021). Additionally, technologies such as carbon capture and storage can help to reduce emissions from industrial processes (Dziejarski et al., 2023). Yet, it also seems to be accepted that problems arising from global environmental change cannot be fixed by technology alone (e.g. Dobson, 2003). There is a growing awareness that not only the factor T (technology) of the IPAT equation needs to be addressed but also factor A (affluence). This belief is usually labelled as "degrowth" (Busk, 2023). Based on the IPAT equation Hickel & Kallis (2020) discuss the theoretical possibility of green growth and the potential for efficiency improvements. They conclude that existing empirical evidence does not support the theory of green growth neither in terms of Domestic Material Consumption (DMC) nor in terms of carbon emissions. The authors suggest that policies relying on green growth assumptions need to be revisited. They propose to explore alternative strategies, such as degrowth to shift away from growth-focused development agendas. In line with several authors (Ekins, 1993) they recommend a focus on decoupling prosperity and development from growth.

7.7 The Great Acceleration of the Anthropocene

Another example of mainstream debates about environment and development which could profit from the application of the IPAT equation and its decomposition relates to the so-called Anthropocene. The flagship publication by Steffen et al. of 2015 presents a collection of graphs to underpin the hypothesis of a "Great Acceleration" (Steffen et al., 2015). As contribution to the International Geosphere-Biosphere Program (IGBP) synthesis project, inspired by Paul Crutzen's introduction of the term "Anthropocene", the graphs track socio-economic and earth system trends from 1750 to 2010. They aim at capturing the comprehensive human impacts on earth systems, particularly after 1950, which marks a significant acceleration in human activity and its impacts on earth system trends. It connects to the Anthropocene discourse by noting the continued post-industrial shifts in the state and functioning of the earth systems beyond Holocene variability. Based on the graphs the authors conclude that the beginning of the Great Acceleration in 1950 would be the most compelling start date for the Anthropocene. Given the importance of the Great Acceleration for the Anthropocene concept it is remarkable that the authors simply stress the correlation between socio-economic trends and Earth system changes but offer no convincing systemic understanding with a causal explanation for the Great Acceleration. This weakens the argument of a Great Acceleration, because correlations cannot substitute for causality. In addition, the authors stress the importance of comparative analysis of socio-economic trends to address equity issues in the OECD, BRICS, and the rest of the world. Even though the authors realize the emerging shift in production and consumption towards BRICS nations they claim that OECD countries drive most of the Earth system impacts by dominating global consumption. The Great Acceleration graphs are an example, how the analysis and evidence of the GRO 2024 presented in this paper could enrich the Anthropocene research as well as teaching on global environmental change in general, especially if comparative analysis of four income groups according to the World Bank methodology would be applied:

1. The causality of the IPAT equation could replace the simple correlation of socio-economic and earth systems trends. Not as a general theory but as robust and frugal heuristics the IPAT equation could introduce an evidence-based perspective on the drivers of the Great Acceleration in the different regions of the world.
2. Introducing IPAT causality in portraying the Great Acceleration would be necessary to critically reflect existing values and objectives related to technological development, economic growth and population. Consistently using frugal IPAT heuristics could raise awareness on the problem that affluence and population are not only the main drivers of resource use and environmental destruction, but also the most widely accepted and popular indicators of collective strength. In contrast, declining population and GDP are seen as signs of weakness. As long as sufficiency, degrowth and depopulation remain political taboos, the only logical option left is disruptive technological shifts that aim at an overall dematerialization of economies in the order of magnitude of a Factor 10 (Schmidt-Bleek, 2008). However, this is also unlikely, not only because of the scientific arguments against green growth and technology fixes quoted above. Poor and middle-income economies are currently developing resource-intensive large-scale infras-

tructure and housing schemes with little concern for resource efficiency and green agendas.

3. Persistent misconceptions on the dominance of OECD consumption of natural resources could be corrected to clear the view on the new realities of a world after the successful industrialization of many middle-income economies. This could also lead to realistic assessments of the continuous expansion of populations and economies as well as the likelihood of emerging new waves of the Great Acceleration of human activity and global environmental change.

Targeting the consumption of the rich parts of humanity is understandable and may be a moral necessity, but it will not contribute to decrease environmental pressure generated by the vast majority of middle-income households. On the contrary, focus on high income usually results in calls for a redistribution of income to poorer segments of the population, which would eventually fuel further consumption. This may have positive effects on social cohesion and justice, which may accelerate demographic shifts towards lower birth rates. However, the main message of the GRO 2024 is not that global resource consumption is primarily driven by the high-income countries but more than ever from the successful attempt to raise income and quality of life for the majority of people, who live in middle-income countries. In other words, global environmental change is not primarily a result of greater inequality. Rather, it is the result of greater equality in terms of rising income for people and states, enabling increased production and consumption including the development of infrastructure, housing, education and healthcare.

References

Busk, L. A. (2023). Degrowth and the future of capitalism: A critical review of recent literature. *Emancipations: A Journal of Critical Social Analysis, 2*(1), Article 10.

Commoner, B., Corr, M., & Stamler, P. J. (2010). The causes of pollution. *Environment: Science and Policy for Sustainable Development, 13*(3), 2–19. (Original work published 1971)

Costanza, R., Cumberland, J., Daly, H., Goodland, R., & Norgaard, R. (1997). The relationship between affluence and environmental degradation: A review of the literature. *Ecological Economics, 21*(3), 199–213. https://doi.org/10.1016/S0921-8009(96)00100-5

Dobson, A. (2003). *The technological fix: Why technology won't save us from environmental disaster*. Routledge.

Dziejarski, B., Krzyżyńska, R., & Andersson, K. (2023). Current status of carbon capture, utilization, and storage technologies in the global economy: A survey of technical assessment. *Fuel, 342*, 127776. https://doi.org/10.1016/j.fuel.2023.127776

Ekins, P. (1993). 'Limits to growth' and 'sustainable development': Grappling with ecological realities. *Ecological Economics, 8*(3), 269–288. https://doi.org/10.1016/0921-8009(93)90062-Z

Giljum, S., Bruckner, M., & Martinez, A. (2015). Material footprint assessment in a global input-output framework. *Journal of Industrial Ecology, 19*(5), 792–804. https://doi.org/10.1111/jiec.12214

Hertwich, E. G. (2005). Consumption and the environment: A review of the literature on the environmental impact of consumption. *Journal of Economic Psychology, 26*(3), 261–274. https://doi.org/10.1016/j.joep.2005.06.005

Hertwich, E. G. (2010). *Assessing the environmental impacts of consumption and production: Priority products and materials*. UNEP/Earthprint.

Hickel, J., & Kallis, G. (2020). Is green growth possible? *New Political Economy, 25*(4), 469–486. https://doi.org/10.1080/13563467.2019.1598964

Jackson, T., & Michaelis, L. (2003). Consumption and the environment: A review of the literature on the environmental impact of consumption. *Journal of Economic Psychology, 24*(3), 257–274. https://doi.org/10.1016/S0167-4870(02)00165-5

López, H., & Gill, M. S. (2015). *The World Bank's classification of countries by income* (Policy Research Working Paper No. 7528). World Bank. https://doi.org/10.1596/1813-9450-7528

Muratori, M., Alexander, M., Arent, D., Bazilian, M., Cazzola, P., Dede, E. M., … & Ward, J. (2021). The rise of electric vehicles—2020 status and future expectations. *Progress in Energy, 3*(2), 022002. https://doi.org/10.1088/2516-1083/abe0ad

Myers, N., & Kent, J. (2003). New consumers: The influence of affluence on the environment. *Proceedings of the National Academy of Sciences, 100*(8), 4963–4968. https://doi.org/10.1073/pnas.0438061100

Rosling, H., Rosling, O., & Rosling Rönnlund, A. (2018). *Factfulness: Ten reasons we're wrong about the world—and why things are better than you think*. Sceptre.

Satterthwaite, D., McGranahan, G., & Tacoli, C. (2010). Global environmental change and human well-being: A review of the literature. *Journal of Environmental Planning and Management, 53*(4), 419–433. https://doi.org/10.1080/09640561003737375

Scheidler, F. (2021). *Der Stoff, aus dem wir sind: Warum wir Natur und Gesellschaft neu denken müssen*. Piper.

Schepelmann, P., Vercalsteren, A., Acosta-Fernandez, J., Saurat, M., Boonen, K., Christis, M., Marin, G., Zoboli, R., & Maguire, C. (2020). Driving forces of changing environmental pressures from consumption in the European food system. *Sustainability, 12*(19), 1–20. https://doi.org/10.3390/su12198137

Schepelmann, P., Fischer, S., Drews, M., Bastein, T., Kropp, J., Krummenauer, L., & Augenstein, K. (2021). Evidence-based narratives in European research programming. *European Journal of Futures Research*, 9(1), 6. https://doi.org/10.1186/s40309-021-00175-2

Schmidt-Bleek, F. (2008). Factor 10: The future of stuff. *Sustainability: Science, Practice and Policy*, 4(1), 1–4.

Steffen, W., Broadgate, W., Deutsch, L., Gaffney, O., & Ludwig, C. (2015). The trajectory of the Anthropocene: The great acceleration. *The Anthropocene Review,* 2(1), 81–98. https://doi.org/10.1177/2053019614564785

Suri, V., & Chapman, D. (1998). The environmental Kuznets curve: A survey of the literature. *Journal of Economic Surveys, 12*(4), 423–447. https://doi.org/10.1111/1467-6419.00056

Tukker, A., & Jansen, B. (2006). Environmental impacts of products: A detailed review of studies. *Journal of Industrial Ecology, 10*(3), 159–182. https://doi.org/10.1162/jiec.2006.10.3.159

United Nations Environment Programme. (2021). *The use of natural resources in the economy: A global manual on economy wide material flow accounting*. United Nations Environment Programme.

United Nations Environment Programme (2024): *Global Resources Outlook 2024: Bend the Trend – Pathways to a liveable planet as resource use spikes*. International Resource Panel. https://wedocs.unep.org/20.500.11822/44901

Wiedmann, T., Lenzen, M., Keyßer, L. T., & Steinberger, J. K. (2020). Scientists' warning on affluence. *Nature Communications, 11*, 3107. https://doi.org/10.1038/s41467-020-16941-y

Wiedmann, T. O., Schandl, H., Lenzen, M., Moran, D., Suh, S., West, J., & Kanemoto, K. (2015). The material footprint of nations. *Proceedings of the National Academy of Sciences, 112*(20), 6271–6276. https://doi.org/10.1073/pnas.1220362110

Part II—Challenging the Status Quo

Infrastructures as Catalysts for Ecological Transformation

Christian Hein

Abstract: *In a globalized world, infrastructures act as catalysts for cultural progress and economic development as well as essential instruments for fighting climate change. However, it is essential to always take an ambivalent view of the technology used and to continuously question the need for infrastructural expansion. A particular challenge lies in the inherent characteristics of infrastructure projects, which emphasize the need for far-reaching future ethics. Infrastructure decisions typically involve lengthy planning phases, considerable financial expenditure and a wide range of environmental and social interventions, the long-term, unintended consequences of which are often not fully foreseeable. Political decision-makers can be guided by a variety of sustainability approaches in order to assess the resulting conflicts of objectives. However, the plurality of sustainability itself raises the question of how a necessary framework for action can be developed from a political perspective in order to resolve the dilemma of conflicting objectives. This plurality raises a guiding question: How can a policy and infrastructure governance framework for the ecological transformation of heavy goods road transport—exemplified by the eHighway system—reconcile ecological effectiveness, social justice, and economic efficiency under conditions of uncertainty and natural-monopoly characteristics? The following section uses the case study of the ecological transformation of heavy goods transport and the associated infrastructures to show which understandings of sustainability are suitable for promoting an ecological transformation of the transport sector and at the same time enabling inclusive mobility. A particular focus is on analyzing barriers to market entry, user accessibility and the importance of a resilient infrastructure in a networked world in the course of the ecological transformation. This analysis shows the central role of infrastructure as a key component for social, ecological and economic transformation processes and emphasizes the need for a holistic approach that integrates technical, cultural and social dimensions. The introduction of new infrastructures such as the eHighway system is associated with complex challenges that must be addressed* *through targeted measures and transparent communication. To ensure social justice, a fair distribution of costs and benefits as well as targeted support for smaller players and lower-income groups is essential. The development of resilient and sustainable infrastructures requires flexible, adaptive and open-technology approaches that ensure both short-term efficiency and long-term adaptability. In conclusion, it is clear that balanced regulation is necessary to enable innovation and at the same time ensure social and ecological objectives in the transformation process. The case analysis indicates that reconciliation is feasible through a balanced governance architecture that combines transparent communication, targeted distributive instruments to safeguard equity, adaptive regulation of natural-monopoly elements to ensure fair and efficient market development, and modular, technology-open design to enhance resilience.*

1. Methodology

The methodology follows an integrated mixed-methods approach that systematically captures the entire technological value chain—from energy generation through transmission and storage to use in road freight transport—and triangulates quantitative governance analyses. Quantitatively, market structure in the subsystems of power generation, transmission and distribution grids, storage infrastructure, and stationary and dynamic charging infrastructure is represented using the Herfindahl-Hirschman Index, with market shares consolidated and interpreted from official and industry-specific secondary sources (e.g., BDEW, Federal Network Agency/Monopolies Commission, operator registries, industry statistics). The socio-economic impact analysis differentiates along a clear impact pathway between energy-affected persons, exposed persons, and disaster victims. It combines heuristic risk parameters from the literature on mortality and morbidity in energy and grid infrastructures, a meta-analytic evaluation of publicly documented BESS incidents (including the EPRI database) to derive normalized indicators per unit of energy or storage capacity, as well as model-based exposure estimates using population densities and near-source emission dispersion radii for typical plant configurations. Primary data come from the ELISA field trial (2018–2025): usage and availability data on dynamic charging and previously published work in the context of doctoral theses and scholarly journals. The statistical evaluation comprises descriptive analyses, correlation analyses, and multivariate procedures to identify perceived barriers to market entry; scales were harmonized and, where necessary, examined via sensitivity analysis.

2. Interdisciplinary understanding of infrastructures

In the course of scientific progress, the understanding of infrastructure has changed significantly and in many ways. Historically, the term was initially reduced to singularly networked technical structures that played a central role in the development of human civilization. The water supply infrastructure is one of the oldest and most essential forms created by early societies (BfG, 2023, 212). At the same time, transportation and energy supply infrastructures emerged, which together laid the foundation for the technology-centric perspective on infrastructure (Thacker et al., 2019, 251–252). For a long time, this technology-induced view shaped the general understanding of the term, which is still closely associated with physical structures such as roads, power grids and bridges. However, these physical infrastructures only represent a subset of the broader concept of infrastructure.

Since the industrial revolution, the technical conditions of physical infrastructures have changed fundamentally. Energy infrastructures, which had their origins in the simple supply of wood to small groups of people, have developed over the course of history into highly complex systems that today supply cities with millions of inhabitants via widely ramified electricity and gas networks (Bridge et al., 2018, 1–7). A comparable transformation process can also be observed in the transportation infrastructure. Paths and roads originally constructed from simple materials, which primarily served regional trade and logistical mobility, now form the basis of global supply chains that span the entire planet (David Daniels and Sonia Yeh, 2022, 1–2). These developments are complemented by modern phenomena such as mass mobility and advancing digitalization, which open up new dimensions of infrastructure and networking.

The availability of mobility services and energy supply is considered a central factor for social development in numerous system theories and guidelines (Wang et al., 2025, 49–51; Sovacool et al., 2021, 218–222). A prominent example of this is the Kardashov scale, which classifies civilizations according to their energy consumption. It postulates that societies with higher energy availability are able to develop more advanced technologies and establish more complex social structures (Nikolai S. Kardashev, 1964, 217–221). This close link between energy, technology and social development is also reflected in the global sustainability goals. For example, the United Nations Sustainable Development Goal (SDG) 8 entitled "Decent Work and Economic Growth" refers to the reciprocal relationship between economic progress and social transformation, whereby sustainable infrastructures are considered an essential basis for both areas from the perspective of the SDG (United Nations General Assembly, 2015). However, technological developments and population growth are leading to increasing consumption of planetary resources.

In addition to physical infrastructures, social infrastructures occupy central areas of human life. System theories such as those of Urry (2012) or Simmel (1997) see infrastructures and mobility in their centrality not as a direct physical connection between two places, but as a complex system in between (Urry, 2012, 47–48; Simmel, 1997, 171; O'Neill et al., 2018, 88–95). Social infrastructures define the space for social interactions and emphasize their multidimensional relevance, from the microcosm to the macrocosm of human life. Social infrastructures are therefore essential components of a functioning society and help to ensure that people can participate in social life regardless of their economic situation or physical location. Modern approaches to the conceptualization of infrastructure question the historically evolved, primarily economic perspective on infrastructure and view it as discursively constructed, i.e. as the result of specific social, political and cultural negotiation processes. In this context, an expanded understanding of mobility and infrastructure is suggested that goes beyond purely economic interests and includes social, ecological and cultural dimensions. The so-called "new mobility paradigm", for example, emphasizes that mobility is not only to be understood as the physical movement of people and goods, but as a complex network of social practices, technologies and infrastructures that reflects and influences social inequalities and power relations (Urry, 2012, 20–32).

Similarly, the Economy for the Common Good (exemplified by Felber (2015)) focuses on infrastructures as central elements of a sustainable and common good-oriented society, in which the provision and use of infrastructures does not primarily follow market logic, but serves the goal of promoting social justice, ecological sustainability and collective well-being (Felber, 2015). Arne Næss (1986), for example, addresses the oldest and at the same time most fundamental form of infrastructure, namely natural, ecological systems, whose inherent value and central importance for human life and social development have long been underestimated or even ignored. In his deep ecology perspective, Næss emphasizes that ecological systems not only serve as a resource base for economic activities, but must be seen as independent, complex networks that enable and sustain life on earth (Næss, 1986, 1–3).

This holistic understanding of infrastructure calls for a shift away from sectoral approaches towards a systemic perspective that focuses on the interactions between ecological, social and economic dimensions. As part of an expanded understanding of infrastructure, it is increasingly recognized that ecological, social and economic infrastructures are closely intertwined and interdependent.

3. Objectives and questions of the work

The infrastructures described above have a profound and multi-layered impact on human life. In particular, rapid technological development, coupled with continuous population growth, is leading to more intensive use of physical infrastructures. One result of this is the increasing consumption of natural resources, which in turn has far-reaching and often irreversible effects on global ecosystems (Wang et al., 2022, 1–15). At the same time, access to infrastructure is essential, as it forms the basis not only for social participation, but also for economic development and individual fulfillment (Thacker et al., 2019, 113–119). Against this backdrop, the key question is how infrastructures can be made more sustainable without jeopardizing inclusivity and accessibility for all social groups.

In order to shed light on this issue, a case study from the mobility sector is used below, namely road-based catenary line technology. This example is used to analyze the challenges and ambivalences associated with the introduction of a technological innovation. In particular, the barriers to market entry and consequences for third parties are examined in order to develop a comprehensive understanding of the dynamics that occur when new technologies are implemented in infrastructures. The methodology of this study is based on an integrative and systemic approach. Not only the primary infrastructures, but also downstream and supporting systems are included in the analysis. The first step is a quantitative assessment of the market structure in order to identify the intensity of competition and potential monopoly positions.

A particular focus is on identifying the causal link between specific socio-political instruments—for example liberalization measures such as unbundling, regulated third-party access, and retail competition—and market density and structure. For this purpose, the Herfindahl-Hirschman Index (HHI) is calculated, which serves as an established indicator for measuring market concentration. The analysis covers several key areas: the energy generation infrastructure, the electricity grid infrastructure, the storage infrastructure and the dynamic charging infrastructure. This comprehensive view makes it possible to capture the interactions between the various infrastructure levels and to identify potential social inequalities and initial user accessibility restrictions.

The next step is a detailed evaluation of which groups of people could potentially be disadvantaged by the introduction or transformation of infrastructures. The analysis is carried out along the entire impact chain in order to comprehensively identify the effects. The focus is on two central groups in particular: exposed persons, potential disaster victims and those affected in terms of energy. Exposed persons are those who are exposed to an increased risk due to their professional, social or geographical position, for example due to direct dependence on certain infrastructures or proximity to critical energy facilities. Energetically affected persons, on the other hand, are those whose quality of life, economic situation or social participation is significantly influenced by changes in the infrastructure chain, such as rising energy costs or restricted access to energy. Disaster victims, meaning fatalities and injured persons, who are particularly vulnerable due to extreme events such as technical incidents are also taken into account. The analysis of these groups is differentiated and serves to evaluate the distribution effects and identify possible social inequalities or disadvantages.

Based on this, a detailed analysis of the accessibility and availability of the infrastructure components under consideration is carried out, based on the results previously obtained from the case study. The aim of this evaluation is to systematically examine the possible uses for both market participants and end customers. In particular, it looks at the conditions under which the various facilities and technologies are accessible, what restrictions exist, and what external factors influence their use. The methodology of this study is based on a combination of qualitative and quantitative analysis. First, the infrastructural and regulatory framework conditions that determine access to the systems are identified. In addition, a usage analysis is carried out based on empirical data from the ELISA[1] field trial. This data includes the availability of connection options and the cost structures associated with usage. A particular focus is placed on identifying barriers that could restrict accessibility. These include technical

1 The ELISA project (2018–2025) tests the real-world use of hybrid and electric trucks powered by catenary lines on a pilot section of the German A5 motorway, aiming to demonstrate technical feasibility and gather data for future electrified freight transport concept (Hein, Knezevic et al. 2023, 57).

hurdles, such as compatibility with existing systems, and socio-economic factors, such as the financial resilience of end customers. In addition, the study examines the extent to which external conditions, such as regional energy infrastructure or the availability of resources, influence usage possibilities.

The systematic investigation of these obstacles makes it possible to identify key challenges and develop targeted solutions that can promote use of the technology.

4. Technology portfolio for road-based catenary line technology

In the political and social discourse on sustainable development, there are a variety of solutions and technological alternatives for mitigating the long-term effects of harmful greenhouse gases on the climate. Technological developments in the transport sector are also ambivalent. On the one hand, they cause problems, but on the other hand, without them, it is often impossible to solve problems. Over time, some technological developments have helped to conserve natural resources. Significant sections of politics, business, and research attest to the promising potential of electrifying roads using catenary lines for the sustainable development of the transport sector (Prof. Dr.-Ing. Manfred Boltze et al., 2022, 2–15) (Hein, Petermann et al., 2023). However, this raises the question of which elements of sustainability and which sustainability approaches should be used for evaluation.

The technological basis for the functioning of road-based catenary lines, also known as dynamic charging, is based on adapted pantograph technology, which was originally developed for trams and trolleybuses and is still used by them (Hein and Wauri, 2024, 8–11). The principle of dynamic charging is based on supplying energy to electrically powered trucks via a catenary above the right lane of a highway. The catenary line system to be installed can be integrated into the existing road infrastructure without major intervention (Hein and Wauri, 2024, 14–17). In addition to an electric motor (and combustion engine), the purely electric (or hybrid) vehicles are equipped with an energy storage device and a pantograph (Hein and Wauri, 2024, 8–11). This enables electrical energy to be transferred from the catenary line system to the vehicle's electric drive system. The trucks can connect to and disconnect from the catenary line at any speed, which ensures the usual driving flexibility. Overtaking maneuvers are therefore still possible without any problems (Prof. Dr.-Ing. Manfred Boltze et al., 2022, 2–15).

Figure 1: BEV+PAN during the charging process.

Source: (Own illustration)

As can be seen in Figure 1, dynamic charging uses a pantograph integrated into the driver's cab (marked in blue) to draw power from the catenary line (marked in orange). With the current state of technology, the batteries of catenary line trucks are charged with a voltage of 600 volts (V) to 750 V and an electric current of 1000 amps (A) while traveling along the route This means that both the traction current and the charging current are provided by the catenary line technology within a section of the route.

Due to the size of the battery installed in the "Battery Electric Vehicle + Pantograph" (BEV+PAN), a continuous route network is not necessary. Additionally, the battery can be smaller than if only traction current were available, which in turn saves resources. The battery capacity enables the last few kilometers on the federal highway and cyclical gaps on the highway to be bridged. System sections of 10–15 km in length are recommended (ibid.).

Battery capacities currently vary depending on the vehicle generation. The first vehicles were still plug-in hybrids and had a battery capacity of 90 kWh. The latest purely electric BEV+PAN have a battery capacity of 300 kWh (ibid.).

The SDGs currently serve as a central framework for the development of political strategies, development plans, and legislation to promote sustainable development globally. Taking these goals into account, key aspects of inclusive mobility can already be identified. In particular, free access to highways, in principle, enables all persons with vehicles that have the necessary technical resources to use these infrastructures. This is in line with the goal of reducing inequalities and ensuring access to basic services for all, as formulated in SDG 10 "Reduced Inequalities" (United Nations General Assembly, 2015; LfU, 2020, 10). In this context, the first step is to examine the extent to which free market and user accessibility is guaranteed in the areas of sustainable mobility use in the form of dynamic charging. This includes energy generation, energy transport, catenary line infrastructure, and the use of dynamic charging infrastructure.

5. Economic perspectives on infrastructure-driven progress and change

The HHI is a measure of market concentration and is often used to analyze the intensity of competition in a market. A high HHI value indicates a high degree of market concentration, with a few companies dominating the market, while a low HHI value indicates a highly competitive market with many evenly distributed players (Palan, 2015, 10–14). Low competitive intensity suggests significant barriers to market entry, which should be removed in the context of inclusive use.

On the one hand, the centralization of market conditions among a few participants enables economic focus, as exemplified by the railway sector in the 1990s (Esposito et al., 2017). By focusing on increasing efficiency and optimizing costs, companies can increase their economic performance and strengthen their market position. On the other hand, however, this development often leads to social injustices, such as the introduction of a three-class system that treats different customer groups unequally and makes access to mobility more difficult for lower-income groups (Urry, 2012, 90–112). Such inequalities undermine the goal of an inclusive infrastructure that should be accessible to all people, regardless of their social or financial situation. Furthermore, such measures can jeopardize the long-term social acceptance of centralized infrastructures and contradict a sustainable and fair infrastructure solution that takes equal account of ecological, social, and economic aspects. Infrastructure should not be evaluated solely from an economic perspective and labeled a "natural monopoly," but should also take into account environmental impacts and social relevance.

In the context of sustainable energy production, for example through wind and photovoltaic systems, the HHI can help to evaluate the market structure and identify possible monopoly or oligopoly positions. In order to calculate the HHI, the market shares of the individual companies or players in energy production are required. The HHI is calculated by squaring the market shares (s) of all players (N) and then summing them.

The formula is as follows:

Equation 1: Calculation of HHI (Herfindahl 1950; Hirschman 1945)

$$HHI = \sum_{i=1}^{N} s_i^2$$

There are currently 1,331 electricity suppliers in Germany, with four large companies accounting for 50% of the market share. For the purposes of the calculation, it is assumed that the remaining 50% of the market is distributed evenly among the other 1,327 suppliers. As shown in Equation 2, the HHI for energy supply for the year 2024 (HHI_{EV2024}) is 626.87 (BDEW 2024). This value indicates low market concentration, as it is well below the threshold of 1,500, which is generally used as an indicator of moderate concentration.

Equation 2: Calculation of HHI for energy suppliers 2024 (own calculation, data from (BDEW 2024))

$$HHI_{EV2024} = 4 \cdot (12.5)^2 + 1{,}331 \cdot (0.0378)^2 \approx 626.87$$

A low HHI indicates that the market is highly competitive and that no single player has excessive dominance (Brezina et al., 2016, 49–72). Despite the strong position of the four major suppliers, which together control half of the market, the large number of smaller players ensures market diversification and maintains competition. This suggests that although the German electricity market is dominated by a few large companies, there is still room for smaller suppliers, whose market presence increases the intensity of competition. This suggests moderate barriers to competition, which do not completely prevent new providers from entering the market, but nevertheless pose certain challenges. Currently, the high complexity of energy industry processes and the highly dynamic purchasing market are worth mentioning here.

As shown in Figure 2, two key factors can be identified that explain the declining HHI and the associated increase in competitive intensity in the energy market. The opening of the electricity market in Germany, which began in the 1990s, was intended to lead to fairer competition. However, the market effect was the opposite. Deregulation significantly lowered the barriers to market entry for new providers, enabling small and medium-sized enterprises to enter the market. The economic dominance of the four major providers initially led to an increase in market density, as can be seen in Figure 2. It was only in the following years that the number of market participants and their associated market share increased. The diversity of supply and the pace of innovation in the energy sector were strengthened, and consumers benefited from a wider choice of electricity tariffs, while competition forced providers to operate more efficiently and in a more customer-oriented manner.

The structure of the energy market has undergone fundamental change due to the increasing relevance of decentralized energy supply. Technological advances, particularly in the field of renewable energies such as photovoltaics and wind power, now make it possible to generate electricity locally and individually. This has significantly reduced traditional economic barriers to market entry, such as the high capital requirements for the construction of large coal or gas-fired power plants. This development has paved the way for smaller providers and even private individuals to actively participate in the energy market, for example by operating solar panels or small wind turbines. At the same time, decentralized energy supply enables greater regional value creation and contributes to the resilience of the energy system.

The HHI for energy production currently stands at 626.87, a significant reduction compared to the 1990s, when it was still above 1,000. This development is primarily attributable to the expansion of renewable energies and the gradual liberalization of the energy market. In particular, the decentralization of energy production has led to a noticeable reduction in market concentration. This transformation has not only increased the intensity of competition, but has also brought ecological and social benefits by promoting sustainable energy sources, strengthening the diversity of market players, and facilitating access to energy for various social groups.

In addition to energy generation, market concentration and the resulting barriers to market entry for energy infrastructure must be examined. A distinction is made here between transmission system operators and distribution system operators.

Figure 2: HHI vs. market share of the big 4 and renewables. (Own representation)

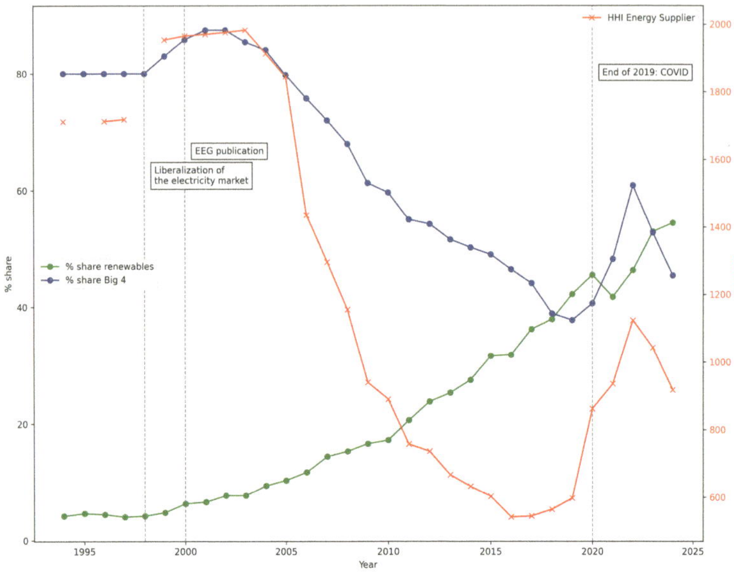

Source: see Appendix 1 for data sources

A transmission system operator (TSO) is responsible for the operation, maintenance, and expansion of interregional and transnational high-voltage and extra-high-voltage grids. These grids transport electrical energy over long distances and connect large generation facilities, such as power plants or offshore wind farms, to regional distribution grids. There are four transmission system operators in Germany: 50Hertz, Amprion, TenneT, and TransnetBW (Tripathi and Mackensen, 2017). They play a central role in ensuring grid stability and the integration of renewable energies.

A distribution system operator (DSO), on the other hand, operates the regional and local power grids that transmit energy from the transmission grid to end consumers, such as households, businesses, and public institutions. These grids operate at medium and low voltage levels and are responsible for the granular distribution of energy. Distribution system operators are often municipal companies or public utilities and ensure that electricity reaches consumers reliably and in the quantities required. There are currently 866 distribution system operators (Bundesnetzagentur 2025).

Equation 3: Calculation of HHI for TSOs (own calculation, data from (Statista GmbH))

$$HHI_{TSO2024} = (0{,}3636)^2 + (0{,}2740)^2 + (0{,}2118)^2 + (0{,}1507)^2 \approx 2{,}749.05$$

The current market shares of the transmission system operators, based on revenue, are as follows: Amprion: 36.36%, TenneT: 27.40%, 50Hertz: 21.18%, and TransnetBW: 15.07%. This gives a HHI of 2.749,05 (Statista GmbH). A HHI of 2,749.05 indicates a high degree of market concentration. This is not surprising, as the market for transmission grids in Germany is dominated by just four major players, with TenneT holding the largest share at over 50%. The high concentration is typical for natural monopolies such as transmission grids, as the operation of such infrastructure is severely limited due to significant investment costs and regulatory requirements. Projects such as the north-south routes preserve the existing market density, as their technical and logistical complexity and the financial and regulatory hurdles maintain barriers to market entry. These secure the dominance of the established transmission system operators and underscore the market's characteristic as a natural monopoly with structurally limited competition.

In contrast, the distribution network market, with an HHI of 269.6 indicates lower market concentration in 2024. This underscores the highly fragmented structure of the German distribution network market, which is characterized by a large number of players, including numerous municipal and regional network operators. Although some larger distribution network operators such as Westnetz (13,6%), Bayernwerk (12,1%), Netze BW (7,6%), Avacon (6,6 %), E.DIS (6,2%), Mitnetz Strom (3,3%), Stromnetz Berlin (2,8%), LEW-Verteilnetz (2,7%), Hamburg Netz (2,3%) and Süwag Netz (2,3%) have significant market shares, the market as a whole remains highly fragmented, as many smaller operators (e.g., municipal utilities) also play an important role (Westnetz GmbH, 2025) (Netze BW GmbH, 2025) (E.DIS Netz GmbH, 2025) (Bayernwerk Netz GmbH, 2025) (Avacon Netz GmbH, 2025) (Süwag Energie AG, 2025) (Stromnetz Berlin GmbH, 2025) (Hamburger Energienetze GmbH, 2025) (LEW Verteilnetz GmbH, 2025) (Mitteldeutsche Netzgesellschaft Strom GmbH, 2025) (Bundesnetzargentur | Bundeskartellamt, 28.02.2025, 109). In contrast to the infrastructure level of energy generation, the increasing costs associated with the expansion of renewable energies at the distribution network level are leading to increasing market concentration, as can be seen in Figure 3.

The energy transition is primarily taking place at the low-voltage level, as this is where photovoltaic systems and new consumers such as heat pumps and electric vehicles are connected (Hein, C. R., Lerchl-Mitsch, K., Petermann, D.,

Simon, L. et al., 2024, 51). The high investment costs for the necessary digitization of the grids and compliance with environmental requirements pose considerable economic challenges, particularly for smaller distribution system operators, which often leads to their takeover by larger market players (Hein, C. R., Lerchl-Mitsch, K., Petermann, D., Simon, L. et al., 2024, 51). The HHI is 2,749 at the TSO network level, while it is 269.6 for DSOs. The increasing expansion of controllable consumers and generators, such as wall boxes, heat pumps, and photovoltaic systems, poses considerable technical and organizational challenges for distribution system operators. However, an unintended consequence of this development is increasing market concentration at the distribution grid level, as the complexity of grid control and infrastructure requirements increasingly disadvantage smaller players.

The increased use of renewable energies and the transformation in the mobility sector are giving rise to supporting sub-infrastructures. The storage infrastructure and charging infrastructure must be considered central here. Energy storage systems form the essential core for effectively compensating for and stabilizing the volatility of electricity generation from renewable energy sources such as wind and solar energy (e-netz Südhessen AG, 2024, 110). Due to the close link with energy generation, it can be assumed that market concentration in the battery storage sector is similar. Battery storage can basically be divided into three categories: large-scale storage with a capacity of over 1,000 kWh, commercial storage with a capacity between 30 and 1,000 kWh, and home storage with a capacity of up to 30 kWh (Pawlik 23.06.2025). In Germany, a total of 270 large-scale storage systems, 10,936 commercial storage systems, and 1,651,520 home storage systems were installed as of December 18, 2024 (Pawlik 23.06.2025). Market concentration in this sector is described by an HHI of 626.87.

Figure 3: HHI for DSOs vs. renewable energy market share. (Own representation)

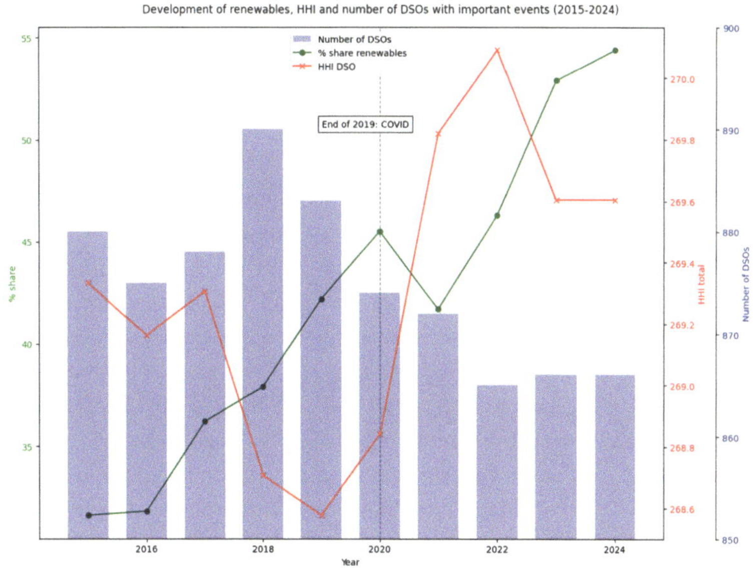

Source: see Appendix 2 for data sources

The transformation of energy and mobility systems is leading to the emergence of a new market for energy storage. Due to its close links with energy generation, this market exhibits a comparable level of market concentration, as described by an HHI of 626.87.

Finally, the market concentration of charging systems is examined. For comparison purposes, stationary and dynamic charging are considered. There are currently 161,700 charging stations and 2,487 charging station operators in Germany, of which 9,086 stations are operated by EnBW mobility+ AG und Co. KG, 4,396 by E.ON Drive GmbH, 3,194 by Tesla Germany GmbH, 2,670 by EWE Go GmbH, and 2,603 by Mercedes-Benz AG (Impey 23.06.2025).

Equation 4: Calculation of HHI for Charging Stations (own calculation, data from (Impey 23.06.2025))

$$HHI_{LS} = (0.0562)^2 + (0.0272)^2 + (0.0198)^2 + (0.0165)^2 + (0.0161)^2 + 2482 \cdot (0.000348)^2 \approx 51.2$$

The HHI for the stationary charging market in Germany is 51.2. This indicates very low market concentration, which is typical of a highly competitive market. The stationary electric mobility market is subject to increased monitoring by the Monopoly Commission. The competition model underlying this market currently comprises the provision of locations for charging points, the market stage of operating publicly accessible charging stations by so-called charge point operators (CPOs), and the market stage of electric mobility providers (EMPs) and roaming platforms (Hein, Knezevic et al., 2023, 20–22). The upstream market stage of electricity production follows an independent competition model and is not directly integrated into the charging point infrastructure. As competition can develop in the charging point infrastructure sector, this economic sector is not considered a classic network sector based on a natural monopoly. The competition parameters at the infrastructure level of electric mobility are complex and include aspects such as charging time, charging capacity, location availability, transparency, and accessibility of charging points. In regions where CPOs have a dominant market position, end customers may not have a choice between different providers or charging points, which can significantly restrict competition (Hein, Knezevic et al., 2023, 14–48).

The HHI for stationary charging is 51.2. The strong focus on a socially acceptable and economically oriented market means that efforts to transform the transport sector in an environmentally friendly way are being significantly hampered.

As described above, there are currently three catenary lines in pilot operation with a single catenary line operator for dynamic charging. The HHI for the dynamic charging market with a single catenary line operator is 10,000, which indicates a complete monopoly. From a competitive economics perspective, the catenary line infrastructure also represents a natural monopoly in the long term, as the parallel construction of several catenary line networks would not be efficient from either an economic or a resource-related point of view. However, this is not solely due to economic market barriers (Hein, Knezevic et al., 2023, 14–48). Regulatory measures are necessary to ensure fair competition in network sectors. Regulatory law serves as the legal implementation of the findings of network economics, whose principles are primarily based on the logic of networks and not on the logic of the goods transported within these networks (Hein, Knezevic et al., 2023, 14–48). Specific regulatory requirements apply to energy supply networks, defined as electricity and gas supply networks according to Section 3 No. 16 EnWG, such as unbundling, access regulation, and tendering. However, these requirements cannot be readily transferred in their current form to the new network sector of "catenary lines on highways" (Malmendier and Schendel, 2006, 362–383). Instead, an independent market for traction current should be created with specific regulatory mechanisms that can be flexibly adapted to the respective market situation.

In this context, it must be ensured that the regulatory requirements of the EnWG do not apply to the Electrified Road System (ERS) and its operators. Simply classifying the catenary line infrastructure as a highway or energy facility does not create sufficient legal certainty. In addition, either the ERS operator should be classified as a final consumer (as in the basic and ELISA models[2]) or the catenary line infrastructure should be classified as a special type of energy facility (as in the AMELIE 2 model) (Hein, Knezevic et al., 2023, 49–60). A four-stage market ramp-up plan is recommended, which provides for the gradual introduction of market players and regulatory mechanisms. The individual stages should be designed depending on the degree of expansion of the catenary line network. In each phase of the market ramp-up, the billing option that best balances ease of market entry (through low regulatory and technical requirements) and acceptance (through user-friendliness and fairness of consumption) should be selected.

The value creation level of traction power supply is particularly important, as there is no location competition in the ERS, as is the case with charging points, for example. The basic and ELISA models provide for a lower degree of regulation than the AMELIE 2 model and are therefore more suitable for the initial phase of the market ramp-up (Hein, Knezevic et al., 2023, 88–89). Specific studies are therefore necessary for the ERS in order to identify the appropriate market regulation approaches for the different market phases. Even with new technologies and natural monopolies, a complete monopoly does not usually exist. This applies in particular to catenary line infrastructure, which is considered part of the highway system. Under German law, in particular Article 90 of the Basic Law (Grundgesetz, GG) and the provisions of the Federal Trunk Road Act (Bundesfernstraßengesetz, FStrG), trunk roads are owned by the state. Since catenary lines can be regarded as an integral part of the trunk road infrastructure, they are also reserved for state ownership.

2 Further information on the basic, ELISA and AMELIE models are to be found in Hein, Knezevic et al. (2023).

Equation 5: Calculation of HHI for dynamic charging (own calculation, data from ELISA)

$$HHI = (s_1)^2$$
$$= (1)^2 = 1$$

This legal basis prevents private actors from gaining a complete monopoly over the catenary line infrastructure, as the state, as the owner of the highways, retains control over the use and expansion of catenary lines. Instead, private companies can only operate as operators or service providers under concessions or public-private partnerships (PPPs). This ensures that the use of the catenary line infrastructure is in line with the principles of public service and fair competition, while at the same time preserving state sovereignty over the highways.

The HHI for dynamic charging is 1. This market constellation is based, among other things, on the regulatory basis of Article 90 of the GG, which assigns sovereignty over highways to the state and thus ensures central control and planning. The state's focus on social interests and its independence from individual regional interests enables more objective and overarching planning and implementation, but at the same time, this orientation means that the ecological and economic potential of dynamic charging is not fully exploited. Prioritizing social and administrative aspects can thus significantly slow down the pace of innovation and the expansion of this forward-looking technology.

Infrastructure not only shapes social coexistence, but also reflects fundamental values such as justice, inclusion, and sustainability. The HHI analysis shows that infrastructure is often associated with natural monopolies, whereby market concentration is not necessarily motivated by economic factors alone. However, sustainable infrastructure development requires a balance between social justice, environmental goals, and economic efficiency.

The German electricity market, which has a medium level of market concentration with an HHI of 626.87, illustrates how deregulation and decentralization in the 1990s successfully lowered barriers to market entry, increased the number of market participants, and strengthened the pace of innovation. It is particularly noteworthy that the originally socially motivated intervention paradoxically led to an intensification of monopoly formation in the energy market. Only through the introduction of innovative technologies such as photovoltaics and wind power, which also promote ecological objectives, was it possible to achieve a real reduction in market concentration.

Comparable challenges can be seen in the area of charging infrastructure for electric mobility. The current market design is geared toward enabling intense competition, which is intended to ensure socially acceptable access to charging infrastructure. This applies to both stationary and dynamic charging systems. However, from an economic perspective, this competitive structure in both technological approaches is delaying the market ramp-up, which means that the ecological potential of electric mobility cannot yet be fully exploited. While the market for stationary charging has a very low market concentration and is therefore competitive, with an HHI of 51.2, the market for dynamic charging, for example via catenary lines, is a complete monopoly with an HHI of 10,000. This monopoly position, which is based on state control in accordance with Article 90 of the Basic Law, secures social interests and overarching planning, but can hamper the pace of innovation and ecological progress. Flexible regulatory approaches are therefore needed to exploit the potential of such technologies while promoting social and ecological goals. The transformation of energy and mobility systems requires supporting sub-infrastructures such as energy storage and charging points, which are essential for the integration of renewable energies and the stabilization of the energy system. Despite moderate market concentration in the energy storage sector (HHI: 626.87), promoting smaller players remains a key challenge. Sustainable infrastructure development must therefore not only drive technological innovation and environmental goals, but also ensure social justice and fair competition in order to enable long-term progress and change. From an economic perspective, low market penetration can lead to economies of scale, resulting in significant cost reductions. This also has social relevance, as it makes products and services more affordable for low-income households. Improved quality of life can be achieved, for example, through lower energy prices or access to innovative technologies. These effects result from the standardization of processes and more efficient planning of production volumes. However, achieving such effects is challenging, especially in transformation phases, such as the transition to a sustainable energy and mobility infrastructure. In these phases, fundamental processes must first be established, while products are often associated with high engineering, research, and development costs. This leads to the opposite social effect. Sustainable technologies often remain unaffordable for low-income households, which can exacerbate social inequalities. High market penetration also carries risks. It can lead to the formation of monopolies that limit consumer choice and exacerbate social disparities. In addition, ecological consequences can arise, as high market penetration is often accompanied by increased resource consumption, especially if the products are not designed sustainably. To meet these challenges, regulatory intervention is needed to provide sustainable products with a protected market space before they have to compete with established, unsustainable alternatives. The energy industry is a prime example of how the expansion of renewable energies can deliver both ecological and economic benefits. Companies with a small market share also have the opportunity to specialize in environmentally friendly niche markets and offer sustainable solutions there. Lower market penetration can also strengthen social resilience, as society is less dependent on individual suppliers. Table 1 shows a summary of the latest HHI figures.

Table 1: HHI overview

Market segment	**HHI (0–10,000)**	**Concentration interpretation**	**Reference year**
Electricity suppliers (retail)	626.87	Low	2024
Transmission system operators (TSO)	2,749.05	High	2024
Distribution system operators (DSO)	269.6	Very low	2023/2024
Charging infrastructure (stationary, CPO shares)	51.2	Very low	2025
Dynamic charging (overhead line, pilot stage)	10,000	Monopoly	2025

Source: Data according to the sources cited in the chapter

6. Social ambivalence of technological developments

As previously outlined, the introduction of renewable energies and the liberalization of the energy industry have both beneficial and challenging effects on market penetration and the various dimensions of sustainability. A key aspect in this context is the importance of the current transformation process toward an ecologically oriented infrastructure chain. In the economic and social context in particular, this change first requires the comprehensive implementation of new structures before the desired positive effects can be realized. Technological developments play an ambivalent role here. On the one hand, they contribute to existing problems; on the other hand, they are essential for enabling sustainable solutions and overcoming long-term challenges. In the following, we will examine who is negatively or positively affected by new ecological technologies from a purely social perspective, based on their social consequences. We will start again with energy production. Figure 4 shows the number of global deaths caused by different energy sources (Markandya and Wilkinson, 15.09.2007; Sovacool et al., 20.01.2016; UNSCEAR, 2008, 2018). Death rates are measured based on direct deaths, such as accidents, or indirect deaths, such as air pollution per terawatt hour of electricity. It is positive to note that renewable energies in particular are responsible for only a low death rate.

Figure 4: Death rate per TWh of generated energy by energy source. (Own representation)

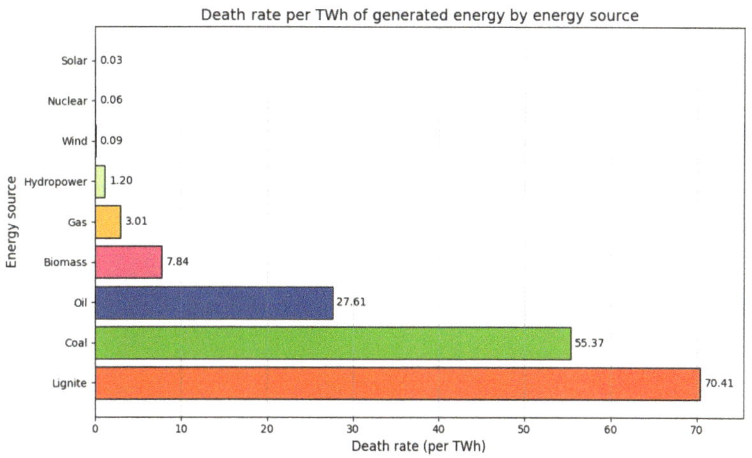

Source: see Appendix 3 for data sources

Figure 5: Death rate based on the case study. (Own representation)

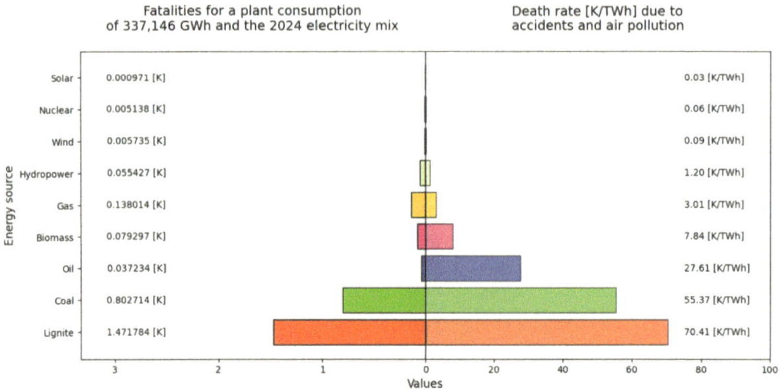

Source: see Appendix 3 for data sources

In the short term, the current electricity mix must be taken into account when introducing a new technology. Taking into account the evaluation results shown in Figure 4 and an assumed prospective utilization of dynamic charging of 100%, the statistical forecast is that, with the current electricity mix, two people would die each year as a result of the introduction of this mobility solution, based on a single section of road alone. Looking at a future scenario in which the predicted system consumption of 337.146 GWh per year is covered exclusively by renewable energies, the number of disaster victims could be reduced to 0.020229 per year. Currently, the global annual number of fatalities amounts to 2.596314.

In addition to the devastating consequences in the form of disaster victims caused by the use of energy sources, there are two other key figures that must be considered in the context of social consequences. These are, on the one hand, those affected by energy and, on the other hand, those exposed to energy. Those affected by energy are individuals or population groups who are directly or indirectly affected by the effects of energy production. This includes people who are economically or socially affected by energy prices, increased local grid fees, increased local and temporary supply interruptions due to the fluctuating nature of renewable energies, or political measures (e.g., CO_2 pricing). Examples include households suffering from energy poverty or companies affected by rising energy costs.

To illustrate the burden of casualties in the electrical grid infrastructure, the systematic review by (Shih et al., 2018) was used, which comprises 41 publications with a total of 5,485 adult patients (18.0% low voltage, 38.3% high voltage, 43.7% voltage not specified) and documented higher morbidity and mortality in the clinical collective at high voltage (hospital mortality: 2.6% at low voltage, 5.2% at high voltage, 3.7% not specified). Aggregated across all voltage levels, normalizing to an assumed global electricity consumption of 26,000 TWh results in a nominal mortality rate of approximately 0.0072 deaths per TWh. Applying this heuristically to an energy consumption of 0.337 TWh, the expected number of victims is

$$0.0072 \frac{K}{TWh} \bullet 0.337\,TWh \approx 0.00243\,K$$

based on this exact amount of energy.

This figure should be understood as a global approximation and primarily reflects individual events; large-scale, simultaneous damage events caused by grid infrastructure are extremely rare. The high level of safety of power grids in public spaces is the result of extensive technical and organizational protective measures, meaning that relevant residual risks exist primarily in professional activities with direct access to the equipment. In countries with high safety standards and a low proportion of overhead lines, even lower values can be assumed, although no country-specific disaggregated meta-analyses are available for this to date.

Exposed persons are people who are exposed to a specific burden or risk arising from energy infrastructure or projects. The term "exposed" refers to physical, health, or social hazards caused by certain influences, i.e., people who live near energy facilities and are potentially exposed to hazards such as electromagnetic fields (from high-voltage power lines), noise emissions (from wind turbines or storage facilities), or accident risks. Also affected are people whose health may be impaired by pollutants, noise, or other environmental impacts, such as residents living near coal-fired power plants who are exposed to health risks from particulate matter or sulfur dioxide. People who experience social disadvantages as a result of the construction or operation of energy projects, such as resettlement, loss of property, or restrictions on their quality of life, are also exposed persons.

The analysis of exposed and energy-affected persons requires a differentiated approach. Focusing on the locally affected population in Germany, there is an increase in the number of people affected, as a larger proportion of energy is generated by locally installed plants, such as wind turbines. However, if these figures are put into relation to the population already affected by the use of oil, lignite, or other fossil fuels, there is an overall reduction in the number of exposed persons.

Wind power and photovoltaic systems expose affected individuals to different types of impact. In the case of wind turbines, the main issues are noise emissions, infrasound, and shadow flicker, which can impair the quality of life of local residents. In addition, visual impairments and potential hazards such as ice throw are often perceived as a nuisance. Photovoltaic systems, on the other hand, mainly cause conflicts due to glare, the reflection of sunlight, and the use of large areas. The measurable effect, i.e., how many exposed persons are affected, depends heavily on the location, the technical generation used, and the population density. The majority of wind and ground-mounted PV systems in Germany are located in suburban, predominantly hilly areas and should serve as an example here.

To calculate the number of people exposed per megawatt (MW), the total number of people affected within the sound and noise radius of the plant is divided by the installed capacity of the plant. For a 3-megawatt wind turbine, a noise radius of 1 kilometer is typically assumed, which corresponds to an area of approximately 3.14 square kilometers (Lewis et al., 2002, 82–83). Renewable energies, especially wind turbines, are primarily installed in rural areas (Bovet et al., 2019). In this area, the population density in the Rhine-Main region is 400 people per square kilometer, which results in the following total number of people affected (Regionalverband FrankfurtRheinMain, 2022):

Equation 6: Calculation of exposed persons in energy supply incidents. (own calculation)

$$\textit{Number of exposed persons} = \textit{Population density} \cdot \textit{Visibility and noise radius}$$

$$\textit{Number of exposed persons } EV = 400\frac{\textit{People}}{km^2} \cdot 3{,}14km^2$$

$$\approx 1.256 \textit{ Exposed persons}$$

As can be seen from Equation 6, around 418.67 people per MW are exposed here. This figure can be used as an indicator of the social and spatial compatibility of wind and PV projects in suburban areas.

In addition to the exposed persons, approximately 1,000,000 persons would be affected in terms of energy in the scenario under consideration, as all persons living in the adjacent grid area would be directly affected by the effects of a decentralized energy supply (e-netz Südhessen AG, 2025). Persons affected in terms of energy are all those who are directly dependent on the energy supply because they cover their electricity needs from the corresponding distribution grid section. This figure includes private households, commercial enterprises, and industrial consumers who depend on a reliable and stable energy supply. In addition, the energy supply also has financial implications for all those affected by energy, particularly through grid fees. These may increase as a result of the expansion of the grid infrastructure required for the integration of new technologies such as wind turbines and dynamic charging infrastructure. Such cost increases affect not only those directly exposed in the vicinity of the facilities, but also the entire population in the grid area. In this case study, the figure of 1,000,000 people affected by energy highlights the far-reaching significance and potential social and economic impacts of energy infrastructure on the region.

Fluctuating generators add another level of consideration. The need for storage capacity and the people exposed to it and affected by energy, as well as potential disaster victims, must also be taken into account. To this end, a meta-analysis of all disaster cases was first carried out. The present study is based on a comprehensive data collection using the BESS Failure Incident Database. According to the definition of the Federal Emergency Management Agency (FEMA), an "incident" is a natural or man-made event that requires an emergency response to protect life or property in direct connection with large-scale electricity storage facilities (≥0.5 MW). The collected data was used for a meta-analysis to gain systematic insights into the effects of incidents related to large-scale electricity storage systems.

In contrast to the analysis of the global BESS database, which focuses primarily on technical causes and their analysis, this study took an alternative approach. The focus was on reports in the local and trade press, which were evaluated not in terms of technical details, but rather in terms of the health consequences and impacts on the local population. Despite the significant global expansion of large-scale electricity storage capacity from 10.3 GWh in 2018 to 304 GWh in 2024, a well-founded assessment in this context remains lacking (Kurtz and Haegel, 2025, 206–214). To better categorize the consequences, the reports were first divided into two main groups, namely injuries and fatalities. In the further course of the analysis, these categories were merged to enable a uniform consideration of those affected as "disaster victims." This approach allows the social and health consequences of battery storage to be viewed in a differentiated manner and placed in the context of emergency management and prevention. The entire value chain was evaluated, from manufacturing to the final use of storage capacities. Due to insufficient data, the extraction of raw materials could not be taken into account, but should be identified as a relevant research gap. Nevertheless, the present analysis can be used as an initial indicator.

As can be seen in Figure 6, the global number of people injured and killed rose significantly, particularly in the ramp-up years 2023 and 2024. While the storage capacity increased by 113.87% in 2023 (25 injured and 1 fatality) in 2023 and by 104.6% (25 injured and 26 fatalities) in 2024 compared to the previous year, the number of disaster victims also increased dramatically during the same period. In 2023, the number of victims doubled compared to 2022, representing an increase of 100%. In 2024, the number of victims rose again by 96.15%, which represents a further doubling compared to the previous year. In the first quarter of 2025, 11.25% of the previous year's victim numbers were already recorded, indicating a continuation of this trend.

Figure 6: Injuries and fatalities vs. installed energy storage capacity[3]

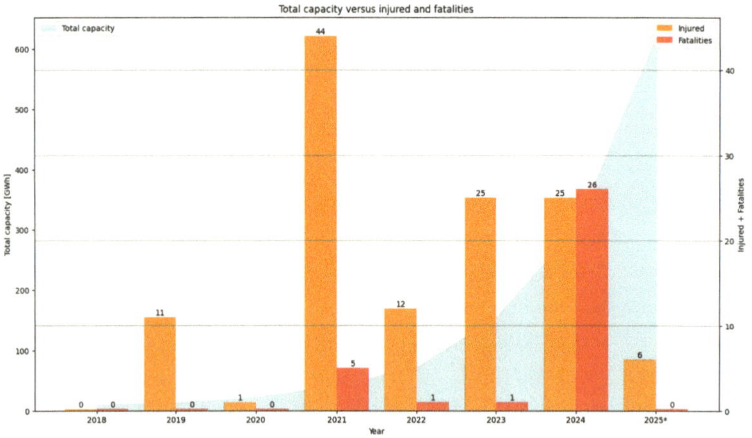

Source: Own representation, see Appendix 4 for data sources

3 The data for 2025 covers only January to May.

The current boom in renewable energies and the associated increase in demand for flexibility in the energy market require a parallel expansion of storage technologies. These are essential, for example, to support electromobility and, in particular, dynamic charging (Hein, C. R., Lerchl-Mitsch, K., Petermann, D., Büchau, N. et al., 2024). Despite the ecological and economic potential associated with the introduction of these technologies, the social impacts must not be ignored. The increase in disaster victims highlights the need to systematically analyze the social consequences of technological transformation and to incorporate them into decision-making processes. Only through a holistic approach can risks be minimized and long-term acceptance by society be ensured.

At this point in the analysis, the unintended consequences of an integrative view of the value chain of mobility solutions, especially dynamic charging, are already becoming apparent. An isolated view of the technology and its effects is no longer appropriate in the context of technology assessment and should not have been taken historically either. It should also be noted that a purely sector-coupling perspective is not sufficient, as central aspects remain unaddressed in the transition areas between sectors. Rather, it is necessary to analyze socially relevant issues along the entire technological value chain—from energy generation to energy transport and intermediate storage to mobility use. The causes of many of the negative effects were and often remain outside the immediate perception of mobility users. Those who are particularly affected are often those who have no direct connection to the mobility solution used, but suffer disproportionately from its consequences.

The problem is further exacerbated when the case study is revisited. To ensure full supply in the case study and to compensate for the fluctuating behavior of renewable energies, a storage facility with a capacity of 25 MWh and an output of 25 MW (type C1) is required. Looking at the ratio of disaster victims (K) to globally available storage capacities, the figure is 0.000302835 K/MWh. This corresponds to 0.007570876 K per plant for dynamic charging. While these figures appear uncritical at first glance, a consideration of the social consequences, as shown in Figure 6, reveals a significant problem in absolute terms.

In addition to those directly affected by the energy supply, there are also exposed persons who are adversely affected by the side effects of storage technologies. Similar to renewable energies, storage facilities cause noise, which is primarily attributable to ventilation systems, as well as waste heat, which can be perceived locally. The integration of large storage parks also often requires an expansion of the local grid infrastructure, which is reflected in increased grid fees that may also affect uninvolved third parties. In the case study, approximately 1,000,000 people are affected in terms of energy, as the entire grid area is integrated into the supply system. The number of people exposed depends heavily on the population density in the respective region and the location of the storage facility. A storage facility can cause noise emissions of up to 70 dB in the short term, which can already be perceived as disturbing. Taking into account sound propagation and population density in the Rhine-Main area, which is around 2,000 people per square kilometer in urban areas, this results in a figure of 6,276 people who are directly affected by noise emissions (TROX TLT GmbH, 2013; Regionalverband FrankfurtRheinMain, 2022). This figure illustrates that even with moderate emissions and a limited number of plants, social and health impacts can occur that must be taken into account in the planning and implementation of such projects. In summary, it is also evident at this level that the introduction and operation of storage technologies pose not only technical and economic challenges, but also social ones. It is therefore essential to take into account social consequences such as noise pollution, waste heat, and the impact on grid fees.

The mobility transition strengthens the polluter pays principle by shifting responsibility for providing the necessary infrastructure and energy supply more toward national circumstances. While oil production and diesel refining have historically taken place predominantly outside Germany, electricity generation from renewable energies, the expansion of transmission infrastructure, such as in the case of the SüdLink project, and the implementation of storage technologies for supplying electric mobility are increasingly taking place within Germany. However, these developments are increasingly causing discontent among the population, as the associated impacts on the environment and quality of life are directly felt at the local level.

In order to complete the evaluation of the social impacts of dynamic charging, it is necessary to assess the consequences for various exposed persons, those affected by energy issues, and potential disaster victims in the context of mobility provision.

In this context, those affected by energy are primarily those who live within the network area of a specific network section. The planned ramp-up of dynamic charging will be limited to central corridors along highways. As already explained, this requires the expansion of the local electricity infrastructure. The associated costs will be passed on to the grid fees, which will lead to a local financial burden for individual energy-affected persons. Based on the size of the affected grid area in the case study, the number of energy-affected persons can be estimated at around 1,000,000.

The negative impacts and the resulting number of people exposed can be derived from the following aspects. The construction phase will lead to restrictions in the road infrastructure, such as traffic jams and traffic restrictions, which may cause increased stress for those affected. With catenary line technology, maintenance work can usually be carried out during operation, reducing the number of people exposed and the severity of the disruption to everyday life. During normal operation, the restrictions are considered less severe and are primarily limited to visual impairments caused by the catenary line. Nevertheless, the number of people directly or indirectly affected is considerable due to the high traffic density on the highways. In 2024, an estimated 172.3 million people were affected by visual impairments along the highway. However, studies conducted as part of the field trial show that after multiple trips on the route, no significant changes in driving behavior or visual stress on road users could be detected.

Figure 7: Affected, exposed and injured/fatalities for different infrastructures.[4]

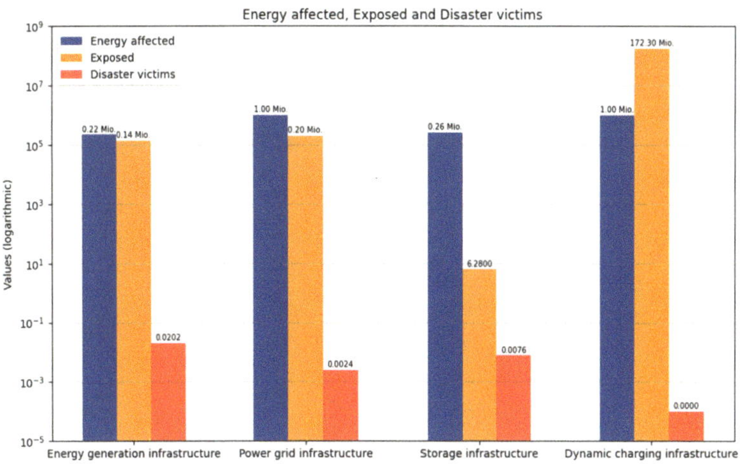

Source: (Own representation)

4 Please note that the "Disaster victims" value for dynamic charging infrastructure is actually 0, however this can not be displayed accurately on a logarithmic scale.

During the six-year field trial, there were no injuries or fatal accidents that could be directly attributed to the catenary line system. The sophisticated safety concept, which consists of a restraint system that allows vehicles to bounce off in a controlled manner and an automated contact wire shutdown in the event of damage, means that the technology can be classified as very safe (Gurske et al., 2023). The complete figures from the analysis can be found in Figure 7.

7. Discussion and recommendations for action

This discussion revisits the guiding question of how a policy and infrastructure governance framework for the ecological transformation of heavy goods road transport—exemplified by the eHighway system—can reconcile ecological effectiveness, social justice, and economic efficiency under conditions of uncertainty and natural-monopoly characteristics. This analysis underscores the central importance of infrastructure as a driving force for social, ecological, and economic transformation. At the same time, it becomes clear that the introduction of new infrastructure, such as the eHighway system, is associated with a multitude of challenges that encompass technical, social, cultural, and economic dimensions. To meet these challenges, targeted recommendations for action and approaches to discussion are needed to enable a sustainable and equitable transformation.

First, a holistic assessment of infrastructure is essential. Infrastructure is not just a technical system, but is deeply embedded in cultural and social practices. Decisions about its expansion or transformation must therefore be made systematically and take into account the interactions between ecological, social, and economic dimensions. A striking example of this is the liberalization of the energy industry, which was originally aimed at promoting social justice and strengthening competition by opening up the market. However, high barriers to market entry and existing market concentration initially had the opposite effect, as they consolidated the dominance of a few large players. It was only with the rise of renewable energies that a decisive decentralization of energy supply was achieved, which not only increased competition but also made a significant contribution to strengthening social justice.

An integrative perspective is necessary to take into account both long-term climate goals and the social acceptance and cultural significance of existing structures. In this context, the question arises as to how assessment frameworks can be developed that adequately reflect both the ecological advantages of new technologies and the social and cultural costs of their introduction. Another key aspect is promoting acceptance through transparent communication. The analysis shows that acceptance of new infrastructure depends heavily on the perception of its benefits and risks. Although scientific studies classify most concerns as unfounded, the survey results indicate that both the general public and affected populations express reservations regarding the visual impact of the catenary line infrastructure. To promote acceptance, broad-based information campaigns are needed to explain the functioning and advantages of the eHighway system in an understandable way. In addition, the population should be involved in planning processes at an early stage in order to identify and address such reservations.

However, the transformation of infrastructure must not lead to an exacerbation of social inequalities. The analysis shows that smaller players and lower-income population groups in particular could be disadvantaged by high investment costs or local burdens. At the same time, the decentralization of energy and mobility systems offers opportunities for greater regional value creation. Support programs that specifically target smaller players and low-income households, as well as a fair distribution of the costs and benefits of new infrastructure, for example through socially acceptable and decentralized network charges, are therefore of central importance. This raises the question of how social justice and economic efficiency can be reconciled in infrastructure planning.

In addition, the long-term planning and high investment costs of infrastructure projects require a forward-looking and flexible design that can respond to unforeseen developments. Resilient infrastructures must not only meet current requirements, but also anticipate future technological and societal changes. Modular and adaptive infrastructure solutions that enable gradual expansion and adaptation, as well as the integration of scenario analyses into planning processes, are crucial in this regard. It remains to be discussed how infrastructure projects can be designed to ensure both short-term efficiency and long-term resilience.

Another key aspect concerns the regulation and design of market mechanisms. The HHI analysis shows that natural monopolies—such as in the case of catenary line infrastructure—require targeted regulatory intervention. This is necessary to ensure fair competition and social justice on the one hand, and to guarantee both ecological transformation and economic sustainability in the long term on the other. At the same time, regulation must not hinder the pace of innovation and market ramp-up. Specific regulatory mechanisms are needed for new infrastructure sectors, such as dynamic charging, which can be flexibly adapted to the respective market situation. A balanced market ramp-up that takes into account both economies of scale and social and ecological goals is essential. It is important to examine which regulatory approaches are suitable for exploiting the potential of natural monopolies without jeopardizing social and ecological goals.

Technological openness and diversification are also decisive factors. A one-sided focus on a single technology carries the risk of increasing social resistance and neglecting alternative solutions. A technology-neutral approach that develops and evaluates different solutions in parallel, as well as support for pilot projects and field trials to test the practical suitability are therefore of great importance. The central question is how to design a technology-neutral strategy that, on the one hand, taps into innovation potential, while at the same time ensuring the urgently needed transformation toward an ecologically sustainable future.

In summary, the transformation of infrastructure in the context of climate protection requires a careful balance between ecological, social, and economic goals. The eHighway system offers promising potential for making road freight transport more sustainable, but faces challenges in terms social justice and regulatory framework conditions. Successful implementation therefore requires an integrative approach that reconciles technological innovations with societal needs and cultural practices.

References

Arne Næss (1986). There is No Point of No Return // Why vegan?: Green Ideas. Penguin Books.

Avacon Netz GmbH. (2025). Das Unternehmen Avacon Netz.https://www.avacon-netz.de/de/avacon-netz/das-unternehmen-avacon-netz.html

Bayernwerk Netz GmbH. (2025). Netze für neue Energien. https://www.bayernwerk-netz.de/de/bayernwerk-netz-gmbh/ueber-bayernwerk-netz-gmbh/unternehmensportrait.html

BDEW. (2024). Anzahl der Unternehmen am Energiemarkt in Deutschland nach Bereichen im Jahr 2024 [Graph].https://de.statista.com/statistik/daten/studie/173884/umfrage/zahl-der-unternehmen-in-den-einzelnen-marktbereichen-des-energiemarktes

BfG, ed. (2023). Hydrologischer Atals von Deutschland.

Bovet, J., Thrän, D., Bunzel, K., Eichhorn, M. (2019). Hidden outlaws in the forest? A legal and spatial analysis of onshore wind energy in Germany. Energy Research & Social Science, https://doi.org/10.1016/j.erss.2019.04.009

Brezina, I., Pekár, J., Cicková, Z., Reiff, M. (2016). Herfindahl–Hirschman index level of concentration values modification and analysis of their change. Central European Journal of Operations Research 24, https://doi.org/10.1007/s10100-014-0350-y

Bridge, G., Özkaynak, B., Turhan, E. (2018). Energy infrastructure and the fate of the nation: Introduction to special issue. Energy Research & Social Science 41, 1–11, https://doi.org/10.1016/j.erss.2018.04.029

Bundesnetzagentur. (2025). Anzahl der Ladesäulen für Elektroautos in Deutschland nach Betreibern im Jahr 2025 [Graph]. https://de.statista.com/statistik/daten/studie/1407386/umfrage/groesste-betreiber-von-ladepunkten-in-deutschland/

Bundesnetzargentur | Bundeskartellamt. (28.02.2025). Monitoringbericht 2024 Monitoringbericht gemäß § 63 Abs. 3 i. V. m. § 35 EnWG und § 48 Abs. 3 i. V. m. § 53 Abs. 3 GWB.

David Daniels, Sonia Yeh (2022). Complexities in the energy-transport co-transformation. *Progress in Energy*, 4(4). https://doi.org/10.1088/2516-1083/ac88b1

E.DIS Netz GmbH. (2025). Ihr Partner für regionale Energielösungen – E.DIS Netz GmbH. https://www.e-dis-netz.de/de.html

e-netz Südhessen AG. (2024). „MobiGrid" – Integration von Elektromobilität in die Verteilnetze durch Nutzung dezentraler Flexibilitä: internes Dokument.

e-netz Südhessen AG. (2025). Karriere bei e-netz Südhessen AG – Gestalten Sie mit uns die Zukunft der Region.https://www.e-netz-suedhessen.de/unternehmen/wir-in-der-region/karriere

Esposito, G., Urban-Kozłowska, J., Kaloud, T., Doleschel, J., Mariotti, M. (2017). The European Railway Sectors: Understanding and Assessing Change.

Felber, C. (2021). Change everything: Creating an economy for the common good. Zed Books; Bloomsbury Publishing.

Gurske, D., Wauri, D., Wilke, J., Öztürk, Ö. (2023). Hinweispapier für Straßeninfrastrukturbetreiber.

Hamburger Energienetze GmbH. (2025). Wie sicher ist meine Stromversorgung? https://www.hamburger-energienetze.de/energie-der-zukunft/stromnetz-der-zukunft/verteilnetzbetreiber

Hein, C., Knezevic, G., Claes, F., Burger, M., Schwarz, J., Korpis, N., Stockmann, I., Feistenauer, L., Petermann, D., Lerchl-Mitsch, K., & Chesi, K. (2023). Die Abrechnung elektrischer Energie für Oberleitungs-LKW: Modellvergleich ELISA II-B und AMELIE 2.

Hein, C., Petermann, D., Lerchl-Mitsch, K., Chesi, K., Hepp, A., Schneider, M., Oelke, L. P., Schwarz, J., Burger, M., Stenner, C., Erdmann, R., & Wilke, J. K. (2023). Hinweispapier für Energieversorgungsunternehmen.

Hein, C. R., Lerchl-Mitsch, K., Petermann, D., Büchau, N., Simon, L., Spies, V., Winter, A., Igel, M., Laxman, N., Wolschke, C. (2024). Forschungsprojekt MobiGrid: Marktgestützte Beschaffung von Flexibilitätsdienstleistungen im Verteilnetz.

Hein, C. R., Lerchl-Mitsch, K., Petermann, D., Simon, L., Spies, V., Winter, A., Prof. Dr.-Ing. Michael Igel, Laxman, N., Wolschke, C. (2024). Marktgestützte Beschaffung von Flexibilitätsdienstleistungen im Verteilnetz. ew Magazin (9), 50–53.

Hein, C. R., Wauri, D. (2024). Potentialanalyse: Synergieeffekte dynamischer und stationärer Ladesysteme entlang von Fernstraßen.

Herfindahl (1950). Concentration in the U.S. Steel Industry.

Hirschman (1945). National Power and the Structure of Foreign Trade.

Impey, B. (23.06.2025). Größte Betreiber von Ladesäulen für E-Autos in Deutschland 2025. https://de.statista.com/statistik/daten/studie/1407386/umfrage/groesste-betreiber-von-ladepunkten-in-deutschland/

Kurtz, S., Haegel, N. (2025). Global Progress Toward Renewable Electricity: Tracking the Role of Solar (Version 4). *IEEE Journal of Photovoltaics*, 15, 206–214, https://doi.org/10.1109/JPHOTOV.2024.3450020

LEW Verteilnetz GmbH. (2025). Unser Unternehmen im Überblick.https://www.lew-verteilnetz.de/lew-verteilnetz/ueber-lew-verteilnetz/lvn-im-ueberblick

Lewis, A., DeGagne, D., May, C. (2002). Evaluation of wind turbine noise. Canadian Acoustics 30, 82–83.

Malmendier, B., Schendel, J. (2006). Unbundling Germany's Energy Networks. *Journal of Energy & Natural Resources Law*, 24, 362–383. https://doi.org/10.1080/02646811.2006.11433442

Markandya and Wilkinson (15.09.2007). Electricity generation and health: The Lancet. Energy and Health (370), 979–990.

Mitteldeutsche Netzgesellschaft Strom GmbH. (2025). Wir zeigen Transparenz – Informationen für das Geschäftsjahr 2024. https://www.mitnetz-strom.de/ver%C3%B6ffentlichungspflichten/zahlen-fakten/netzdaten

Netze BW GmbH. (2025). Über uns: Wir kümmern uns drum. https://www.netze-bw.de/unternehmen/ueber-uns#1-1

Nikolai S. Kardashev (1964). Transmission of Information by Extraterrestrial Civilizations. Soviet Astronomy (8), 217–221.

O'Neill, D. W., Fanning, A. L., Lamb, W. F., Steinberger, J. K. (2018). A good life for all within planetary boundaries. *Nature Sustainability*, *1*(2), 88–95. https://doi.org/10.1038/s41893-018-0021-4

Palan, N. (2015). Konzentrations- und Ungleichheitsindizes – ein Überblick am Beispiel der Textilindustrie. https://static.uni-graz.at/fileadmin/sowi/Working_Paper/2015-02_Palan.pdf

Pawlik, V. (23.06.2025). Anzahl der Batteriespeicher in Deutschland nach Größe 2024. https://de.statista.com/statistik/daten/studie/1548677/umfrage/anzahl-der-batteriespeicher-in-deutschland-nach-groesse/

Prof. Dr.-Ing. Manfred Boltze, Linke, R., Öztürk, Ö., Schöpp, F., Wauri, D., Wilke, J. K. (2022). ELISA II-B – Vorbereitung, Durchführung und Evaluation eines realitätsnahen Probebetriebs von OH-Lkw auf der ELISA-Versuchsanlage: Ergebniszwischenbericht. https://www.autobahn.de/storage/user_upload/qbank/20220311_ELISA_Ergebniszwischenbericht_Band_0.pdf

Regionalverband FrankfurtRheinMain. (2022). Bevölkerungsdichte der Landkreise und Städte der Metropolregion FrankfurtRheinMain im Jahr 2021 (Einwohner je km²) [Graph]. https://de.statista.com/statistik/daten/studie/1186755/umfrage/bevoelkerungsdichte-landkreise-metropolregion-frankfurt-rhein-main/

Shih, J., Shahrokhi, S., (2017). Review of adult electrical burn injury outcomes worldwide: An analysis of Iow- voltage versus high-voltage electrical injury.

Simmel, G. (1997). Simmel on Culture. Frisby, D., Featherstone, M. (eds).

Sovacool, B. K., Kim, J., Yang, M. (2021). The hidden costs of energy and mobility: A global meta-analysis and research synthesis of electricity and transport externalities. Energy Research & Social Science **72**, 101885, https://doi.org/10.1016/j.erss.2020.101885

Sovacool et al. (20.01.2016). Balancing safety with sustainability: assessing the risk of accidents for modern low-carbon energy systems. Journal of Cleaner Production (Volume 112, Part 5), 3952–3965

Statista GmbH Umsatz der vier deutschen Übertragungsnetzbetreiber im Jahr 2024 (in Millionen Euro). https://de.statista.com/statistik/daten/studie/316698/umfrage/umsatz-deutscher-stromnetzbetreiber/

Stromnetz Berlin GmbH. (2025). Roadmap 2030, Sinn & Zweck und Vision. https://www.stromnetz.berlin/uber-uns/

Süwag Energie AG. (2025). Versorgungssicherheit. https://www.suewag.com/corp/ueber-uns/nachhaltigkeit/sozial/versorgungssicherheit#: :text=Wir%20sind%20zuverl%C3%A4ssiger%20Energiepartner,und%20somit%20die%20Versorgungssicherheit%20sicherzustellen.

Thacker, S., Adshead, D., Fay, M., Hallegatte, S., Harvey, M., Meller, H., O'Regan, N., Rozenberg, J., Watkins, G., Hall, J. W. (2019). Infrastructure for sustainable development. *Nature Sustainability*, 2(4). https://doi.org/10.1038/s41893-019-0256-8

Tripathi, S., Mackensen, R. (2017). Virtual Power Plants-Renewable Energy Production of the Future.

TROX TLT GmbH. (2013). Technische Publikationen: Grundlagen der Schalltechnik – Luftschall, Schallfeldgrößen, Schallgeschwindigkeit, Schalldruck, Schallleistung, Dezibel, Oktavspektrum, Terzspektrum, Phon und Schallausbreitung etc. https://www.trox-tlt.de

United Nations General Assembly. (2015). Transforming our world: the 2030 Agenda for Sustainable Development: Resolution adopted by the General Assembly on 25 September 2015 (A/RES/70/1). https://undocs.org/A/RES/70/1

UNSCEAR. (2008). Report to the General Assembly with Scientific Annexes.

UNSCEAR. (2018). Report to the General Assembly with Scientific Annexes.

Urry, J. (2012). Mobilities (Reprint). Polity Press.

Wang, H., Wang, J., Lyu, Y., Li, X. (2025). The impact of supply chain digitisation on sustainable development in global panel data. Does the energy efficiency matter? Energy Economics, 141, 108147. https://doi.org/10.1016/j.eneco.2024.108147

Wang, W., Deng, X., Wang, Y., Peng, L., Yu, Z. (2022). Impacts of infrastructure construction on ecosystem services in new-type urbanization area of North China Plain. Resources, Conservation and Recycling, 185, 106376. https://doi.org/10.1016/j.resconrec.2022.106376

Westnetz GmbH. (2025). Westnetz – wir bewegen Energie. https://www.westnetz.de/de/ueber-westnetz/unser-unternehmen/wir-ueber-uns.html

Appendix

Scan the QR-Code to easily access every appendix of this paper.

https://tvl.ink/9783839424506

Carbon Pricing in Practice

Interdisciplinary Insights to Improve the Effectiveness of CO_2 Pricing

Michelle Alfers & Elias-Johannes Schmitt

Abstract: *Following economic theory, carbon pricing is generally regarded as the optimal policy to achieve a reduction in CO_2 emissions. In theory, a carbon price is characterized by its cost-effectiveness, its flexibility as a market-based solution, and its relatively straightforward implementation compared to other regulatory approaches. Moving from theory to practice, however, any political intervention inevitably encounters a complex interplay of political, economic, and social dynamics, leading to unintended consequences that often undermine its effectiveness. Studying these dynamics is crucial to avoid negative outcomes and re-evaluate the policy design to ensure its intended impact. By analyzing existing carbon pricing measures, this chapter aims to address disciplinary blind spots that hinder their effectiveness in reducing carbon emission. In doing so, we identify two key areas: (1) Political feasibility as a concept that can be used to analyze the implementation of carbon pricing depending on key social actors, and (2) behavioral barriers, which result from actual behavior systematically deviating from the rational actor assumptions typically assumed in economic models. We demonstrate that recognizing these dimensions is crucial for designing effective and socially acceptable climate policies.*

Keywords: *Carbon pricing; climate policy effectiveness; political feasibility; public acceptance; behavioral barriers; policy design*

1. Introduction

Climate change and the associated environmental crises are undoubtedly the central challenges of the coming years. For several decades, climate researchers have been warning of the negative effects on humanity and calling on politicians and society to act quickly and profoundly.

From an economic perspective, the answer appears straightforward: to address climate change and place societies on a sustainable path, putting a price on carbon is regarded as the optimal (and often sufficient) solution. However, several challenges arise in the development and implementation of carbon prices (Stoll & Mehling, 2021):

First, the role of carbon pricing is increasingly questioned in scientific discourse—either as a standalone instrument or, in some cases, as a viable solution at all. Concerns have been raised about its capacity to drive the structural transformations required for deep decarbonization.

Second, in political practice, strong resistance often hinders the introduction of new carbon pricing schemes. Once introduced, carbon prices usually remain well below levels considered necessary for meaningful impact.

Third, empirical studies investigating the effectiveness of existing carbon prices report mixed results, but most indicate insufficient emission reductions to meet serious climate targets.

In this article, we argue that the focus on an 'optimal' carbon price is the result of a purely economic perspective. By focusing on a supposedly optimal carbon price, central aspects concerning its effectiveness are neglected and implementation problems arise in practice. To support this argument, we first introduce the standard-economic understanding of emissions as an externality and show how a carbon price is determined on this basis (section 2.1). Following this theoretical introduction, we briefly review the empirical evidence on the effectiveness of carbon pricing policies in section 2.2. As we will show, there is a significant inconsistency between theoretical predictions and the realized effects of these measures. We then use the remainder of this chapter to discuss two central issues contributing to this discrepancy. First, we show how the implementation of carbon prices is influenced by political feasibility. Whether and to what extent a carbon price is implemented depends on various social actors and their political power (section 3). Second, the effectiveness of carbon prices as an instrument for reducing emissions crucially depends on human behavior. In Section 4, we show how the assumption of rationality hinders the design of an effective carbon price. Section 5 summarizes the central insights.

The aim of this article is to show that interdisciplinary cooperation is necessary to design effective carbon prices and complementary policies. Students and young economists in particular must broaden their disciplinary view at an early stage in order to uncover blind spots and to be able to support the design of effective measures to mitigate climate change.

2. Carbon pricing in theory and practice

This section introduces the basic economic understanding of carbon emissions as an externality. We show that current carbon prices can be traced back to the theoretical work of Arthur C. Pigou and the modeling of William D. Nordhaus. We then review the effectiveness of real carbon prices and show that they differ greatly from those modeled.

2.1 The economic theory of carbon pricing

CO2 emissions are a typical example of a negative externality. In economics, negative externalities refer to costs imposed on third parties who are not directly involved in the production or consumption of a good or service. Starting with the standard textbook example, consider a factory that produces near a settlement and emits polluting substances that harm the inhabitants of the adjacent settlement (Coase, 1960). The damage caused in this way should be part of the production costs of the factory, but the manufacturer only takes into account the capital and wage costs of production. As a result, the market price does not reflect the true social costs of the good, preventing the economy from reaching a social optimum through the interplay of supply and demand.

Pigou (1920) argued that in such cases, state intervention is legitimate to correct this market failure. By imposing a tax equal to the social cost on the manufacturer, the state forces it to internalize the damage caused by pollution into the cost of production. Due to the higher market price, production and consumption will be reduced until market equilibrium reaches the socially optimal level. Alternatively, the manufacturer can invest in technologies that reduce pollution until the marginal cost of prevention equals the marginal cost of its damage. The Pigouvian tax is therefore understood as the most efficient market solution as it provides incentives for a change in behavior at the lowest absolute cost (Stern, 2006).

The Pigouvian model provides the theoretical foundation for modern attempts to calculate an optimal price on carbon emissions (Nordhaus, 1991; Stern, 2006). Accordingly, the carbon price is intended to reflect the social costs of carbon (SCC). The SCC is defined as the negative change in the discounted value of economic prosperity resulting from an additional unit of CO_2 emissions (Nordhaus, 2017; Nordhaus & Sztorc, 2013). Nordhaus developed a model framework in the 1990s in which he links economic activity, greenhouse gas emissions, the carbon cycle and the resulting economic damage of climate change (Nordhaus, 1991). The Dynamic Integrated Climate-Economy (DICE) model is built on a neoclassical growth framework and forecasts global production from capital accumulation, job growth, and exogenous technological progress, minus mitigation expenditures that reduce CO_2 emissions (Nordhaus, 1991, 2017). The emissions are entered into a simplified sub-model of the carbon cycle, which converts them into atmospheric concentrations, and into a reduced climate module, which translates the concentrations into global mean temperature changes. A damage function then maps these temperature increases in fractions of gross production, resulting in net consumption. Net consumption is aggregated over time via a social welfare function that includes a pure time preference and an inequality aversion parameter to generate a present value measure of well-being. The model then determines the intertemporal allocation of resources between mitigation and consumption by equating the marginal cost of emission reduction with the marginal welfare loss due to additional warming. The carbon price from the DICE model thus corresponds to the marginal discounted welfare loss from emitting an additional ton of CO_2.

To determine the optimal price, a cost-benefit analysis is carried out within the DICE model. Here, the selection of a carbon price is understood as an intertemporal maximization problem where the economic costs of mitigation are weighed against the benefits of preventing climate damage.

In theory, the carbon price determined in this way is the economically optimal price. However, the DICE model is extremely sensitive with regard to central model functions and parameter values (Dietz & Stern, 2015; Nordhaus, 2018; Stern, 2006). For example, the estimated carbon price for 2025 varies between values of $37 per ton of CO_2 to $4185 per ton of CO_2 depending on assumptions such as the discount rate of future damages or the weighting of low-risk high-impact events (Barrage & Nordhaus, 2024). Therefore, it is not possible to determine a clear carbon price, as the parameter values are subject to great uncertainty (Heal, 2017).

While Nordhaus's SCC is the best-known approach to calculating the optimal carbon price, harsh criticism on its modeling assumptions and overall premise have led some researchers to develop alternative methods. For instance, instead of developing the price based on a cost-benefit analysis to determine its economically optimal value, some researchers suggest starting with a specific climate target and 'back-calculating' the price that is necessary to reach this target (Marron & Toder, 2014). This method therefore prioritizes ecological effectiveness over economic optimality, often rejecting the usage of future discounting and putting higher emphasis on low-risk high-impact scenarios. According to the model proposed in the well-known "Stern and Stiglitz Report" (High-Level Commission on Carbon Prices, 2017), for example, a global carbon price of $40-80 in 2020 would be necessary to keep global warming below 2°C.

While many attempts have been made to calculate the 'correct' price, reality often paints a different picture: Instead of careful cost-benefit assessments or climate targets, real carbon prices are the result of political processes and vary in the real world. Consequently, a substantial gap emerges between the theoretically predicted and empirically observed effects of carbon pricing measures, as we will show in the following section.

2.2 Effectiveness of carbon pricing in practice

Following the theoretical discourse and increasing urgency to keep global warming well below 2°C (IPCC, 2021), carbon pricing policies have been implemented all around the world. At the time of writing, 80 pricing schemes—43 taxes and 37 emission trading systems (ETS)—have been implemented by sub-national, national and supranational jurisdictions, covering 28% of global carbon emissions (World Bank, 2025). The average carbon price is roughly $19 per ton of CO2, with prices ranging from less than $1 up to $158. The global emissions-weighted price, which calculates the average price for all priced and non-priced emissions, is around $5.

Despite the increasing adoption of carbon pricing schemes, only a minority of prices reach the level predicted to be necessary for effective climate change mitigation. In fact, less than 4% of priced emissions are covered by the aforementioned $40-80 range (Pryor et al., 2021) and about half are priced with a level below $10 (World Bank & Ecofys, 2018).

These differences in policy schemes and the existence of additional climate policies make it difficult to assess and compare the effectiveness of these pricing schemes in reducing carbon emissions. However, a growing body of ex-post evaluations aims to quantify the impact on carbon emissions, and some review papers and meta-analyses have been published to compare the results of individual case studies.

One of the first comprehensive meta-reviews by Green (2021) analyzes thirty-seven quantitative ex-post evaluations, 70% of which focus on European schemes such as the European Union Emissions Trading System (EU-ETS). Her review finds that, in most instances, the introduction of a carbon price yields only moderate average emissions reductions of 0–2 percent per year. Among some notable exceptions is the United Kingdom's carbon price support mechanism, which reportedly achieved a 41–49 percent decline in power-sector emissions between 2013 and 2017. Green attributes these generally weak outcomes to the low price levels in most schemes, as well as to political constraints and industry lobbying that have limited both the ambition and public acceptance of more rigorous pricing policies. Overall, the review suggests that carbon pricing can only promote marginal emission reductions, mostly via fuel switching and incremental efficiency improvements, but is insufficient to induce the transformation needed to substantially mitigate climate change.

Döbbeling-Hildebrandt et al. (2024) build on this foundation with a comprehensive quantitative meta-analysis covering 21 distinct carbon-pricing programs, synthesizing 483 individual effect sizes from 80 ex-post evaluations. After correcting for publication bias, they estimate an average cumulative emissions reduction of 6.8 percent since policy implementation, with individual reductions ranging from 4 to 15 percent. Their findings also suggest that heterogeneity in observed effectiveness arises mainly from differences in policy design and from contextual factors, including the duration of the pricing policy, the availability of complementary policies, and local economic conditions. In contrast, price levels across countries, sectoral coverage, and the choice between tax and cap-and-trade explain relatively little of the variation in policy effectiveness. The authors interpret this to be the result of heterogeneous abatement costs, leading price levels to have vastly different effects in different countries. They also highlight that differences in effectiveness across schemes do not negate the benefits of increasing carbon prices within schemes. However, due to the limited empirical evidence on high-level carbon prices, the effect of tax increases within pricing schemes cannot be adequately assessed.

Köppl and Schratzenstaller (2023) further complement these insights by analyzing not only the ecological effectiveness, but also economic impacts of various carbon pricing schemes. In terms of effectiveness, their findings confirm the evidence discussed so far—most pricing schemes result in some emission reductions, but effectiveness differs greatly across schemes and most effect sizes found so far are insufficient to achieve substantial changes in carbon emissions on their own. They also find that the use of revenues to finance improvements in energy efficiency can significantly contribute to carbon reductions. Finally, the authors highlight the importance of economic conditions, including the structure of the energy system and availability of low-carbon alternatives, for successful mitigation practices.

The observed findings on the economic impact of carbon pricing are more inconclusive, however—while no reductions in GDP or employment could be observed in the reviewed literature, the findings on competitiveness and innovation are found to be rather sparse, partially due to measurement issues. However, the evidence concerning the effect on innovation suggests that carbon pricing alone is insufficient to drive the structural and technological changes needed for deep decarbonization; instead, carbon taxes need to be complemented by a wider policy mix, including subsidies, standards, and infrastructure investments.

Overall, four recurring insights emerge from these reviews:

1. While carbon pricing seems to have the intended negative effect on emissions, the reductions observed so far are far below the reductions needed to reach any serious climate target.
2. Effect sizes vary greatly. Statistical analyses suggest that policy context (e.g. the presence of other climate policies, the (macro)economic conditions and emission-intensity of national industries, or the potential for carbon leakage) plays a vital role in determining the effectiveness of carbon pricing.
3. Carbon pricing seems to be a useful tool to incentivize substitution away from carbon-intensive technologies and products *as long as* cleaner alternatives are available or efficiency improvements achievable. Its potential for initiating the structural transformations needed for deep decarbonization, however, remains questionable.
4. Despite rigorous efforts to calculate the optimal carbon price, few pricing schemes come close to the supposedly optimal or necessary price levels discussed above. Instead, political feasibility often determines (and limits) the price level implemented in practice. As Green (2021, 11–12) puts it, "after nearly four decades of experience with carbon pricing, the empirical evidence to date suggests that low prices are a feature of this policy, rather than a bug.".

Based on these findings, two problems of current pricing schemes become evident. On the one hand, political feasibility is a core issue, preventing prices from being in ranges necessary to keep global warming below 2°C. On the other hand, even high carbon prices do not seem to work as effectively as predicted by economic models. Thus, the behavioral incentives intended by carbon pricing seem to face some barriers that are not accounted for in those models.

We will discuss these two issues in more detail in the remainder of this paper.

3. The general concept of political feasibility

The concept of political feasibility is prominently addressed in areas of transition research and focuses on possible pathways from a fossil to a decarbonized society (Roberts et al., 2018). Techno-economic scenarios provide starting points for what a sustainable society based on renewable energies could look like. However, these scenarios are assessed with regard to their feasibility by means of an economic cost-benefit analysis, and aspects of social and political feasibility tend to be omitted (Hoffart, 2022; Hoffart et al., 2021; Jewell & Cherp, 2020). It is precisely these political and social factors that are decisive for the successful implementation and long-term stability of climate policy measures (Cherp et al., 2018; Kallbekken, 2023). In particular, the long-term stability of climate policy measures is demonstrated by the example of the promotion of renewable energies in Germany. In the period from the 1990s to the beginning of the 2010s, the expansion of renewable energies in Germany was promoted across the board and received broad political and social support (Kern & Markard, 2016). In the wake of the Euro crisis, political support for the promotion of renewable energies declined as political will waned due to the economic recession (Meckling, 2019).

This shows that the concept of political feasibility cannot be defined universally and instead depends on the social environment and temporal developments (Gilabert & Lawford-Smith, 2012). In contrast to technical or economic feasibility, political feasibility is often used less precisely, sometimes vaguely equated with political costs or judgments about political possibilities (Meltsner, 1972). However, its analytical usefulness depends on explicitly naming the political constraints at play. Political feasibility is not just about whether something is desirable, but whether it is feasible in practice (Jewell & Cherp, 2020; Peng et al., 2021).

Majone (1975) classifies these constraints on the basis of three dimensions. First, a policy measure must have the necessary resources in terms of support within politics: In order for a policy measure to be implemented in general, policymakers must support it (Majone, 1975; Meltsner, 1972).

Second, policies are subject to distributional constraints. A political proposal must be evaluated according to how it benefits and disadvantages different groups of people. Coercing individuals or groups to accept decisions that they see as unfair or overly burdensome can lead to appeal, litigation, and ineffectiveness. This, in turn, can jeopardize the policy measure or the implementing body itself. Thus, political feasibility is significantly influenced by the distribution of costs and benefits across different social actors (Pierson, 1993).

As a third constraint, Majone (1975) refers to the institutional framework. The implementation of policies follows certain institutional rules that exist in the form of parliamentary procedures, rule of law and also cultural norms (North, 1990). These institutional constraints are beyond the direct influence of political decision-makers and represent structures that have grown over the long term. They are understood as soft constraints that do not make the feasibility of a policy measure impossible, but can make its implementation less likely (Gilabert & Lawford-Smith, 2012).

These three aspects are the basic prerequisites for the conditions under which a policy can be considered politically feasible. In the case of carbon pricing, however, its political feasibility is not just central for the introduction, but also the long-term perpetuation of the policy. Thus, two challenges emerge: On the one hand, there must be the social and political will to implement carbon prices. On the other hand, carbon prices must be accepted by society in the long term. Since the introduction and existence of a carbon price is an inherently political endeavor, various social actors must be brought into focus.

In the following subsections, we apply these three constraints to societal actor groups that play central roles in the long-term implementation of climate policies. In doing so, we will first address political actors, which, through their role in government and opposition, determine the legislative implementation and policy design of these measures.

3.1 Political feasibility within politics

In Western democracies, most states consist of parties that form the government and parties that act in the opposition. Within this construct, there are formal and informal frameworks that influence legislation and the political process in general. In order to initiate a carbon price, parties in government must create majorities within the political process. Such majorities in the form of coalitions can be understood as political resources as defined by Majone (1975).

With a carbon price, the negative effects of the use of fossil fuels are to be priced into the economic process and at the same time further economic growth is to be made possible. Thus, political actors are exposed to a conflict of goals within fossil economies. Their central task is to moderate different interests. On the one hand, the state pursues the containment of climate-damaging emissions and strives to comply with international obligations. Emissions must be reduced throughout the economic system and at the same time continuous economic growth must be sought. On the other hand, the state must moderate different and often conflicting economic interests and meet the expectations of voters in order to continue to be able to act.

This conflict of goals is reflected in the design of a carbon price. To be ecologically effective, it must make the use of fossil fuels unprofitable. As explained earlier, the carbon price would be significantly higher than its current level and lead to massive conflicts within society that prevent the implementation or existence of a carbon price. For a long-term effective climate policy, politicians and bureaucrats must design measures in such a way that they at least weaken opposition and, in the best case, promote support (Edmondson et al., 2019, 2020). In order to make policies resistant to negative pressures, a carbon price must be flanked by other climate and social policies (Jordan & Matt, 2014).

A central aspect here is the fundamentally regressive character of a carbon price, which negatively affects acceptance. To ensure that broad sections of the population do not oppose a carbon price, it is necessary to link state revenues through a carbon price with redistributive measures. On the part of industry representatives, funding programs are being demanded for a phase-out of fossil fuels and the further development of renewable alternatives. At the same time, such funding programs run the risk of manifesting technologies that contribute to further conflicts and open up the space for further influence by interest groups (Rosenbloom et al., 2019). In addition, the state has the potential to determine economic development paths for long periods of time through support programs (Pierson, 2000). For example, there is a risk that after the phase-out of coal and nuclear energy in Germany, the expansion of the natural gas infrastructure could delay the transition to a decarbonized economy (Kemfert et al., 2022). The state must therefore ensure a long-term perspective for the transformation path with the help of climate policy measures, anticipating possible obstacles due to a lack of acceptance and resistance (Edmondson et al., 2020).

This again highlights the complex interplay between politics, business and the broader public. The introduction and maintenance of a carbon price is the subject of constant social negotiation processes that are determined by the structure of the political process.

In the following, another social actor group in the political process is discussed. The focus here is on interest groups that are influenced differently by the distributional effect of a carbon price and therefore try to influence the design of a carbon price.

3.2 Political feasibility and organized interests

The introduction or adjustment of a carbon price influences the cost structure of companies or entire industries. For example, a carbon price increases the production costs of carbon-intensive industries, whereas carbon-efficient industries are relatively better off. Based on these distributional effects, either support for or opposition to a carbon price can form (Edmondson et al., 2019; Pierson, 1993). Interest groups[1] are particularly interesting from a political science and politico-economic perspective because, in contrast to the general population, they have direct access to the political process through lobbying (Klüver & Zeidler, 2019; Pierson, 1993).

In this context, the formation, mobilization and political influence of interest groups do not only depend on the re-allocation of resources, but are also conditioned by the market structure of the affected industries (Peng et al., 2021). Klüver and Zeidler (2019) show that both the size, measured in terms of the number of companies, and the value added are reliable predictors of lobbying activity within an economic sector. Interest groups in these sectors benefit from synergy effects and the financial resources invested in political influence. Notably, the results also show a reciprocal relationship between lobbying and

1 *The term interest groups includes not only economic interest groups, but also NGOs and trade unions. These are omitted from this consideration, as they are not considered here as direct representatives of the economic interests of affected industries. Nevertheless, these interest groups are also important actors in the political process and can support the implementation of a socio-ecological transformation (Cremer 2024; Trappmann et al., 2024).*

parliamentary initiatives—as the number of administrative requirements increases, so does lobbying, and the same applies vice versa.

In this way, established industries generally have an advantage over newer industries in influencing the political process. This advantage in the basic economic endowment and the resulting influence of interest groups can consolidate existing power structures over time and lead to path dependencies (Pierson, 1993; 2000). This hinders the introduction or increase of a carbon price due to the relatively strong power position of interest groups of fossil fuel industries. Michaelowa (2013) outlines the shift in the positioning of fossil interest groups since the 1990s in Germany. Initially, exemptions from climate policy regulations were obtained for certain industries. When pollution rights were then freely distributed within the framework of the EU ETS and unexpected profits could be achieved, the headwind weakened somewhat. In addition, an industry formed around renewable energies and a broader social commitment to environmental protection emerged.

On the part of industrial and corporate interest groups, the opposition to climate policies uses common lines of argumentation. Possible losses in sales, the reduction of investments, layoffs of employees or even the relocation of the production site are cited as threatening scenarios in order to directly influence the political process or to mobilize the general population against climate policy intervention via the media (Lockwood, 2013; Meckling, 2019). Thus, interest groups of carbon-intensive industries generally have an effective lever and can actively influence the political process.

The last actor group to be addressed is the broader public. Similar to economic interest groups, it is also affected by distributional effects. The special feature here is that the broader public does not directly influence the political process. However, it can express its interests through its voting behavior.

3.3 Political feasibility and the broader public

The distributional effect of a carbon price has a significant impact on the broader public in the form of income effects, the intensity of which varies across the income distribution. On average, wealthier households cause more CO_2 emissions than low-income households. But these low-income households bear a higher burden from carbon pricing, as they have to spend a higher proportion of their income on necessary consumption (Grainger & Kolstad, 2010). Thus, a carbon price in an unequal society has a regressive effect and places a greater burden on those households that have fewer opportunities to adapt their consumption behavior (Muth, 2023).

Survey studies on the acceptance of carbon prices show that acceptance depends largely on the social compatibility of a carbon price and the reuse of government revenues. In general, a progressive distribution of costs is preferred, in which wealthier households pay relatively more and poorer or vulnerable ones are compensated proportionately (Klenert et al., 2018; Maestre-Andrés et al., 2019). In addition, a targeted use of the revenues collected for further climate protection measures is appreciated. (Levi, 2021; Maestre-Andrés et al., 2019). If the revenues from carbon pricing simply flow into the state budget, this tends to reduce the acceptance of carbon pricing (Klenert et al., 2018; Mildenberger et al., 2022).

Certainly, the public acceptance of carbon prices depends on other factors, such as the fundamental political attitude, confidence in the state's ability to act and the public debate (Maestre-Andrés et al., 2019; Mildenberger et al., 2022; Savin et al., 2024). Nevertheless, a socially acceptable design of carbon pricing is crucial in order not to risk the support of the population or strengthen political forces that oppose climate protection.

Depending on the social compatibility of carbon prices, acceptance among the broader public can lead to ecologically progressive political parties being elected to government. To this end, however, socio-economic lines of conflict must be considered and mechanisms of social cushioning included in the design of carbon pricing schemes.

4. Behavioral barriers

The previous chapter has addressed the question of how to implement and maintain a sufficient carbon price given political interests and their influence on the realizability of the measure. However, chapter 2 has shown that even some historical carbon prices that have come close to or even exceeded the presumed optimal price level fail to induce the necessary emission reductions. Apparently, therefore, there seems to exist an ongoing discrepancy between theoretical predictions and the realized outcomes of carbon pricing policies.

We argue that part of this misprediction lies in the way the standard economic model portrays human behavior and behavioral change. Building on the rational actor, the model describes a form of decision-making that, as empirical studies have shown, can only be observed in some contexts and is not adequate to describe the everyday behavior that is ultimately resulting in most carbon emissions (Frederiks et al., 2015). Instead, human behavior depends on a multitude of both internal (e.g. values, perceptions, habits) and external factors (e.g. resources, infrastructure, social norms), which are interdependent and shape behavior to different degrees based on the relevant context (Milfont & Markowitz, 2016; Wang et al., 2021).

The following sections summarize the literature on how real-world behavior differs from the standard economic model in the context of carbon pricing and sustainable behavior. We start by investigating the role of the rational actor in the standard-economic model of carbon pricing in more detail. Afterwards, we discuss various empirical findings of 'imperfect' decision-making and the role of voluntary pro-environmental behavior to understand how the ineffectiveness of carbon pricing can be counterbalanced by additional, behaviorally informed policies.

4.1 Rationality in Pigou's model

Like most standard-economic models, Pigou's model (1920) places humans in a world where markets are the only place of interaction and all decisions to be made are economic in nature. The economic agent (homo economicus) follows the basic principle of optimization—consumers maximize their private utility and firms maximize their private profits. In a free market with full information and no market power, the coordination of supply and demand via price signals produces a pareto-efficient allocation of resources such that costs will be minimized and welfare maximized. By means of a Pigouvian tax (here as carbon price), the social costs are internalized into the individual cost calculations and a welfare-maximizing equilibrium is achieved again.

The initial idea of carbon pricing is therefore fundamentally based on the assumptions of a rational, optimizing agent whose welfare depends exclusively on economic cost-benefit considerations. While it cannot be denied that people make cost-benefit assessments and that prices do in fact influence firm and consumer behavior, behavioral research shows that there is far more to (economic) decision-making (Milfont & Markowitz, 2016). But how do deviations from the rational model affect the effectiveness of carbon pricing?

To answer this, we will first examine the basic characteristics of the rational actor and consider how, in theory, a violation of these characteristics might affect his reaction to a carbon price.

Urbina and Ruiz-Villaverde (2019) define homo economicus based on five distinct characteristics: Individualism, optimizing behavior, full rationality, exogenous preferences and universality. We discuss each of these in turn.

First, *individualism* describes the assumption that the economic agent exclusively considers his own interest. While this does not exclude social preferences per se, pro-social behavior itself can only be the result of self-interest. In addition, the agent's social environment does not influence the decision-making process, i.e. his decisions are made in a 'vacuum'.

Individualism is a central assumption for the economic model of carbon pricing because it constitutes the fundamental source of the externality problem: Since agents only consider their own welfare, private costs and social costs can deviate and need to be aligned by the Pigouvian tax. And as an agent's social environment does not influence his choices, prices are the only way to alter behavior.

A deviation from the individualism assumption itself must not necessarily reduce the effectiveness of carbon pricing, but taxing emissions might be less crucial to solving the climate problem. If we assume that most people care about others and are willing to forego personal gains in order to act pro-socially, other measures might be just as important to motivate sustainable behavior—information provision, norm-based messaging or collective projects could encourage behavioral change without having to rely on the continued upkeep of a monetary incentive. Even more, if unsustainable patterns of behavior are the result of people's social context, price signals might actually be less effective—in this case, motivating sustainable behavior via non-market interventions would be even more crucial.

The second characteristic, *optimizing behavior*, expresses the utility- and profit-maximizing motive described above. By this assumption, each decision is made based on an elaborate, often intertemporal, cost-benefit-analysis to optimize private gains. When social costs are adequately represented in market prices, individual optimization will also lead to collective welfare optimization.

If people do not optimize, price changes alone may fail to induce the predicted shifts in behavior. Instead, people might rely on simple rules of thumb (heuristics) or follow a "good enough" approach (satisficing), as has been studied extensively by behavioral economists (Mullainathan & Thaler, 2000). In such cases, choice-architecture interventions—like setting green options as defaults or providing targeted nudges—can compensate for the lack of optimization and induce low-carbon behavior more effectively (Frederiks et al., 2015).

Third, the rational actor is assumed to possess *full rationality*, allowing him to perfectly process all available information and choose the best option available. In the case of carbon pricing, it follows that agents are immediately aware of the change in prices and instantly switch to a more sustainable (i.e. cheaper) alternative. If the government communicates a fixed price path for the carbon tax, the rational actor can flawlessly integrate those expected future prices into his investment and consumption plans. Finally, homo economicus is not interested in the origin of the increased price, but will adapt his behavior to the tax in exactly the same way as he does to usual market-based price changes.

If we loosen the assumption of full rationality, people either have incomplete access to the relevant information or they are not able to perfectly process them. Consequently, they might not notice or care about the price changes. Moreover, they might be unable to identify or access lower-carbon alternatives—in this case, the tax would merely raise costs without lowering emissions, reducing material welfare without the environmental gain.

In addition, the concept of tax aversion shows that people do not react to taxes the same way as they do to regular price changes (Kallbekken et al., 2011). If they refuse to accept the tax, they might also deliberately ignore it and resist the behavioral adjustment.

Fourth, the standard-economic framework treats individual *preferences as exogenous*. While strong assumptions about the structure of preferences are made to ensure the consistency needed for mathematical optimization—they are usually assumed to be complete, transitive, and monotonic—the initial process of forming preferences is beyond the scope of traditional economics. Under the assumption of stable preferences, shifting relative prices is therefore the only viable lever for influencing consumption patterns.

Treating preferences as endogenous, on the other hand, might show that personal needs, desires and tastes are not stable, but shaped by context, learning or socialization (O'Hara & Stagl, 2002). If the formation of preferences depends on such external factors, carbon pricing would not be the only (or even most effective) strategy to motivate more sustainable behavior. It would even be possible that modern economic activity, expressing current socially-shaped preferences, might be sub-optimal in terms of well-being compared to an economy in which other things are valued and other goals pursued.

Lastly, the *universality* assumption claims that every person acts according to the rational actor model, independent from context, culture or personality.

Thus, if everyone applies the same rational decision-making process in every situation, a global and universal carbon price is the best instrument to achieve the social optimum.

If instead we assume that people apply varying decision processes in different social roles, economic contexts and stages of life, policy instruments too would need to consider these differences. For instance, promoting sustainable consumption choices might require a different strategy from decarbonizing the energy sector.

To summarize, we have demonstrated how the theoretical superiority of carbon pricing fundamentally relies on assumptions of a perfectly rational actor. If those assumptions are violated, efficiency and effectiveness might be strongly diminished, and other sustainability strategies and policy instruments gain significance.

4.2 Price signals and behavioral change

Behavioral economics has indeed shown that people do not always act rationally, but that our behavior is often guided, for instance, by cognitive biases and heuristics (Shogren & Taylor, 2008). This can lead to individuals not recognizing or caring about price changes, or not having the willingness or capacity to adjust their behavior. Consequently, people tend to stick to high-carbon consumption patterns despite the additional cost of a carbon tax (Stoll & Mehling, 2021).

To solve the persistence of unsustainable patterns of behavior, understanding its root causes can help guide decision-makers in designing adequate responses and interventions to complement the financial incentive of carbon pricing.

The range of cognitive biases and behavioral anomalies studied by behavioral economists has grown steadily in recent decades and found application in various fields (Mullainathan & Thaler, 2000). The strand of literature focusing on sustainable behavior such as household energy use (Wilson & Dowlatabadi, 2007), low-carbon transport (Gaker et al., 2010) or green consumer choice (Sunstein & Reisch, 2014) has identified a subset of these biases that seem particularly relevant to these contexts. We categorize them in two groups according to how they influence the effect of carbon pricing: First, they affect whether any behavioral changes are made at all, and second, they influence the kind of behavior that is adopted instead.

The first challenge then lies in ensuring that the carbon price provides sufficient incentive for individuals to adjust their behavior in the first place. Empirical research indicates that people exhibit strong *inertia*, favoring familiar routines and only reluctantly modifying their existing habits even when behavioral changes would benefit them (Marechal & Lazaric, 2010). The cognitive component of the same phenomenon has been studied under the notion of *status-quo bias* – a systematic preference to maintain or repeat prior choices even when better alternatives are available (Samuelson & Zeckhauser, 1988). In general, habituation arises from a cognitive mechanism designed to minimize mental effort, reduce learning costs, and preserve one's sense of competence and self-control (Galla & Duckworth, 2015; Jager, 2003). Such strong habits are especially relevant in every-day activities such as personal mobility, dietary choices, and residential energy use (Wang et al., 2021) and have been found to impede switches to low-carbon behaviors in these contexts (R & Perumandla, 2023; Watkins & Musselwhite, 2025). This highly habitual nature of most carbon-intensive consumer behaviors has led some authors to declare habits as the most important barrier to sustainable behavior (Huebner et al., 2013; Wang et al., 2021).

The second challenge lies in ensuring that individuals who do respond to the carbon price by altering their behavior do so in ways that effectively reduce their carbon footprint.

Behavioral economics shows that the optimization assumption of traditional economic models does not apply to many real-world behaviors, but that most decision processes are guided by heuristics, satisficing and social cues (Frederiks et al., 2015). *Satisficing* refers to the human tendency to exert only the effort needed to achieve a satisfactory rather than an optimal result. Instead of systematically processing all available information to maximize utility, people often settle for 'good enough' or the first available option that meets minimum requirements (ibid). Similarly, heuristics describe choice strategies that do not rely on careful cost-benefit analyses, but use simple rules of thumb to reduce the complexity of decision-making processes.

Consequently, consumers facing a carbon price might reduce high-carbon behaviors or switch to less carbon-intensive goods, but do so in ways that are not as effective as predicted. For example, consumers might rely mainly on product marketing to choose more sustainable products, which can lead them to overestimate the carbon reductions from products labeled as 'eco-friendly', ultimately causing only minimal environmental impact despite the intention to act more environmentally-friendly (Hossain et al., 2022). Indeed, survey evidence indicates that many consumers misjudge the carbon-reduction potential of various actions (Ipsos, 2021).

These findings underscore the difficulty of influencing consumption patterns that have been reinforced by habit and familiarity, as well as encouraging behavior change that truly decreases consumer's carbon footprint. Consequently, for carbon pricing to trigger meaningful emission reductions, a carbon price must be complemented by interventions that directly lower these behavioral barriers. Promising approaches include implementing green default settings and opt-out programs that leverage inertia in favor of sustainable outcomes—for instance, making renewable energy the standard option in new electricity contracts (Pichert & Katsikopoulos, 2008) or offering plant-rich meals in school cafeterias by default (Marcano-Olivier et al., 2020). Similarly, providing consumers with clear information on effective carbon-reduction strategies can steer their decision-making toward more sustainable practices.

4.3 Carbon taxes meet pro-environmental behavior

While the behavioral economics perspective is concerned with strategies to correct behavioral failures and promote decisions that resemble that of the rational agent, it still follows the standard-economic argument that consumer behavior must be regulated from the "outside" to achieve the social optimum. In doing so, the economic perspective assumes that people have no intrinsic incentive to make decisions for the sake of sustainability itself—a direct consequence of the individualism assumption discussed above.

While most economists probably would not deny the existence of pro-environmental values, one argument for carbon pricing is that we do not *have to* rely on moral considerations to solve the climate crises (Baranzini et al., 2017).

However, this argument faces two major problems.

First, carbon pricing and the focus on a purely economic solution has been shown to interfere with pro-environmental behavior. Experimental research shows that people's intrinsic motivation to act pro-environmentally can be diminished or replaced by an extrinsic incentive that is aimed at promoting the same behavior, such as the carbon price (Gowdy, 2008). This *crowding-out effect* has been studied in other contexts by both psychologists (e.g. Deci, 1971) and behavioral economists (e.g. Gneezy & Rustichini, 2000), but has gained more attention with regards to carbon pricing in recent years.

Experimental studies confirm that the price effect of a carbon tax intended to reduce consumption is partially offset by an (openly communicated) carbon tax (Grieder et al., 2021; Lanz et al., 2018), suggesting that consumer's intrinsic motivation to reduce emissions is indeed reduced by their awareness of the tax. One explanation is so-called 'moral licensing'—paying a higher price for carbon-intensive goods can make consumers feel they have 'earned' the right to continue harmful behavior, as the extra cost is perceived as compensating for the environmental damage (Stoll & Mehling, 2021).

This line of argument is further supported by evidence that earmarking the tax revenues, i.e. using them to finance green projects or subsidize sustainable alternatives, further increases the willingness to buy a high-carbon good (Grieder et al., 2021). Again, it is assumed that part of the perceived moral obligation to act pro-environmentally is crowded out by the knowledge that the tax revenues are utilized for sustainable purposes. In addition, consumers might actively believe the product to be 'greener' as their purchase is indirectly used to mitigate climate change elsewhere.

Interestingly, the observed negative effect of earmarked carbon taxes on sustainable behavior mirrors the evidence that earmarking carbon prices increases the acceptance of the policy. While the latter finding is often used to recommend implementing carbon taxes and using the revenues for environmental purposes, the former literature suggests avoiding explicit earmarking to not reduce the effectiveness of the tax. Thus, the question of revenue use seems to face a trade-off between public acceptance and behavioral effectiveness.

In addition to the crowding-out effect, the economic focus on monetary incentives might have another downside with respect to pro-environmental behavior: Experimental evidence indicates that money itself can undermine cooperative behavior, with the mere mention of money resulting in more self-regarding attitudes and reduced pro-social decisions (Vohs et al., 2006). Therefore, arguing that behavior is best regulated via economic incentives because people inherently follow their own interest might turn out to be a self-fulfilling prophecy.

Concluding the first problem of exclusive reliance on carbon taxes to mitigate climate change: In cases where people are self-motivated to reduce their environmental impact, a carbon price that undermines this motivation can lead to less effective emission reductions than would occur through their unaided, voluntary actions.

Second, the economic perspective ignores the fact that extrinsic and intrinsic motivation have qualitatively different behavioral consequences.

Extrinsic motivation, on the one hand, faces the disadvantage that it often needs to be permanently maintained in order to trigger a lasting change in behavior; once the incentive is removed, behavior is often found to revert back to baseline levels, especially when the behavior change has not resulted in new habits (James, 2005). Moreover, some studies find that the behavioral effect of the incentive declines over time as individuals get used to it, resulting in the need to increase the size of the incentive to maintain persistent behavioral adjustments (ibid).

Intrinsic and autonomous motivation, on the other hand, have been shown to produce long-lasting behavioral patterns that are not only independent from the existence of an extrinsic incentive, but which also deepen investment in the behavior itself and improve peoples' psychological well-being (Ryan & Deci, 2000). Indeed, individuals who act out of genuine concern for the environment have been found to develop stronger habits and green lifestyles, which can positively influence others and foster a collective culture of sustainability (Faraz et al., 2021). Research on the determinants of persistent pro-environmental behavior also confirm the importance of moral conviction, environmental values and voluntary action (Bamberg & Möser, 2007).

Unfortunately, pro-environmental attitudes do not always translate into pro-environmental behavior, as extensive research on the value-action-gap, attitude-action-gap and intention-action-gap shows (Kollmuss & Agyeman, 2002). To bridge these gaps, efforts need to be made to remove structural and institutional barriers hindering the adoption of sustainable behaviors. For instance, providing a safe bicycle infrastructure, reliable public transport and walkable environments have been found to be the key instruments for reducing transport-related carbon emissions (Javaid et al., 2020). Similarly, governments can promote longer product life spans by setting standards on product durability and repairability or promoting business models that specialize on repair, refurbishment and repurposing of products (Milios, 2021). Lastly, subsidies or 'green' loans can help lower-income households overcome financial barriers that might otherwise prevent them from investing in energy-efficient technologies (Wilson & Dowlatabadi, 2007).

In light of these findings, it becomes evident that placing singular focus on carbon prices risks missing the chance to encourage meaningful, long-term behavioral change through policies designed to close the value–action gap and promote collective sustainable action.

5. Conclusion

This article has outlined the basic, economic foundations of carbon pricing. Its origins go back to Pigou, whose idea of taxing an externality to correct the market failure it caused has laid the foundation for how economists understand the problem of (and solution to) climate change today. Decades later, William Nordhaus advanced Pigou's idea by integrating it into formal climate-economy models to derive a carbon price that balances the economic benefits of fossil fuel use with the costs of climate change. Despite criticism on core modelling assumptions, as well as on the overall approach that prioritizes economic optimality over effective environmental protection, Nordhaus's work forms the basis for most of today's carbon prices.

As empirical evaluations show, however, the majority of carbon prices implemented to date are neither as high as supposedly necessary, nor as effective as predicted. We argued that two aspects, among others, lack in the economic conceptualization of carbon pricing which hinder its effectiveness in practice: The issue of political feasibility and the diversity of human behavior beyond the assumptions of the rational actor model.

From a politico-economic perspective, the introduction and implementation of a carbon price are shaped by the heterogeneous interests and influence of societal actors. Political feasibility depends on the support of these actors, typically divided into the mass public, interest groups, and the political elite. Consumers, who experience carbon pricing mainly through income effects, represent the central actors of the mass public. Social support depends less on the price level itself than on compensatory measures that offset income losses and facilitate sustainable choices. Interest groups, representing firms and sectors, are likewise affected by distributional effects but can shape political decisions through lobbying; their resources and interests must therefore be considered in policy design. Finally, the state, composed of diverse political actors, seeks to represent voter interests. The design of a carbon price can thus create path dependencies that either reinforce or mitigate social inequalities.

The analysis of psychological and behavioral factors shows that carbon pricing models fundamentally rely on the rational actor assumption, which is central to their conclusion that putting a price on CO2 is the most efficient solution to climate change. Real-life behavior, however, has been shown to regularly deviate from these assumptions, which ultimately reduces the observed effectiveness of the policy. These findings highlight the need for behaviorally informed and complementary policies to make the theoretical efficiency work in practice. This includes removing behavioral and structural barriers from low-carbon choices, as well as fostering the sense of collective action and pro-social attitudes necessary for people to practice sustainable behaviors on their own volition and conviction. Finally, for those behaviors that are not easily accessible or have high initial costs, subsidies and increased availability can foster behavioral changes that carbon pricing alone cannot achieve.

In sum, our analysis of the political-economic, psychological and behavioral economic factors shows that a carbon price alone is not an effective measure to sufficiently reduce carbon emissions. Based on these findings, we argue that, in addition to economic factors, a broader, interdisciplinary view is crucial when designing a carbon price in order to make the policy both socially acceptable and ecologically effective. Economists must include such interdisciplinary factors in their analyses if they want to make a goal-oriented contribution to the socio-ecological transformation of our societies.

References

Bamberg, S., & Möser, G. (2007). Twenty years after Hines, Hungerford, and Tomera: A new meta-analysis of psycho-social determinants of pro-environmental behaviour. *Journal of Environmental Psychology*, *27*(1), 14–25. https://doi.org/10.1016/j.jenvp.2006.12.002

Baranzini, A., van den Bergh, J. C. J. M., Carattini, S., Howarth, R. B., Padilla, E., & Roca, J. (2017). Carbon pricing in climate policy: Seven reasons, complementary instruments, and political economy considerations. *Wiley Interdisciplinary Reviews: Climate Change*, *8*(4). https://doi.org/10.1002/wcc.462

Barrage, L., & Nordhaus, W. (2024). Policies, projections, and the social cost of carbon: Results from the DICE-2023 model. *Proceedings of the National Academy of Sciences*, *121*(13), e2312030121. https://doi.org/10.1073/pnas.2312030121

Cherp, A., Vinichenko, V., Jewell, J., Brutschin, E., & Sovacool, B. (2018). Integrating techno-economic, socio-technical and political perspectives on national energy transitions: A meta-theoretical framework. *Energy Research & Social Science*, *37*, 175–190. https://doi.org/10.1016/j.erss.2017.09.015

Coase, R. H. (1960). The Problem of Social Cost. *The Journal of Law and Economics*, *3*, 1–44.

Cremer, J. C. (2024). Collective actors and potential alliances for eco-social policies in Germany. *Zeitschrift Für Politikwissenschaft*, 34, 183–206. https://doi.org/10.1007/s41358-024-00374-w

Deci, E. L. (1971). Effects of externally mediated rewards on intrinsic motivation. *Journal of Personality and Social Psychology*, *18*(1), 105–115. https://doi.org/10.1037/h0030644

Dietz, S., & Stern, N. (2015). Endogenous Growth, Convexity of Damage and Climate Risk: How Nordhaus' Framework Supports Deep Cuts in Carbon Emissions. *The Economic Journal*, *125*(583), 574–620. https://doi.org/10.1111/ecoj.12188

Döbbeling-Hildebrandt, N., Miersch, K., Khanna, T. M., Bachelet, M., Bruns, S. B., Callaghan, M., Edenhofer, O., Flachsland, C., Forster, P. M., Kalkuhl, M., Koch, N., Lamb, W. F., Ohlendorf, N., Steckel, J. C., & Minx, J. C. (2024). Systematic review and meta-analysis of ex-post evaluations on the effectiveness of carbon pricing. *Nature Communications*, *15*(1), 4147. https://doi.org/10.1038/s41467-024-48512-w

Edmondson, D. L., Kern, F., & Rogge, K. S. (2019). The co-evolution of policy mixes and socio-technical systems: Towards a conceptual framework of policy mix feedback in sustainability transitions. *Research Policy*, *48*(10), 103555. https://doi.org/10.1016/j.respol.2018.03.010

Edmondson, D. L., Rogge, K. S., & Kern, F. (2020). Zero carbon homes in the UK? Analysing the co-evolution of policy mix and socio-technical system. *Environmental Innovation and Societal Transitions*, *35*, 135–161. https://doi.org/10.1016/j.eist.2020.02.005

Faraz, N. A., Ahmed, F., Ying, M., & Mehmood, S. A. (2021). The interplay of green servant leadership, self-efficacy, and intrinsic motivation in predicting employees' pro-environmental behavior. *Corporate Social Responsibility and Environmental Management*, *28*(4), 1171–1184. https://doi.org/10.1002/csr.2115

Frederiks, E. R., Stenner, K., & Hobman, E. V. (2015). Household energy use: Applying behavioural economics to understand consumer decision-making and behaviour. *Renewable and Sustainable Energy Reviews*, *41*, 1385–1394. https://doi.org/10.1016/j.rser.2014.09.026

Gaker, D., Zheng, Y., & Walker, J. (2010). Experimental Economics in Transportation: Focus on Social Influences and Provision of Information. *Transportation Research Record*, *2156*(1), 47–55. https://doi.org/10.3141/2156-06

Galla, B. M., & Duckworth, A. L. (2015). More than resisting temptation: Beneficial habits mediate the relationship between self-control and positive life outcomes. *Journal of Personality and Social Psychology*, 109(3), 508–525. https://doi.org/10.1037/pspp0000026

Gilabert, P., & Lawford-Smith, H. (2012). Political Feasibility: A Conceptual Exploration. *Political Studies*, 60(4), 809–825. https://doi.org/10.1111/j.1467-9248.2011.00936.x

Gneezy, U., & Rustichini, A. (2000). A Fine Is a Price. *The Journal of Legal Studies*, 29(1), 1–17. https://doi.org/10.1086/468061

Gowdy, J. M. (2008). Behavioral economics and climate change policy. *Journal of Economic Behavior & Organization*, 68(3), 632–644. https://doi.org/10.1016/j.jebo.2008.06.011

Grainger, C. A., & Kolstad, C. D. (2010). Who Pays a Price on Carbon? *Environmental and Resource Economics*, 46(3), 359–376. https://doi.org/10.1007/s10640-010-9345-x

Green, J. F. (2021). Does carbon pricing reduce emissions? A review of ex-post analyses. *Environmental Research Letters*, 16(4), 043004. https://doi.org/10.1088/1748-9326/abdae9

Grieder, M., Bärenbold, R., Schmitz, J., & Schubert, R. (2021). *The Behavioral Effects of Carbon Taxes – Experimental Evidence* (SSRN Scholarly Paper 3628516). Social Science Research Network. https://doi.org/10.2139/ssrn.3628516

Heal, G. (2017). The Economics of the Climate. *Journal of Economic Literature*, 55(3), 1046–1063. https://doi.org/10.1257/jel.20151335

High-Level Commission on Carbon Prices. (2017). *Report of the high-level commission on carbon prices*. World Bank.

Hoffart, F. M. (2022). *What Is a Feasible and 1.5°C-Aligned Hydrogen Infrastructure for Germany? A Multi-Criteria Economic Study Based on Socio-Technical Energy Scenarios*. RWI. https://doi.org/10.4419/96973144

Hoffart, F. M., Schmitt, E.-J., & Roos, M. (2021). Rethinking Economic Energy Policy Research – Developing Qualitative Scenarios to Identify Feasible Energy Policies. *Journal of Sustainable Development of Energy, Water and Environment Systems*, 9(2), 1–28. https://doi.org/10.13044/j.sdewes.d8.0331

Hossain, I., Nekmahmud, M., & Fekete-Farkas, M. (2022). How Do Environmental Knowledge, Eco-Label Knowledge, and Green Trust Impact Consumers' Pro-Environmental Behaviour for Energy-Efficient Household Appliances? *Sustainability*, 14(11), Article 11. https://doi.org/10.3390/su14116513

Huebner, G. M., Cooper, J., & Jones, K. (2013). Domestic energy consumption—What role do comfort, habit, and knowledge about the heating system play? *Energy and Buildings*, 66, 626–636. https://doi.org/10.1016/j.enbuild.2013.07.043

IPCC. (2021). *Climate Change 2021: The Physical Science Basis. Contribution of Working Group I to the Sixth Assessment Report of the Intergovernmental Panel on Climate Change* (V. Masson-Delmotte, P. Zhai, A. Pirani, S. L. Connors, C. Péan, Y. Chen, L. Goldfarb, M. I. Gomis, J. B. R. Matthews, B. Sophie, M. Huang, O. Yelekçi, R. Yu, B. Zhou, E. Lonnoy, T. K. Maycock, T. Waterfield, K. Leitzell, & N. Caud, Eds.). Cambridge University Press.

Ipsos. (2021, April 17). *Perils of Perception: Climate change*. https://www.ipsos.com/en/ipsos-perils-perception-climate-change

Jager, W. (2003). Breaking bad habits: A dynamical perspective on habit formation and change. *Human Decision-Making and Environmental Perception–Understanding and Assisting Human Decision-Making in Real Life Settings. Libor Amicorum for Charles Vlek, Groningen: University of Groningen.*

James, H. S. (2005). Why did you do that? An economic examination of the effect of extrinsic compensation on intrinsic motivation and performance. *Journal of Economic Psychology*, *26*(4), 549–566. https://doi.org/10.1016/j.joep.2004.11.002

Javaid, A., Creutzig, F., & Bamberg, S. (2020). Determinants of low-carbon transport mode adoption: Systematic review of reviews. *Environmental Research Letters*, *15*(10), 103002. https://doi.org/10.1088/1748-9326/aba032

Jewell, J., & Cherp, A. (2020). On the political feasibility of climate change mitigation pathways: Is it too late to keep warming below 1.5°C? *WIREs Climate Change*, *11*(1), e621. https://doi.org/10.1002/wcc.621

Jordan, A., & Matt, E. (2014). Designing policies that intentionally stick: Policy feedback in a changing climate. *Policy Sciences*, *47*(3), 227–247. https://doi.org/10.1007/s11077-014-9201-x

Kallbekken, S. (2023). Research on public support for climate policy instruments must broaden its scope. *Nature Climate Change*, *13*(3), 206–208. https://doi.org/10.1038/s41558-022-01593-1

Kallbekken, S., Kroll, S., & Cherry, T. L. (2011). Do you not like Pigou, or do you not understand him? Tax aversion and revenue recycling in the lab. *Journal of Environmental Economics and Management*, *62*(1), 53–64. https://doi.org/10.1016/j.jeem.2010.10.006

Kemfert, C., Präger, F., Braunger, I., Hoffart, F. M., & Brauers, H. (2022). The expansion of natural gas infrastructure puts energy transitions at risk. *Nature Energy*, *7*(7), 582–587. https://doi.org/10.1038/s41560-022-01060-3

Kern, F., & Markard, J. (2016). Analysing Energy Transitions: Combining Insights from Transition Studies and International Political Economy. In T. Van de Graaf, B. K. Sovacool, A. Ghosh, F. Kern, & M. T. Klare (Eds.), *The*

Palgrave Handbook of the International Political Economy of Energy (pp. 291–318). Palgrave Macmillan UK. https://doi.org/10.1057/978-1-137-55631-8

Klenert, D., Mattauch, L., Combet, E., Edenhofer, O., Hepburn, C., Rafaty, R., & Stern, N. (2018). Making carbon pricing work for citizens. *Nature Climate Change*, *8*(8), 669–677. https://doi.org/10.1038/s41558-018-0201-2

Klüver, H., & Zeidler, E. (2019). Explaining Interest Group Density Across Economic Sectors: Evidence from Germany. *Political Studies*, *67*(2), 459–478. https://doi.org/10.1177/0032321718774685

Kollmuss, A., & Agyeman, J. (2002). Mind the Gap: Why do people act environmentally and what are the barriers to pro-environmental behavior? *Environmental Education Research*, *8*(3), 239–260. https://doi.org/10.1080/13504620220145401

Köppl, A., & Schratzenstaller, M. (2023). Carbon taxation: A review of the empirical literature. *Journal of Economic Surveys*, *37*(4), 1353–1388. https://doi.org/10.1111/joes.12531

Lanz, B., Wurlod, J.-D., Panzone, L., & Swanson, T. (2018). The behavioral effect of Pigovian regulation: Evidence from a field experiment. *Journal of Environmental Economics and Management*, *87*, 190–205. https://doi.org/10.1016/j.jeem.2017.06.005

Levi, S. (2021). Why hate carbon taxes? Machine learning evidence on the roles of personal responsibility, trust, revenue recycling, and other factors across 23 European countries. *Energy Research & Social Science*, *73*, 101883. https://doi.org/10.1016/j.erss.2020.101883

Lockwood, M. (2013). The political sustainability of climate policy: The case of the UK Climate Change Act. *Global Environmental Change*, *23*(5), 1339–1348. https://doi.org/10.1016/j.gloenvcha.2013.07.001

Maestre-Andrés, S., Drews, S., & van den Bergh, J. (2019). Perceived fairness and public acceptability of carbon pricing: A review of the literature. *Climate Policy*, *19*(9), 1186–1204. https://doi.org/10.1080/14693062.2019.1639490

Majone, G. (1975). ON THE NOTION OF POLITICAL FEASIBILITY*. *European Journal of Political Research*, *3*(3), 259–274. https://doi.org/10.1111/j.1475-6765.1975.tb00780.x

Marcano-Olivier, M. I., Horne, P. J., Viktor, S., & Erjavec, M. (2020). Using Nudges to Promote Healthy Food Choices in the School Dining Room: A Systematic Review of Previous Investigations. *Journal of School Health*, *90*(2), 143–157. https://doi.org/10.1111/josh.12861

Marechal, K., & Lazaric, N. (2010). Overcoming inertia: Insights from evolutionary economics into improved energy and climate policies. *Climate Policy*, *10*(1), 103–119. https://doi.org/10.3763/cpol.2008.0601

Marron, D. B., & Toder, E. J. (2014). Tax Policy Issues in Designing a Carbon Tax. *American Economic Review*, *104*(5), 563–568. https://doi.org/10.1257/aer.104.5.563

Meckling, J. (2019). Governing renewables: Policy feedback in a global energy transition. *Environment and Planning C: Politics and Space*, *37*(2), 317–338. https://doi.org/10.1177/2399654418777765

Meltsner, A. J. (1972). Political Feasibility and Policy Analysis. *Public Administration Review*, *32*(6), 859–867. https://doi.org/10.2307/974646

Michaelowa, A. (2013). The politics of climate change in Germany: Ambition versus lobby power. *WIREs Climate Change*, *4*(4), 315–320. https://doi.org/10.1002/wcc.224

Mildenberger, M., Lachapelle, E., Harrison, K., & Stadelmann-Steffen, I. (2022). Limited impacts of carbon tax rebate programmes on public support for carbon pricing. *Nature Climate Change*, *12*(2), 141–147. https://doi.org/10.1038/s41558-021-01268-3

Milfont, T. L., & Markowitz, E. (2016). Sustainable consumer behavior: A multilevel perspective. *Current Opinion in Psychology*, *10*, 112–117. https://doi.org/10.1016/j.copsyc.2015.12.016

Milios, L. (2021). Overarching policy framework for product life extension in a circular economy—A bottom-up business perspective. *Environmental Policy and Governance*, *31*(4), 330–346. https://doi.org/10.1002/eet.1927

Mullainathan, S., & Thaler, R. H. (2000). *Behavioral Economics* (Working Paper 7948). National Bureau of Economic Research. https://doi.org/10.3386/w7948

Muth, D. (2023). Pathways to stringent carbon pricing: Configurations of political economy conditions and revenue recycling strategies. A comparison of thirty national level policies. *Ecological Economics*, *214*, 107995. https://doi.org/10.1016/j.ecolecon.2023.107995

Nordhaus, W. (1991). To Slow or Not to Slow: The Economics of The Greenhouse Effect. *The Economic Journal*, *101*(407), 920–937.

Nordhaus, W. (2017). Revisiting the social cost of carbon. *Proceedings of the National Academy of Sciences*, *114*(7), 1518–1523. https://doi.org/10.1073/pnas.1609244114

Nordhaus, W. (2018). Evolution of modeling of the economics of global warming: Changes in the DICE model, 1992–2017. *Climatic Change, 148*(4), 623–640. https://doi.org/10.1007/s10584-018-2218-y

Nordhaus, W., & Sztorc, P. (2013). *DICE 2013R: Introduction and User's Manual*. http://www.econ.yale.edu/ nordhaus/homepage/homepage/documents/DICE_Manual_100413r1.pdf

North, D. C. (1990). *Institutions, institutional change, and economic performance*. Cambridge University Press.

O'Hara, S. U., & Stagl, S. (2002). Endogenous preferences and sustainable development. *The Journal of Socio-Economics, 31*(5), 511–527. https://doi.org/10.1016/S1053-5357(02)00134-8

Peng, W., Kim, S. E., Purohit, P., Urpelainen, J., & Wagner, F. (2021). Incorporating political-feasibility concerns into the assessment of India's clean-air policies. *One Earth*, 4(8), 1163–1174. https://doi.org/10.1016/j.oneear.2021.07.004

Pichert, D., & Katsikopoulos, K. V. (2008). Green defaults: Information presentation and pro-environmental behaviour. *Journal of Environmental Psychology, 28*(1), 63–73. https://doi.org/10.1016/j.jenvp.2007.09.004

Pierson, P. (1993). When Effect Becomes Cause: Policy Feedback and Political Change. *World Politics*, 45(4), 595–628. https://doi.org/10.2307/2950710

Pierson, P. (2000). Increasing Returns, Path Dependence, and the Study of Politics. *American Political Science Review*, 94(2), 251–267. https://doi.org/10.2307/2586011

Pigou, A. C. (1920). *The economics of welfare* (4th ed.). Macmillan, London.

Pryor, J. D. C., Gadde, H., Pigato, M. A., Sinha, C. S., & Timilsina, G. R. (2021). *Carbon Pricing for Climate Action*.

R, S. D., & Perumandla, S. (2023). Do individuals resist green home investment decisions? An empirical study from status quo bias and inertia perspective. *Frontiers in Sustainable Cities*, 5. https://doi.org/10.3389/frsc.2023.1295357

Roberts, C., Geels, F. W., Lockwood, M., Newell, P., Schmitz, H., Turnheim, B., & Jordan, A. (2018). The politics of accelerating low-carbon transitions: Towards a new research agenda. *Energy Research &Social Science*, 44, 304–311. https://doi.org/10.1016/j.erss.2018.06.001

Rosenbloom, D., Meadowcroft, J., & Cashore, B. (2019). Stability and climate policy? Harnessing insights on path dependence, policy feedback, and transition pathways. *Energy Research & Social Science*, 50, 168–178. https://doi.org/10.1016/j.erss.2018.12.009

Ryan, R. M., & Deci, E. L. (2000). Self-determination theory and the facilitation of intrinsic motivation, social development, and well-being. *American Psychologist, 55*(1), 68–78. https://doi.org/10.1037/0003-066X.55.1.68

Samuelson, W., & Zeckhauser, R. (1988). Status quo bias in decision making. *Journal of Risk and Uncertainty, 1*(1), 7–59. https://doi.org/10.1007/BF00055564

Savin, I., Drews, S., & Van Den Bergh, J. (2024). Carbon pricing – perceived strengths, weaknesses and knowledge gaps according to a global expert survey. *Environmental Research Letters, 19*(2), 024014. https://doi.org/10.1088/1748-9326/ad1c1c

Shogren, J. F., & Taylor, L. O. (2008). On Behavioral-Environmental Economics. *Review of Environmental Economics and Policy, 2*(1), 26–44. https://doi.org/10.1093/reep/rem027

Stern, N. (Ed.). (2006). *The Economics of Climate Change: The Stern Review*. Cambridge University Press.

Stoll, C., & Mehling, M. A. (2021). Climate change and carbon pricing: Overcoming three dimensions of failure. *Energy Research & Social Science, 77*, 102062. https://doi.org/10.1016/j.erss.2021.102062

Sunstein, C. R., & Reisch, L. A. (2014). Automatically Green: Behavioral Economics and Environmental Protection. *Harvard Environmental Law Review, 38*, 127.

Trappmann, V., Eversberg, D., & Schulz, F. (2024). Conjunctures of eco-social partnership unionism: The German Trade Union Confederation's climate policies over three decades. *Industrielle Beziehungen, 31*(1), 35–62. https://doi.org/10.5771/0943-2779-2024-1-35

Urbina, D. A., & Ruiz-Villaverde, A. (2019). A Critical Review of Homo Economicus from Five Approaches. *The American Journal of Economics and Sociology, 78*(1), 63–93. https://doi.org/10.1111/ajes.12258

Vohs, K. D., Mead, N. L., & Goode, M. R. (2006). The Psychological Consequences of Money. *Science, 314*(5802), 1154–1156. https://doi.org/10.1126/science.1132491

Wang, T., Shen, B., Han Springer, C., & Hou, J. (2021). What prevents us from taking low-carbon actions? A comprehensive review of influencing factors affecting low-carbon behaviors. *Energy Research & Social Science, 71*, 101844. https://doi.org/10.1016/j.erss.2020.101844

Watkins, S. J., & Musselwhite, C. (2025). Recognised cognitive biases: How far do they explain transport behaviour? *Journal of Transport & Health, 40*, 101941. https://doi.org/10.1016/j.jth.2024.101941

Wilson, C., & Dowlatabadi, H. (2007). Models of Decision Making and Residential Energy Use. *Annual Review of Environment and Resources, 32*(Volume 32, 2007), 169–203. https://doi.org/10.1146/annurev.energy.32.053006.141137

World Bank. (2025). *State and Trends of Carbon Pricing 2025*. https://doi.org/10.1596/978-1-4648-2255-1

World Bank & Ecofys. (2018). *State and Trends of Carbon Pricing 2018*. https://doi.org/10.1596/978-1-4648-1292-7

The Ecological Price of Inequality
How Wealth Disparities Shape Sustainable Development

Michelle Alfers

Abstract: *Environmental degradation and global income inequality are widely recognized as two of the defining crises of the 21st century. In political practice, they are usually treated as two separate challenges, requiring separate sets of interventions. Growing research, however, suggests that both are deeply interconnected and that economic inequality is not just a separate concern, but a core component of sustainable development. This chapter provides an overview of the literature investigating the effect of economic inequality on environmental degradation. Theory suggests that various channels drive this relationship via political, economic and social pathways. After discussing each of these pathways, the chapter reviews empirical findings on the inequality-environment link from a wide range of national contexts. Although studies report mixed findings, some patterns emerge with respect to national income levels and environmental indicators. By mapping the three underlying pathways and synthesizing results across countries, the chapter shows where equality can serve as a lever for environmental improvement and where trade-offs must be managed, pointing to integrated policy designs and priorities for future research.*

1. Inequality and environmental degradation—two separate crises?

Environmental degradation and increasing economic inequality are among the most pressing crises of current times.

Ecological crises, including climate change, biodiversity loss, pervasive pollution and growing freshwater scarcity, are tightly linked and accelerate rapidly. The IPCC's latest report shows warming of about 1.1 °C, already with escalating, widespread risks from extremes and slow-onset changes (Calvin et al., 2023). Global biodiversity is in steep decline, with IPBES estimating about 1 million species at risk of extinction due to land and sea-use change, overexploitation, pollution, invasive species and climate change (Watson et al., 2019). Pollution remains the largest environmental risk to health, causing about 9 million premature deaths annually (Fuller et al., 2022). Synthesizing these trends, the updated planetary boundaries assessment concludes that six of nine Earth-system limits are already transgressed (Richardson et al., 2023). Overall, the continuous increase in global economic activity poses a serious threat to the planet.

Despite the associated growth in global wealth, not everyone benefits equally from it—in most countries, economic inequality continues to intensify (Milanovic, 2024), leading to numerous adverse social and economic outcomes. The persistence of absolute poverty, inadequate access to basic needs, and lack of social inclusion remain a fundamental problem, especially in low-income countries. Studies demonstrate that both absolute and relative poverty seriously undermine physical and mental health (Pickett & Wilkinson, 2015), making it even more difficult for individuals to escape persistent poverty.

Beyond its impact on individual well-being, inequality is linked to a variety of macroeconomic and societal challenges. For instance, it is associated with weakened resilience against recessions and economic crises (Kumhof et al., 2015). On a societal level, socioeconomic inequality has been shown to contribute to the destabilization of systems by deepening social fragmentation and polarization, leaving room for populism (Engler & Weisstanner, 2021) and fostering violent crime rates (Fajnzylber et al., 2002).

In sum, both individual well-being and systemic stability are significantly impacted by strong degrees of inequality.

Moreover, solving these two crises is severely complicated by the fact that both are deeply interconnected. As research on the issue of carbon inequality shows, both the responsibility for and the burden of environmental degradation are distributed highly unequally: Globally, the richest 10 percent are responsible for nearly half of consumption-based CO_2 emissions, while the bottom 50 percent emit only a tenth of global CO_2 (Bruckner et al., 2022). Historically, the countries that are now among the richest in the world have contributed most to the current carbon budget: The USA, UK and today's EU countries have emitted nearly half of global cumulative emissions since 1751 (Ritchie, 2019), a share that increases even more when colonial rule is taken into account (Evans & Viisainen, 2023). At the same time, the consequences of climate change and environmental degradation have a disproportionate impact on the poorest households, as people in low-income countries are exposed more frequently to climate disasters, have fewer resources to protect themselves against them, and rely more heavily on natural resources and ecosystem services for their everyday living (Adger et al., 2003; Barbier & Hochard, 2018).

In the context of environmental protection, inequality further intensifies the trade-offs between economic interests and mitigation efforts: When sustainability requires changes in lifestyles and investments in cleaner technology and infrastructure, negotiations about who carries which share of the burden are often unavoidable. Consequently, issues of social fairness and acceptability have become a crucial component of (and obstacle to) environmental policies (Maestre-Andrés et al., 2019).

In addition to the questions of climate justice and the feasibility of environmental policies, a growing strand of literature has emerged over the last 30 years studying the direct linkages between economic inequality and ecological degradation. The overarching goal of this line of research is to understand whether income inequality, on an aggregate level, is conducive or obstructive to sustainability—or, as a result, whether policymakers can either utilize a win-win relationship to achieve both higher levels of equality and sustainability or whether they have to carefully manage a trade-off between both goals.

This strand of literature focuses on two questions: *1) What are the underlying pathways through which inequality affects the environment? and 2) What is the empirical evidence of the inequality-environment relationship across countries and time?*

The first question has been discussed extensively on a theoretical basis. While various mechanisms have been proposed, the literature focuses on three pathways, two of which act through households' consumption patterns and one through the distribution of political power. Since these pathways suggest contradictory effects, however, they alone cannot provide a definite answer.

As a result, more attention is being paid to the empirical evidence. Despite a growing number of studies, the results do not provide a clear picture, either. In addition to mixed findings, estimates have been found to be sensitive to country-specific contexts, use of indicators for inequality and environmental impacts, as well as choices of data and methodology.

The aim of this chapter is to review this literature addressing the effect of economic inequality on environmental degradation. While neither theoretical considerations nor empirical evidence provide a definitive answer, the chapter attempts to provide a structured overview of the current state of research. Section 2 discusses possible political, economic and social pathways underlying the inequality-environment link. In section 3, I summarize the empirical evidence on the relationship, highlighting some patterns that emerge despite the overall mixed findings. Section 4 concludes with a summary of policy implications and open points for future research.

2. The pathways from inequality to sustainability

While many studies try to establish a general link between inequality and environmental degradation, this aggregate relationship seems to emerge from an interaction between various underlying mechanisms. Several approaches have been used to study these mechanisms, e.g. by investigating the role of different societal actors and decision instances (Islam, 2015), using a scale-composition-technique approach (Berthe & Elie, 2015; Clement & Meunie, 2010) or taking a complex adaptive systems perspective (Leach et al., 2018). Most papers, however, explain the inequality-environment link by distinguishing between *economic* and *political* pathways.

From this analytical perspective, the economic pathways operate via the consumption and investment decisions of households, whereas the political pathways investigate the role of power, voter interests and political priorities in the determination of environmental policies. In more recent papers, the social dimension is discussed as well, showing how social and cultural consequences of inequality shape environmental attitudes.

As not only the theoretical, but also most empirical papers are guided by this classification, I will discuss the three pathways in more detail in the following sections.

2.1 Political pathways

Among the first authors to link environmental degradation and economic inequality was Boyce (1994). Using a political economy framework, he demonstrated how inequality can exacerbate environmental harm through power dynamics favoring the wealthy.

He adopts the standard welfare-economic model of externalities as his point of departure. In this framework, polluting activities yield short-term economic gains but also impose costs on the general public. When these gains and costs are unevenly distributed across the population, certain actors derive net benefits from such activities, while others bear net costs. In equilibrium, the level of pollution should be set to maximize overall welfare. Given diminishing marginal benefits from the pollution-generating activity and increasing marginal costs from pollution, the socially optimal level of activity is determined by the standard condition in which marginal benefit equals marginal cost.

Boyce contends that this optimal outcome can only be achieved if no power asymmetries exist between net beneficiaries and net cost bearers. Where such asymmetries do exist, the level of pollution is no longer determined by the optimal benefit-cost criterion, but instead by the so-called '*power-weighted social decision rule*' (PWSDR) whereby more powerful actors have greater influence over public decision-making. Depending on whether power is concentrated among the winners or losers of polluting activities, the resulting pollution level will deviate upward or downward from the social optimum. Consequently, greater power inequality leads to larger deviations from the socially optimal level.

Building on this formal model, Boyce argues that a) political power is usually correlated with income and b) income correlates with being a net beneficiary of polluting activities. As a result, powerful actors who benefit from pollution are able to assert their interests via the PWSDR, resulting in higher pollution levels.

Boyce justifies the assumption that wealthy individuals have a stronger preference for pollution on two grounds (Torras & Boyce, 1998). First, he argues that the wealthy benefit disproportionately from polluting activities because they are more likely to own polluting firms, hold greater asset portfolios and maintain higher levels of consumption. As a result, they generate greater producer and consumer surplus, which they have an interest in protecting. Second, wealthy individuals are more likely able to protect themselves from the consequences of pollution, for example by relocating to less polluted areas or by using their financial resources to secure priority access to otherwise scarce goods and services.

Accordingly, strong inequality creates conditions in which high levels of pollution persist, with the associated costs disproportionately borne by low-income groups that lack the political influence to prevent them. In the context of political decision-making, this dynamic manifests as insufficient environmental protection and inadequate climate mitigation policies.

Boyce's line of argument, also known as the *equality hypothesis*, is prominently challenged by Scruggs (1998), who argues that the link between inequality and environmental quality is more complex and mediated by institutional structures and the distribution of preferences.

Scruggs mainly challenges Boyce's claim that the wealthy systematically prefer environmental degradation. He argues that, if the environment is considered a normal or superior good, higher-income individuals may instead demand more protection, meaning inequality could under some conditions improve environmental outcomes. He also questions the assumption that the wealthy can fully shield themselves from pollution, noting that global problems like climate change are public, not private, bads.

Empirically, Scruggs points to evidence that environmental concern is often stronger among higher-income groups, drawing on Inglehart's theory of culture shift according to which post-materialist values can only emerge once a minimum level of prosperity and material security is acquired. He concludes that environmental preferences cannot be reduced to income alone but result from a complex interplay of economic, cultural, and individual factors.

Finally, Scruggs disputes Boyce's notion that political outcomes simply reflect power-weighted preferences. Instead, institutional rules, advocacy dynamics and voting behavior shape the outcome of democratic processes. Thus, even if higher equality strengthened pro-environmental interests, the resulting collective choices might not automatically lead to more environmental protection.

Considering both positions, the political economy arguments can thus lead to inequality being either conducive or obstructive to environmental quality, depending on which assumptions about environmental interests and the mechanisms of political influence are true in a given empirical context. Berthe and Elie (2015) summarize this point by identifying three questions that need to be asked in order to test the suitability of the different arguments:

1. What are different social groups' overall interests in terms of protecting the environment?
2. How have these interests been transformed into political positions?
3. Are these positions reflected in political decisions?

While these two theoretical positions dominate the inequality-environment literature, other political pathways may play a role as well.

First, both positions investigate how political interests directly translate into public decision-making. However, political decisions are not only influenced by contemporary interests and institutional structures, but also by general beliefs about welfare, economic dynamics and the role of the government. In the short term, public opinion has been shown to be significantly affected by the media (DellaVigna & Kaplan, 2007), which can be biased towards the interests of the wealthy if media ownership is concentrated in these groups. Indeed, studies confirm this influence of elite and business interests in various contexts (e.g. Gilens & Page, 2014; Popiel, 2018).

In the long run, political and economic thinking is strongly influenced by academia, think tanks and policy networks, often reflecting the interests of privileged groups and contributing to the preservation of existing power balances (Campbell & Pedersen, 2014). Therefore, existing power asymmetries do not only influence which interests are prioritized in political decision-making, they can also influence the *formation* of interests in the first place.

Second, inequality can shape environmental policy by shifting political priorities from long-term concerns to short-term issues. The social consequences of inequality—lacking access to necessities in low-income groups, increased support needs in times of crises, unequal opportunities in education and employment, etc.—require political attention and resources that could be reduced in the long run if structural changes were implemented to permanently reduce inequality (O'Neill, 2020). Instead, policies prioritizing the preservation of the status quo tend to apply short-term 'damage control' measures to cushion the consequences of inequality (Stiglitz, 2015), forcing political attention away from other long-term concerns such as environmental protection.

In sum, most of these political pathways suggest that inequality acts as a barrier to sustainable development, making reductions in income and power disparities an important tool to combat environmental degradation. However, the role of environmental preferences across the income distribution plays in an important role in these dynamics—if high-income groups with significant political power care more about the environment than lower-income groups, inequality could actually lead to better environmental protection.

2.2 Economic pathways

The economic pathways underlying the inequality-environment link focus on how households' consumption patterns would be affected by income redistribution measures.

As discussed earlier, high-income groups are responsible for the majority of resource use and pollution, both within and across countries. For instance, Bruckner et al. (2022) find that carbon footprints of the top 10 percent incomes in the US are about 40 times higher than those of the top 10 percent in Nigeria, and over 500 times higher than the footprints of Nigeria's bottom 10 percent.

Globally, they report that the top 1 percent emit more CO_2 than the bottom 50 percent combined.

These extreme degrees of carbon inequality should undoubtedly serve as a warning to recognize the role and responsibility of high-income groups in the ongoing global environmental crisis. Nevertheless, they are more indicative of the impact of *extreme wealth* on the environment rather than the impact of *wealth inequality* per se. Wealthy households have a disproportionately higher ecological footprint than poorer households, but they also have disproportionately high incomes. Whether redistributing this income would mitigate or exacerbate the environmental footprint of consumption depends on the extent to which lower-income households spend the additional income on more or less resource-intensive goods. In other words, it depends on the resource intensity of the average dollar spent across the income distribution.

The inequality-environment literature addresses this problem using the *marginal propensity to emit (MPE)* framework (Holtz-Eakin & Selden, 1995), describing how emissions associated with each dollar earned change with increasing income. In the case of constant MPE, redistribution should not affect consumption-based emissions because each dollar 'contains' the same amount of emissions. If the MPE is increasing, redistribution would benefit the environment as a dollar used in lower income groups is associated with fewer emissions than one in higher income groups. If it is diminishing, redistribution would worsen environmental degradation as more money is spent on emission-intensive goods after redistributing it.

Studies investigating the environmental impact of consumption patterns in Western countries tend to support the *diminishing* marginal propensity to emit (DMPE) hypothesis, i.e. the average carbon intensity of consumption decreases with higher income (Grunewald et al., 2017; Wan et al., 2022). This observation is linked to two underlying effects:

First, the *marginal propensity to consume (MPC)* usually diminishes with increasing income (Drescher et al., 2020). Compared to lower-income households, higher incomes devote a smaller proportion of their income to consumption, directing more towards savings or investment instead. Wealthy households spending less income on consumption therefore have a lower ecological footprint of consumption *relative to their income* than households with higher MPC.

Second, the *composition* of consumption patterns also changes across the income distribution. Analyses of household expenditure data suggest that, at least in high- and middle-income countries, the average carbon and resource intensity (i.e. the impact per dollar) tends to diminish with increasing income as well (Ivanova et al., 2016). Lower-income households usually spend a larger share of their income on carbon-intensive necessities such as food and housing, while higher-income households tend to buy more services, higher-quality (i.e. more durable) goods, as well as high-efficiency appliances (Bjelle et al., 2021; Druckman & Jackson, 2016). Rich households also tend to have a higher willingness to pay for expensive products and brand mark-ups (Fassnacht & Dahm, 2021), which have a lower environmental impact per dollar compared to less expensive substitutes with comparable material and energy inputs.

While most studies support the evidence of diminishing MPC and MPE, estimates of exact elasticities vary considerably across countries (Berthe & Elie, 2015), indicating that other economic and socio-cultural factors might play a role in determining consumption patterns in a given context. Static analyses using data of historical consumption patterns to test the effect of redistribution may therefore fail to capture dynamic connections between inequality and consumption. Consequently, understanding how inequality itself shapes consumption patterns via economic and social mechanisms is crucial to assess the ecological effect of redistribution.

One of these dynamic effects is captured by the concepts of *conspicuous consumption* and *status competition*, representing the second economic pathway frequently discussed in the inequality-environment literature. Based on Veblen's *Theory of the Leisure Class* (1899), conspicuous consumption describes the purchase of expensive and highly visible goods that are not consumed for individual utility, but to signal wealth, status and social position to others. According to Veblen, wealthy individuals engage in conspicuous consumption to differentiate themselves from lower social classes. In doing so, they create status competition that lower-income groups respond to by trying to emulate the consumption patterns of the rich—'Keeping up with the Joneses'—resulting in a 'consumption arms race' across income groups.

Veblen's theory is applied to the inequality-environment relationship to describe how inequality affects consumption patterns via social norms. In highly unequal societies, differences in social status are more pronounced and visible, which intensifies status competition and therefore demand for status goods. This can lead to more resource-intensive consumption patterns via three direct effects: First, status competition can cause a scale effect by stimulating total demand—as demand for status goods rises across all income groups, overall consumption levels increase (Bertrand & Morse, 2016). Second, the environmental impact of consumption increases if status goods are more resource- or emission-intensive than the average non-status good. Evidence for this composition effect has been found in the context of SUV purchases (Grinblatt et al., 2008), travel (Josiassen & George Assaf, 2013) and housing (Fligstein et al., 2017). Third, there is some evidence that status competition can increase people's working hours, affecting both economic growth and individual consumption levels (Bowles & Park, 2005).

As before, the consumption pathways lead to conflicting implications: On the one hand, the DMPE findings suggest that reducing income disparities will harm the environment by allocating income towards households with more resource-intensive consumption patterns. On the other hand, the Veblen approach indicates that higher equality can mitigate status competition and overconsumption, leading to lower absolute and possibly less resource-intensive lifestyles. The total impact of redistribution would thus depend on the net effect between the two.

Finally, it should be noted that the arguments surrounding the economic pathway focus mostly on consumption, ignoring the role of *investments* in a household's environmental footprint. Although it is difficult to assign the environmental impact of production processes to investors rather than final consumers, the role of capital income cannot be ignored in a discussion on the effects of inequality. Compared to labor income, it is significantly more concentrated among the population, with the top 10 percent receiving a disproportionate share of dividends and profits (Bengtsson & Waldenström, 2018). Hence, lower marginal propensities to consume among the rich may be offset by higher investment shares. Indeed, Chancel (2022) finds that most emissions caused by the top 1 percent stem from investments rather than consumption.

The environmental effects of redistribution via changes in investment behavior are hard to predict, mainly because of the interaction of scale and technique effects: While investments contribute to expanding production levels, they can also promote efficient production processes via innovation and technology. Nonetheless, incorporating investment and capital income alongside consumption in the analysis may reveal an important piece in the inequality-environment puzzle.

2.3 Social pathways

Income inequality can affect environmental degradation through several social pathways, which explain how inequality influences environmental concern via social norms, societal cohesion, and environmental awareness. As before, several mechanisms stand out.

The first one directly builds on the conspicuous consumption pathway discussed above. In addition to the effects of status competition on demand, it has been argued that cultures expressing social hierarchies mainly though material goods foster materialism and consumerism (Kasser, 2003), influencing not only individual consumption choices but general attitudes on life and well-being. As such, they can also feed back into attitudes on sustainability. For instance, materialism has been shown to be related to lower environmental concern, possibly because people view sustainability and the necessary changes in lifestyles as a direct threat to their social status and identity (Kilbourne & Pickett, 2008).

Second, inequality has been found to reduce pro-environmental attitudes by weakening social cohesion and a sense of solidarity. Research suggests that societies with higher economic inequality and steeper social hierarchies show lower levels of trust in institutions and among citizens, strongly mediated by perceived societal (un)fairness (Rothstein & Uslaner, 2005). This can reduce people's desire to advocate for others and be concerned with the common good (Power et al., 2016).

There is strong evidence that this effect also feeds into environmental concern, behavior and policy support. Generalized trust, for example, is linked to general pro-environmental behavior (Zheng et al., 2025) and has been found to reduce the gap between environmental concern and action (Tam & Chan, 2018). Similarly, Harring & Jagers (2013) report that higher interpersonal trust increases support for carbon taxes. With respect to social norms, Vesely et al. (2020) find that pro-environmental acts are perceived as signals of cooperativeness that, in turn, elicit more cooperation from others. Overall, this evidence suggests that societies with strong social cohesion produce a sense of collective responsibility for current and future generations, which is an essential prerequisite for mobilizing collective efforts toward environmental sustainability (Wilkinson et al., 2010).

The third social pathway concerns the role of education. Economic inequality is typically associated with inequality in educational attainment (Gregorio & Lee, 2002). Education, in turn, is related to environmental awareness, attitudes and behaviors, (Meyer, 2015), including behaviors such as organic food choice (Dimitri & Dettmann, 2012), bicycle-use (Cole-Hunter et al., 2015) and green voting (Schumacher, 2014).

Table 1: Overview of theoretical pathways

Type of pathway	Mechanism	Hypothesized effect
Political	**Equality hypothesis and PWSDR** (Boyce, 1994)	+
	PWSDR with increasing environmental preferences over income (Scruggs, 1998)	–
	Influence of elites on political and economic beliefs	+
	Political priorities and short-termism	+
Economic	**Diminishing marginal propensity to emit (DMPE)**	–
	Veblen effect and status competition	+
Social	Materialism and consumerism	+
	Social cohesion and collective responsibility	+
	Education	+

Description: Overview of political, economic and social pathways. The three main mechanisms discussed in the literature are printed in bold. Positive effects of inequality on environmental degradation represent a 'win-win' relationship, negative ones a trade-off between improved equality and environmental quality.

How does education raise pro-environmental attitudes? While the role of environmental knowledge itself is smaller than commonly expected (Kollmuss & Agyeman, 2002), the process of engaging with environmental topics generally seems increase awareness (Zsóka et al., 2013). Furthermore, there is evidence that education can foster civic engagement and voter participation (Dee, 2004), which can increase environmental concern via the social cohesion pathway. Indeed, Meyer's (2015) observed positive effect of education on several pro-environmental behaviors suggest a higher concern with social welfare as one of the underlying mechanisms.

Summarizing the findings on the three types of pathways, this chapter illustrated the multidimensionality and context-dependency of the inequality-environment relationship. The social and most political pathways indicate that higher equality is beneficial for the environment, whereas the economic pathways suggest conflicting effects (see table 1 for an overview).

To gain insights into the overall net effect of these pathways, the next section turns to studies investigating the relationship empirically across countries and for various measures of environmental degradation.

3. Evidence of the inequality-environment relationship

Empirical studies investigating the inequality-environment relationship have been growing steadily since the 1990s. Starting with the pioneering study by Torras and Boyce (1998), who aimed to test Boyce's (1994) equality hypothesis, many papers followed to empirically investigate the relationship in various national contexts.

3.1 Research designs and methods

Most of the empirical studies discussed below use panel data to test the relationship within or across countries.

To measure inequality, the majority of analyses apply the Gini coefficient. Theoretically, a coefficient of 0 reflects perfect equality, a value of 1 means all income would be concentrated in one person. Empirically, national Gini coefficients lie in a range from 0.2 to 0.8, with a global pre-tax average of 0.67 (Chancel, 2022; WID, 2025). Income redistribution can significantly lower this value—in OECD countries, for instance, the Gini coefficient changes from 0.46 to 0.32 after taxes and transfers (OECD, 2025).

Environmental impacts are measured with a variety of indicators. A small, early group of studies investigates the role of local pollutants such as water or air pollution, as well as deforestation and biodiversity loss. Over time, more analyses started focusing on per-capita CO_2 emissions or footprints, now making up the majority of papers in this branch of literature. Some more recent studies further apply the ecological footprint, which measures the amount of biologically productive land and water required to sustain a person's or population's consumption patterns (Wackernagel & Lin, 2023). I will discuss each group of studies in turn.

All models control for GDP or GDP per capita. Other common control variables include urbanization rates or population density, share of manufacturing as % of GDP, energy consumption, measures for political rights and trade openness.

3.2 Local pollutants and biodiversity loss

In order to test Boyce's (1994) equality hypothesis, Torras and Boyce (1998) are the first to empirically examine the relationship between inequality and pollution. They analyze the effect on seven indicators of water and air pollution, including sulfur dioxide (SO_2), smoke, heavy particles, dissolved oxygen (O_2) and fecal coliform, in an international sample of 58–82 countries. Apart from using the Gini coefficient as a measure of income inequality, they also include indicators for political rights, literacy and civil liberties to test for the role of inequality in political power.

Their results show a clear difference between low- and high-income countries. In low-income countries, income inequality has a significant positive effect on most pollution indicators, confirming Boyce's equality hypothesis. In high-income countries, however, effects are either non-significant or negative. With respect to political rights and literacy, results generally show positive significant effects on nearly all pollution indicators, although the relationship is stronger in low-income countries. The authors conclude that the hypothesized role of power inequalities in environmental protection is confirmed, though its channel through income inequality is weaker than the direct channel via political rights, especially in high-income countries.

Other studies build on this initial analysis to test the effect of inequality on pollution across a variety of contexts (see table 2 for an overview).

Some studies support the hypothesized positive relationship. In an investigation of 113 Chinese cities, Wang et al. (2021) find that inequality correlates with increased smog and pollution levels. Persson et al. (2023) report that smoke rises with higher inequality across countries, while SO_2 depends on country context: in rich democracies, inequality is associated with higher SO_2, but in poor non-democracies, the Gini index is non-significant, suggesting other factors are more relevant. Similarly, Clement and Meunie (2010) confirm a positive effect on water pollution in developing countries, but a negative one in transitioning countries.

However, other studies do not support the inequality-pollution link. Kasuga and Takaya (2017) test it in Japanese cities and find that inequality was associated with worse air quality in the 1990s, but the effect disappeared in the 2000s. They find no significant effect for water pollution. Clement and Meunie (2010) likewise report no significant effects for SO_2 across developing and transitioning countries. They do, however, find a positive effect for the interaction between income inequality and power inequality, suggesting that income inequality may indirectly increase pollution via power relations, as posited in Boyce's equality hypothesis.

Several studies further investigate inequality's effects on biodiversity loss. Mikkelson et al. (2007) show that higher inequality exacerbates biodiversity loss across countries and US states, a finding confirmed by Holland et al. (2009) in a larger cross-country sample. Heerink et al. (2001) also find a positive relationship for deforestation in a cross-country analysis. Similarly, Ceddia (2019) reports that income, land and wealth inequality significantly increases agricultural expansion in 10 Latin American countries.

In sum, the evidence linking inequality to water and air pollution is mixed, with most results indicating either positive or non-existing associations depending on the geographical context. All evidence on biodiversity loss and its proximate drivers, however, points towards positive connection, confirming the detrimental effect of inequality on the environment.

Table 2: Empirical studies (local pollution and biodiversity loss)

Study	**Environmental indicators**	**Sample**	**Time span**	**Effect**
Torras and Boyce (1998)	Water pollution	58 countries	1977–1991	+ (LIC) *ns* (HIC)
Heerink et al. (2001)	Water pollution	33–46 countries	1985	+
Clement and Meunié (2010)	Water pollution	83 developing and transition countries	1988–2003	+ (LIC) – (MIC)
Kasuga and Takaya (2017)	Water pollution	Japanese cities	1990–2009	*ns*, but indirect effect
Torras and Boyce (1998)	Air pollution	19–42 countries	1977–1991	+ (LIC) *ns* (HIC)
Heerink et al. (2001)	Air pollution	31–38 countries	1985	*ns*
Clement and Meunié (2010)	Air pollution	83 developing and transition countries	1988–2003	*ns*

Study	Environmental indicators	Sample	Time span	Effect
Kasuga and Takaya (2017)	Air pollution	Japanese cities	1990–2012	+ in 1990s *ns* in 2000s
Persson et al. (2023)	Air pollution	35 countries	1971–1992	*ns* (LIC) + (HIC)
Heerink et al. (2001)	Deforestation	52 countries	1961–1986	+
Ceddia (2019)	Agricultural expansion	10 Latin American countries	1990–2010	+
Mikkelson et al. (2007)	Biodiversity loss	US states; 45 countries	1969–2004 (time lag)	+
Holland et al. (2009)	Biodiversity loss	US states, 50 countries	1975–2007 (time lag)	+

Description: Overview of studies investigating the effect of inequality on local pollution or biodiversity loss. '+' = positive effect (win-win); '–' = negative effect (trade-off); 'ns' = non-significant; LIC, MIC, HIC = low-, middle- and high-income countries.

3.3 CO_2 emissions

While earlier studies focus on local types of pollution, a larger body of literature investigating the link between inequality and CO_2 emissions has emerged from the 2010s on. Overall, the studies yield mixed findings, though some patterns can be observed—most noticeably with respect to countries' development level (table 3).

Among studies reporting exclusively positive associations between inequality and emissions, the majority analyze medium- or low-income contexts. Zhang and Zhao (2014) and Hao et al. (2016) confirm the positive relationship for China, noting substantial regional variation and particularly strong effects in the developed eastern provinces. Baloch et al. (2020) report that both poverty and income inequality increased CO_2 emissions in 40 African countries, a finding they further validate for consumption-based emissions in the BRICS countries (Baloch & Danish, 2022). Yang et al. (2022) corroborate this finding in a sample of 42 developing countries. In the US context, two studies lend support to the equality hypothesis, though with variation: Baek and Gweisah (2013) find positive effects in both the short and long run, while Liu et al. (2019) identify a reversal to negative effects in the long run.

Conversely, a few studies provide evidence for a negative association, indicating a trade-off relationship between climate change mitigation and inequality reduction. Heerink et al. (2001) and Wan et al. (2022) report this negative relationship using cross-sectional data of 64 and 217 countries, respectively. Ravallion et al. (2000) confirm this finding in 42 countries but note that the effect is weaker in high-income economies. They conclude that, in the long run, low inequality combined with high income growth may reduce emissions and eventually eliminate the inequality-emissions trade-off.

A third group of cross-country analyses provides evidence for different effect directions depending on the national income of the countries involved. Among these, Ehigiamusoe et al. (2022) examine the relationship in 70 countries, finding a positive effect of inequality in low-income countries, but a negative one in high-income countries. They also investigate the effect of poverty, which was related to higher CO_2 emissions in low-income countries. Chen et al. (2020) provide evidence for a positive inequality-emissions link in developing countries as well, but apart from a few negative effects in countries with very high per-capita emissions, inequality in most developed countries is found to be unrelated to emissions. Similarly, Wu and Xi (2020) observe that higher inequality reduces CO_2 emissions in high-income countries, but cannot confirm any significant association in low-income countries.

Interestingly, Grunewald et al. (2017) and Rojas-Vallejos and Lastuka (2020) come to the opposite conclusion; in a panel dataset of 158 and 68 countries, respectively, their findings indicate a trade-off between equality and emission reductions in low- and middle-income countries, and a win-win relationship in high-income countries.

Table 3: Empirical studies (CO2 emissions)

Study	Environmental indicators	Sample	Time span	Effect
Baek and Gweisah (2013)	CO_2 per capita	US states	1967–2008	+
Zhang and Zhao (2014)	CO_2	Chinese provinces	1995–2010	+
Hao et al. (2016)	CO_2 per capita	Chinese provinces	1995–2012	+
Liu et al. (2019)	CO_2 per capita	US states	1997–2015	+(short term) – (long term)
Baloch et al. (2020)	CO_2 per capita	40 African countries	2010–2016	+
Khan and Yahong (2022)	CO_2 per capita	18 Asian developing countries	2006–2017	+
Baloch and Danish (2022)	Consumption-based CO_2	BRICS	1994–2018	+
Yang et al. (2022)	CO_2 per capita	42 developing countries	1984–2016	+
Grunewald et al. (2017)	CO_2 per capita	158 countries	1980–2007	– (LIC) + (HIC)
Rojas-Vallejos and Lastuka (2020)	CO_2 per capita	68 countries	1961–2010	– (LIC) + (HIC)
Chen et al. (2020)	CO_2 per capita	17 G20 countries	1988–2015	+ (LIC) – or *ns* (HIC)
Wu and Xi (2020)	CO_2 per capita	78 countries	1990–2017	*ns* (LIC) – (HIC)
Ehigiamusoe et al. (2022)	CO_2 per capita	70 countries	2000–2018	+ (MIC) – (HIC)
Hübler (2017)	CO_2 per capita	149 countries	1985–2012	*ns* or –

Study	Environmental indicators	Sample	Time span	Effect
Jorgenson et al. (2017)	CO_2	US states	1997–2012	*ns* (Gini) + (income top 10%)
Kasuga and Takaya (2017)	CO_2	Japanese cities	1990–2012	*ns*
Wolde-Rufael and Idowu (2017)	CO_2 per capita	China, India	1971–2010	*ns*
Khan et al. (2018)	CO_2 per capita	Bangladesh, India, Pakistan	1980–2014	+ (Bangladesh) – (India / Pakistan)
Mader (2018)	CO_2 per capita	28 countries, US states	2000–2014 1997–2014	*ns*
Baležentis et al. (2020)	Consumption-based GHG emissions p.c.	109 countries	1990–2014	Non-linear
Ravallion et al. (2000)	CO_2 per capita	42 countries	1975–1992	– (+ long term)
Heerink et al. (2001)	CO_2 per capita	64 countries	1985	–
Wan et al. (2022)	CO_2 per capita	217 countries	1960–2021	–

Description: Overview of studies investigating the effect of inequality on CO_2 emissions. '+' = positive effect (win-win); '–' = negative effect (trade-off); 'ns' = non-significant; LIC, MIC, HIC = low-, middle- and high-income countries, respectively.

Lastly, some studies report mixed or non-significant results. Khan et al. (2018) find a positive association in Bangladesh, but negative ones in Pakistan and India. Baležentis et al. (2020) identify a non-linear relationship in a sample of 109 countries, where the effect depends on the level of inequality. Jorgenson et al. (2017) find no effect of the Gini coefficient on US state-level emissions, but using the top 10 percent income share shows a positive association with CO_2 emissions, leading the authors to assume that this indicator is more accurate to capture the underlying Veblen and political economy effects.

Generally non-significant results, however, have been found for China and India (Wolde-Rufael & Idowu, 2017) and Japanese cities (Kasuga & Takaya, 2017), as well as in two cross-country analyses (Hübler, 2017; Mader, 2018).

Overall, the inequality-emissions link remains unclear despite the growing body of empirical analyses. Some studies indicate that reducing inequality may lead to emission reductions, mainly in low- and middle-income countries, but this result is not universally supported. Likewise, the negative (trade-off) association found for some high-income countries cannot be supported by all studies, either. In the CO_2 context, therefore, there is no evidence for a universal or linear relationship, but likely a strong impact of context-dependent factors and dynamics.

3.4 Ecological footprints

The last group of studies focuses on the general environmental impact of economic activity. Interestingly, these studies paint a somewhat clearer picture than those covering only CO_2-Emissions, although some areas of uncertainty remain (table 4).

Again, Boyce and colleagues conduct the first analysis using a composite measure of environmental degradation, the environmental stress indicator, which includes water and air pollution, energy use, waste production, and others (Boyce et al., 1999). Instead of using a single-equation model, they apply a recursive model to test the multiple hypothesized stages from income inequality over political inequality to environmental stress. Their results support the equality hypothesis across US states in the early 1990s—higher income and racial inequality predict higher power inequality, which in turn predicts less environmental policy, resulting in higher environmental stress. Taken together, these effects match the political pathway proposed by Boyce (1994).

Table 4: Empirical studies (composite environmental indicators)

Study	Environmental indicators	Sample	Time span	Effect
Boyce et al. (1999)	Environmental stress index	US states	1990s	+
Ekeocha (2021)	Ecological footprint	46 African countries	1996–2014	+
Khan and Yahong (2022) / Khan et al. (2022)	Ecological footprint	18 Asian developing countries	2006–2017	+
Uzar and Eyuboglu (2023)	Ecological footprint	US states	1965–2017	+ *(via cropland component)*
Kazemzadeh et al. (2021)	Ecological footprint	25 countries	1970–2016	+ (lower quantiles) *ns* (higher quantiles)
Ehigiamusoe et al. (2022)	Ecological footprint	70 countries	2000–2018	+ (MIC) – (HIC)

Description: Overview of studies investigating the effect of inequality on environmental stress and ecological footprints. '+' = positive effect (win-win); '–' = negative effect (trade-off); 'ns' = non-significant; MIC, HIC = middle- and high-income countries.

While no follow-up study applies a recursive model, some more recent papers test the inequality-environment relationship using the ecological footprint (EF) as another composite indicator of environmental degradation.

Uzar & Eyuboglu (2023) examine the impact of inequality on EF in the United States as well, finding a positive effect over the entire period of 1965–2017. However, an investigation of the components of the EF reveals that the positive association is mainly related to cropland use, not fishing grounds or the carbon footprint. In contrast, Khan and Yahong (2022) find that inequality increases both CO_2 emissions and EF among Asian developing countries. They also find the reverse effect of environmental degradation on increased income inequality, suggesting a reinforcing feedback loop between inequality and deteriorating environmental quality. Khan et al. (2022) extend the analysis by including the role of poverty, which is also found to increase ecological footprints. Likewise, the positive effect of inequality on EF and CO_2 emissions is confirmed by Ekeocha (2021) in a sample of 46 African countries.

Finally, two studies yield somewhat mixed results. Kazemzadeh et al. (2022) find that inequality results in higher EF across 25 countries, but the effect turns non-significant in higher quantiles. Similarly, Ehigiamusoe et al. (2022) investigate a sample of 70 countries, finding that inequality increases EF, but only in middle-income countries. In high-income countries, on the other hand, the effect turns negative.

Therefore, the evidence suggest that for environmental footprints, too, a country's national income level seems to be a relevant factor in the inequality-environment relationship.

3.5 Synthesizing the findings

As shown in this section, the link between inequality and various measures of environmental degradation is everything but clear, depending heavily on context, time, and type of environmental indicator. Despite the large number of contradictory findings and mixed results, though, some patterns can be observed across studies.

First, results are less diverse in the case of local pollutants, biodiversity loss and ecological footprints compared to CO_2 emissions. Apart from the negative effect in Ehigiamusoe et al. (2022) for high-income countries, all other studies in these groups find either positive or non-significant associations. These results suggest that in cases where the effect of environmental degradation is directly perceived, such as in the case of local pollution, inequality plays a larger role in preventing mitigation efforts. Several authors have linked this finding to a strong political pathway: Powerful individuals can shield themselves from the effects of local pollutants, leaving less powerful groups to bear the burden. By contrast, in more equal settings, where the interests of all are considered, general improvements in environmental quality are more easily achieved (Berthe & Elie, 2015; Clement & Meunie, 2010; Uzar & Eyuboglu, 2023).

Second, inequality is more frequently associated with increased environmental degradation in low- and middle-income countries, whereas the reverse pattern is more commonly observed in high-income countries. The underlying pathways therefore seem to hold different weight depending on the national income or development level of a country. Some authors attribute this finding to the influence of institutions and regulations, as well as the role of absolute poverty, which tends to exacerbate environmental pressures as low-income populations often rely on resource-intensive means of subsistence (Barrett et al., 2011). Indeed, three empirical studies in the current sample (Baloch et al., 2020; Ehigiamusoe et al., 2022; Khan et al., 2022) test the role of poverty as an underlying mechanism in the inequality-environment link, unanimously confirming the detrimental impact of poverty on CO_2 emissions and ecological footprints.

Third, in terms of study design and interpretation, surprisingly little attention has been paid to social and cultural factors. The majority of studies only discusses the three dominant pathways—the role of political power and influence, the marginal propensity to emit, and the Veblen effect – and use them to interpret their results. Understanding the social effects of inequality and how they lead to sustainable lifestyles or increased environmental protection might shed some light on the persistence of mixed findings in the empirical literature.

Fourth, very few studies in the current sample explicitly test the underlying pathways, focusing only on the significance and effect signs of the general inequality-environment link. Among those studies that do investigate underlying mechanisms, most focus on the political pathway. As discussed above, Torras and Boyce (1998) and Boyce et al. (1999) find support for Boyce's equality hypothesis in low-income countries and the US. Additional studies confirm the importance of political power and rights for local pollution (Clement & Meunie; Kasuga & Takaya, 2017; Persson et al., 2023) and ecological footprints (Ekeocha, 2021). In contrast, research explicitly testing mechanisms for CO_2 emissions remains more limited. Two studies (Baloch & Danish, 2022; Jorgenson et al., 2017) employ the income share of the top 10 percent as an alternative measure of inequality, arguing that it more accurately reflects political economy dynamics and Veblen effects. Both find this measure to be positively associated with CO_2 emissions. In addition, Yang et al. (2022) show that institutional quality moderates the positive link between inequality and emissions, thereby indirectly supporting Boyce's hypothesis that the limited political influence of poorer groups contributes to environmental degradation.

Beyond that, only one study in the current sample, Rojas-Vallejos and Lastuka (2020), tests the interaction between multiple pathways. They observe that the consumption effect dominates for most income levels, but its magnitude diminishes as income rises, with the political effect dominating at higher-income levels—explaining their somewhat divergent finding of a positive effect in high-income and a negative one in low-income countries.

All in all, this review emphasizes the importance of further empirical research into the mechanisms—particularly the economic and social pathways—underpinning the inequality-environment relationship, rather than focusing solely on the aggregate link.

4. The way forward

Overall, the empirical evidence confirms the complex and context-dependent nature of the inequality-environment relationship. Although a variety of underlying political, economic and social pathways has been proposed and investigated, they alone do not seem sufficient to explain the mixed findings. To further advance the understanding of this topic, future research is needed to a) examine the dynamic interplay between the different pathways, b) understand which societal conditions activate individual pathways to different degrees, and c) investigate other mechanisms besides the three pathways dominating the literature.

The question of whether income redistribution measures lead to beneficial outcomes for the environment or whether they result in a trade-off with environmental protection cannot be answered with certainty. Still, the literature has provided some suggestions.

For lower-income economies, where inequality poses a serious humanitarian challenge due to its association with absolute poverty, evidence indicates that inequality reductions can directly or indirectly lead to better environmental quality. Consequently, policymakers can use a win-win strategy to achieve both social equity and environmental protection to a certain degree.

In higher-income countries, the opposite seems to be the case, suggesting that policymakers need to find strategies that specifically combat social inequality without exacerbating environmental destruction. Given that these countries are responsible for the majority of resource use and greenhouse gas emissions, it is crucial to consider the environmental consequences of inequality reductions.

When it comes to designing these policies, the literature discussed in this article can help identify important features, as well as measures to avoid. On the one hand, the findings regarding the diminishing marginal propensity to emit point towards the danger of using progressive taxation to exclusively boost households' disposable income in lower- and especially middle-income brackets. Instead, using a share of the revenues for environmental protection, sustainable infrastructure and clean technologies could contribute to weakening the trade-off between inequality and environmental degradation. In addition, a variety of public investments can increase well-being without relying on economic gains and resource use—education, healthcare, social protection and community services, accessibility, or culture and arts can significantly curb welfare for the entire population.

On the other hand, policymakers could aim to strengthen the pathways leading from higher equality to better environmental outcomes. By making use of the social pathway, for instance, investments in procedural fairness, public goods and civic infrastructure could be used to restore a sense of solidarity and trust, which can increase support for sustainable policies as well.

Taken together, this chapter has shown that global income disparities and environmental degradation are not separate crises, but that the path to sustainable development is shaped by political, economic and social consequences of inequality. Whether this path is enhanced or impeded by narrowing the income gap depends on a variety of factors. Some of these factors are known and explored, others are yet to be identified.

The chapter has presented a synthesis of existing research on the links between inequality and the environment. Although the literature on this topic is expanding, many of the underlying dynamics remain unclear. Further investigation is needed to develop more robust policy guidance on managing trade-offs and enhancing synergies between inequality reduction and environmental protection. Only by designing policies that deliberately align distributional fairness with environmental protection can we achieve equity, well-being, and a livable planet for all.

References

Adger, W. N., Huq, S., Brown, K., Conway, D., & Hulme, M. (2003). Adaptation to climate change in the developing world. *Progress in Development Studies*, 3(3), 179–195. https://doi.org/10.1191/1464993403ps060oa

Baek, J., & Gweisah, G. (2013). Does income inequality harm the environment?: Empirical evidence from the United States. *Energy Policy*, 62, 1434–1437. https://doi.org/10.1016/j.enpol.2013.07.097

Baležentis, T., Liobikienė, G., Štreimikienė, D., & Sun, K. (2020). The impact of income inequality on consumption-based greenhouse gas emissions at the global level: A partially linear approach. *Journal of Environmental Management*, 267, 110635. https://doi.org/10.1016/j.jenvman.2020.110635

Baloch, M. A. & Danish. (2022). The nexus between renewable energy, income inequality, and consumption-based CO2 emissions: An empirical investigation. *Sustainable Development*, *30*(5), 1268–1277. https://doi.org/10.1002/sd.2315

Baloch, M. A., Danish, Khan, S. U.-D., Ulucak, Z. Ş., & Ahmad, A. (2020). Analyzing the relationship between poverty, income inequality, and CO2 emission in Sub-Saharan African countries. *Science of The Total Environment*, *740*, 139867. https://doi.org/10.1016/j.scitotenv.2020.139867

Barbier, E. B., & Hochard, J. P. (2018). The Impacts of Climate Change on the Poor in Disadvantaged Regions. *Review of Environmental Economics and Policy*, *12*(1), 26–47. https://doi.org/10.1093/reep/rex023

Barrett, C. B., Travis, A. J., & Dasgupta, P. (2011). On biodiversity conservation and poverty traps. *Proceedings of the National Academy of Sciences*, *108*(34), 13907–13912. https://doi.org/10.1073/pnas.1011521108

Bengtsson, E., & Waldenström, D. (2018). Capital Shares and Income Inequality: Evidence from the Long Run. *The Journal of Economic History*, *78*(3), 712–743. https://doi.org/10.1017/S0022050718000347

Berthe, A., & Elie, L. (2015). Mechanisms explaining the impact of economic inequality on environmental deterioration. *Ecological Economics*, *116*, 191–200. https://doi.org/10.1016/j.ecolecon.2015.04.026

Bertrand, M., & Morse, A. (2016). Trickle-Down Consumption. *The Review of Economics and Statistics*, *98*(5), 863–879. https://doi.org/10.1162/REST_a_00613

Bjelle, E. L., Wiebe, K. S., Többen, J., Tisserant, A., Ivanova, D., Vita, G., & Wood, R. (2021). Future changes in consumption: The income effect on greenhouse gas emissions. *Energy Economics*, *95*, 105114. https://doi.org/10.1016/j.eneco.2021.105114

Bowles, S., & Park, Y. (2005). Emulation, Inequality, and Work Hours: Was Thorsten Veblen Right? *The Economic Journal*, *115*(507), F397–F412. https://doi.org/10.1111/j.1468-0297.2005.01042.x

Boyce, J. K. (1994). Inequality as a cause of environmental degradation. *Ecological Economics*, *11*(3), 169–178. https://doi.org/10.1016/0921-8009(94)90198-8

Boyce, J. K., Klemer, A. R., Templet, P. H., & Willis, C. E. (1999). Power distribution, the environment, and public health: A state-level analysis. *Ecological Economics*, *29*(1), 127–140.

Bruckner, B., Hubacek, K., Shan, Y., Zhong, H., & Feng, K. (2022). Impacts of poverty alleviation on national and global carbon emissions. *Nature Sustainability*, *5*(4), 311–320. https://doi.org/10.1038/s41893-021-00842-z

Calvin, K., Dasgupta, D., Krinner, G., Mukherji, A., Thorne, P. W., Trisos, C., Romero, J., Aldunce, P., Barrett, K., Blanco, G., Cheung, W. W. L., Connors, S., Denton, F., Diongue-Niang, A., Dodman, D., Garschagen, M., Geden, O., Hayward, B., Jones, C., … Péan, C. (2023). *IPCC, 2023: Climate Change 2023: Synthesis Report. Contribution of Working Groups I, II and III to the Sixth Assessment Report of the Intergovernmental Panel on Climate Change [Core Writing Team, H. Lee and J. Romero (eds.)]. IPCC, Geneva, Switzerland.* (First). Intergovernmental Panel on Climate Change (IPCC). https://doi.org/10.59327/IPCC/AR6-9789291691647

Campbell, J. L., & Pedersen, O. K. (2014). *The National Origins of Policy Ideas: Knowledge Regimes in the United States, France, Germany, and Denmark*. Princeton University Press. https://www.jstor.org/stable/j.ctt5hhrcq

Ceddia, M. G. (2019). The impact of income, land, and wealth inequality on agricultural expansion in Latin America. *Proceedings of the National Academy of Sciences of the United States of America*, *116*(7), 2527–2532. https://doi.org/10.1073/pnas.1814894116

Chancel, L. (2022). Global carbon inequality over 1990–2019. *Nature Sustainability*, *5*(11), 931–938.
https://doi.org/10.1038/s41893-022-00955-z

Chen, J., Xian, Q., Zhou, J., & Li, D. (2020). Impact of income inequality on CO2 emissions in G20 countries. *Journal of Environmental Management*, *271*, 110987. https://doi.org/10.1016/j.jenvman.2020.110987

Clement, M., & Meunie, A. (2010). Is Inequality Harmful for the Environment? An Empirical Analysis Applied to Developing and Transition Countries. *Review of Social Economy*, *68*(4), 413–445. https://doi.org/10.1080/00346760903480590

Cole-Hunter, T., Donaire-Gonzalez, D., Curto, A., Ambros, A., Valentin, A., Garcia-Aymerich, J., Martínez, D., Braun, L. M., Mendez, M., Jerrett, M., Rodriguez, D., de Nazelle, A., & Nieuwenhuijsen, M. (2015). Objective correlates and determinants of bicycle commuting propensity in an urban environment. *Transportation Research Part D: Transport and Environment*, *40*, 132–143. https://doi.org/10.1016/j.trd.2015.07.004

Dee, T. S. (2004). Are there civic returns to education? *Journal of Public Economics*, *88*(9), 1697–1720. https://doi.org/10.1016/j.jpubeco.2003.11.002

DellaVigna, S., & Kaplan, E. (2007). The Fox News Effect: Media Bias and Voting*. *The Quarterly Journal of Economics*, *122*(3), 1187–1234. https://doi.org/10.1162/qjec.122.3.1187

Dimitri, C., & Dettmann, R. L. (2012). Organic food consumers: What do we really know about them? *British Food Journal*, *114*(8), 1157–1183. https://doi.org/10.1108/00070701211252101

Drescher, K., Fessler, P., & Lindner, P. (2020). Helicopter money in Europe: New evidence on the marginal propensity to consume across European households. *Economics Letters*, *195*, 109416. https://doi.org/10.1016/j.econlet.2020.109416

Druckman, A., & Jackson, T. (2016). Understanding households as drivers of carbon emissions. In *Taking stock of industrial ecology* (pp. 181–203). Springer International Publishing Cham.

Ehigiamusoe, K. U., Majeed, M. T., & Dogan, E. (2022). The nexus between poverty, inequality and environmental pollution: Evidence across different income groups of countries. *Journal of Cleaner Production*, *341*, 130863. https://doi.org/10.1016/j.jclepro.2022.130863

Ekeocha, D. O. (2021). Urbanization, inequality, economic development and ecological footprint: Searching for turning points and regional homogeneity in Africa. *Journal of Cleaner Production*, *291*, 125244. https://doi.org/10.1016/j.jclepro.2020.125244

Engler, S., & Weisstanner, D. (2021). The threat of social decline: Income inequality and radical right support. *Journal of European Public Policy*, *28*(2), 153–173. https://doi.org/10.1080/13501763.2020.1733636

Evans, S., & Viisainen, V. (2023). Revealed: How Colonial Rule Radically Shifts Historical Responsibility for Climate Change. *Carbon Brief. November*. https://www.carbonbrief.org/revealed-how-colonial-rule-radically-shifts-historical-responsibility-for-climate-change/

Fajnzylber, P., Lederman, D., & Loayza, N. (2002). Inequality and Violent Crime. *The Journal of Law & Economics*, *45*(1), 1–39. https://doi.org/10.1086/338347

Fassnacht, M., & Dahm, J.-M. (2021). Growing luxury brands by increasing the price: Does the Veblen effect exist? *Luxury Research Journal*, *2*(1–2), 99–139. https://doi.org/10.1504/LRJ.2021.116292

Fligstein, N., Hastings, O. P., & Goldstein, A. (2017). Keeping up with the Joneses: How Households Fared in the Era of High Income Inequality and the Housing Price Bubble, 1999–2007. *Socius*, *3*, 2378023117722330. https://doi.org/10.1177/2378023117722330

Fuller, R., Landrigan, P. J., Balakrishnan, K., Bathan, G., Bose-O'Reilly, S., Brauer, M., Caravanos, J., Chiles, T., Cohen, A., Corra, L., Cropper, M., Ferraro, G., Hanna, J., Hanrahan, D., Hu, H., Hunter, D., Janata, G., Kupka, R., Lanphear, B., ... Yan, C. (2022). Pollution and health: A progress update. *The Lancet Planetary Health*, 6(6), e535–e547. https://doi.org/10.1016/S2542-5196(22)00090-0

Gilens, M., & Page, B. I. (2014). Testing Theories of American Politics: Elites, Interest Groups, and Average Citizens. *Perspectives on Politics*, 12(3), 564–581. https://doi.org/10.1017/S1537592714001595

Gregorio, J. D., & Lee, J. (2002). Education and Income Inequality: New Evidence From Cross-Country Data. *Review of Income and Wealth*, 48(3), 395–416. https://doi.org/10.1111/1475-4991.00060

Grinblatt, M., Keloharju, M., & Ikäheimo, S. (2008). Social Influence and Consumption: Evidence from the Automobile Purchases of Neighbors. *The Review of Economics and Statistics*, 90(4), 735–753. https://doi.org/10.1162/rest.90.4.735

Grunewald, N., Klasen, S., Martínez-Zarzoso, I., & Muris, C. (2017). The Trade-off Between Income Inequality and Carbon Dioxide Emissions. *Ecological Economics*, 142, 249–256. https://doi.org/10.1016/j.ecolecon.2017.06.034

Harring, N., & Jagers, S. C. (2013). Should We Trust in Values? Explaining Public Support for Pro-Environmental Taxes. *Sustainability*, 5(1), 210–227. https://doi.org/10.3390/su5010210

Heerink, N., Mulatu, A., & Bulte, E. (2001). Income inequality and the environment: Aggregation bias in environmental Kuznets curves. *Ecological Economics*, 38(3), 359–367. https://doi.org/10.1016/S0921-8009(01)00171-9

Holtz-Eakin, D., & Selden, T. M. (1995). Stoking the fires? CO2 emissions and economic growth. *Journal of Public Economics*, 57(1), 85–101. https://doi.org/10.1016/0047-2727(94)01449-X

Hübler, M. (2017). The inequality-emissions nexus in the context of trade and development: A quantile regression approach. *Ecological Economics*, 134, 174–185. https://doi.org/10.1016/j.ecolecon.2016.12.015

Islam, S. N. (2015). *Inequality and environmental sustainability*. United Nations.

Ivanova, D., Stadler, K., Steen-Olsen, K., Wood, R., Vita, G., Tukker, A., & Hertwich, E. G. (2016). Environmental Impact Assessment of Household Consumption. *Journal of Industrial Ecology*, 20(3), 526–536. https://doi.org/10.1111/jiec.12371

Jorgenson, A., Schor, J., & Huang, X. (2017). Income Inequality and Carbon Emissions in the United States: A State-level Analysis, 1997–2012. *Ecological Economics*, *134*, 40–48. https://doi.org/10.1016/j.ecolecon.2016.12.016

Josiassen, A., & George Assaf, A. (2013). Look at me—I am flying: The influence of social visibility of consumption on tourism decisions. *Annals of Tourism Research*, 40, 155–175. https://doi.org/10.1016/j.annals.2012.08.007

Kasser, T. (2003). *The high price of materialism*. MIT press.

Kasuga, H., & Takaya, M. (2017). Does inequality affect environmental quality? Evidence from major Japanese cities. *Journal of Cleaner Production*, *142*, 3689–3701. https://doi.org/10.1016/j.jclepro.2016.10.099

Kazemzadeh, E., Fuinhas, J. A., & Koengkan, M. (2022). The impact of income inequality and economic complexity on ecological footprint: An analysis covering a long-time span. *Journal of Environmental Economics and Policy*, *11*(2), 133–153. https://doi.org/10.1080/21606544.2021.1930188

Khan, A. Q., Saleem, N., & Fatima, S. T. (2018). Financial development, income inequality, and CO2 emissions in Asian countries using STIRPAT model. *Environmental Science and Pollution Research*, *25*(7), 6308–6319. https://doi.org/10.1007/s11356-017-0719-2

Khan, S., & Yahong, W. (2022). Income inequality, ecological footprint, and carbon dioxide emissions in Asian developing economies: What effects what and how? *Environmental Science and Pollution Research*, *29*(17), 24660–24671. https://doi.org/10.1007/s11356-021-17582-4

Khan, S., Yahong, W., & Zeeshan, A. (2022). Impact of poverty and income inequality on the ecological footprint in Asian developing economies: Assessment of Sustainable Development Goals. *Energy Reports*, *8*, 670–679. https://doi.org/10.1016/j.egyr.2021.12.001

Kilbourne, W., & Pickett, G. (2008). How materialism affects environmental beliefs, concern, and environmentally responsible behavior. *Journal of Business Research*, *61*(9), 885–893. https://doi.org/10.1016/j.jbusres.2007.09.016

Kollmuss, A., & Agyeman, J. (2002). Mind the gap: Why do people act environmentally and what are the barriers to pro-environmental behavior? *Environmental Education Research*, *8*(3), 239–260. https://doi.org/10.1080/13504620220145401

Kumhof, M., Rancière, R., & Winant, P. (2015). Inequality, Leverage, and Crises. *American Economic Review*, *105*(3), 1217–1245. https://doi.org/10.1257/aer.20110683

Leach, M., Reyers, B., Bai, X., Brondizio, E. S., Cook, C., Díaz, S., Espindola, G., Scobie, M., Stafford-Smith, M., & Subramanian, S. M. (2018). Equity and sustainability in the Anthropocene: A social–ecological systems perspective on their intertwined futures. *Global Sustainability*, *1*, e13. https://doi.org/10.1017/sus.2018.12

Liu, C., Jiang, Y., & Xie, R. (2019). Does income inequality facilitate carbon emission reduction in the US? *Journal of Cleaner Production*, *217*, 380–387. https://doi.org/10.1016/j.jclepro.2019.01.242

Mader, S. (2018). The nexus between social inequality and CO2 emissions revisited: Challenging its empirical validity. *Environmental Science & Policy*, *89*, 322–329. https://doi.org/10.1016/j.envsci.2018.08.009

Maestre-Andrés, S., Drews ,Stefan, & and van den Bergh, J. (2019). Perceived fairness and public acceptability of carbon pricing: A review of the literature. *Climate Policy*, *19*(9), 1186–1204. https://doi.org/10.1080/14693062.2019.1639490

Meyer, A. (2015). Does education increase pro-environmental behavior? Evidence from Europe. *Ecological Economics*, *116*, 108–121. https://doi.org/10.1016/j.ecolecon.2015.04.018

Milanovic, B. (2024). The three eras of global inequality, 1820–2020 with the focus on the past thirty years. *World Development*, *177*, 106516. https://doi.org/10.1016/j.worlddev.2023.106516

OECD. (2025). *Government at a Glance 2025*. OECD Publishing. https://doi.org/10.1787/0efd0bcd-en

O'Neill, M. (2020). Power, Predistribution, and Social Justice. *Philosophy*, *95*(1), 63–91. https://doi.org/10.1017/S0031819119000482

Persson, J., Eriksson, C., & Mobäck, R. (2023). Does income inequality worsen pollution? The GEMS air pollution data revisited. *Journal of Cleaner Production*, *422*, 138478. https://doi.org/10.1016/j.jclepro.2023.138478

Pickett, K. E., & Wilkinson, R. G. (2015). Income inequality and health: A causal review. *Social Science & Medicine*, *128*, 316–326. https://doi.org/10.1016/j.socscimed.2014.12.031

Popiel, P. (2018). The Tech Lobby: Tracing the Contours of New Media Elite Lobbying Power. *Communication, Culture and Critique*, *11*(4), 566–585. https://doi.org/10.1093/ccc/tcy027

Power, M., Wilkinson, R., & Pickett, K. (2016). 37. Inequality, economic democracy and sustainability. *World Social Science Report*, 160.

Ravallion, M., Heil, M., & Jalan, J. (2000). Carbon emissions and income inequality. *Oxford Economic Papers*, *52*(4), 651–669. https://doi.org/10.1093/oep/52.4.651

Richardson, K., Steffen, W., Lucht, W., Bendtsen, J., Cornell, S. E., Donges, J. F., Drüke, M., Fetzer, I., Bala, G., von Bloh, W., Feulner, G., Fiedler, S., Gerten, D., Gleeson, T., Hofmann, M., Huiskamp, W., Kummu, M., Mohan, C., Nogués-Bravo, D., … Rockström, J. (2023). Earth beyond six of nine planetary boundaries. *Science Advances*, *9*(37), eadh2458. https://doi.org/10.1126/sciadv.adh2458

Ritchie, H. (2019). Who has contributed most to global CO2 emissions? *Our World in Data*. https://ourworldindata.org/contributed-most-global-co2

Rojas-Vallejos, J., & Lastuka, A. (2020). The income inequality and carbon emissions trade-off revisited. *Energy Policy*, *139*, 111302. https://doi.org/10.1016/j.enpol.2020.111302

Rothstein, B., & Uslaner, E. M. (2005). All for All: Equality, Corruption, and Social Trust. *World Politics*, *58*(1), 41–72. https://doi.org/10.1353/wp.2006.0022

Schumacher, I. (2014). An Empirical Study of the Determinants of Green Party Voting. *Ecological Economics*, *105*, 306–318. https://doi.org/10.1016/j.ecolecon.2014.05.007

Scruggs, L. A. (1998). Political and economic inequality and the environment. *Ecological Economics*, *26*(3), 259–275. https://doi.org/10.1016/S0921-8009(97)00118-3

Stiglitz, J. E. (2015). *Rewriting the rules of the American economy: An agenda for growth and shared prosperity*. WW Norton & Company.

Tam, K.-P., & Chan, H.-W. (2018). Generalized trust narrows the gap between environmental concern and pro-environmental behavior: Multilevel evidence. *Global Environmental Change*, *48*, 182–194. https://doi.org/10.1016/j.gloenvcha.2017.12.001

Torras, M., & Boyce, J. K. (1998). Income, inequality, and pollution: A reassessment of the environmental Kuznets curve. *Ecological Economics*, *25*(2), 147–160.

Uzar, U., & Eyuboglu, K. (2023). Does income inequality increase the ecological footprint in the US: Evidence from FARDL test? *Environmental Science and Pollution Research*, *30*(4), 9514–9529. https://doi.org/10.1007/s11356-022-22844-w

Veblen, T. (with Project Gutenberg). (1899). *Theory of the Leisure Class*. http://archive.org/details/theoryoftheleisu00833gut

Vesely, S., Klöckner, C. A., & Brick, C. (2020). Pro-environmental behavior as a signal of cooperativeness: Evidence from a social dilemma experiment.

Journal of Environmental Psychology, 67, 101362. https://doi.org/10.1016/j.jenvp.2019.101362
Wackernagel, M., & Lin, D. (2023). Ecological Footprint. In N. Wallenhorst & C. Wulf (Eds), *Handbook of the Anthropocene: Humans between Heritage and Future* (pp. 585–590). Springer International Publishing. https://doi.org/10.1007/978-3-031-25910-4_93
Wan, G., Wang, C., Wang, J., & Zhang, X. (2022). The income inequality-CO2 emissions nexus: Transmission mechanisms. *Ecological Economics, 195*, 107360. https://doi.org/10.1016/j.ecolecon.2022.107360
Wang, F., Yang, J., Shackman, J., & Liu, X. (2021). Impact of Income Inequality on Urban Air Quality: A Game Theoretical and Empirical Study in China. *International Journal of Environmental Research and Public Health, 18*(16), 8546. https://doi.org/10.3390/ijerph18168546
Watson, R., Baste, I., Larigauderie, A., Leadley, P., Pascual, U., Baptiste, B., Demissew, S., Dziba, L., Erpul, G., & Fazel, A. (2019). Summary for policymakers of the global assessment report on biodiversity and ecosystem services of the Intergovernmental Science-Policy Platform on Biodiversity and Ecosystem Services. *IPBES Secretariat: Bonn, Germany*, 22–47.
WID. (2025). *Gini index of national income*. World Inequality Database. https://wid.world/
Wilkinson, R. G., Pickett, K. E., & Vogli, R. D. (2010). Equality, sustainability, and quality of life. *BMJ, 341*, c5816. https://doi.org/10.1136/bmj.c5816
Wolde-Rufael, Y., & Idowu, S. (2017). Income distribution and CO2 emission: A comparative analysis for China and India. *Renewable and Sustainable Energy Reviews, 74*, 1336–1345. https://doi.org/10.1016/j.rser.2016.11.149
Wu, R., & Xie, Z. (2020). Identifying the impacts of income inequality on CO2 emissions: Empirical evidences from OECD countries and non-OECD countries. *Journal of Cleaner Production, 277*, 123858. https://doi.org/10.1016/j.jclepro.2020.123858
Yang, B., Ali, M., Hashmi, S. H., & Jahanger, A. (2022). Do Income Inequality and Institutional Quality affect CO2 Emissions in Developing Economies? *Environmental Science and Pollution Research, 29*(28), 42720–42741. https://doi.org/10.1007/s11356-021-18278-5
Zheng, W., Gao, Y., & Xi, J. (2025). When Does Generalized Trust Promote Pro-Environmental Behavior? A Multilevel Analysis. *Scandinavian Journal of Psychology, 66*(4), 571–577. https://doi.org/10.1111/sjop.13102
Zsóka, Á., Szerényi, Z. M., Széchy, A., & Kocsis, T. (2013). Greening due to environmental education? Environmental knowledge, attitudes, consumer

behavior and everyday pro-environmental activities of Hungarian high school and university students. *Journal of Cleaner Production*, *48*, 126–138. https://doi.org/10.1016/j.jclepro.2012.11.030

Individual-Level Predictors of Climate Misinformation Susceptibility

Marvin Fendt[1], *Fabian Reinwarth*[2] *and Peter Adriaan Edelsbrunner*[3]

Abstract: *Misinformation poses a substantial challenge for consensus on critical issues like climate change. While research has identified numerous psychological drivers of misinformation susceptibility, the interplay between belief systems, knowledge, and deliberation may benefit from further investigations. This study (N = 675) investigates these factors to better understand individual differences in judging and sharing climate-related information. Participants reported their manipulation judgement, sharing intentions, and analytic thinking for posts that contained manipulation strategies (ad hominem attacks, false dichotomies, cherry-picking data, setting impossible expectations, pseudo-experts) and credible control posts. Participants also reported predictors including political opinion, conspiracy thinking, climate knowledge, and persuasion knowledge (i.e. awareness of persuasive attempts). Using Bayesian regression models, we found that, while our participants were generally better at identifying manipulative than credible content, a more progressive political opinion, higher formal education, higher climate knowledge, and higher persuasion knowledge were associated with better sharing decisions, better manipulation judgements, and more analytic thinking.*

1 Marvin Fendt and Peter Adriaan Edelsbrunner: Department of Psychology, Ludwig Maximilian University of Munich; The authors have no conflict of interest. Correspondence concerning this article should be addressed to Marvin Fendt, Department of Educational Psychology, Ludwig Maximilian University, Leopoldstr. 13, D-80802 München, Email: marvin.fendt@psy.lmu.de.

2 Fabian Reinwarth: Chair of Educational Psychology, Technical University of Munich. The author has no conflict of interest.

3 Marvin Fendt and Peter Adriaan Edelsbrunner: Department of Psychology, Ludwig Maximilian University of Munich; The authors have no conflict of interest. Correspondence concerning this article should be addressed to Marvin Fendt, Department of Educational Psychology, Ludwig Maximilian University, Leopoldstr. 13, D-80802 München, Email: marvin.fendt@psy.lmu.de.

Findings on the Big Five personality traits were mixed with less agreeable participants making better sharing decisions and less conscientious participants engaging more in analytic thought. While we found that longer deliberation times were connected to more analytic thinking, they were not credibly associated with manipulation judgments and even slightly worse average sharing decisions. These findings support the idea that for polarized topics such as climate change, belief may be at least as important as objective knowledge. Interventions should address the complex interplay between identity, beliefs, knowledge, and deliberation.

1. Introduction

The Internet is a rich repository of curious, harmless, and valuable content, but it is also home to malicious actors propagating falsehoods to manipulate unsuspecting recipients (Kbaier et al., 2024). Misinformation can often outpace countermeasures, such as fact-checking, which take time to produce and distribute (Roozenbeek et al., 2022). Misconceptions derived from misinformation range from harmless inaccuracies to drivers of notable problems, including undesirable behaviors, increased polarization, and distrust in science and credible institutions (Cook et al., 2023; Van Bavel et al., 2024). Misinformation therefore poses a substantial societal challenge that necessitates a multidisciplinary response to mitigate its impact (Kozyreva et al., 2024).

Climate change misinformation presents a peculiar case: Climate change is a complex, high-stakes scientific issue that has been targeted by organized, well-funded disinformation campaigns for decades (Herasimenka et al., 2025). However, most citizens do no longer believe outright climate denial (Leiserowitz et al., 2025). Disinformation campaigns have therefore moved from denial to delay, strategically exploiting the inherent uncertainties of scientific modeling and public discourse to sow doubt, confuse the public, and ultimately delay or prevent policy action (Lamb et al., 2020). Exposure to misleading information, such as cherry-picked statistics, can lower public support for climate mitigation policies (Cook, 2022).

Belief in climate misinformation is not an isolated fallacy but often entrenched in a broader belief system (Ziegler, 2017). Therefore, this cross-sectional study aims to investigate the individual drivers of belief in climate change misinformation. We focus on conspiracy beliefs (Uscinski et al., 2017), climate knowledge (Visschers, 2018), skepticism towards persuasive attempts (Fendt, Scheibenzuber, et al., 2025), and analytic thinking (Pennycook & Rand,

2019). Furthermore, we explore the ongoing debate over whether judging falsehoods and detecting credible information are two distinct processes (Kiili et al., 2023) or one overarching process (Pennycook et al., 2024).

2. Theoretical Framework

Misinformation refers to any false or inaccurate information, including errors, misunderstandings, or unverified content, that people may create and share (Ecker et al., 2022). Unlike disinformation, which is deliberately deceptive, misinformation can arise innocently or unintentionally. While some types of misinformation arguably cause little harm, such as hoaxes by satirical outlets, disinformation can have devastating impact on societies (Abudu et al., 2023). Although the content examined in this study largely qualifies as disinformation, we use the broader term "misinformation" because it is often difficult to undoubtedly prove a spreader's intent to deceive.

While high-quality information often requires time for thorough quality control and states the limitations of current knowledge, misinformation often presents holistic solutions quickly (Ecker et al., 2022). Consequently, misinformation can spread quickly in situations of uncertainty, where countermeasures and high-quality information have yet to be implemented (Van Der Linden, 2022). Since it is impossible to reach the entire audience of initial misinformation with debunking, research has also focused on measures to prevent and slow the spread of misinformation by reducing the intention to share (Roozenbeek et al., 2022). While spreading misinformation can have monetary benefits, ideological motives, like sowing social discord, are arguably a larger threat to society (Bakir & McStay, 2018; Lazer et al., 2018).

Misinformation can be found about the same topics as credible information, including but not limited to health, politics, nutrition, and climate change (Ecker et al., 2022). If people are exposed to misinformation, they may develop false beliefs that range from simple misconceptions to the outright rejection of factual evidence. Climate change misinformation is a well-researched example where disinformation campaigns have increased polarization and opposition to climate change policies (Lamb et al., 2020; Ziegler, 2017). While research argues that belief in misinformation does not necessitate undesirable actions, there have been numerous incidents where misinformation has sparked resistance to renewable energy projects like wind turbines (Winter et al., 2022).

Beyond defining misinformation, a central challenge in its study is how to conceptualize and measure an individual's susceptibility to it.

Research has debated whether *discriminating information quality* should be conceptualized as an overarching ability (e.g. Roozenbeek et al., 2022), two distinct processes (e.g. Fendt et al., 2023), or something else (Tay et al., 2024). An overarching credibility discernment score that indicates a tendency to trust credible information and distrust dubious information is compelling and arguably easy to interpret—a higher score indicates greater tendency for a person to believe credible information over misinformation (Pennycook et al., 2024). However, discernment can also yield ambiguous results, because people who distrust all information would still receive a medium score, since they do not favor unreliable over credible information. Furthermore, discernment does not indicate whether people trust information too easily. Meta-analytic evidence by Sultan et al. (2024) illustrates this limitation: discernment ability appears to increase with age which originates from a lower level of trust in all information that is more pronounced for dubious than credible information. Conversely, more educated people seem to trust credible information disproportionately more than misinformation. And lastly, discernment, often scored by equally weighing credible and dubious information, may not resemble people's information diet that mainly leans towards credible information (Altay et al., 2023; Kbaier et al., 2024).

Separate scores on credible information and misinformation may be harder to interpret but come closer to recent findings that detecting credible and dubious information may be two separate processes (Fendt et al., 2023; Fendt, Scheibenzuber, et al., 2025; Kiili et al., 2023). However, dichotomously categorizing information may still not capture the nuances of real-world misinformation that often uses ambiguous language, greyscales, and logical fallacies instead of presenting outright falsehoods (Lazer et al., 2018; Tay et al., 2024). Apart from the theoretical lens through which belief in misinformation can be measured, individual characteristics are essential for identifying predictors of misinformation susceptibility.

Decades of research (e.g. Ecker et al., 2022; Sultan et al., 2024) have identified numerous factors, which we group into cognitive abilities, belief systems, and stable personal traits. Perhaps the most studied factors relate to how people think, including their tendency for analytical thought and their existing knowledge. Higher *analytic skills* are robustly associated with better credibility discernment (Sultan et al., 2024). Drawing from dual-process theories of cognition, individuals tend to either follow a route of analytic, slow, and motivated investigation or intuitive, fast, and unmotivated reception. According to this view, people often fall for misinformation because they rely on their initial, intuitive gut reactions (Bago et al., 2020; Pennycook & Rand, 2019). People mostly engage analytically with information if their intuitive flow is interrupted or if the information contradicts their beliefs or is utterly unbelievable (Schwarz et al., 2021). While intuitive assessments are fast and often reasonably accurate (Modirrousta-Galian et al., 2025), this unmotivated route can leave people prone to biases exploited by misinformation, as they rely on cognitive shortcuts based on familiarity or belief consistency (Ecker et al., 2022; Epstein et al., 2023). The analytical path requires high motivation and cognitive resources to scrutinize claims and sources (Fendt, Muth, et al., 2025; Swami et al., 2014). This can also be indicated by the *time taken to reflect* on information credibility, which can notably improve the accuracy of credibility assessments (Fazio, 2020).

In general, studies have found a relationship between higher *content knowledge* and the ability to correctly judge the credibility of information in that domain (Fendt, Scheibenzuber, et al., 2025; Flanagin et al., 2020; Lucassen et al., 2013). However, recent studies have yielded mixed findings on the protective role of knowledge on politicized topics such as climate change (Ecker et al., 2022; Edelson et al., 2024). In other words, people with higher science literacy and education may not be the most concerned about climate change (Kahan et al., 2012). Formal education may also serve as an indicator of prior knowledge, again without a credible relationship (Sultan et al., 2024). Knowledge and education may not be neutral tools, but instead serve primarily to effectively seek out, interpret, and argue for evidence that supports a person's pre-existing position on politicized topics. In some cases prior knowledge may even be counterproductive if misinformation blends novel, false claims with known, correct claims (Benegal & Scruggs, 2018).

While cognitive style explains *how* people process information, their pre-existing belief systems often determine *why* they accept or reject it, particularly for politicized topics (Benegal & Scruggs, 2018; Compton et al., 2021; Faragó et al., 2023; Fendt, Scheibenzuber, et al., 2025). One such system is a person's *persuasion knowledge*. The process of reading misinformation can be conceptualized as an episode in which a malicious actor (persuader) tries to persuade a reader (recipient) of a claim (Cuteanu, 2024). Persuasion attempts are not exclusive to misinformation, but malicious actors often employ manipulative strategies such as logical fallacies or outright falsehoods, while credible actors mostly root their attempts in facts and logic (Arce, 2024; Cook et al., 2023). Over the course of their lives, people develop a lay theory of persuasion attempts, encompassing their tactics, goals, and agents. When people recognize such an attempt, persuasion knowledge is activated and triggers coping behaviors such as increased skepticism, critical evaluation, and counter-arguing (Eisend & Tarrahi, 2022). This is directly related to misinformation, where knowledge about the persuasive nature of malicious actors can help people remain skeptical of dubious information and resist persuasion attempts (Chen & Cheng, 2019).

Belief in *conspiracy theories* is another factor deeply intertwined with misinformation susceptibility (O'Mahony et al., 2023). Conspiracy theories offer holistic yet misleading explanations during times of uncertainty, often providing a false sense of control and closure in response to existential threats or stressful situations (Liekefett et al., 2023). They can also serve as a vehicle for social belonging by making people feel part of a knowledgeable in-group, often doubting the cognitive abilities and motives of the out-group (Bowes et al., 2023). Research has found that a conspiratorial mindset is one of the few factors that is consistently associated with general misinformation susceptibility, including both political and non-political content (Bowes et al., 2023). Their compelling nature makes conspiracy theories particularly persuasive and resistant to correction. As a result, a large fraction of the global population, including nearly half of the citizens in the United States of America, endorses at least one conspiracy theory, while few interventions can permanently reduce these beliefs (Oliver & Wood, 2014; Van Prooijen & Douglas, 2018; Walter & Drochon, 2022). As argued by Imhoff and Bertlich (2024), conspiratorial worldviews form a self-sealing belief system of epistemic distrust towards official sources (e.g. governments, science, and mainstream media) and trust in alternative, anti-establishment sources. This system is almost impossible to correct due to a deeply entrenched distrust in most correction institutions (Lewandowsky et al., 2013).

Finally, on politicized topics like climate change, an individual's *political opinion* and overarching worldview may be more influential determinants than cognitive abilities alone. For politicized information, the primary goal of information processing often shifts from determining credibility to affirming identity (Swire-Thompson et al., 2020). In general, if information is coherent with a person's political views, they are more likely to accept it as true, regardless of its actual credibility, as long as it is not utterly unbelievable (Sultan et al., 2024).

Stable characteristics such as demographics and core personality traits provide a context for an individual's susceptibility to misinformation. The influence of *demographic* variables is often more complex than popular narratives suggest. Several studies found that older people make worse overall sharing decisions but judge information credibility slightly better, mostly because of a higher skepticism towards information in general (Sultan et al., 2024). Contrary to common belief, most studies find no credible education effects, because even people involved in higher education are often susceptible to misinformation (Breakstone et al., 2021; Sultan et al., 2024). Lastly, most studies have not found a credible gender effect, even though some studies found that men may be more susceptible to climate misinformation due to a higher average climate susceptibility (Larzabal-Fernandez et al., 2025; Sultan et al., 2024).

When it comes to other stable characteristics, some explanations for why people fall prey to misinformation point to specific *personality traits*. The Big Five model is the most widely accepted model for personality traits, comprising the five factors of openness to experience, conscientiousness, extraversion, agreeableness, and neuroticism (John et al., 2012; Johnson, 2017). Openness to experience is the willingness to engage with new things and think outside the box. Conscientiousness is the tendency to be organized and plan carefully. Extraversion is the tendency to draw energy from social interactions and is characterized by sociability and assertiveness. Agreeableness is the tendency to be cooperative and considerate in interpersonal relationships. Neuroticism is characterized by emotional instability and a tendency toward negative emotions such as anxiety and stress. A review by Calvillo et al. (2024) found modest correlations between personality traits and a tendency for believing and sharing misinformation: Believing and sharing misinformation was associated with higher extraversion, lower conscientiousness and lower agreeableness, while higher neuroticism was associated with sharing misinformation. While ideology may primarily explain the motivation for believing and sharing misinformation, personality traits may better explain how people approach information in general.

3. Current Study

Building on the outlined theoretical framework, our present study aims to investigate the individual-level drivers of credibility judgments about climate change information. We focus on manipulative strategies as a measurable component of misinformation (similar to Cook et al., 2023). Specifically, we examine the ability to identify manipulative and credible content (manipulation discernment) and the willingness to share credible over manipulative content (sharing discernment). While analytic thinking is a known predictor of discernment, less is known about the individual factors that promote an analytical mindset. Therefore, we also examine analytic thinking as an outcome. We will assess the predictive power of several individual characteristics including demographic variables (age, gender, educational background), cognitive and belief-system factors (conspiracy thinking, persuasion knowledge, political opinion and prior content knowledge) and stable personality traits (the Big Five). We report discernment for clarity, but our formal hypotheses are tested by including an interaction on the trustworthiness of the content being evaluated (manipulative vs. credible).

Our investigation is guided by the following research questions:

Research Question 1: To what extent do demographic, cognitive, and belief-system factors predict participants' a) manipulation discernment, b) sharing discernment, and c) analytic thinking?

This question addresses the combined influence of our selected predictors on credibility assessment, sharing intention and analytic thinking. Given mixed findings on demographics, we expect that age will be positively associated with general skepticism but do not expect gender or education to be credible predictors of manipulation and sharing (Sultan et al., 2024). In line with robust evidence, we expect that higher conspiracy beliefs and lower analytic thinking will be associated with lower manipulation and sharing discernment (O'Mahony et al., 2023; Pennycook & Rand, 2019). Based on initial findings by Fendt et al. (2025), we expect that higher persuasion knowledge will be associated with better manipulation and sharing discernment. Finally, because climate change is a highly politicized topic where worldviews can supersede factual knowledge (Edelson et al., 2024; Flanagin et al., 2020; Swire-Thompson et al., 2020), we expect that more conservative political opinion will be associated with lower manipulation and sharing discernment, but that there will be no credible effect of content knowledge.

Research Question 2: What is the predictive power of the Big Five personality traits to explain a) manipulation discernment, b) sharing discernment, and c) analytic thinking?

While Research Question 1 (RQ1) primarily examines demographic, cognitive, and belief factors, this question focuses on the role of stable dispositional traits via the Big Five. Based on prior research (Calvillo et al., 2024), we expect that lower conscientiousness, indicating less thoroughness and lower agreeableness, indicating higher antagonism, will predict worse manipulation and sharing discernment.

Research Question 3: What is the predictive power of the time spent evaluating information to explain a) manipulation discernment, b) sharing discernment, and c) analytic thinking?

Drawing from dual-process theories that contrast fast, intuitive thinking with slow, deliberate thinking (Pennycook & Rand, 2019), we use the time participants spend on each judgment as a behavioral proxy for cognitive deliberation. This aligns with recent studies suggesting that misinformation susceptibility may be related to a failure to engage with information analytically (Bago et al., 2020). We therefore expect that individuals who spend more time evaluating information will better identify manipulative content and less likely share it.

To answer these questions, our study presented participants with eight synthetic social media posts. These posts either contained one of five manipulative strategies (false dichotomies, ad hominem attacks, cherry-picking data, setting impossible expectations, and pseudo-experts) or were presented as a non-manipulative control version. We calculate two of our primary outcomes, manipulation and sharing discernment, using scores of participants' ratings for manipulative and non-manipulative (control) social media posts (similar to Roozenbeek et al., 2022). The third outcome, analytic thinking, is operationalized as a sum of participants' self-reports of analytically assessing each stimulus. Our predictors for research question 1 are age, gender, conspiracy thinking (Uscinski et al., 2017), persuasion knowledge (Fendt, Scheibenzuber, et al., 2025), political opinion, and content knowledge (Visschers, 2018). To answer research question 2, we use the Big Five personality traits (Rammstedt et al., 2017) which were measured in only a subsample of $n = 224$ participants due to data loss. To answer research question 3, we will use the task time on each stimulus as the predictor variable, serving as a behavioral proxy of cognitive reflection. We will analyze the data in R using a multivariate Bayesian linear regression model for each research question.

4. Methods

This study employed a cross-sectional design to investigate the factors related to discerning and sharing online information. This study was approved by the university's ethics committee prior to data collection and preregistered as part of a larger project. All participants gave informed consent. Supplementary materials including analysis script and dataset are available on osf.io/rt6p8/.[4]

4.1 Participants

We collected 697 complete responses in a science museum in Southern Germany. We asked participants at the end of the study whether they had answered every question honestly and carefully, assuring them this would not result in any penalty, and excluded those who stated they had not ($n = 22$). This resulted in a final sample of $N = 675$ participants, spanning a wide age range from 9 to 80 years ($M = 33.67$, $SD = 15.51$). Gender distribution was balanced (53% male, 45% female, 1% non-binary). Most of the participants were involved in higher education (18% lower secondary education degree, 18% A-levels, 48% university degree, 7% PhD). Our sample size allowed us to detect a smallest predictor effect of $\beta = .03$ with either BF > 5 or BF < 0.5 with above 90% power. Due to unforeseen data loss, only 224 participants provided Big Five personality covariates. This subsample allowed us to detect a smallest predictor effect of $\beta = .10$ with either BF > 5 or BF < 0.5 with above 90% power.

4.2 Measures

Dependent variables are manipulation discernment, sharing discernment, and analytic thinking. Predictors are age, gender, political opinion, conspiracy thinking, persuasion knowledge, content knowledge, the Big Five personality traits, and trustworthiness. We report the raw scores for descriptive statistics but use the z-standardized scores in our analyses for easier interpretation.

Manipulation. Participants' ability to discern manipulative intent was assessed by randomly showing them 8 stimuli in a version that randomly either did or did not contain a manipulative strategy. Participants rated each post on a 7-point Likert scale from 1 = absolutely not manipulative to 7 = absolutely manipulative. We then summed the ratings on control items to a control score

4 Retrieved November 1, 2025.

and the reverse coded ratings of manipulative items to a misinformation score. That means, rating a manipulative item with a '7' (absolutely manipulative) contributed to a higher *misinformation score*, while rating a control item with a '1' (absolutely not manipulative) contributed to a higher *control score*. *Discernment* ($M = 0.98$, $SD = 1.64$) was calculated as the sum of the manipulative and the control score. A higher discernment score indicates a tendency to correctly judge whether information is manipulative or not (Roozenbeek et al., 2022). Our formal inferential test of discernment is modeled via an interaction term, as detailed in the Analysis section.

Sharing. Participants indicated for each post how likely they would share it (1 = absolutely not to 7 = absolutely). Ratings for misinformation and control posts were summed separately. *Discernment* ($M = 0.87$, $SD = 1.35$) was again calculated as the sum of the manipulative and the control score. That means, higher discernment indicates a tendency to share more trustworthy posts instead of manipulative ones. Again, our primary analysis tests this effect using an interaction term in the regression model.

Analytic thinking. Participants indicated for each post whether they had judged it intuitively (= 0) or analytically (= 1). The answers were then summed ($M = 5.31$, $SD = 2.11$), with higher scores indicating more analytic verdicts and lower scores indicating more intuitive judgments.

Predictor variables. We measured age, gender (female, male, non-binary), political opinion, conspiracy thinking, content knowledge, the Big Five personality traits, and trustworthiness as covariates. We measured *political opinion* ($M = 3.49$, $SD = 1.29$) with a single item on a 7-point Likert scale (1 = very progressive to 7 = very conservative). We assessed participants' *climate knowledge* ($M = 15.91$, $SD = 2.63$, $\omega = .74$), on a 4-item scale by Visschers (2018) with 5-point Likert responses (1 = totally disagree, 5 = totally agree). We measured *conspiracy thinking* on a 4-item scale by Uscinski et al. (2017) with 5-point Likert responses (1 = totally agree, 5 = totally disagree) that were then summed ($M = 14.48$, $SD = 3.81$, $\omega = .84$). We measured *persuasion knowledge*, which we conceptualize as participants' knowledge of persuasive attempts by misinformation creators, on a short scale derived from Fendt et al. (2025) with 5 items on a 7-point Likert scale (1 = totally disagree, 7 = totally agree), which were then scored ($M = 25.25$, $SD = 6.05$, $\omega = .85$).

We recorded the *time* ($M = 15.07$, $SD = 16.51$) participants took to answer for each post, which we logarithmized due to a right-skew (4.45).

We included the *Big Five personality traits* using the 10-item scale by Rammstedt et al. (2017) with 2 items on a 5-point Likert scale, each for openness

($M = 4.72$, $SD = 1.97$, $\omega = .68$), conscientiousness ($M = 7.17$, $SD = 1.54$, $\omega = .40$), extraversion ($M = 6.33$, $SD = 1.70$, $\omega = .64$), agreeableness ($M = 5.90$, $SD = 1.57$, $\omega = .39$), and neuroticism ($M = 5.51$, $SD = 1.80$, $\omega = .64$).

4.3 Materials and Procedure

We administered the study via Qualtrics. Participants were recruited face-to-face by the researchers in a science museum in Southern Germany and participated voluntarily. After providing informed consent, participants provided demographic information. Then, participants saw 8 stimuli that were designed to look like social media posts (following the principles of Cook et al., 2023; Roozenbeek et al., 2022).

These posts (see Figure 1) either contained or did not contain one of five manipulative strategies: false dichotomies, ad hominem attacks, cherry-picking data, setting impossible expectations, and presenting pseudo-experts as credible sources.

- *False dichotomies* imply that only two options exist, often diametrically opposed, with one depicted as undesirable (e.g., "Either we save the climate or our hardworking citizens will lose their jobs and starve").
- *Ad hominem attacks* unfairly target an opponent's credibility instead of their argument, often implying hypocrisy (e.g., "You can't believe such a ridiculous-looking person").
- *Cherry-picking data* involves selecting only supportive cases, often favoring anecdotal evidence over statistics (e.g., "Climate change can't be that bad because there was still snow in the alps last winter").
- *Impossible expectations* set unattainable standards for proof (e.g., "I only believe in climate change, if 100% of the experts agree").
- *Pseudo-experts* are individuals with expertise in unrelated fields who use their academic titles to spread misinformation (e.g., someone with a PhD in computer science pretending to be a scientific expert in climate change).

Figure 1: Sample post containing a false dichotomy.

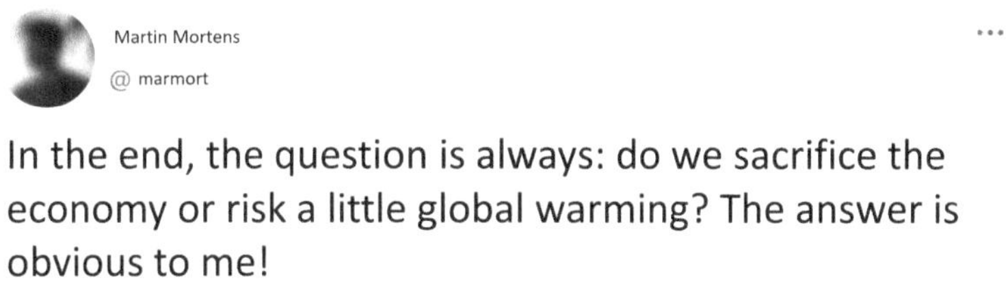

Note. The false dichotomy can be identified by only presenting two viable options (economy vs. climate). This technique is often accompanied by steering the audience towards the desired option (i.e., risk a little global warming).

These synthetic social media posts were randomly drawn from a pool of stimuli in a planned missing-data design following this procedure:

1) Each participant randomly saw stimuli related to two out of five manipulation strategies (false dichotomies, ad hominem arguments, cherry-picking, impossible expectations, pseudo-experts).
2) For each strategy, four out of six possible stimuli were randomly selected.
3) Each of these four posts was then randomly shown in a version that contained a manipulation strategy or the non-manipulative control version.

For each of the eight posts presented, participants indicated their manipulation rating, sharing intention, and analytic thinking. After seeing the stimuli, participants provided data for the covariates and feedback before they were debriefed.

To illustrate the randomization, we outline a hypothetical participant Adam. The randomizer selected that Adam receives posts that may contain false dichotomies or cherry-picking. The randomizer selected the cherry-picking posts 1, 3, 4, and 6. Adam receives post 1 in the misinformation version, which says: “If global warming really exists, why was last winter colder than the previous one?”. He rates the credibility of the post as absolutely not credible (1) and would never share such a post (7) based on his gut feeling (0). He would then receive the post 4 in a control version that says: “Ralf says he works a lot. I still think short breaks are important to stay as productive as possible”. Adam is fairly sure that this post does not contain a manipulative strategy (2) and would therefore potentially also share it (3), but still analytically thinkings whether the post contains a manipulative strategy (1). After filling out the cherry-picking posts, Adam fills out four posts that may contain false dichotomies to finally provide covariates and feedback. Since Adam said to have answered carefully and in good faith, we include his response in our analysis.

4.4 Analysis

All statistical analyses were conducted in R 4.5 using the brms 2.23 package. After scoring the individual scales, we z-standardized all continuous predictors and dependent variables prior to analysis, implying that the parameter estimates can be interpreted as effect sizes. We estimated a multivariate regression model for each research question using Bayesian statistics, which provides advantages in model estimation, but features parameters that can be interpreted like those in frequentist models (Edelsbrunner et al., 2024).

For research question 1, we estimated a multivariate multilevel regression model in which the dependent variables were the scores on credible and manipulative stimuli (manipulation, sharing, and analytic thinking), nested within participants. The multilevel structure allowed us to include scores akin to discernment as well as an interaction between trustworthiness and the predictors to assess whether judgment on credible and dubious stimuli might differ. The predictors were age, gender, political opinion, conspiracy thinking, persuasion knowledge, and content knowledge as well as their interaction with trustworthiness.

For research question 2, due to a misconfiguration of the platform the first two thirds of our participants did not see the Big Five covariates. Since imputing such a large percentage of missing variables would have greatly reduced the meaningfulness of the predictor estimates, we estimated a separate model for this partial sample (n = 224) that included the Big Five covariates but was otherwise identical to the previous one. We compared the demographics and performance of the subsample with our other participants to find no credible differences.

For research question 3, we estimated a model in which the ratings of individual posts (manipulation, sharing, and analytic thinking) were the dependent variables, nested for each participant. The predictors were the logarithmized task time and its interaction with trustworthiness.

For model estimation, we used four chains with 5,000 draws each (1,000 of which were treated as burn-in). We specified weakly informative priors, which are Student t-distributions with 3 degrees of freedom, locations of 0, and scales of 10 for variance parameters. All models converged without issues, indicated by $\hat{R} = 1.00$ for all parameters, no divergent transitions during estimation and visual inspection of posteriors (which were all strongly unimodal), and mixing in posterior trace plots.

Regarding *model interpretation*, we assessed overall model fit with a Bayesian R^2, which can be interpreted like the frequentist equivalent (R^2_{adj}). We interpret the medians of posterior distributions as parameter estimates. Because Bayesian models do not rely on *p* values, we instead examined highest density intervals, representing the range of parameter values covering the central 90% of the posterior (90% HDIs). If the 90% HDI does not include 0.00, we interpret this as evidence that the effect deviates from zero (Sorensen et al., 2016). While there is no scientific consensus on the range for reporting HDIs yet, we decided to use 90% intervals because recent research increasingly favors these intervals and they are also more reliable than 95% intervals (Edelsbrunner et al., 2024; McElreath, 2018).

5. Results

The **main model** (RQ1) for predictors of manipulation discernment ($R^2 = .226$), sharing discernment ($R^2 = .543$), and analytic thinking ($R^2 = .053$) explained a moderate amount of variance (see Table 1). Manipulation and sharing discernment correlated weakly, $r = .19$, $SE = .03$, manipulation discernment and analytic thinking, $r = .03$, $SE = .02$, as well as sharing discernment and analytic thinking, $r = .06$, $SE = .03$, shared no meaningful correlation.

Several individual characteristics were associated with better overall performance on *manipulation discernment*. Participants were better at identifying manipulative content than credible content, $\beta = -.99$. A more progressive political opinion, $\beta = -.08$, higher conspiracy thinking, $\beta = .09$, higher climate knowledge, $\beta = .12$, higher persuasion knowledge, $\beta = .08$, and higher formal education, $\beta = .05$, were associated with better manipulation discernment.

Higher *sharing discernment* was associated with a more progressive political opinion, $\beta = -.07$, higher conspiratory thinking, $\beta = .14$, more climate knowledge, $\beta = .05$, and more persuasion knowledge, $\beta = .07$.

More *analytic thinking* was associated with a more progressive political opinion, $\beta = -.05$, more climate knowledge, $\beta = .10$, more persuasion knowledge, $\beta = .08$, and higher formal education, $\beta = .03$.

We found several *interaction* effects. For manipulation discernment, there was an interaction between trustworthiness and climate knowledge, $\beta = -.11$, indicating that people with more climate knowledge were better at judging credible content than manipulative content. For sharing discernment, higher conspiracy thinking interacted with trustworthiness, $\beta = .11$, suggesting those high in conspiracism were better at making sharing decisions for manipulative content than for credible content. The interaction with climate knowledge was negative, $\beta = -0.24$, indicating that those with more knowledge were particularly better at making appropriate sharing decisions for credible content.

Table 1: Regression results of the main model.

	Manipulation			**Sharing**			Analytic Thinking		
Parameter	β	**SE**	**HDI**	β	**SE**	**HDI**	β	SE	HDI
Intercept	.61	.13	**[.40; .81]**	.79	.10	**[.63; .95]**	-.12	.14	[-.35; .11]
Trustworthiness	-.99	.14	**[-1.22; -.75]**	-1.79	.11	**[-1.97; -1.61]**	-.09	.16	[-.35; .17]
Political Opinion	-.08	.03	**[-.13; -.04]**	-.07	.02	**[-.10; -.03]**	-.05	.03	**[-.10; .00]**
Conspiracy Thinking	.09	.04	**[.03; .15]**	.14	.03	**[.09; .18]**	.02	.04	[-.05; .08]
Climate Knowledge	.12	.04	**[.06; .18]**	.05	.03	**[.01; .10]**	.10	.04	**[.04; .17]**
Persuasion Knowledge	.08	.04	**[.02; .14]**	.07	.03	**[.02; .11]**	.08	.04	**[.01; .14]**
Gender	.03	.05	[-.05; .10]	.01	.04	[-.04; .08]	-.02	.05	[-.10; .07]
Age	.00	.00	[-.01; -.00]	.00	.00	[.00; .01]	.00	.00	[.00; .01]
Education	.05	.02	**[.02; .07]**	.01	.01	[-.02; .03]	.03	.02	**[.01; .07]**
Trustworthiness * Political Opinion	.04	.04	[-.02; .10]	.11	.03	**[.06; .16]**	.01	.04	[-.05; .09]
Conspiracy Thinking	-.11	.05	**[-.20; -.02]**	-.24	.04	**[-.30; -.17]**	-.06	.06	[-.15; .03]
Climate Knowledge	-.08	.05	[-.17; .00]	-.03	.04	[-.10; .03]	-.04	.06	[-.13; .05]
Persuasion Knowledge	-.07	.05	[-.16; .01]	-.14	.04	**[-.21; -.08]**	.02	.06	[-.08; .11]
R^2	.226	.02		.543	.01		.053	.01	

Table 2: Regression results of the Big Five model.

	Manipulation			**Sharing**			**Analytic Thinking**		
Parameter	β	SE	HDI	β	SE	HDI	β	SE	HDI
Intercept	.77	.21	**[.43; 1.11]**	.85	.16	**[.59; 1.12]**	-.14	.26	[-.54; .29]
Trustworthiness	-1.02	.25	**[-1.45; -.64]**	-1.73	.19	**[-2.04; -1.42]**	.02	.30	[-.46; .51]
Political Opinion	-.08	.05	[-.16; .00]	-.04	.04	[-.10; .02]	-.10	.06	[-.19; .00]
Conspiracy Thinking	.08	.07	[-.03; .19]	.08	.05	**[.00; .17]**	-.07	.08	[-.20; .06]
Climate Knowledge	.14	.06	**[.05; .24]**	.06	.05	[-.02; .13]	.16	.07	**[.04; .28]**
Persuasion Knowledge	.04	.06	[-.06; .14]	.09	.05	**[.01; .16]**	.06	.07	[-.05; .18]
Gender	-.03	.08	[-.16; .10]	-.01	.06	[-.11; .09]	.01	.10	[-.15; .16]
Age	.00	.00	[-.01; .00]	.01	.00	[.00; .01]	.01	.00	[.00; .01]
Education	.05	.03	**[.00; .10]**	-.04	.02	**[-.07; -.00]**	.05	.03	[-.01; .10]
Openness	-.04	.06	[-.13; .05]	-.04	.04	[-.11; .03]	-.03	.07	[-.14; .08]
Conscientiousness	.04	.06	[-.05; .13]	.00	.04	[-.07; .07]	-.14	.07	**[-.26; -.04]**
Extraversion	-.05	.06	[-.15; .04]	-.02	.04	[-.10; .05]	.03	.07	[-.09; .15]
Agreeableness	.02	.06	[-.07; .11]	-.10	.04	**[-.17; -.02]**	.05	.07	[-.06; .16]

	Manipulation			Sharing			Analytic Thinking		
Neuroticism	-.04	.06	[-.14; .06]	-.01	.05	[-.09; .06]	.01	.07	[-.11; .13]
Trustworthiness * Political Opinion	.03	.07	[-.08; .15]	.05	.05	[-.03; .14]	.00	.08	[-.14; .13]
Conspiracy Thinking	-.19	.09	**[-.34; -.04]**	-.21	.07	**[-.33; -.10]**	-.01	.11	[-.18; .18]
Climate Knowledge	-.11	.08	[-.25; .02]	-.05	.05	[-.16; .05]	-.17	.10	**[-.34; -.01]**
Persuasion Knowledge	.04	.08	[-.09; .18]	-.06	.06	[-.17; .04]	-.06	.10	[-.23; .10]
Openness	.08	.08	[-.05; .21]	.18	.06	**[.08; .28]**	.01	.10	[-.14; .17]
Conscientiousness	-.17	.08	**[-.29; -.04]**	-.07	.06	[-.16; .03]	.28	.09	**[.12; .43]**
Extraversion	.05	.08	[-.09; .18]	.08	.06	[-.02; .19]	.00	.10	[-.17; .16]
Agreeableness	-.10	.08	[-.23; .03]	.18	.06	**[.08; .28]**	.02	.10	[-.14; .18]
Neuroticism	.02	.08	[-.12; .16]	.05	.06	[-.05; .15]	.08	.10	[-.09; .25]
R^2	.336	.03		.658	.02		.140	.03	

The **response time model** (R^2 = .069) indicated a small association between longer response time and worse sharing decisions, β = -.04, 90% HDI [-.07, -.01] and more analytic thinking, β = .23, 90% HDI [.17, .29], but not manipulation discernment, β = -.02, 90% HDI [-.04, .01].

In the **Big Five model** with our subsample (see Table 2), we observed several effects. For manipulation discernment, there was a negative interaction between trustworthiness and conscientiousness, $\beta = -.17$. Higher sharing discernment was associated with lower agreeableness, $\beta = -.10$. There were *interactions* with trustworthiness for openness, $\beta = .18$, and agreeableness, $\beta = .18$, indicating that more agreeable and open participants were better at identifying reliable information than misinformation. Furthermore, lower conscientiousness was associated with more analytic thinking, $\beta = -.14$, and interacted with trustworthiness, $\beta = .28$.

6. Discussion

In our information-driven world, the ability to critically evaluate information and make responsible sharing decisions is essential to reduce susceptibility to and the spread of misinformation. After decades of research, many predictors have been assessed to form a notable research body (e.g. Calvillo et al., 2024; Ecker et al., 2022; Sultan et al., 2024). However, open questions about the interplay of beliefs, stable individual characteristics demographics and their influence on judging and sharing information remain.

This study sought to address these questions by assessing how cognitive abilities, belief systems, and personality traits predicted participants' ability to discern manipulative content, their intention to share it, and their use of analytic thinking. Overall, we found three key patterns. First, in line with recent research, participants were generally skeptical of manipulative content and often identified it more readily than credible content (similar to Modirrousta-Galian et al., 2025). Second, belief systems, particularly political orientation, and conspiracy thinking, were powerful predictors, often in complex and interactive ways. Third, less agreeable participants made more accurate sharing decisions, while more conscientious participants reported judging information more intuitively. Constantly, taking more time to scrutinize information yielded slightly better average results.

6.1 The Influence of Beliefs and Demographics

Our first research question sought to identify the strongest predictors of manipulation discernment, sharing discernment and analytic thinking. When it comes to demographics, we observed negligible gender and age effects. While the meta-analysis by Sultan et al. (2024) suggested that older individuals may exhibit greater general skepticism toward all information, we did not find such a tendency in our study. This may indicate that effects driven by social identity and beliefs can overshadow age-related skepticism, especially on highly polarized and domain-specific topics like climate change. However, higher formal education predicted better manipulation discernment and analytic thinking, suggesting that formal education could be a protective factor against climate misinformation. This may be because formal education teaches the mechanisms behind climate change which could result in a deeper understanding of the issue.

When it comes to beliefs, *political opinion* played a role in predicting performance. More politically progressive participants showed better manipulation discernment, made better sharing decisions and approached information more analytically. In line with meta-analytic findings, our participants' credibility assessment may have been partially motivated by their worldview as climate change is a topic where scientific consensus aligns more closely with a progressive mindset (Pfänder & Altay, 2025). This explanation is further supported by the finding that progressive participants reported engaging more analytically with the posts. While the relationship between analytic thinking and better credibility discernment is well-researched (e.g. Faragó et al., 2023; Swami et al., 2014), this could indicate that progressive participants were simply more motivated to engage with posts on such topic analytically.

However, conservative participants detected misinformation better than credible information. This does not necessarily mean conservatives spot falsehoods better overall, but rather that their performance on the two types of content was different (in line with Sultan et al., 2024). This may indicate that conservative participants were reluctant to share information on climate change in general, but this aversion was strongest for content that appears manipulative (Benegal & Scruggs, 2018).

Counterintuitively, *conspiracy thinking* was associated with better discernment. However, the interaction with trustworthiness suggests a more complex situation: While individuals low in conspiracy thinking distinguished between sharing credible and manipulative content, this effect diminishes for those with a more conspiratorial mindset. This supports theories that frame conspiracies as a self-sealing system of epistemic distrust (Imhoff & Bertlich, 2024; Lewandowsky et al., 2013). We interpret the higher average discernment score not as pro-social accuracy, but as an artifact of broad-spectrum distrust:

Participants with a conspiratorial mindset were reluctant to share and believe any posts.

In line with our expectations, *climate knowledge* predicted more meaningful sharing decisions and better manipulation discernment, while participants also approached information more analytically. This may align with aforementioned effect of ideological congruency, since climate knowledge is a highly polarized topic. Furthermore, this effect seemed to be weaker for identifying dubious information. Knowledge alone may therefore not suffice to withstand manipulation in general, which again raises the need for complementary support to meaningfully scrutinize information (Breakstone et al., 2021; Sultan et al., 2024).

Similarly, higher *persuasion knowledge* was linked to more analytic thinking, more meaningful sharing decisions, and better manipulation discernment. This is in line with the findings of Fendt et al. (2025), who also found a straightforwardly positive role for persuasion knowledge. This does not come as a surprise, since persuasion knowledge also indicates skeptical awareness towards persuaders (Eisend & Tarrahi, 2022). In other words, participants who had already been skeptical towards misinformation outlets better recognized and withstood their persuasion attempts. However, the negative interaction for sharing discernment suggests that while knowledge of persuasive tactics helps to correctly evaluate credible posts, it appears less effective when deciding whether to share manipulative content.

Beyond the predictors for each outcome, we found that believing and sharing information was only weakly connected in our sample. This suggests that accurately judging information as manipulative does not automatically translate into a reluctance to share it and vice-versa. First, in line with Baribi-Bartov et al. (2024), many people may be "few-sharers" who rather err on the side of caution. Our sample may therefore have already been rather careful about their decisions. Second, individual may not feel the need to share such information if they grew up with a deep believe that anthropogenic climate change is common knowledge—as much as they wouldn't share a post outlining that the earth is not flat. Third, sharing motives are complex and not always driven by accuracy; people may ironically share information they know is false to ridicule it or warn peers.

6.2 Big Five Personality Traits

Our second research question focused on the role of the *Big Five personality traits*. We found only a credible association between higher agreeableness and lower sharing discernment. This is consistent with Calvillo et al (2024), who also identified mostly inconsistent correlations and may suggest that personality traits are less influential drivers than belief systems. While paradoxical at first, this effect may indicate a particular skepticism towards dubious information, since more agreeable participants detected credible information better than misinformation. This aligns with the core idea that agreeable individuals are motivated by trust, compassion, and harmony (Reizer et al., 2023), rather than distrust and suspicion, the former being potentially more useful drivers in our society (Altay et al., 2023).

The positive interaction effect for openness on sharing discernment aligns well with theory, suggesting that open-minded individuals shared credible information more than dubious content. Unexpectedly, lower conscientiousness was associated with more self-reported analytic thinking. We can only speculate on the reasons for that finding, but maybe analytic thought is the "modus operandi" for more conscientious people, whereas for less conscientious people deliberate thought is a notable event that they actively remember and report. However, the reliability of our agreeableness and conscientiousness subscales was low, which calls for caution in interpreting these results.

6.3 The Role of Deliberation Time

Our third question examined task time as a behavioral proxy for deliberation. Counterintuitively, we found no meaningful association between deliberation time and manipulation discernment and a negative association with sharing discernment. This finding does not seem to align with previous research supporting the idea that misinformation susceptibility may often be a failure of deliberation, where individuals rely on their fast, intuitive gut reactions rather than more effortful analytical thought (Faragó et al., 2023; Pennycook & Rand, 2019). However, longer deliberation time was still associated with more analytic thinking.

Analytic thinking may have been triggered by motivated reasoning, where people investigate analytically only when information contradicts their beliefs (similar to Kahan et al., 2012). In that case, participants may not have used analytical thought for accuracy-focused evaluation but to justify their pre-existing positions—a rationalization that participants would have experienced as analytic thought. In line with our previous arguments, participants' cognitive effort may have been hijacked to serve ideological goals on a polarized topic such as climate change.

6.4 Implications for Research and Practice

While our study was mainly exploratory, the results contribute to misinformation research in several ways. First, they provide another datapoint against purely information-deficit models, especially in the context of politically polarized topics, supporting motivated reasoning as one central driver for beliefs in this domain (Swire-Thompson et al., 2020). This may suggest that practitioners, for example at schools, should consider the social environment and beliefs of learners to incorporate more holistic approaches that include character development in long-term curricula rather than a sole content-focus.

Second, we found that participants identified misinformation more accurately than credible information, strengthening the argument that these might be two distinct processes. Future research should investigate the specific cognitive processes required to identify different types of information. This could especially inform the design of meaningful interventions that do not foster general skepticism but also increase trust in established institutions and credible information (similar to Altay et al., 2024). Persuasion knowledge remains a plausible influence on detecting certain manipulation strategies, but its measurement may need to be more specific to the manipulation tactics being deployed.

Third, our results demonstrate that there appears to be no single strong predictor of recognizing manipulation. Instead, we found a constellation of small effects involving climate knowledge, persuasion knowledge, and political opinion. This complexity may underscore the need for multifaceted approaches to explain and combat misinformation susceptibility.

6.5 Limitations and Future Directions

This exploratory study, while carefully prepared and conducted, has several limitations. First and foremost, we found only small effects for our predictors, which may indicate that we overlooked crucial variables, such as social media behavior or media literacy. Furthermore, we assessed political opinion on a one-item scale, whereas recent discussions shift towards a multi-dimensional assessment.

Our data was collected from visitors at a science museum, resulting in a highly educated sample that limits the generalizability of our findings. Furthermore, the museum setting may have primed participants to be more analytical or, conversely, caused cognitive fatigue after a day of learning.

We experienced substantial data loss for the Big Five personality traits, limiting the predictive quality of these results. Also, the reliability of the conscientiousness and agreeableness subscales was very low. Additionally, our synthetic stimuli may not have captured the complexity and emotional resonance of real-world misinformation as they were lacking most of the surrounding information, such as the author. Future studies may want to recreate more authentic environments like clickable mock social media pages.

Finally, the cross-sectional nature of our data does not allow for causal claims. For example, we cannot determine whether a conspiratorial worldview causes a particular sharing style or if that style is merely one component of a broader conspiratorial identity. Future research should employ experimental designs, for example, by training participants to direct skepticism towards suspicious actors rather than all information.

7. Conclusion

Our study contributes to a deeper understanding of the factors driving judgments about climate misinformation. The findings support the conclusion that a person's political identity and belief systems are as powerful as their objective knowledge in predicting their judgments. Interventions aimed at mitigating the spread of misinformation should address the complex interplay of identity, ideology, and the social motivations that govern our behavior online.

CRediT Statement

Marvin Fendt: Conceptualization, Methodology, Data curation, Formal analysis, Investigation, Writing—original draft, Writing—Review & Editing. **Fabian Reinwarth**: Investigation; Writing—original draft. **Peter Adriaan Edelsbrunner**: Conceptualization, Methodology, Writing—original draft, Writing—Review & Editing, Supervision.

References

Abudu, H., Wesseh, P. K., & Lin, B. (2023). Does political propaganda matter in mitigating climate change? Insights from the United States of America. *Journal of Management Science and Engineering*, *8*(3), 386–397. https://doi.org/10.1016/j.jmse.2022.12.006

Altay, S., Berriche, M., & Acerbi, A. (2023). Misinformation on Misinformation: Conceptual and Methodological Challenges. *Social Media + Society*, *9*(1), 20563051221150412. https://doi.org/10.1177/20563051221150412

Altay, S., De Angelis, A., & Hoes, E. (2024). Media literacy tips promoting reliable news improve discernment and enhance trust in traditional media. *Communications Psychology*, *2*(1), 74. https://doi.org/10.1038/s44271-024-00121-5

Arce, D. (2024). Disinformation Strategies. *Defence and Peace Economics*, *35*(6), 659–672. https://doi.org/10.1080/10242694.2024.2302236

Bago, B., Rand, D. G., & Pennycook, G. (2020). Fake news, fast and slow: Deliberation reduces belief in false (but not true) news headlines. *Journal of Experimental Psychology: General*, *149*(8), 1608–1613. https://doi.org/10.1037/xge0000729

Bakir, V., & McStay, A. (2018). Fake news and the economy of emotions. *Digital Journalism*, *6*(2), 154–175. https://doi.org/10.1080/21670811.2017.1345645

Baribi-Bartov, S., Swire-Thompson, B., & Grinberg, N. (2024). Supersharers of fake news on Twitter. *Science*, *384*(6699), 979–982. https://doi.org/10.1126/science.adl4435

Benegal, S. D., & Scruggs, L. A. (2018). Correcting misinformation about climate change: The impact of partisanship in an experimental setting. *Climatic Change*, *148*(1–2), 61–80. https://doi.org/10.1007/s10584-018-2192-4

Bowes, S. M., Costello, T. H., & Tasimi, A. (2023). The conspiratorial mind: A meta-analytic review of motivational and personological correlates. *Psychological Bulletin*, *149*(5–6), 259–293. https://doi.org/10.1037/bul0000392

Breakstone, J., Smith, M., Wineburg, S., Rapaport, A., Carle, J., Garland, M., & Saavedra, A. (2021). Students' civic online reasoning: A national portrait. *Educational Researcher*, *50*(8), 505–515. https://doi.org/10.3102/0013189X211017495

Calvillo, D. P., León, A., & Rutchick, A. M. (2024). Personality and misinformation. *Current Opinion in Psychology*, *55*, 101752. https://doi.org/10.1016/j.copsyc.2023.101752

Chen, Z. F., & Cheng, Y. (2019). Consumer response to fake news about brands on social media: The effects of self-efficacy, media trust, and persuasion knowledge on brand trust. *Journal of Product & Brand Management*, 29(2), 188–198. https://doi.org/10.1108/JPBM-12-2018-2145

Compton, J., van der Linden, S., Cook, J., & Basol, M. (2021). Inoculation theory in the post-truth era: Extant findings and new frontiers for contested science, misinformation, and conspiracy theories. *Social and Personality Psychology Compass*, *15*(6), 1–16. https://doi.org/10.1111/spc3.12602

Cook, J. (2022). Understanding and Countering Misinformation About Climate Change. In *Research Anthology on Environmental and Societal Impacts of Climate Change* (pp. 1633–1658). IGI Global. https://doi.org/10.4018/978-1-6684-3686-8.ch081

Cook, J., Ecker, U. K. H., Trecek-King, M., Schade, G., Jeffers-Tracy, K., Fessmann, J., Kim, S. C., Kinkead, D., Orr, M., Vraga, E., Roberts, K., & McDowell, J. (2023). The cranky uncle game—Combining humor and gamification to build student resilience against climate misinformation. *Environmental Education Research*, 29(4), 607–623. https://doi.org/10.1080/13504622.2022.2085671

Cuteanu, C. (2024). Fake News as a Persuasion Attempt, in a Post-Globalization Context. Extrapolations from Friestad and Wright's Persuasion Knowledge Model. In S. L. Fotea, S. A. Văduva, & I. Ş. Fotea (Eds.), *Reimagining Capitalism in a Post-Globalization World* (pp. 145–157). Springer Nature Switzerland. https://doi.org/10.1007/978-3-031-59858-6_11

Ecker, U. K. H., Lewandowsky, S., Cook, J., Schmid, P., Fazio, L. K., Brashier, N., Kendeou, P., Vraga, E. K., & Amazeen, M. A. (2022). The psychological drivers of misinformation belief and its resistance to correction. *Nature Reviews Psychology*, *1*(1), 13–29. https://doi.org/10.1038/s44159-021-00006-y

Edelsbrunner, P. A., Schumacher, R., Hänger-Surer, B., Schalk, L., & Stern, E. (2024). Preparation for future conceptual learning: Content-specific long-term effects of early physics instruction. *Journal of Educational Psychology*, *116*(8), 1479–1499. https://doi.org/10.1037/edu0000887

Edelson, S. M., Reyna, V. F., Singh, A., & Roue, J. E. (2024). The Psychology of Misinformation Across the Lifespan. *Annual Review of Developmental Psychology*, 6(1), 425–454. https://doi.org/10.1146/annurev-devpsych-010923-093547

Eisend, M., & Tarrahi, F. (2022). Persuasion Knowledge in the Marketplace: A Meta-Analysis. *Journal of Consumer Psychology*, *32*(1), 3–22. https://doi.org/10.1002/jcpy.1258

Epstein, Z., Sirlin, N., Arechar, A., Pennycook, G., & Rand, D. (2023). The social media context interferes with truth discernment. *Science Advances*, *9*(9), eabo6169. https://doi.org/10.1126/sciadv.abo6169

Faragó, L., Krekó, P., & Orosz, G. (2023). Hungarian, lazy, and biased: The role of analytic thinking and partisanship in fake news discernment on a Hungarian representative sample. *Scientific Reports*, *13*(1), 178. https://doi.org/10.1038/s41598-022-26724-8

Fazio, L. (2020). Pausing to consider why a headline is true or false can help reduce the sharing of false news. *Harvard Kennedy School Misinformation Review*. https://doi.org/10.37016/mr-2020-009

Fendt, M., Muth, X., & Edelsbrunner, P. A. (2025). Judging a text by its author—A meta-analysis of interventions to foster source credibility assessment. *Learning and Individual Differences*, *124*, 102782. https://doi.org/10.1016/j.lindif.2025.102782

Fendt, M., Nistor, N., Scheibenzuber, C., & Artmann, B. (2023). Sourcing against misinformation: Effects of a scalable lateral reading training based on cognitive apprenticeship. *Computers in Human Behavior*, *146*, 107820. a9h. https://doi.org/10.1016/j.chb.2023.107820

Fendt, M., Scheibenzuber, C., Edelsbrunner, P. A., & Nistor, N. (2025). Read Between the Li(n)es: Pedagogical Lateral Reading Training to Enhance Information Discernment. *Submitted for Publication*.

Flanagin, A. J., Winter, S., & Metzger, M. J. (2020). Making sense of credibility in complex information environments: The role of message sidedness, information source, and thinking styles in credibility evaluation online. *Information, Communication & Society*, *23*(7), 1038–1056. https://doi.org/10.1080/1369118X.2018.1547411

Herasimenka, A., Wang, X., & Schroeder, R. (2025). A Systematic Review of Effective Measures to Resist Manipulative Information About Climate Change on Social Media. *Climate*, *13*(2), 32. https://doi.org/10.3390/cli13020032

Imhoff, R., & Bertlich, T. (2024). Are conspiracy beliefs a sign of flawed cognition? Reexamining the association of cognitive style and skills with conspiracy beliefs. *Harvard Kennedy School Misinformation Review*. https://doi.org/10.37016/mr-2020-168

John, O. P., Donahue, E. M., & Kentle, R. L. (2012). *Big Five Inventory* [Dataset]. https://doi.org/10.1037/t07550-000

Johnson, J. A. (2017). Big-Five Model. In V. Zeigler-Hill & T. K. Shackelford (Eds.), *Encyclopedia of Personality and Individual Differences* (pp. 1–16).

Springer International Publishing. https://doi.org/10.1007/978-3-319-28099-8_1212-1

Kahan, D. M., Peters, E., Wittlin, M., Slovic, P., Ouellette, L. L., Braman, D., & Mandel, G. (2012). The polarizing impact of science literacy and numeracy on perceived climate change risks. *Nature Climate Change*, *2*(10), 732–735. https://doi.org/10.1038/nclimate1547

Kbaier, D., Kane, A., McJury, M., & Kenny, I. (2024). Prevalence of Health Misinformation on Social Media—Challenges and Mitigation Before, During, and Beyond the COVID-19 Pandemic: Scoping Literature Review. *Journal of Medical Internet Research*, *26*, e38786. https://doi.org/10.2196/38786

Kiili, C., Räikkönen, E., Bråten, I., Strømsø, H. I., & Hagerman, M. S. (2023). Examining the structure of credibility evaluation when sixth graders read online texts. *Journal of Computer Assisted Learning*, *39*(3), 954–969. https://doi.org/10.1111/jcal.12779

Kozyreva, A., Lorenz-Spreen, P., Herzog, S. M., Ecker, U. K. H., Lewandowsky, S., & Hertwig, R. (2024). Toolbox of Interventions Against Online Misinformation and Manipulation. *Nature Human Behaviour*, *8*(6), 1044–1052. https://doi.org/10.1038/s41562-024-01881-0

Lamb, W. F., Mattioli, G., Levi, S., Roberts, J. T., Capstick, S., Creutzig, F., Minx, J. C., Müller-Hansen, F., Culhane, T., & Steinberger, J. K. (2020). Discourses of climate delay. *Global Sustainability*, *3*, e17. https://doi.org/10.1017/sus.2020.13

Larzabal-Fernandez, A., Castrechini Trotta, A., & Vázquez, A. (2025). Gender and ideological orientation moderate the influence of climate misinformation on pro-environmental behavioural intentions. *British Journal of Social Psychology*, *64*(3). https://doi.org/10.1111/bjso.70000

Lazer, D. M. J., Baum, M. A., Benkler, Y., Berinsky, A. J., Greenhill, K. M., Menczer, F., Metzger, M. J., Nyhan, B., Pennycook, G., Rothschild, D., Schudson, M., Sloman, S. A., Sunstein, C. R., Thorson, E. A., Watts, D. J., & Zittrain, J. L. (2018). The science of fake news. *Science*, *359*(6380), 1094–1096. https://doi.org/10.1126/science.aao2998

Leiserowitz, A., Maibach, E., Rosenthal, S., & Kotcher, J. (2025). *Climate change in the american mind: Politics & policy, fall 2024*. Yale Program on Climate Change Communication. https://coilink.org/20.500.12592/2m3ew8m

Lewandowsky, S., Gignac, G. E., & Oberauer, K. (2013). The Role of Conspiracist Ideation and Worldviews in Predicting Rejection of Science. *PLoS ONE*, *8*(10), e75637. https://doi.org/10.1371/journal.pone.0075637

Liekefett, L., Christ, O., & Becker, J. C. (2023). Can Conspiracy Beliefs Be Beneficial? Longitudinal Linkages Between Conspiracy Beliefs, Anxiety, Uncertainty Aversion, and Existential Threat. *Personality and Social Psychology Bulletin*, 49(2), 167–179. https://doi.org/10.1177/01461672211060965

Lucassen, T., Muilwijk, R., Noordzij, M. L., & Schraagen, J. M. (2013). Topic familiarity and information skills in online credibility evaluation. *Journal of the American Society for Information Science and Technology*, 64(2), 254–264. https://doi.org/10.1002/asi.22743

McElreath, R. (2018). *Statistical Rethinking: A Bayesian Course with Examples in R and Stan* (1st ed.). Chapman and Hall/CRC. https://doi.org/10.1201/9781315372495

Modirrousta-Galian, A., Higham, P. A., & Seabrooke, T. (2025). Wordless wisdom: The dominant role of tacit knowledge in true and fake news discrimination. *Journal of Applied Research in Memory and Cognition*, 14(2), 231–240. https://doi.org/10.1037/mac0000151

Oliver, J. E., & Wood, T. J. (2014). Conspiracy Theories and the Paranoid Style(s) of Mass Opinion. *American Journal of Political Science*, 58(4), 952–966. https://doi.org/10.1111/ajps.12084

O'Mahony, C., Brassil, M., Murphy, G., & Linehan, C. (2023). The efficacy of interventions in reducing belief in conspiracy theories: A systematic review. *PLOS ONE*, 18(4), e0280902. https://doi.org/10.1371/journal.pone.0280902

Pennycook, G., Berinsky, A. J., Bhargava, P., Lin, H., Cole, R., Goldberg, B., Lewandowsky, S., & Rand, D. G. (2024). Inoculation and accuracy prompting increase accuracy discernment in combination but not alone. *Nature Human Behaviour*, 8(12), 2330–2341. https://doi.org/10.1038/s41562-024-02023-2

Pennycook, G., & Rand, D. G. (2019). Lazy, not biased: Susceptibility to partisan fake news is better explained by lack of reasoning than by motivated reasoning. *Cognition*, 188, 39–50. https://doi.org/10.1016/j.cognition.2018.06.011

Pfänder, J., & Altay, S. (2025). Spotting false news and doubting true news: A systematic review and meta-analysis of news judgements. *Nature Human Behaviour*, 9(4), 688–699. https://doi.org/10.1038/s41562-024-02086-1

Rammstedt, B., Kemper, C. J., Klein, M. C., Beierlein, C., & Kovaleva, A. (2017). A Short Scale for Assessing the Big Five Dimensions of Personality: 10 Item Big Five Inventory (BFI-10). *Methods, data*, 17 Pages. https://doi.org/10.12758/MDA.2013.013

Reizer, A., Harel, T., & Ben-Shalom, U. (2023). Helping Others Results in Helping Yourself: How Well-Being Is Shaped by Agreeableness and Perceived Team Cohesion. *Behavioral Sciences*, *13*(2), 150. https://doi.org/10.3390/bs13020150

Roozenbeek, J., van der Linden, S., Goldberg, B., Rathje, S., & Lewandowsky, S. (2022). Psychological inoculation improves resilience against misinformation on social media. *Science Advances*, *8*(34), eabo6254. https://doi.org/10.1126/sciadv.abo6254

Schwarz, N., Jalbert, M., Noah, T., & Zhang, L. (2021). Metacognitive experiences as information: Processing fluency in consumer judgment and decision making. *Consumer Psychology Review*, 4(1), 4–25. https://doi.org/10.1002/arcp.1067

Sorensen, T., Hohenstein, S., & Vasishth, S. (2016). Bayesian linear mixed models using Stan: A tutorial for psychologists, linguists, and cognitive scientists. *The Quantitative Methods for Psychology*, *12*(3), 175–200. https://doi.org/10.20982/tqmp.12.3.p175

Sultan, M., Tump, A. N., Ehmann, N., Lorenz-Spreen, P., Hertwig, R., Gollwitzer, A., & Kurvers, R. H. J. M. (2024). Susceptibility to online misinformation: A systematic meta-analysis of demographic and psychological factors. *Proceedings of the National Academy of Sciences*, *121*(47), e2409329121. https://doi.org/10.1073/pnas.2409329121

Swami, V., Voracek, M., Stieger, S., Tran, U. S., & Furnham, A. (2014). Analytic thinking reduces belief in conspiracy theories. *Cognition*, *133*(3), 572–585. https://doi.org/10.1016/j.cognition.2014.08.006

Swire-Thompson, B., Ecker, U. K. H., Lewandowsky, S., & Berinsky, A. J. (2020). They Might Be a Liar But They're My Liar: Source Evaluation and the Prevalence of Misinformation. *Political Psychology*, *41*(1), 21–34. a9h.

Tay, L. Q., Lewandowsky, S., Hurlstone, M. J., Kurz, T., & Ecker, U. K. H. (2024). Thinking clearly about misinformation. *Communications Psychology*, 2(1), 4. https://doi.org/10.1038/s44271-023-00054-5

Uscinski, J. E., Douglas, K., & Lewandowsky, S. (2017). Climate Change Conspiracy Theories. In J. E. Uscinski, K. Douglas, & S. Lewandowsky, *Oxford Research Encyclopedia of Climate Science*. Oxford University Press. https://doi.org/10.1093/acrefore/9780190228620.013.328

Van Bavel, J. J., Rathje, S., Vlasceanu, M., & Pretus, C. (2024). Updating the identity-based model of belief: From false belief to the spread of misinformation. *Current Opinion in Psychology*, *56*, 101787. https://doi.org/10.1016/j.copsyc.2023.101787

Van Der Linden, S. (2022). Misinformation: Susceptibility, spread, and interventions to immunize the public. *Nature Medicine*, *28*(3), 460–467. https://doi.org/10.1038/s41591-022-01713-6

Van Prooijen, J., & Douglas, K. M. (2018). Belief in conspiracy theories: Basic principles of an emerging research domain. *European Journal of Social Psychology*, *48*(7), 897–908. https://doi.org/10.1002/ejsp.2530

Visschers, V. H. M. (2018). Public Perception of Uncertainties Within Climate Change Science. *Risk Analysis : An Official Publication of the Society for Risk Analysis*, *38*(1), 43–55. https://doi.org/10.1111/risa.12818

Walter, A. S., & Drochon, H. (2022). Conspiracy Thinking in Europe and America: A Comparative Study. *Political Studies*, *70*(2), 483–501. https://doi.org/10.1177/0032321720972616

Winter, K., Hornsey, M. J., Pummerer, L., & Sassenberg, K. (2022). Anticipating and defusing the role of conspiracy beliefs in shaping opposition to wind farms. *Nature Energy*, *7*(12), 1200–1207. https://doi.org/10.1038/s41560-022-01164-w

Ziegler, A. (2017). Political orientation, environmental values, and climate change beliefs and attitudes: An empirical cross country analysis. *Energy Economics*, *63*, 144–153. https://doi.org/10.1016/j.eneco.2017.01.022

Part III—Reimagining Transformation

Who owns the present, owns the future?
Rethinking socio-ecological transformations through infrastructure ownership

Carlotta Terhorst

Abstract: *In the face of rising global temperatures and their devastating consequences, the urgency of socio-ecological transformation is increasingly evident. However, transformative change remains difficult to achieve. This contribution attempts to examine how infrastructure ownership influences the speed and direction of the socio-ecological transformation. An initial theoretical discussion on the role of infrastructure ownership in the transformation is empirically exemplified by an analysis of the European Union's strategic turn toward hydrogen as a key energy carrier, despite scientific debates about its scalability and capacity. A thematic analysis of selected documents during the policy-making process reveals that the narrative of private, profit-oriented incumbent companies mirrors the policy shift on the EU level. Thus, it shows that private, profit-oriented ownership of incumbent infrastructures and related power dynamics can delay transformative change. Ultimately, the contribution emphasizes the need for critical research to start with material conditions and their subsequent power dynamics when examining the reality of socio-ecological transformations.*

1. Introduction

Recent heat waves, wild fires, and devastating floods in Europe and many other places in the world, have demonstrated the urgency of socio-ecological transformation. The Intergovernmental Panel on Climate Change (IPCC) has repeatedly warned that incremental changes are not enough; only transformative shifts in energy, production, and consumption patterns can keep global warming below critical thresholds (IPCC, 2023). Yet, despite widespread recognition of this imperative, today, transformative change towards a climate-friendly future seems further away than ever. Even without taking current developments in the US, and their drastic consequences, into account, the 1,5 °C goal is now almost impossible to achieve (IPCC, 2023). So, the question remains: Why do transformation efforts often fail?

A growing body of scholarship has sought to answer this question by focusing on the role of infrastructures as possible barriers to socio-ecological transformation by creating "carbon lock-ins" (Unruh, 2000; Geels et al., 2016). While this perspective provides a first valuable insight in the dynamics at work, it treats technical infrastructures as mere socio-technical systems. More recent work in various disciplines of the social sciences hints at seeing infrastructures rather as socio-political objects that are politically chosen and heavily shape questions of costs and burdens in the transformation (Malm, 2016; Kropp, 2024; Wansleben & Terhorst, 2025). Building on Chancel & Rehm (2024), this contribution highlights the interplay between inequality and the climate crisis by looking at the ways in which infrastructure ownership shapes both the possibilities and limits of socio-ecological transformation. In the following sections, the contribution first gives an overview of how social science literature engages with the role of infrastructures in the socio-ecological transformation. Then it expands this literature by revisiting Chancel & Rehm's (2024) notion of ownership carbon inequality. Their study shows that carbon emissions are not distributed equally among individuals or countries but are deeply linked to ownership structures: those who own and control productive assets, e.g. factories, vehicles, power plants, also own the means by which carbon is emitted. This insight compels us to look beyond individual consumption patterns and toward ownership emissions. In addition, ownership shapes not only who profits from infrastructures but also whose interests guide their design, deployment, and maintenance. Finally, the contribution refers to an empirical example of a policy decision for a certain infrastructure where profit-driven and centralized ownership hindered deep ecological transformation: The European Union's turn towards hydrogen as a key energy carrier in the beginning of the 2020s. This empirical example is analyzed by a first consideration of ownership structures of incumbent infrastructure and points to an important forum for policy influence: The Gas Regulatory Forum, or Madrid Forum. In a second step, a thematic analysis of the presentations of this forum is conducted. By theoretically discussing the role of ownership in socio-ecological transformation and showing empirically how influential this incumbent forum was in the policy-making process, this contribution aims to lay the groundwork for a more materially grounded answer to the question of why transformation efforts fail.

2. Infrastructures & the socio-ecological transformation: an emerging topic in the social sciences

Infrastructures have become increasingly central to debates on climate protection across a wide range of social science disciplines. Across social science disciplines, infrastructures are often understood as interconnected systems and facilities designed to provide, store, and transform goods and services for collective use, forming the foundation for essential public services like water, energy, healthcare, and transportation. The longest tradition of looking at infrastructures can be found in the *transition studies* literature. Transition scholars emphasize that infrastructures are not merely technical, but deeply embedded socio-technical systems that can both enable and constrain sustainability transitions. Publications in this field of study have established the idea of "lock-in"-effects of existing systems, highlighting how material, institutional, and economic path dependencies constrain the pace and direction of change (Unruh, 2000; Geels et al., 2016; Seto et al. 2016). Critically reflecting on those lock-in effects, Andreas Malm (2016) powerfully argues that fossil-fuel infrastructure is not a neutral structure but a material force that actively shapes and constrains social choices. He writes:

> "The choice to travel in [cars] rather than in trams or buses or on bicycles is conditioned by a vast infrastructure of oil terminals, petroleum refineries, asphalt plants, road networks, gasoline stations—not to [mention] the film industry, the lobbying groups, the billboards—which did not fall from the sky in this moment but was built up over time, eventually amassing such weight and inertia that other modes of transportation are now excluded, or at least prevented from rising to predominance. This is what some refer to as 'carbon lock-in': a cementation of fossil-fuel–based technologies, deflecting alternatives and obstructing policies of climate-change mitigation." (Malm, 2016, 7)

The concept of carbon lock-in underscores how deeply entrenched infrastructures privilege carbon-intensive technology and obstruct climate mitigation. But existing infrastructures are not creating carbon lock-in by their mere existence, rather, it's a political choice which infrastructure is chosen and how it is designed. This point of view is often claimed by scholars in the field of heterodox economics. The foundational economy gives importance to infrastructures because they shape the social, economic, and ecological conditions of specific regions and are crucial for ensuring equal access and societal participation. Thus, it situates infrastructures at the core of a politics of provisioning and advocates for socio-ecological infrastructures (Bärnthaler et al., 2021; Foundational Economy Collective, 2022). Relating to this call to revalue the everyday infrastructure that sustains social life, Kohei Saito's work pushes these insights into a more radical ecological and systemic critique. Drawing on Marx's theory of the metabolic rift, he argues for a shift away from mass consumption and toward public goods that serve collective needs: compact, energy-efficient cities with strong public transit, minimal packaging and advertising sectors, and a greater focus on properly maintained, socially owned infrastructure (Saito, 2020). Recently also more and more sociological literature has acknowledged that only a profound change in infrastructure systems will limit climate change and its consequences (Neckel 2022; Kropp, 2024; van Dyck et al., 2024; Wansleben & Terhorst, 2025). Those sociological discussions of the role of infrastructures in the socio-ecological transformation highlight their immense relevance for understanding the nexus between inequality and the climate crisis. Kropp (2024) holds that social differences between rich and poor and between the provision of resources in the Global South and their use in the Global North are anchored and perpetuated in infrastructure systems. Similarly, Wansleben & Terhorst (2025) argue for the strategic importance of infrastructures for the investigation of inequality in the climate crisis. By distinguishing between 'upstream' concentrated versus diffuse investment requirements and between profit-oriented versus public welfare-oriented institutional embedding of infrastructures, they also offer an initial analytical framework for analyzing such infrastructure-related distributional effects (Wansleben & Terhorst, 2025). This interdisciplinary body of work highlights that infrastructures are not neutral structures, but they shape who benefits from transformation, who bears its costs, and which futures remain viable. In this light, infrastructures must be understood not only as technical challenges, but as political objects—and the investigation of such is essential, especially to understand the nexus between climate crisis and inequality.

3. On inequality and ownership of infrastructures

Interlinkages between inequality and the climate crisis have empirically been demonstrated by the team around Lucas Chancel associated with the World Inequality Lab for the past years (Chancel & Piketty, 2015; Chancel et al., 2023). Chancel's recent work with his colleague Yannick Rehm adds one dimension of inequality that is especially interesting to look at within the discussion of infrastructures in the socio-ecological transformation: ownership-based carbon inequality. Their research explores the carbon footprint of individuals by incorporating emissions from both consumption and asset ownership, such as real estate, equities, and pensions and introduces a novel framework: ownership-based emissions (Chancel & Rehm, 2024). Key findings reveal significant inequality in carbon emissions across wealth groups in the United States, Germany, and France. The wealthiest 10% emit far more CO_2-equivalent annually when ownership emissions are included, compared to their consumption-only emissions.[1] According to their study, the top 10% wealthiest people on the planet are responsible for 70–85% of emissions tied to capital ownership, with wealth-related emissions being more unequal than wealth distribution itself due to the carbon intensity of assets owned by the wealthy. Looking at future developments of such inequality, Chancel and his team argue in a recent publication that the way capital for the green transition is funded and owned, whether by the public or private sector, could significantly impact the global distribution of wealth in the future (Chancel et al., 2025). If governments take the lead and retain ownership of climate-related infrastructure, public wealth could grow substantially. In contrast, if private actors dominate these investments, the wealth gap could widen, with the top 1% potentially capturing an even larger share of global assets (Chancel et al., 2025). Thus, decisions made today about how to finance climate investments, especially in renewable infrastructure, will have long-lasting effects on economic inequality. But not only do incumbent ownership structures deeply affect future inequality scenarios, they also heavily influence how socio-ecological transformation is taking place. Van Dyk et al. (2024) make the claim that the ownership of infrastructures, such as energy supply, transport systems, and digital networks, can represent key obstacles to achieving a sustainable and just transformation. In

1 Ownerhip-based emissions: 102 tonnes in the US, 50 tonnes in Germany, and 38 tonnes in France vs. Comsumption-based emissions: of 52 tonnes in the US, 18 tonnes in Germany, and 16 tonnes in France.

their work, private ownership of infrastructure is critically examined, as it is often geared toward profit maximization, which can exacerbate social inequalities and ecological damage. At the same time, they discuss how alternative forms of ownership, such as commons or public infrastructure, could play a crucial role in advancing the socio-ecological transformation (van Dyck et al., 2024). A prominent example of their claim is the continued existence of fossil fuel infrastructure, particularly natural gas facilities, in regions where private companies have a strong interest in maintaining these assets. This vested interest can significantly slow down the transition to renewable energy sources, a point that will be discussed in more detail later in this text. Taking these considerations together, they hint at a research avenue for understanding barriers for socio-ecological transformation: The way infrastructures, the interconnected systems and facilities designed to provide, store, and transform goods and services for collective use, are organized and owned. Especially looking at ownership and organization of those infrastructures that need to be transformed for an ecological future, such as energy infrastructure, seems essential. Therefore, to understand the processes of socio-ecological transformations, it appears crucial to pose the following questions: Who owns the incumbent infrastructures today, and how do these ownership structures influence the possibilities for transformation?

4. The European Union's turn to hydrogen

One productive line of inquiry to find out how ownership structures influence the possibilities for transformation is to investigate policy cases that delay or divert deep transformation, particularly where incumbent actors succeed in reshaping climate agendas to preserve their assets and influence.

4.1 Case selection & description

A compelling case to explore in light of the posed question is the European Union's strategic turn[2] toward hydrogen as a key energy carrier. In her 2022

2 Important to note here is that this shift, that is explained in detail below, does not necessarily describe a shift within the European industry sector towards using hydrogen, it only describes a noticeable shift of focus on hydrogen and other renewable gases in the strategy documents and directives of the European Union from 2020 onwards.

State of the Union address, European Commission President Ursula von der Leyen highlighted that hydrogen could be a potential game-changer for Europe's energy system. However, before 2020, unlike the steady rise of the importance of renewables in policy discourse over the decades, hydrogen had not been a central focus in the EU's renewable energy transition. While interest in hydrogen dates back to the 1970s oil crisis, technological and structural challenges kept it on the sidelines, with investments favouring other energy solutions. Recently, this has shifted. Many EU member states have introduced national hydrogen strategies, increased funding for hydrogen projects, and integrated hydrogen more prominently into energy policies. Germany has, for example, even set up a National Hydrogen Council and a Hydrogen Coordination Office to follow through on its goals of producing, importing and using hydrogen in all industry sectors.[3] At the EU level, strategy documents like the "A Hydrogen Strategy for a Climate-Neutral Europe" and "REPower EU" reflect this growing emphasis. New is also the European Hydrogen Bank, which has awarded nearly €1 billion to 15 renewable hydrogen projects through its second auction.[4] Yet, the rapid embrace of hydrogen as a "solution fuel" overlooks ongoing scientific debates about its scalability and capacity. Fossil fuels dominate current hydrogen production due to the availability of energy inputs and the higher costs and limited technology associated with alternative hydrogen production methods (Moraga et al., 2019; Nikolaidis and Poullikkas, 2017). As of 2023, most hydrogen is produced using natural gas and coal without carbon capture and storage (CCS) technology, while less than 1% is derived from renewable energy electrolysis. Notably, carbon dioxide emissions from hydrogen production have risen by 1.5% compared to 2022 levels (IEA, 2024, 2022, 2021; Lagioia et al., 2023). This hydrogen is primarily used in heavy industries like refining and steel production. Critics highlight the lack of scalable, cost-competitive technology for clean hydrogen production in the short term (Löffer et al., 2022). In Europe, challenges in producing green hydrogen domestically have prompted energy partnerships with regions such as Latin America and MENA. Concerns persist about future hydrogen availability and pricing relative to other fuels, especially as integrating hydrogen into energy grids requires substantial investment. This includes either building new hydrogen-specific

3 Germany's National Hydrogen Strategy: https://www.bundeswirtschaftsministerium.de/Redaktion/EN/Hydrogen/Dossiers/national-hydrogen-strategy.html

4 More information on the European Hydrogen Bank: https://energy.ec.europa.eu/topics/eus-energy-system/hydrogen/european-hydrogen-bank_en

infrastructure or retrofitting existing gas systems, which is complicated by hydrogen's unique chemical properties. These factors increase the risk of leaks, require higher system pressure, and necessitate significant retrofitting or reconstruction, potentially entrenching reliance on fossil fuels for transportation (Baasch et al., 2024; Hollenhorst, 2023; Lagioia et al., 2023; Moraga et al., 2019). Thus, framing hydrogen as a green solution for the EU's sustainable future remains highly contentious. Rather, it might lead to the cementation of an energy infrastructure relying on natural gas for decades to come, instead of transforming the European energy system sustainably.

4.2 Method

If analyzed through the lens of infrastructures as socio-technical systems, the described case could be simply interpreted as a case of carbon lock-in: the incumbent gas infrastructure in Europe functions here as a barrier to deep transformation and steers the European Commission towards a decision that keeps the infrastructure alive. However, and here is the critical point, such an explanation completely misses an understanding of why this happens. Here, the look at ownership structures and power is essential. Especially in this case, where the shift toward hydrogen came so suddenly, ownership structures of incumbents and their power in political decision-making might also explain the suddenness of the turn. To understand why the European Commission opted to shift its focus on hydrogen as an energy carrier, the analysis thus started with what was argued for previously: the ownership structures of incumbent infrastructure. Those were examined through already existing literature. This contextual analysis led to the focus one specific event: the Gas Regulatory Forum, also called the "Madrid Forum", a forum set up by the European Commission, to meet with the gas industry twice a year. A systematic thematic analysis of all presentations held at the 32nd Madrid Forum in 2019, which took place on June 5th–6th, 2019 and the 33rd Madrid Forum on October 23rd–24th, 2019, was then employed to reveal the discursive strategy and narratives of the gas industry prior to the noticeable shift in 2020 in EU strategy papers. Those presentations were held by representatives of think tanks, companies, or business associations invited to the forum by the European Commission. All 65 available documents were collected from the official website of the European Commission.[5] The collected texts were prepared for analysis by converting them into .txt files and then imported into the MAXQDA software[6] for coding and analysis. The thematic analysis of this data set was then conducted following the six-phase framework proposed by Braun and Clarke (2006):

> First, the researcher immersed herself in the data by reading and rereading the transcripts to gain a deep understanding of the content.
> Second, the researcher coded the data systematically by inductively identifying meaningful segments of text.
> Third, the researcher then grouped the codes into broader themes by identifying patterns and relationships across the data.
> Fourth, the researcher reviewed and refined the themes to ensure they accurately represent the data.
> Fifth, the researcher named the themes.
> Sixth, the researcher organized the themes into a coherent narrative and supported it by illustrative quotes from the data.

It is acknowledged that thematic analysis is an inherently interpretive method, and the findings may be influenced by the researcher's own biases. But to minimize the biases and ensure reliability, another researcher independently coded a subset of the texts.

4.3 Context & Ownership

In 2019, Corporate Europe Observatory published the results of its study on the ownership of gas infrastructure in Europe. The report shows that gas pipelines are concentrated in the hands of a few powerful Transmission System Operators (TSOs), many of which are partially or fully state-owned, while also involving major institutional investors. Companies like Italy's Snam, Spain's Enagás, France's GRTgaz, Belgium's Fluxys, and Germany's Open Grid Europe control large portions of the continent's pipeline networks and Liquefied Natural Gas (LNG) terminals. These operators are often backed by

---

5 Documents were retrieved from: https://commission.europa.eu/publications/32nd-madrid-forum-presentations_en & https://commission.europa.eu/publications/33rd-madrid-forum-presentations_en

6 MAXQDA is a software program for analyzing various types of data, including text, audio, video, images, and survey results. MAXQDA helps organizing, coding, and analyzing data, as well as visualizing relationships and patterns within the data.

sovereign investment arms—such as Cassa Depositi e Prestiti Reti S.p.A. (CDP Reti) in Italy—and global financial actors like BlackRock and Lazard Asset Management, which hold significant shares. Furthermore, these companies are not merely passive infrastructure managers; they play an active role in shaping EU energy policy through bodies like ENTSO-G, the European Network of Transmission System Operators for Gas. This dual position, owning physical infrastructure while participating in regulatory planning, enables them to safeguard and extend their assets, often pushing for continued gas investments under the guise of energy security or transition. Consequently, Corporate Europe Observatory comes to the conclusion that the result is a structurally embedded system where gas interests can delay decarbonization efforts and influence the trajectory of Europe's energy transition (Corporate Europe Observatory, 2019). In addition, Szabo (2022) notes that a unified industry coalition emerged around the idea that gas infrastructure could support the transition by transporting decarbonized fuels, such as hydrogen. This narrative shift also allowed gas incumbents to position natural gas as the foundation for a low-carbon future through blue hydrogen. According to Szabo (2023), industry actors, particularly transmission system operators and gas producers, used forums like the European Gas Regulatory Forum, where critical voices are systematically excluded, to influence the European Commission. Therefore, to understand how the gas industry influenced the policy-making process, it is essential to look at what happened at the European Gas Regulatory Forum. The turn towards hydrogen in EU strategy papers happened between 2019 and 2020. In the European Green Deal, published in 2019, hydrogen only had a minimal role, while it gained prominence in the policy discussion on the transition in 2020 with the publication of the 'Hydrogen Strategy for a Climate-Neutral Europe'. Thus, the following analysis will focus on the European Gas Regulatory Forums in 2019. In 2019, the European Gas Regulatory Forum met twice, once in June and once in October.

4.4 Findings of thematic analysis

The thematic analysis revealed six distinct themes that were discussed most in the presentations: "Hydrogen and Low-Carbon Gases", "Gas Infrastructure", "Market-Based Solutions", "Potential Sectors for Hydrogen Use", "Sector Coupling and Integration" and "Carbon Capture and Storage (CCS)". However, there is a significant difference in the frequency of their occurrence within the Madrid Forum presentations (see Figure 1).

Figure 1: The figure shows how often concepts that were clustered in the 6 themes were coded throughout the 65 documents.

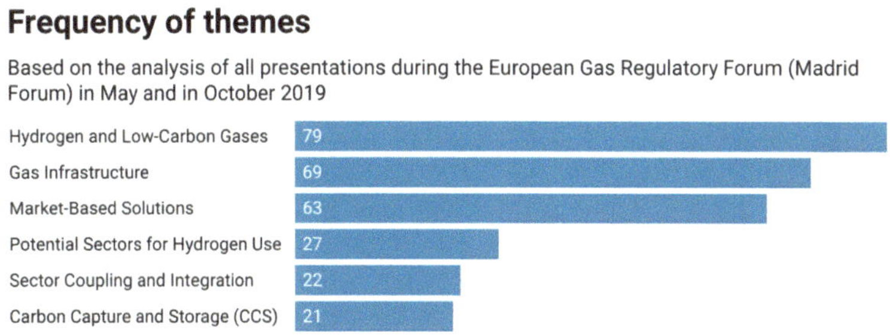

Source: own illustration of results with www.datawrapper.de

The theme that came up the most throughout the documents was named *Hydrogen and Low-Carbon Gases*. It summarizes all segments of the texts that dealt with hydrogen and low-carbon gases and their role in the decarbonization of European industries. Decarbonized, low-carbon gas, such as blue hydrogen, is often discussed as a good solution to reduce emissions. *Gas Infrastructure Europe (GIE)* writes, for example: "decarbonized gas which could substantially decrease the emission of greenhouse gases". In addition, equal importance for decarbonization is given to low-carbon cases and renewable gases. The consultancy company *Navigant*, holds, for instance: "Not scaling up renewable and low carbon gas and decommissioning gas infrastructure will lead to unnecessary costs." Here, also cost-efficiency of the use of low-carbon gases is mentioned.

Related to this main theme, additional attention was also given to the CCS technology and its prospects for decarbonizing hydrogen. All segments of the text referring to this technology were summarized in the theme "Carbon Capture and Storage (CCS)". Especially given the scarcity of green hydrogen, CCS is framed as necessary for the energy transition. The voice of Europe's national energy regulators at both the EU and international levels, the *Council of European Energy Regulators (CEER)* writes for example: „Nevertheless, to reach the ambitious 2050 emission target, in the long-term the use of natural gas has to be faded out or, at least, drastically reduced, unless decarbonisation technologies such as Carbon Capture and Storage (CCS) are widely deployed." In addition, it using CCS is also seen as the most cost-effective way of producing hydrogen. The *International Association of Oil & Gas Producers (IOGP)* writes on this for example: "CCS is a proven technology necessary to achieve climate neutrality in Europe in a cost-efficient manner, and to enable negative emissions. All credible scenario modelling shows that CCS will be essential to meeting the targets set by the Paris Agreement."

Hydrogen and low-carbon gases, including those produced with CCS are discussed frequently to be essential in the decarbonization of all so-called hard-to-abate sectors. The theme "Potential Sectors for Hydrogen Use" summarizes text segments that specify certain sectors for hydrogen use. Long-distance transport and energy-intensive industries are mentioned the most. This holds true not only for gas and industry actors, but also for electricity sector participants. *Eurelectic*, the European electricity industry's leading association, even holds: "Europe should strive to maintain leadership in green molecules, including green hydrogen, which are needed to decarbonize, especially specific segments of industrial activity and heavy-duty transport".

A significant amount of attention is also given to the potential application of hydrogen for sector coupling and integration, including discussion of its role as storage and the application of power-to-gas (P2G) technology. All text segments that discussed hydrogen concerning these were summarized in the theme "Sector Coupling and Integration". For many participants in the Madrid Forum, sectoral integration is crucial for decarbonizing the energy sector, and hydrogen is regarded as an especially useful tool. This view is shared across the board, from energy regulators to gas and electricity industry members. *Gas Infrastructure Europe (GIE)* highlights, for example, the "key role of Power to Gas (P2G) in coupling electricity and gas systems as well as between important demand sectors." And even *Eurelectic*, agrees with this and states that "significant benefits and synergies can be found through the coupling of electricity and gas sectors."

One conviction that runs through most of the documents is that market-based solutions are considered more important than regulations for the decarbonization of the European energy systems. Text segments that express this belief are summarized in the theme "Market-Based Solutions". This argument is often expressed as a more general push for a 'technologically neutral' approach to regulation. This insistence on technological neutrality implies levelling the playing field by not ensuring favourable conditions for specific energy carriers over others; for example, not punishing 'low-carbon' solutions in favour of renewables. In this context, Guarantees of Origin (GOs)[7] are discussed as a potential solution. In the presentations of the Madrid Forum, the demand that GOs should also be issued for low-carbon gases appears frequently. The European think tank *Hydrogen Europe* holds, for example, that GOs should be extended to cover renewable and low-carbon gases, because "this would provide a consistent means of proving to final customers the origin of renewable and low-carbon gases, including hydrogen, facilitating greater cross-border trade in such gases."

And lastly, the theme "Gas Infrastructure", relates to all passages that discuss the role of gas infrastructure in energy systems and its readiness for hydrogen. First of all, there is a broad consensus among the analyzed documents that it is important to consider the repurposing of gas infrastructure for decarbonization. The Brussels-based association *Gas Infrastructure Europe (GIE)*, representing the interests of European gas infrastructure operators, argues, for instance, to view "gas infrastructure and green gases as a key pillar of a sustainable energy system." In addition, it is often argued that using the gas infrastructure is the most cost-effective solution to ensure hydrogen integration into the energy sector. The *International Association of Oil & Gas Producers (IOGP)*, a global forum for the upstream oil and gas industry, writes, for example: "CO_2 can be transported in existing steel pipelines, driven by compressors, without the need for costly infrastructure upgrades." This statement also suggests the readiness of existing gas infrastructure to integrate hydrogen. The Brussels-based, non-profit organization that advocates for the widespread adoption of biogas and biomethane as sustainable solutions, the European Biogas Association (EBA), states in its vivid claim: "Gas infrastructure exists—use it!"

In contrast, what appeared only to a limited extent was a critical perspective on the technical capacity and scalability of hydrogen. Critique was limited to the recognition that green hydrogen is scarce. The feasibility of CCS technology also went largely unquestioned. The Madrid Forum participants adhered to the notion that hydrogen can be successfully scaled up; recognition of technological immaturity was only considered in the context of advocating for more financial investment to achieve guaranteed maturity. Furthermore, gas industry actors in the Madrid Forums insisted on the readiness of existing gas in-

7 GOs are electronic certificates that prove a specific amount of energy was produced from renewable energy sources. They are traded and used to demonstrate the renewable origin of electricity, ensuring transparency and preventing double-counting.

frastructure to integrate hydrogen. There were no discussions about the actual feasibility of doing so.

4.5 Discussion

What the findings of the thematic analysis clearly show is that there had indeed, as Szabo (2023), mentioned, been a consensus among industry actors that hydrogen will be one of the key energy carriers for the future. But instead of focusing on renewable hydrogen, most actors promoted low-carbon hydrogen, produced from natural gas, as well as blue hydrogen, produced from gas with Carbon Capture and Storage (CCS) technology. In addition, gas infrastructure is argued to be "hydrogen-ready", even though the scientific community shows that this is not yet the case (Baasch et al., 2024; Hollenhorst, 2023; Lagioia et al., 2023; Moraga et al., 2019). In general, there is little to no reference to controversial discussions in academia. And if we look at the legal translation in the revision of Renewable Energy Directive from 2023, the themes emphasized in the Madrid Forum can be detected. In the legal text, it says that the European Commission encourages Member States to support renewable hydrogen via contracts for difference, subsidies, or quotas and a binding target is set. But only 42% of hydrogen used in industry must be renewable by 2030, and 60% by 2035. And it also allows Member States to issue GOs for low-carbon hydrogen (e.g., blue hydrogen) if emissions are significantly lower than those from fossil fuels (European Union, 2023). Thus, not only did the presented narrative seem to have influenced EU strategy papers, but also legislative action. Now, what does this mean in the context of ownership? The case of the European Union's policy decision to turn towards hydrogen reveals how strong the influence of incumbent infrastructure owners is. The thematic analysis of the Madrid Forum documents shows that the narrative created by the companies owning the pipelines and supplying gas seems to be the one adopted by the European Commission—a narrative that ignored scientific knowledge but secured the material interests of incumbents.

5. Conclusion

Efforts to tackle the climate crisis are often not reaching its goals. A growing body of literature suggests that this could be caused by existing infrastructures and the way they are designed. This chapter expanded on this thought by drawing on the notion of ownership-based emissions (Chancel & Rehm, 2024), and demonstrated how ownership of infrastructures and related power dynamics can hinder transformative change. To illustrate this, it provided the example of the European Union's strategic turn toward hydrogen. With the help of existing research on the gas industry, it has revealed that incumbent actors, particularly those owning gas infrastructure, have leveraged their power to reframe hydrogen as a key energy solution, despite its reliance on fossil fuels and limited scalability. This contribution reminds us that the socio-ecological crisis we are facing today demands critical research that does not ignore the effects of material conditions and related power asymmetries, but puts them at the heart of its work. Who owns the material foundations of societies, such as, for example, gas grids, shapes not only who benefits from current arrangements but also determines who has the power and responsibility to drive or resist change. Thus, to understand current failures in dealing with climate change, we must ask: who owns what, and what does that mean for power, responsibility and resistance? Not addressing this question has far-reaching political implications. The failure to incorporate a clear analysis of ownership in policy has contributed to public backlash. Carbon pricing mechanisms like CO_2 taxes, for example, designed as well-intentioned as tools for emissions reduction, frequently impose disproportionate burdens on low-income households, while leaving large corporate polluters untouched. Moreover, ownership interests can, as discussed in this contribution, act as barriers to transformative change. Fossil fuel companies, and infrastructure providers are not passive stakeholders, but actively shape policy outcomes to protect their assets. To deepen the understanding of such dynamics, efforts in critical research on the socio-ecological transformation should begin with a critical analysis of existing ownership structures. While the analysis in this contribution simply used ownership as a starting point for contextualizing its case and determining crucial events to analyze, future research could expand on this by combining a deep analysis of ownership structures e.g. though ownership mapping with qualitative methods of similar cases. Such a combination might deeply enhance our understanding of the dynamics in socio-ecological transformation. It also allows us to reevaluate the transformation of infrastructures as a political struggle over ownership and to imagine alternative scenarios. Public ownership, cooperative models and community-based governance offer viable alternatives to concentrated corporate control. Reclaiming infrastructure for the common good could redistribute power, reduce inequality and vulnerability, and might even strengthen democracy. Consequently, a social and ecological future begins with the question: Who owns the present?

References

Baasch, S., Maschke, J., & Buhk, J. (2024). An (in-)just transition? Sociotechnical imaginaries of the 'green' hydrogen and steel transition in Bremen, Germany. *Futures, 164*, 103489. https://doi.org/10.1016/j.futures.2024.103489

Bärnthaler, R., Novy, A., & Plank, L. (2021). The Foundational Economy as a Cornerstone for a Social–Ecological Transformation. *Sustainability, 13*(18), 10460. https://doi.org/10.3390/su131810460

Braun, V., & Clarke, V. (2006). Using thematic analysis in psychology. *Qualitative Research in Psychology*. https://www.tandfonline.com/doi/abs/10.1191/1478088706qp063oa

Chancel, L., & Piketty, T. (2015). *Carbon and inequality: From Kyoto to Paris Trends in the global inequality of carbon emissions (1998–2013) & prospects for an equitable adaptation fund World Inequality Lab*. https://shs.hal.science/halshs-02655266

Chancel, L., Bothe, P., & Voituriez, T. (2023). *Climate inequality report 2023*.

Chancel, L., & Rehm, Y. (2024). *The Carbon Footprint of Capital: Evidence from France, Germany and the US based on Distributional Environmental Accounts*.

Chancel, L., Mohren, C., Bothe, P., Semieniuk, G. (2025). Climate changeand the global distribution of wealth. *Nature Climate Change. 15, 364–374 (2025).* https://doi.org/10.1038/s41558-025-02268-3

Corporate Europe Observatory (11th September, 2019). *Who owns all the pipelines?* Retrieved on 10th of July from https://corporateerope.org/en/2019/09/who-owns-all-pipelines

European Union. (2023). *Directive (EU) 2023/2413 of the European Parliament and of the Council of 4 October 2023*. Official Journal of the European Union. Retrieved from https://eur-lex.europa.eu/eli/dir/2023/2413/oj/eng

Geels, F. W., Berkhout, F., & van Vuuren, D. P. (2016). Bridging analytical approaches for low-carbon transitions. *Nature Climate Change*, 6(6), 576–583. https://doi.org/10.1038/nclimate2980

Hickel, J. (2020). *Less is More: How Degrowth Will Save the World*. Random House.

Hollenhorst, J. (2023). Why hydrogen's carbon past matters for hydrogen futures. *GAIA - Ecological Perspectives for Science and Society, 32*(2), 225–229. https://doi.org/10.14512/gaia.32.2.4

IEA. (2021). *Global Hydrogen Review 2021*. IEA.

IEA. (2022). *Global Hydrogen Review 2022*. IEA.

IEA. (2024). *Global Hydrogen Review 2024*. IEA.

IPCC. (2023). *Climate Change 2023: Synthesis Report. Intergovernmental Panel on Climate Change.* Retrieved from https://www.ipcc.ch/report/ar6/syr/

Kropp, C. (2023). Infrastrukturen – Hebel der sozial-ökologischen Transformation. In *Handbuch Umweltsoziologie* (S. 1–16). Springer VS, Wiesbaden. https://doi.org/10.1007/978-3-658-37222-4_67-1

Lagioia, G., Spinelli, M. P., & Amicarelli, V. (2023). Blue and green hydrogen energy to meet European Union decarbonisation objectives. An overview of perspectives and the current state of affairs. *International Journal of Hydrogen Energy*, 48(4), 1304–1322. https://doi.org/10.1016/j.ijhydene.2022.10.044

Löffler, K., Burandt, T., Hainsch, K., Oei, P.-Y., Seehaus, F., & Wejda, F. (2022). Chances and barriers for Germany's low carbon transition—Quantifying uncertainties in key influential factors. *Energy*, *239*, 121901. https://doi.org/10.1016/j.energy.2021.121901

Malm, A. (2016). *Fossil Capital: The Rise of Steam Power and the Roots of Global Warming*. Verso Books.

Moraga, J. L., Mulder, M., & Perey, P. (2019). Future markets for renewable gases & hydrogen: What would be the optimal regulatory provisions? *Centre on Regulation in Europe (CERRE)*.

Neckel, S. (o. J.). *Infrastruktursozialismus: Die Bedeutung der Fundamentalökonomie.*

Nikolaidis, P., & Poullikkas, A. (2017). A comparative overview of hydrogen production processes. *Renewable and Sustainable Energy Reviews, 67,* 597–611. https://doi.org/10.1016/j.rser.2016.09.044

Saito, K. (2020). *Marx's Theory of Metabolism in the Age of Global Ecological Crisis.* https://doi.org/10.1163/1569206X-20202802

Seto, K. C., Davis, S. J., Mitchell, R. B., Stokes, E. C., Unruh, G., & Ürge-Vorsatz, D. (2016). Carbon Lock-In: Types, Causes, and Policy Implications. *Annual Review of Environment and Resources*, *41*(1), 425–452. https://doi.org/10.1146/annurev-environ-110615-085934

Szabo, J. (2022). Energy transition or transformation? Power and politics in the European natural gas industry's trasformismo. *Energy Research & Social Science*, 84, 102391. https://doi.org/10.1016/j.erss.2021.102391

The Foundational Economy Collective (2022). *Foundational Economy: The infrastructure of everyday life, new edition*, Manchester: Manchester University Press. https://doi.org/10.7765/9781526165411

Unruh, G. C. (2000). Understanding carbon lock-in. *Energy Policy*, *28*(12), 817–830. https://doi.org/10.1016/S0301-4215(00)00070-7

van Dyk, S., Reitz, T., & Rosa, H. (2024). *Nach dem Privateigentum?: Güter, Infrastrukturen und Weltverhältnisse im Kapitalismus des 21. Jahrhunderts*. Campus Verlag. https://library.oapen.org/handle/20.500.12657/90984

Wansleben, L. & Terhorst, C. (2025). Ungleichheiten in der grünen Transformation: Die prädistributive Macht von Infrastrukturen. *Zeitschrift für Soziologie*. https://doi.org/10.1515/zfsoz-2025-2023

Qualitative Scenarios for supporting regional public foresight

Insights from practical student projects

Elias-Johannes Schmitt

Abstract: *In the face of mounting challenges such as limited financial and human resources, global forces like climate change and digitalization exert increasing pressure on cities and municipalities. To address the uncertainties inherent in these developments, the qualitative scenario method offers a structured approach for exploring diverse future pathways by involving a broad spectrum of stakeholders. At Ruhr University Bochum, students have collaborated with representatives from the Bochum municipal administration and civic stakeholders to develop forward-looking scenarios that not only communicate scientific insights and raise awareness of potential futures but also serve as a basis for long-term strategic planning. In one case study, students devised four scenarios outlining various impacts of climate change on the city, while in a second, they partnered with the Smart City Innovation Unit to examine the implications of digitalization for municipal governance. This article discusses how qualitative scenarios can support regional public foresight and the value of the scenario planning as participatory method, while also addressing the inherent limitations of the method in the context of regional public foresight.*

Keywords: *qualitative scenarios; public foresight; scenario planning; participatory methods*

1. Introduction

In recent decades, municipalities have been confronted with a wide range of challenges. As climate change progresses, extreme weather events such as heat waves, droughts, and heavy rainfall are occurring more and more frequently

(Stott, 2016). In recent years, for example, more record summers have been recorded in Germany and in 2021, entire parts of municipalities were destroyed by heavy rainfall (Ludwig et al., 2023). In addition, there are extreme situations such as the Corona pandemic, in which cultural institutions, schools, and childcare facilities were closed and employees had to shift to working from home or deal with loss of income in short-time work. In addition, the migration movement from the Middle East since 2015 and the war refugees from Ukraine since 2022, municipalities have been faced with the challenge of offering people accommodation and prospects. At the same time, the precarious financial situation and the increase in cyber-attacks on public institutions further threaten municipalities' room for manoeuvre. Furthermore, municipalities must manage broad structural transformations in the transport sector and energy supply in order to implement the change from a carbon-based to a sustainable society locally. From this, the claim can be derived that municipal management is more difficult today than ever (Roos & Schmitt, 2022).

These areas of tension do not seem to be easing in the near future and present municipal decision-makers with the task of developing long-term strategies to enable democratic and solidary coexistence on the ground.

This article addresses two different groups. On the one hand, it is shown to what extent qualitative scenarios can support municipal decision-makers in the development of long-term strategies to deal with multiple challenges. For this purpose, the scientific method of scenario planning is first introduced (section 2). The focus is on the purpose of scenarios and the emergence of foresight methods since the 1950s. Subsequently, the development process of qualitative scenarios is outlined on the basis of four phases (section 3).

On the other hand, with the help of a detailed description of two student practical projects, it is shown how teachers and lecturers can implement the method of scenario planning in practice (section 4). Both student projects were carried out at the Faculty of Management and Economics at the Ruhr University Bochum. Here, students developed qualitative scenarios together with representatives of the city of Bochum and civil society. In the first practical project, the students developed four qualitative scenarios that describe life in Bochum in the year 2046. In these scenarios, the focus is on the effects of climate change and the associated environmental and social lines of conflict. In the second practical project, students turned to the topic of digitization and the role of Bochum as a smart city. In close cooperation with the Smart City Innovation Unit (SCIU) of the City of Bochum, five scenarios have been created.

Based on the project descriptions, section 5 discusses the implications and limitations of applying scenario planning methods for public foresight. The students' experiences are compared with current discourses in the scientific literature. The article ends with a conclusion.

2. Scenario development as a scientific method

In this section, the concept of *scenarios* will be introduced and the emergence of scenario development as a scientific method will be described. The section concludes with a brief overview of the scientific fields in which scenarios are applied.

2.1 Definition of Scenarios

Scenarios are defined as alternative futures resulting from the combination of current trends and policy measures (Amer et al., 2013). They explore multiple plausible future spaces or alternative perspectives on the future (Chermack et al., 2001; Hoffart et al., 2021; Schmidt-Scheele, 2020). Scenarios describe possible future states of a complex system characterised by a network of influence factors, uncertainty about their development, and the occurrence of potential and perhaps eruptive events (Hoffart et al., 2021). Figure 1 shows the scenario cone. Here it becomes clear that the development of scenarios is about the systematic exploration of the future. Scenarios must first and foremost be possible, regardless of how probable their occurrence is. The goal here is to create a consistent set of futures. It is explicitly not about predicting the most likely future possible (Bradfield et al., 2005). Rather, scenarios serve as a means to an end. The development of scenarios is in the foreground. It is intended to prepare the people involved for possible eventualities and to promote the flexibility and innovative power of organizations and individuals in uncertain and complex contexts (Amer et al., 2013; Schoemaker, 1995).

Figure 1: The scenario cone.

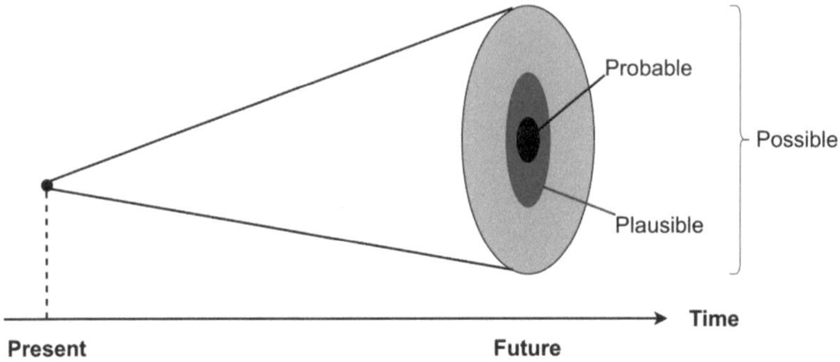

Source: adapted from Pillkahn (2008, 175).

In order for scenarios to support systemic thinking and holistic strategic planning, they must meet various characteristics.

First and foremost, scenarios must be possible. To this end, scenarios must be able to occur in principle and be based on well-founded assumptions about the future (Amer et al., 2013). In addition, the scenarios must paint a plausible picture of the future that is believed and accepted by users of the scenarios (Schmidt-Scheele, 2020). To ensure the plausibility of the scenarios, they must be consistent. Consistency is characterized by the fact that the assumptions about future developments do not contradict each other from present factors. The individual components of the scenarios must therefore be logically compatible (Gausemeier et al., 1998; Schlösser, 2022).

Since qualitative scenarios are often developed with or for organizations such as companies or municipalities, scenarios must be relevant and helpful. They should be able to support decision-makers (Chermack, 2018; Durance & Godet, 2010). To this end, scenarios must systematically and comprehensively prepare complex relationships in a coherent manner (Amer et al., 2013). In addition, the development process of the scenarios must be prepared transparently. This means that the assumptions, materials and conclusions of the scenarios are made available to users (Durance & Godet, 2010).

In the following, the emergence of the scenario method will be briefly outlined and the difference between predictive, normative, and explorative scenarios is described.

2.2 The Origin and Application of scenario development

The following subsection explains three exemplary applications of the term scenario in more detail, highlighting the purpose of three different types of scenarios: *predictive*, *normative*, and *explorative* (Schmidt-Scheele, 2020).

Scenario methods emerged in the 1950s to develop more effective war tactics in military contexts. The main aim was to test different strategies in simulated environments and to use the allocation of scarce resources as efficiently as possible in order to achieve the best possible outcome (Bradfield et al., 2005; Mayer, 2009). In the course of the 1960s, the field of application expanded and scenarios were increasingly used in contexts to improve political and social decision-making processes (Amer et al., 2013; Kahn & Wiener, 1967). Social and political contexts are characterized by complexity and uncertainty (Roos, 2015, 2017). The application of scenario methods to social and political systems marks the beginning of modern scenario methods (Bradfield et al., 2005). Thus, from the 1960s onwards, scenarios were no longer used only to predict well-structured problems. Rather, scenarios are used to examine changes in the entire system. Scenario methods focus on the interactions between the influencing factors and system dynamics in order to gain insights into possible options for decision-makers (Hoffart et al., 2021).

Basically, scenarios can be divided into three categories: predictive, normative, and explorative. These categories are based on three fundamental questions that can be asked of the scenarios from a user perspective.

Predictive scenarios address the question *"What will happen?"* (Börjeson et al., 2006). This question is accompanied by the development of scenarios that assess the probability of each scenario (Hoffart et al., 2021). Computer-aided forecasting models are often developed for this purpose, which extrapolate past and present data into the future (Amer et al., 2013). Examples of such scenarios include emission scenarios that simulate long-term emission pathways (Schmidt-Scheele, 2020). It is important to note that scenarios are generally to be distinguished from forecasts, as they explore a range of possible futures rather than identifying the most likely future possible (Amer et al., 2013; Chermack et al., 2001; Hoffart et al., 2021). Even though predictive scenarios are assigned to scenario planning, they are more traditional forecasts.

Normative scenarios are goal-oriented and address the *question of how a certain goal or scenario can be achieved* (Börjeson et al., 2006; Hoffart et al., 2021). In this context, both desirable and undesirable futures are taken into account in the creation of scenarios. Based on the target state, it is then analyzed which planning steps are necessary to achieve this state. Therefore, normative scenarios are particularly suitable for political and strategic contexts (Durance & Godet, 2010).

Explorative scenarios are designed to address the question *"What can happen?"* (Börjeson et al., 2006) by mapping out a wide spectrum of plausible futures without attempting to predict which will occur. Their construction and selection rest explicitly on the principle of plausibility: each scenario must be internally coherent and grounded in rigorous analysis of past and present trends, yet no scenario is assigned a probability of realization (Schmidt-Scheele, 2020). Instead, they focus on identifying key uncertainty factors—ranging from technological breakthroughs to socio-political shifts—and examining the complex interrelationships among them (Amer et al., 2013; Durance & Godet, 2010). By depicting alternative pathways, explorative scenarios enable us to anticipate how changes from the status quo might unfold and to prepare for a variety of contingencies. Typical examples include context scenarios, which explore possible future social, environmental, and political conditions, and socio-technical scenarios, which illuminate the dynamics of major systemic transitions (Hoffart et al., 2021). Ultimately, the exploratory purpose of these scenarios is not to forecast the most likely future but to reveal the breadth of what could happen, thereby enriching strategic decision-making under deep uncertainty (Amer et al., 2013).

In summary, scenarios can be classified based on their aim: predictive scenarios focus on predicting what will happen (often quantitative and probability-based), normative scenarios focus on achieving a desired future state (goal-directed and value-laden), and explorative scenarios focus on understanding the range of what could plausibly happen (plausibility-based and uncertainty-focused). Scenarios in general serve as a tool to explore multiple possibilities under uncertainty, rather than providing single-point forecasts.

3. The Development Process of Qualitative Scenarios

In general, the development of scenarios can be divided into four phases (Figure 2). In the first phase, the scenario field is identified, the time horizon is set and key factors are defined (Haigh, 2019). In order to be able to develop scenarios that differ from projections of the present and show alternative development paths, a time horizon must be defined that focuses on the long term (Zumbrunn, 2023). Different periods are mentioned here. In the field of long-range planning and strategic foresight, periods of 15–30 years are common (Bradfield et al., 2005; Hoffart et al., 2021). In contexts of public or urban foresight, time horizons of 20–50 years are considered (Dixon & Tewdwr-Jones, 2021; Roos & Schmitt, 2022; Szpilko, 2020).

Figure 2: The four phases of the scenario development process.

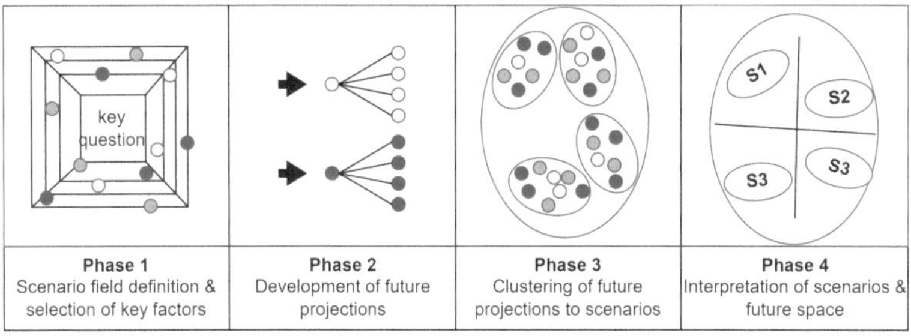

Source: Hoffart et al. (2021, 6).

The scenario field is used to develop a systematic representation of the interdependencies between different levels of the system. These can span different sectors and jurisdictions (Hoffart et al., 2021). In order to systematically capture the scenario field, qualitative methods such as literature analyses, participatory system mapping, or expert interviews are used (Ernst et al., 2018). The aim is to illuminate as broad an environment as possible in order to be able to identify a wide range of influencing factors. By means of the scenario environment, influencing factors are then compiled for the different levels of the system and evaluated according to their influence and uncertainty.

There are two ways to do this. On the one hand, a resource-saving and on the other hand a more resource-intensive method can be used to determine the influence and uncertainty of the factors (Pillkahn, 2008). Both approaches are used to identify key factors that can have the strongest influence on the development of the system. In system field analysis—as a resource-intensive method—all influencing factors are plotted in a matrix and the mutual influence of each factor on the others is assessed on the basis of an ordinal scale (Gausemeier et al., 1998). Since this approach was not used in the practical examples covered in this article, this approach is omitted here. A detailed description and practical application can be found in Hoffart et al. (2021).

Figure 3: A general Wilson Matrix.

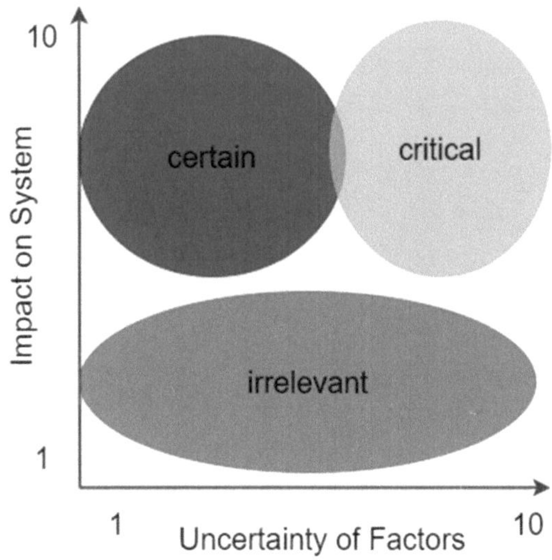

Source: Adapted from Pillkahn (2008, 203).

The Wilson matrix can be understood as a more resource-efficient method (Pillkahn, 2008). Each factor is assessed in terms of its systemic impact and uncertainty with a view to future development. The rating scale is ordinal and extends from 1 to 10, where 10 expresses the strongest impact on system or the highest uncertainty.

In the context of the practical examples presented here, the Wilson matrix was used to classify the influencing factors and thus identify the decisive key factors. Figure 3 shows a Wilson matrix as an example. The impact of the factors is plotted on the ordinate. The abscissa indicates the degree of uncertainty of a factor with regard to its possible development. The matrix can then be divided into different quadrants. A common subdivision can be seen in the Wilson Matrix shown here (Pillkahn, 2008). Factors that have a small impact on the system, regardless of how uncertain their development is assessed, tend to be less relevant for the design of the scenarios. Particularly interesting for the further development of the scenarios are those factors that have a high impact. Depending on the degree of uncertainty, these can be divided into certain and critical factors. Certain factors are factors for which there are relatively precise estimates, even over long periods of time. Critical factors have both a high influence and a high degree of uncertainty. They are particularly interesting from the point of view of scenario development, as they allow great freedom in the further design of the factors. These critical factors tend to be the key factors of the scenarios (Gausemeier et al., 1998). However, certain factors that have a particularly strong impact can also be included in the set of key factors. The selection of key factors is not only based on the structural assessment of their impact and uncertainty. Rather, the selection of key factors also depends on the purpose of the scenarios and the interests of the stakeholders involved (Ernst et al., 2018).

After the key factors have been identified, projections are developed in phase 2. Projections express different possible developments of the key factors. As a rule, at least two projections should be formulated for each key factor (Haigh, 2019; Pillkahn, 2008). When formulating projections, it is important that they reflect contrary developments. For example, if one defines a price as a key factor, two obvious projections would be that the price will either rise or fall. Depending on the key factor and system environment, the number of projections varies (Hoffart et al., 2021).

In phase 3, the projections of the key factors are merged into consistent scenarios. As in phase 1, a resource-saving approach as well as a resource-intensive approach can be used for this purpose. The resource-intensive method is consistency analysis (Pillkahn, 2008; Weimer-Jehle, 2006). This method is based on the pairwise comparison of two projections of different key factors. Here, the simultaneous occurrence of the projections in a future is evaluated. Thus, the logical consistency of the pairwise occurrence of the projections is determined. This evaluation also takes place with an ordinal scale. Depending on the number of projections, consistency analysis can extend over a large set of projections and thus ties up large human resources and, if necessary, computational capacities (Weimer-Jehle, 2023; Weimer-Jehle et al., 2016). As part of the practical examples, we used morphological analysis as a resource-saving method.

In morphological analysis, the goal is to combine the individual projections into plausible and consistent scenarios. As a rule, the scenarios should be developed together with decision-makers and stakeholders. The starting point is a particularly central key factor with an associated projection. In figure 4, for example, this is the projection A of the key factor 1. Based on this projection, further projections of the other key factors [2, 3, 4, ...] are assigned to the first scenario. This process takes place in workshops and discursively determines which combination of projections represents a plausible state of the future (Godet, 2000a, 2000b). To determine the number of scenarios that will be included in the later analysis, each projection should occur in at least one scenario.[1] The stylized example in Figure 4 would therefore reveal four scenarios. In the literature, the number of scenarios differs depending on the methods used. However, three to five scenarios represent a good middle ground between the reduction of complexity and the analytical effort involved in evaluating the scenarios (Amer et al., 2013; Bradfield et al., 2005; Durance/Godet, 2010; Schwartz, 1996; Sharpe/Van der Heijden, 2007).

Figure 4: General example of the morphological analysis.

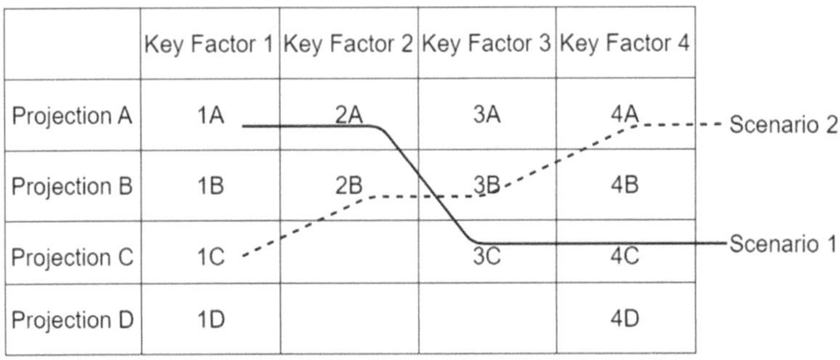

Source: adapted from Pillkahn (2008, 204).

Phase 4 includes the interpretation, preparation, and communication of the scenarios. The depth and design of the visions of the future depends on the desired scope and the area of application. If the scenarios are used for public communication or as educational tools, then the focus is on communicating the scenarios. For this purpose, the scenarios can be prepared into stories in text form or transferred to other creative visualizations. In principle, there are no limits here (Pillkahn, 2008). If the scenarios are further processed in scientific contexts or in strategic planning, the focus is more on the interpretation and analysis of the systemic relationships of the key factors and projections in the individual scenarios. For example, qualitative scenarios are used in the development of emission pathways within the framework of the IPCC (Kriegler

1 In Figure 4, two scenarios are still missing, which contain the projections 1B, 1D, 3A, 4B and 4D. In order not to overload the figure, these scenarios were omitted.

et al., 2014; O'Neill et al., 2014; van Vuuren et al., 2014), in the concrete simulation of transformation paths of energy systems (Hoffart et al., 2021; Pregger et al., 2020; Prehofer et al., 2021; Vögele et al., 2017) or in scientific advice to municipal decision-makers (Nilsson et al., 2017; Volkery & Ribeiro, 2009).

In the following section, two student projects are presented in which master's students from the Faculty of Management and Economics at the Ruhr-University Bochum have developed qualitative scenarios for and with the city of Bochum. These student projects show the didactic added value and strategic potential that lies in the development of qualitative scenarios. Municipalities in particular have a special role to play in times of crisis. They can be understood as representatives of politics and have the opportunity to shape transformation processes in a participatory and inclusive way in the immediate vicinity of the population and to absorb the negative effects of the transformation. (Roos/ Schmitt, 2022).

4. Application of Qualitative Scenario Development for Public Foresight

Due to advancing technological progress, automation, and digitalization, the task profile of universities is shifting. It is no longer just about preparing knowledge and bringing it closer to students. In the digital age, knowledge is archived and easily accessible. Rather, it is about empowering students to deal with complexity and uncertainty. Systemic and critical thinking can be named as two central building blocks here (Roos, 2024). The task profile of universities has thus evolved from the transfer of knowledge to the intertwined transfer of knowledge and skills in dealing with complex and uncertain issues (Ehlers, 2020). In order to meet these new challenges, seminars have been offered at the Faculty of Management and Economics in recent years that deal with the systematic and scientific recording of future developments. The two practical projects presented below take up this claim.

In the first practical project *Climate-resilient Bochum 2046*, the question was "What are the specific impacts of climate change on Bochum and what can be done to prepare for it?". In the second practical project *Smart City Bochum 2040*, the students were confronted with the topic of advancing digitalization. The focus was on the influence of digitization on the municipal administration and its possibilities for action.

To address these topics, students of the Faculty of Management and Economics have developed qualitative and explorative scenarios at the regional level. In the first practical project, the scenarios were developed *for* the city of Bochum. The students worked primarily independently and had the results evaluated by the Climate and Sustainability Unit of the City of Bochum[2]. In addition, the local working group of Scientists for Future provided its assessment of a sustainable city of Bochum in the light of the potential local effects of climate change (Ehrhardt et al., 2022). In the second practical project, scenarios were developed *together* with representatives of the Smart City Innovation Unit (SCIU) of the city of Bochum. The students of the Ruhr University Bochum prepared the development process and developed exploratory scenarios in two workshops with members of the SCIU.

These two projects show how the scientific method of scenario planning can be integrated into university teaching and collaborations between the university and the municipal administration can be established.

In the following section, the course and structure of the two practice projects is outlined. Both practical projects spanned a total of two semesters and focused on different phases of scenario development.

4.1 First practical project: Climate-resilient Bochum 2046

The first practical project spanned from April 2021 to April 2022 and included two seminars. In the first seminar, the students were introduced to the topic of the regional impacts of climate change and familiarized themselves with extensive teaching materials on qualitative scenario development. In the second seminar, the students concentrated on the scientific processing of the scenarios. Table 1 shows the four phases of scenario development and which tasks were implemented by the students in the first and second seminar. A special feature of the seminars was the project-oriented way of working. Instead of frontal teaching in the form of lectures, the teaching materials on the method of qualitative scenario development and the role of sustainability in macroeconomics were made available to the students in an interactive online course. The students and lectures then came together in seminar sessions and discussed

2 The evaluation took place in the form of a presentation of the results of the scenarios and an interview with Sonja Eisenmann as Head of the Climate and Sustainability Unit of the City of Bochum (Püttbach, 2022b).

the teaching materials together and trained practical steps of scenario development. For this purpose, there were several smaller group works in which historical stories from the last 30 years were collected, pop cultural narratives of the future were assessed and one's own attitudes towards the future were discussed. The aim of the joint work phases was not primarily to impart knowledge, but to engage creatively and critically with the future.

Table 1: Overview of development phases for scenarios for the project Climate-resilient Bochum 2046.

Phase 1	Phase 2	Phase 3	Phase 4
1.1. Objective & time horizont provided by lectures 1.2. Students researched responsibilities of municipalities & influence factors 1.3. Applying Wilson Matrix to define key factors	2.1. Students developed projections for key factors 2.2. Discussion of key factors with lecturers	3.1. Morphological analysis to construct scenarios	4.1. Developing narratives in form of persona 4.2. Presentation of scenarios to S4F and CSU Bochum 4.3. Second seminar on scientific preparation of scenarios 4.4. Preparation of student anthology

Source: own contribution based on the seminar documents.

In the first phase, the lecturers gave the students the question of the seminar and the time horizon for the exploratory scenarios. In addition, group work phases were planned in which the students were able to consolidate the method and already collect the first possible influencing factors. In their own work phases, the students researched the areas of action and responsibility of the city of Bochum and collected concrete influencing factors that can impact the scope of action of the city of Bochum against the background of advancing climate change. In order to narrow down the influencing factors collected and identify important drivers, the students applied the Wilson Matrix.

In phase 2, nine key factors covering political, ecological, techno-economic, and social factors could be identified together. In small groups, the students developed projections for the individual key factors, which were then discussed and adapted with the lecturers. In phase 3, the students developed four scenarios together with the lecturers based on morphological analysis. In the end, qualitative scenarios could be developed that define the framework conditions of the city of Bochum in 2046.

The fourth phase of scenario development was ultimately divided into two parts. In the first part, the students each wrote a term paper as part of their final course assessment. These term papers dealt with different aspects of the scenarios. The seminar papers addressed the local effects of climate change, prepared the method of qualitative scenario planning, backed up the scenarios with scientific evidence and developed narratives to communicate the scenarios. In order to communicate the significance of the developed scenarios, so-called personas[3] were designed. This creative form of writing is about fictional characters going about their everyday lives in the respective scenarios and thus bringing the reader closer to the meaning of such a future (Torma/Aschemann-Witzel, 2024).

The second part of the fourth phase includes the second seminar. This seminar came about because the students expressed a desire to continue developing their scenario work beyond the framework of the first seminar by promoting the further processing and communication of the developed scenarios. In this seminar, the students worked almost independently. The aim was to produce a student anthology[4] in which the method and the results are prepared in such a way that they can serve as a working basis for interested parties and employees in the municipal administration. To do this, the students had to partially rewrite the existing texts from the term papers, compile a more solid empirical basis for the individual scenarios and enter into direct communication with the Climate and Sustainability Office of the City of Bochum. The anthology was compiled over seven months. After the publication of the student anthology, excerpts were presented in a public reading at the Bochum Theatre.

---

3 The scenario description in the form of personas can be viewed in the German-language student anthology (see Eckert, 2022; Leusmann, 2022; Püttbach, 2022a; Vollbracht, 2022).

4 The student anthology was edited by the lecturers. The individual contributions were written by the students of the seminars (see Roos et al., 2022).

Table 2 lists the four scenarios that emerged in the practical project. The scenarios describe mixed futures in which the negative effects of advancing climate change take different forms. Particularly interesting are the social upheavals that will emerge in the city of Bochum in 2046 as a result of global developments. The scenarios vividly present the tensions between economic prosperity and socially acceptable redistribution and the dealing with climate refugees.

Table 2: Overview of the four scenarios of the project Climate-resilient Bochum 2046.

Scenarios	Description
Waste Land 2046 – "We Told You So" (Alfers/Ruhfaut, 2022)	This worst-case scenario depicts Bochum in 2046 as the locus of pervasive system and ecosystem collapse. Extreme weather events, failing supply chains, and dwindling natural resources result in severe shortages of water, food, and energy. Widespread unemployment and social unrest dominate daily life, while only affluent households with off-grid power systems maintain reliable access to electricity. Motorized transportation has largely broken down; most inhabitants travel on foot or by bicycle. Trust in political institutions has all but vanished, and public protest remains absent, as citizens have lost all hope in governmental intervention.
Greentopia – "Too Good to Be True" (Alfers, Kruse, et al., 2022)	In this hybrid utopian-dystopian future, a rigorous sustainability agenda in Germany and Bochum has successfully averted major climate catastrophes. A pervasive "sustainability mind-set" combined with stringent consumption and production regulations ensures stable resource provision and a clean environment. However, elevated energy costs and strict usage limits place significant burdens on households and businesses, giving rise to a small yet vocal protest movement. The majority of residents nonetheless accept these constraints as necessary for long-term ecological stability.

Scenarios	Description
Economy First – "Business as Usual" (Alfers, Westhof, et al., 2022)	Under this growth-oriented narrative, policymakers and corporations prioritize "green" innovation-driven expansion without implementing substantive social redistribution. Large firms embrace virtual working models, which exacerbates income and spatial segregation: wealthy populations inhabit secure suburbs or gated communities, while inner-city districts experience increasing poverty. Smart-city technologies are deployed chiefly for efficiency gains and surveillance, and broad segments of the populace see little benefit from overall prosperity. The middle class continues to contract, and public scepticism toward digitalization intensifies.
Rotten Oasis – "Let's Make Things Better" (Alfers, 2022)	This scenario combines moderate climate impacts with a phase of economic stabilization, thereby averting acute systemic crises. A collective awareness of sustainability emerges, yet political urgency and financial resources for adaptation measures remain insufficient. During periods of drought and extreme rainfall, water and energy rationing are enforced, while technical interventions—such as air-conditioning units, façade greening, and communal "cooling shelters"—become commonplace. Local biodiversity suffers, and supply chains for industrial goods are robust but consumer-goods provisioning remains vulnerable. Municipal authorities respond reactively, and citizen-led initiatives assume primary responsibility for climate adaptation and the maintenance of social cohesion.

Source: The summaries and translations of the scenarios were created by the author.

The close and self-organized cooperation between students and lecturers in the practical project Climate-resilient Bochum 2046 and the resulting anthology gave the reason to continue the format. The second practical project will be presented in the next section.

4.2 Second practical project: Smart City Bochum 2040

The second practical project also spanned two seminars from April 2023 to April 2024 and focuses on the Smart City concept of the City of Bochum. Within the concept, innovation scouting and urban foresight on technological potentials and negative consequences for the urban population is planned. At the beginning of the seminar, the students of the practical project familiarized themselves with the topic of the smart city and the method of qualitative scenario development with the help of the methodological self-study course. In this practical project, the focus was on the collaborative development of scenarios *together* with representatives of the SCIU. For this purpose, two one-day workshops were organized, which the students planned and carried out together with the lecturers. Before the workshops took place, the students rehearsed the development of scenarios in fast forward under the guidance of the lecturers. For this purpose, there were several seminar sessions in which the basic concepts of scenario planning were explained and the creation of scenarios was rehearsed. Table 3 shows the course of the practical project with regard to the workshops. The trial run of the students is not explicitly listed.

Table 3: Overview of development phases for scenarios for the project Smart City Bochum 2040.

Phase 1	Phase 2	Phase 3	Phase 4
1.1. Scenario field defined by students & lecturers 1.2. Collection of influence factors with SCIU members 1.3. Applying Wilson matrix with SCIU members	2.1. Developing of projections with SCIU members	3.1. Morphological analysis with members of SCIU to construct scenarios	4.1. Public presentation of scenarios to SCIU 4.2. Second seminar to further develop visual communication of scenarios

Source: own contribution based on the seminar documents.

In phase 1, the students defined the scenario field and the time horizon. The basis for this was public strategy papers of the city of Bochum, in which central topics and development paths of the city up to 2030 are outlined (Stadt Bochum, 2017; 2022). The first workshop took place about 6 weeks after the start of the seminar. At this workshop, influencing factors were collected on the basis of the scenario field. The students used participatory brainstorming methods. The members of the SCIU were divided into two groups and each group was supervised by students. The aim was to collect influencing factors, discuss their systemic significance, and assign them to the PESTEL[5] categories. In the second part of the first workshop, the influencing factors collected in this way were evaluated according to their systemic influence and uncertainty using the Wilson matrix. Finally, the factors classified in this way were discussed together and 12 key factors were identified. In this way, complex and supra-regional trends could be translated to the regional level (Nilsson et al., 2017) and the development of explorative scenarios for the city of Bochum could be prepared. After the first workshop, the students further specified the key factors collected and developed projections for each key factor. For this purpose, the notes from the first workshop from the discussion rounds were used to align the descriptions of the key factors and their projections as closely as possible to the ideas of the members of the SCIU.

In the second workshop, phases 2 and 3 were combined. First, the developed projections were discussed together with representatives of the SCIU and then scenarios were developed by means of morphological analysis. The students took the scenarios developed in this way into the seminar sessions and developed narratives, analysed the systemic relationships and reflected the results back with the SCIU. This resulted in five scenarios.

As before, the fourth phase of the project is divided into two parts. The conclusion of the first seminar was a public presentation of the scenarios, during which the development process was presented and the scenarios were discussed. The second part of phase 4 was implemented in a second seminar. The focus was on the creative preparation and broader communication of the resulting scenarios. Comparable to the creation of the student anthology, the students formed working groups that dealt with different areas of responsibility. The goal was to develop a video that conveys the central aspects of the scenarios in a scientifically sound way. To this end, the students contacted advertising and graphics agencies, drafted a script, interviewed scientists about the various focal points of the scenarios and organized a final event in which the results were presented to a wider public (RUB, 2024).

Table 4 lists the five scenarios developed and includes a brief description. Central topics of the scenarios are the development of the global security situation, the financial situation of the city of Bochum and the structure of digitalization. Both the international geopolitical balance of power and the local

5 PESTEL is an acronym of the terms Political, Economic, Social, Technological, Environmental and Legal and serves as a strategic orientation framework.

implementation of digital services in private or public hands play a central role here. The scenarios can rarely be assigned to a dystopia or utopia and can thus be used as cause for thought for the further development of the smart city concept.

Table 4: Overview of the five scenarios of the project Smart City Bochum 2040.

Scenarios	Description
Plenty of Light with a touch of shadow	By 2040, Bochum benefits from deep global integration and successful digitalization: stable, diversified supply chains and a sustainable energy infrastructure underpin a thriving economy. Key public services have been partly privatized, yet a strong sense of community—fueled by citizen engagement and private foundations—ensures social cohesion and effective crisis management. Although municipal budgets remain tight, widespread trust in digital technologies and robust cybersecurity enable seamless communication and low levels of crime.
The Division	In 2040 the world has fractured into national blocs. "America First" politics and trade conflicts have stalled globalization, leading to deindustrialization in Germany, the disappearance of the middle class, and a surge in populism and right-wing policies. In Bochum, empty coffers and high unemployment have driven privatization of essential infrastructure and pervasive surveillance, while affluent groups seclude themselves in gated communities. Smart-city technologies are deployed primarily to control disadvantaged populations.
We – But not all	Amid climate change and social tensions in the 2040s, tightly knit local communities emerge in Bochum, but mutual mistrust deepens between them. Despite ecological pressures and constrained household budgets, the broader population remains indifferent toward digitalization and smart-city initiatives. Key services such as infrastructure, education, and healthcare are largely privatized, and shortages of skilled workers combined with low urban density hinder progress.
Digitalization as the last hope	By 2040, Bochum faces economic stagnation and depleted municipal funds, yet progressive policies and a creative civil society view digital transformation as the key to renewal. Through targeted partnerships and investments in education and training, the city strengthens its digital competencies and develops innovative solutions for mobility, energy, and administration. Digitalization becomes the driving force behind sustainable growth and renewed social cohesion.

Scenarios	Description
The Great Crash	Following a period of global cooperation to combat climate change, society has become fully digitalized: AI-optimized supply chains, intelligent energy distribution, and interconnected communication define daily life. Then an unforeseen threat—whether an "AI virus" or cyber terror attack—brings all digital infrastructure to its knees within days. In Bochum, supply chains falter, panic buying spreads, and without Internet-based administration and services, societal functions grind to a halt.

Source: The summaries and translations of the scenarios were created by the author.

The description of the two practical projects is intended to show how versatile the scenario planning method can be used. On the one hand, the practical projects have contributed to students of the Faculty of Management and Economics dealing with interdisciplinary issues. On the other hand, the students were able to gain experience in dealing with experts from municipal administration through the independent structure of the seminars and had to organize project management independently. In the following section, the applied method of scenario planning and the experience gained in the two practical projects against the background of regional political decisions will be reflected.

5. Reflections about Qualitative Scenarios for regional public foresight

The description of the two practical projects shows how flexibly the scenario planning method can be applied. It can be applied in various degrees of depth and professional expertise. While scenarios developed by students will inevitably be more superficial than those developed by experts of the respective fields, current debates in the scientific literature can be transferred to the practical projects. Regardless of the depth of the scenarios developed, the process encourages collaborative work between the participants and promotes the reciprocal transfer of knowledge between universities and practice.

In the following section, the core benefits and limitations of qualitative scenario planning as a foresight method will be discussed and the experiences of the two practical projects will be reflected against this background. Project diaries and reflection reports of the students, which they have written to accompany the projects and discussed with the lecturers in feedback meetings, serve as the basis for this reflection.

The work in the practical projects has clearly shown that scenario planning is a method with which complexity and uncertainty of long-term developments can be captured and communicated in a structured form (Durance/Godet, 2010; Hoffart et al., 2021). Particularly in regional contexts such as urban and spatial planning, decision-makers are confronted with complex and transdisciplinary challenges (Dixon/Tewdwr-Jones, 2021). These experiences are also reflected in the students' reports, which highlight the competence development of design thinking and ambiguity tolerance (Ehlers, 2020). In addition, there is a strong focus on the integration of inter- and transdisciplinary dimensions, which are addressed in public foresight in the form of social, technological, economic, environmental, political, legal, and value-based (STEEPVL) factors (Szpilko, 2020). This confronts regional decision-makers with a holistic problem and enables them to develop strategic decisions as a group through the participatory development of shared visions (Burrows/Gnad, 2018; Ravetz/Miles, 2016; Rijkens-Klomp/Van Der Duin, 2014). Here, existing thought patterns and assumptions about the future are challenged and compromise is supported by the joint development of futures (Amanatidou, 2017).

Although this process was not evaluated on the part of the municipal administrative employees in the course of the practical projects, the students report joint learning effects in their project diaries. This showed that the students were able to broaden their economic view from their studies. Above all, the close cooperation with the SCIU in the Smart City Bochum 2040 project showed the students how administrative work processes differ from academic work. These different logics represent a central challenge in the application of scenario planning processes in public foresight. The scientific approach to the future focuses on systemic relationships between inter- and transdisciplinary factors, which are analyzed in time horizons of decades. Whereas the strategic work of administrations and public organizations tends to take place over shorter periods of up to 15 years. This is a structural conflict that can hinder the development process and the practical use of public foresight for political work in municipalities (Bourgeois et al., 2017; Rijkens-Klomp/Van Der Duin, 2014; Tatar et al., 2020). However, the SCIU is a special working unit within the municipal administration. The members of the SCIU work in different areas of the city administration and at the same time belong to a working unit that deals with long-term developments of a smart city and is granted fixed working hours for this purpose. As a result, the SCIU offers great potential for incorporating findings from scenario planning into the day-to-day work of the municipal administration.

In addition to communicating with the city administration, the students had to moderate different perspectives and interests in their own group. Although this also led to tensions because the workload was distributed highly unequally at times and students held conflicting opinions about the contents of the anthology, this was actively addressed in the group and led to the development of communication skills and the strengthening of one's own self-efficacy. The students emphasise the self-organised character of the project work, which strengthens the group structure and encourages students to proactively stand up for themselves and the project. In particular, the acquisition of offers from various publishers for the publication of the student anthology in the project Climate-resilient Bochum 2046, as well as the contact with graphic designers for the preparation of the scenarios in the Smart City Bochum 2040 project, confronted the students with rather unusual tasks that are not required in regular studies. The students reported that they regularly had to leave their comfort zone due to the varied tasks and at the same time had the feeling that the project team supported them in these steps.

Within the practical projects, the lecturers were able to gain insights into the personal development of the students through the diaries and feedback discussions. However, this also reveals a fundamental problem of the scenario planning method. The learning effects described by the students cannot be directly attributed to the scenario planning method itself. Although the collaborative nature of the method promotes democratic decision-making and self-efficacy, these effects are difficult to attribute directly to the scenario method (Amanatidou, 2017; Rijkens-Klomp/Van Der Duin, 2014; Tatar et al., 2020). Especially in economics studies, the focus is often on written exams as a form of examination. Here, scenario planning proves to be a helpful method for breaking up isolated teaching and learning formats and bringing those involved into direct exchange. Especially against the background of advancing digitalization, the mediation and testing of collaborative and transdisciplinary approaches plays a greater role (Ehlers 2020).

In addition to the process-oriented effects of scenario planning, which have a positive effect on group dynamics in an organization and the individual development of strategic thinking in complex and fundamentally uncertain contexts, scenario planning is subject to material limitations. The presentation of the two practical projects shows that scenario planning is a time-consuming and financially intensive method. Both projects lasted one year each. Of course, this is partly due to the university context, where semester times have to be adhered to and exams have to be collected. Nevertheless, well-founded scenario planning can extend over several months to years and requires intensive group processes to be effective (Durance/Godet, 2010; Hoffart et al., 2021). The two practical projects took place as part of regular courses and the publication and visualization were partly co-financed by university funding programs. Thus, in addition to the personnel leave, there were no additional costs for the city of Bochum. Nevertheless, the high intensity of scenario planning can be a central obstacle in the practical application of public foresight. However, this use of time and personnel resources is not inherent in the scenario planning method, but is much more due to the complex challenges of participatory processes and a sound scientific foundation.

6. Conclusions

This article has shown that qualitative scenario planning offers a systematic method for addressing uncertainty in long-term municipal strategy development. The method is based on identifying a scenario field, isolating key factors, formulating projections, and combining them into consistent futures. Rather than predicting the most likely outcome, scenario planning seeks to map out plausible alternatives that can challenge assumptions, highlight systemic interdependencies, and provide a structured basis for strategic reflection.

The two student projects presented here illustrate how this scientific approach can be adapted in practice. In both practical projects, students experimented with the method, engaged with municipal stakeholders, and translated abstract foresight concepts into narratives and visualizations. These projects demonstrate that universities can serve as experimental spaces where exploratory foresight methods are tested, refined, and foster transdisciplinary exchange. They also reveal the dual challenge of linking academic processes—which operate with long time horizons and systemic perspectives—to administrative practice, which is often bound by shorter planning cycles and functions in different institutional logics.

The experiences suggest that the value of scenario planning for regional public foresight lies less in delivering ready-made policy solutions and more in enabling collaborative exploration of uncertainty and in building competencies for systemic thinking. For this potential to unfold, both sides must be receptive: universities need to open their teaching formats to real-world collaboration, while municipal institutions must be willing to engage with exploratory methods whose outcomes are not immediately instrumental. When these conditions are met, qualitative scenarios can serve as a bridge between academic experimentation and municipal strategy, fostering long-term, participatory, and adaptive approaches to local governance.

References

Alfers, M. (2022). Szenariobeschreibung "Rotten Oasis – Let's make things better". In M. Roos, J.-H. Kamlage, & E.-J. Schmitt (Eds.), *Klimaresiliente Kommunalpolitik: Eine Szenarioanalyse für Bochum im Jahr 2046*. Springer Fachmedien Wiesbaden. (pp. 121–132). https://doi.org/10.1007/978-3-658-38393-0

Alfers, M., Kruse, L. M., & Schumacher, S. (2022). Szenarionbeschreibung "Greentopia – Too good to be true". In M. Roos, J.-H. Kamlage, & E.-J. Schmitt (Eds.), *Klimaresiliente Kommunalpolitik: Eine Szenarioanalyse für Bochum im Jahr 2046*. (pp. 75–86). Springer Fachmedien Wiesbaden. https://doi.org/10.1007/978-3-658-38393-0

Alfers, M., & Ruhfaut, M. (2022). Szenariobeschreibung "Waste Land 2046 – We told you so". In M. Roos, J.-H. Kamlage, & E.-J. Schmitt (Eds.), *Klimaresiliente Kommunalpolitik: Eine Szenarioanalyse für Bochum im Jahr 2046* (pp. 53–64). Springer Fachmedien Wiesbaden. https://doi.org/10.1007/978-3-658-38393-0

Alfers, M., Westhof, M. K., & Wieseler, P. (2022). Szenariobeschreibung "Economy First – Business as usual". In M. Roos, J.-H. Kamlage, & E.-J. Schmitt (Eds.), *Klimaresiliente Kommunalpolitik: Eine Szenarioanalyse für Bochum im Jahr 2046* (pp. 99–110). Springer Fachmedien Wiesbaden. https://doi.org/10.1007/978-3-658-38393-0

Amanatidou, E. (2017). Foresight process impacts: Beyond any official targets, foresight is bound to serve democracy. *Futures*, *85*, 1–13. https://doi.org/10.1016/j.futures.2016.11.003

Amer, M., Daim, T. U., & Jetter, A. (2013). A review of scenario planning. *Futures*, *46*, 23–40. https://doi.org/10.1016/j.futures.2012.10.003

Börjeson, L., Höjer, M., Dreborg, K.-H., Ekvall, T., & Finnveden, G. (2006). Scenario types and techniques: Towards a user's guide. *Futures*, *38*(7), 723–739. https://doi.org/10.1016/j.futures.2005.12.002

Bourgeois, R., Penunia, E., Bisht, S., & Boruk, D. (2017). Foresight for all: Co-elaborative scenario building and empowerment. *Technological Forecasting and Social Change, 124*, 178–188. https://doi.org/10.1016/j.techfore.2017.04.018

Bradfield, R., Wright, G., Burt, G., Cairns, G., & Van Der Heijden, K. (2005). The origins and evolution of scenario techniques in long range business planning. *Futures, 37*(8), 795–812. https://doi.org/10.1016/j.futures.2005.01.003

Burrows, M. J., & Gnad, O. (2018). Between 'muddling through' and 'grand design': Regaining political initiative – The role of strategic foresight. *Futures, 97*, 6–17. https://doi.org/10.1016/j.futures.2017.06.002

Chermack, T. J. (2018). An Analysis and Categorization of Scenario Planning Scholarship from 1995–2016. *Journal of Futures Studies, 22*(4). https://doi.org/10.6531/JFS.201806.22(4).0004

Chermack, T. J., Lynham, S., & Ruona, W. (2001). A Review of Scenario Planning Literature. *Futures Research Quartely, 17*(2), 7–31.

Dixon, T. J., & Tewdwr-Jones, M. (2021). *Urban futures: Planning for city foresight and city visions* (1st ed.). Bristol University Press. https://doi.org/10.46692/9781447336297

Durance, P., & Godet, M. (2010). Scenario building: Uses and abuses. *Technological Forecasting and Social Change, 77*(9), 1488–1492. https://doi.org/10.1016/j.techfore.2010.06.007

Eckert, L. (2022). Economy first: Macht kaputt, was euch kaputt macht. In M. Roos, J.-H. Kamlage, & E.-J. Schmitt (Eds.), *Klimaresiliente Kommunalpolitik: Eine Szenarioanalyse für Bochum im Jahr 2046* (pp. 111–120). Springer Fachmedien Wiesbaden. https://doi.org/10.1007/978-3-658-38393-0

Ehlers, U.-D. (2020). *Future Skills: Lernen der Zukunft – Hochschule der Zukunft.* Springer Fachmedien Wiesbaden. https://doi.org/10.1007/978-3-658-29297-3

Ehrhardt, H., Linke, C., & Schüttler, S. (2022). Bochum: Ausblick auf messbare Indikatoren in der fortschreitenden Klimakatastrophe bis 2046. In M. Roos, J.-H. Kamlage, & E.-J. Schmitt (Eds.), *Klimaresiliente Kommunalpolitik: Eine Szenarioanalyse für Bochum im Jahr 2046* (pp. 173–194). Springer Fachmedien Wiesbaden. https://doi.org/10.1007/978-3-658-38393-0

Ernst, A., Biß, K. H., Shamon, H., Schumann, D., & Heinrichs, H. U. (2018). Benefits and challenges of participatory methods in qualitative energy scenario development. *Technological Forecasting and Social Change, 127*, 245–257. http://dx.doi.org/10.1016/j.techfore.2017.09.026

Gausemeier, J., Fink, A., & Schlake, O. (1998). Scenario Management: An Approach to Develop Future Potentials. *Technological Forecasting and Social Change*, *59*, 111–130.

Godet, M. (2000a). How to be rigorous with scenario planning. *Foresight*, 2(1), 5–9. https://doi.org/10.1108/14636680010802438

Godet, M. (2000b). The Art of Scenarios and Strategic Planning: Tools and Pitfalls. *Technological Forecasting and Social Change*, *65*(1), 3–22. https://doi.org/10.1016/S0040-1625(99)00120-1

Haigh, N. (2019). *Scenario planning for climate change: A Guide For Strategists*. Routledge.

Hoffart, F. M., Schmitt, E.-J., & Roos, M. (2021). Rethinking Economic Energy Policy Research – Developing Qualitative Scenarios to Identify Feasible Energy Policies. *Journal of Sustainable Development of Energy, Water and Environment Systems*, 9(2), 1–28. https://doi.org/10.13044/j.sdewes.d8.0331

Kahn, H., & Wiener, A. J. (1967). *The Year 2000 A Framework for Speculation on the Next Thirty-Three Years* (5th ed.). The Macmillan Company.

Kriegler, E., Edmonds, J., Hallegatte, S., Ebi, K. L., Kram, T., Riahi, K., Winkler, H., & van Vuuren, D. P. (2014). A new scenario framework for climate change research: The concept of shared climate policy assumptions. *Climatic Change*, *122*(3), 401–414. https://doi.org/10.1007/s10584-013-0971-5

Leusmann, L. (2022). Rotten Oasis: Woanders is noch mehr schei... In M. Roos, J.-H. Kamlage, & E.-J. Schmitt (Eds.), *Klimaresiliente Kommunalpolitik: Eine Szenarioanalyse für Bochum im Jahr 2046* (pp. 133–144). Springer Fachmedien Wiesbaden. https://doi.org/10.1007/978-3-658-38393-0

Ludwig, P., Ehmele, F., Franca, M. J., Mohr, S., Caldas-Alvarez, A., Daniell, J. E., Ehret, U., Feldmann, H., Hundhausen, M., Knippertz, P., Küpfer, K., Kunz, M., Mühr, B., Pinto, J. G., Quinting, J., Schäfer, A. M., Seidel, F., & Wisotzky, C. (2023). A multi-disciplinary analysis of the exceptional flood event of July 2021 in central Europe – Part 2: Historical context and relation to climate change. *Natural Hazards and Earth System Sciences*, *23*(4), 1287–1311. https://doi.org/10.5194/nhess-23-1287-2023

Mayer, I. S. (2009). The Gaming of Policy and the Politics of Gaming: A Review. *Simulation & Gaming*, 40(6), 825–862. https://doi.org/10.1177/1046878109346456

Nilsson, A. E., Bay-Larsen, I., Carlsen, H., van Oort, B., Bjørkan, M., Jylhä, K., Klyuchnikova, E., Masloboev, V., & van der Watt, L.-M. (2017). Towards extended shared socioeconomic pathways: A combined participatory bottom-up and top-down methodology with results from the Barents region.

Global Environmental Change, 45, 124–132. https://doi.org/10.1016/j.gloenvcha.2017.06.001

O'Neill, B. C., Kriegler, E., Riahi, K., Ebi, K. L., Hallegatte, S., Carter, T. R., Mathur, R., & van Vuuren, D. P. (2014). A new scenario framework for climate change research: The concept of shared socioeconomic pathways. *Climatic Change, 122*(3), 387–400. https://doi.org/10.1007/s10584-013-0905-2

Pillkahn, U. (2008). *Using trends and scenarios as tools for strategy development: Shaping the future of your enterprise*. Publicis Corporate Publishing.

Pregger, T., Naegler, T., Weimer-Jehle, W., Prehofer, S., & Hauser, W. (2020). Moving towards socio-technical scenarios of the German energy transition—Lessons learned from integrated energy scenario building. *Climatic Change, 162*(4), 1743–1762. https://doi.org/10.1007/s10584-019-02598-0

Prehofer, S., Kosow, H., Naegler, T., Pregger, T., Vögele, S., & Weimer-Jehle, W. (2021). Linking qualitative scenarios with quantitative energy models: Knowledge integration in different methodological designs. *Energy, Sustainability and Society, 11*(1), 25. https://doi.org/10.1186/s13705-021-00298-1

Püttbach, K. (2022a). Greentopia: Ohne Grün ist alles nichts, aber Grün ist nicht alles. In M. Roos, J.-H. Kamlage, & E.-J. Schmitt (Eds.), *Klimaresiliente Kommunalpolitik: Eine Szenarioanalyse für Bochum im Jahr 2046* (pp. 87–98). Springer Fachmedien Wiesbaden. https://doi.org/10.1007/978-3-658-38393-0

Püttbach, K. (2022b). "Wir müssen ... Sozial gerechten Klimaschutz und Klimafolgenanpassung auf den Weg bringen" – Ein Interview mit der Leiterin der Stabsstelle Klima und Nachhaltigkeit der Stadt Bochum. In M. Roos, J.-H. Kamlage, & E.-J. Schmitt (Eds.), *Klimaresiliente Kommunalpolitik: Eine Szenarioanalyse für Bochum im Jahr 2046* (pp. 161–172). Springer Fachmedien Wiesbaden. https://doi.org/10.1007/978-3-658-38393-0

Ravetz, J., & Miles, I. D. (2016). Foresight in cities: On the possibility of a "strategic urban intelligence." *Foresight, 18*(5), 469–490. https://doi.org/10.1108/FS-06-2015-0037

Rijkens-Klomp, N., & Van Der Duin, P. (2014). Evaluating local and national public foresight studies from a user perspective. *Futures, 59*, 18–26. https://doi.org/10.1016/j.futures.2014.01.010

Roos, M. (2015). Die Komplexitätsökonomik und ihre Implikationen für die Wirtschaftspolitik. *Perspektiven der Wirtschaftspolitik, 16*(4), 379–392. https://doi.org/10.1515/pwp-2015-0024

Roos, M. (2017). Behavioral and complexity macroeconomics. *European Journal of Economics and Economic Policies: Intervention*, *14*(2), 186–199. https://doi.org/10.4337/ejeep.2017.02.03

Roos, M. (2024). *Principles of Complexity Economics: Concepts, Methods and Applications*. Springer International Publishing. https://doi.org/10.1007/978-3-031-51436-4

Roos, M., Kamlage, J.-H., & Schmitt, E.-J. (Eds.). (2022). *Klimaresiliente Kommunalpolitik: Eine Szenarioanalyse für Bochum im Jahr 2046*. Springer Fachmedien Wiesbaden. https://doi.org/10.1007/978-3-658-38393-0

Roos, M., & Schmitt, E.-J. (2022). Kommunales Management im 21. Jahrhundert. In M. Roos, J.-H. Kamlage, & E.-J. Schmitt (Eds.), *Klimaresiliente Kommunalpolitik: Eine Szenarioanalyse für Bochum im Jahr 2046* (pp. 1–20). Springer Fachmedien Wiesbaden. https://doi.org/10.1007/978-3-658-38393-0

RUB. (2024, April 16). *Bochum Foresight: Wie smart wird unsere City?* [Presseinformation]. News.Rub. https://news.rub.de/presseinformationen/kultur-und-freizeit/2024-04-16-termine-und-veranstaltungen-bochum-anno-2040-gesundheitswesen-gruenden

Schlösser, T. (2022). Methodik der qualitativen Szenarioanalyse. In M. Roos, J.-H. Kamlage, & E.-J. Schmitt (Eds.), *Klimaresiliente Kommunalpolitik: Eine Szenarioanalyse für Bochum im Jahr 2046* (pp. 33–51). Springer Fachmedien Wiesbaden. https://doi.org/10.1007/978-3-658-38393-0

Schmidt-Scheele, R. (2020). 'Plausible' energy scenarios?! How users of scenarios assess uncertain futures. *Energy Strategy Reviews*, *32*, 100571. https://doi.org/10.1016/j.esr.2020.100571

Schoemaker, P. J. H. (1995). Scenario Planning: A Tool for Strategic Thinking. *MIT Sloan Management Review*, *36*(2), 25–40.

Schwartz, P. (1996). *The art of the long view: Paths to strategic insight for yourself and your company* (2nd ed.). Doubleday.

Sharpe, B., & Van der Heijden, K. (Eds.). (2007). *Scenarios for success: Turning insights into action*. John Wiley & Sons, Ltd.

Stadt Bochum (Ed.). (2017, June 19). *Die Bochum Strategie 2030*.

Stadt Bochum (Ed.). (2022). *Bochum Smart City Konzept: Alles rund um die Smart City Bochum*.

Stott, P. (2016). How climate change affects extreme weather events. *Science*, *352*(6293), 1517–1518. https://doi.org/10.1126/science.aaf7271

Szpilko, D. (2020). Foresight as a Tool for the Planning and Implementation of Visions for Smart City Development. *Energies*, *13*(7), 1782. https://doi.org/10.3390/en13071782

Tatar, M., Kalvet, T., & Tiits, M. (2020). Cities4ZERO Approach to Foresight for Fostering Smart Energy Transition on Municipal Level. *Energies*, *13*(14), 3533. https://doi.org/10.3390/en13143533

Torma, G., & Aschemann-Witzel, J. (2024). Sparking stakeholder support: Creating personas for renewable energy innovation adoption based on qualitative data analysis. *Energy Research & Social Science*, *109*, 103407. https://doi.org/10.1016/j.erss.2023.103407

van Vuuren, D. P., Kriegler, E., O'Neill, B. C., Ebi, K. L., Riahi, K., Carter, T. R., Edmonds, J., Hallegatte, S., Kram, T., Mathur, R., & Winkler, H. (2014). A new scenario framework for Climate Change Research: Scenario matrix architecture. *Climatic Change*, *122*(3), 373–386. https://doi.org/10.1007/s10584-013-0906-1

Vögele, S., Hansen, P., Poganietz, W.-R., Prehofer, S., & Weimer-Jehle, W. (2017). Building scenarios for energy consumption of private households in Germany using a multi-level cross-impact balance approach. *Energy*, *120*, 937–946. https://doi.org/10.1016/j.energy.2016.12.001

Volkery, A., & Ribeiro, T. (2009). Scenario planning in public policy: Understanding use, impacts and the role of institutional context factors. *Technological Forecasting and Social Change*, *76*(9), 1198–1207. https://doi.org/10.1016/j.techfore.2009.07.009

Vollbracht, C. (2022). Waste Land 2046: Heute sind wir satt geworden. In M. Roos, J.-H. Kamlage, & E.-J. Schmitt (Eds.), *Klimaresiliente Kommunalpolitik: Eine Szenarioanalyse für Bochum im Jahr 2046* (pp. 65–74). Springer Fachmedien Wiesbaden. https://doi.org/10.1007/978-3-658-38393-0_5

Weimer-Jehle, W. (2006). Cross-impact balances: A system-theoretical approach to cross-impact analysis. *Technological Forecasting and Social Change*, *73*(4), 334–361. https://doi.org/10.1016/j.techfore.2005.06.005

Weimer-Jehle, W. (2023). *Cross-Impact Balances (CIB) for Scenario Analysis: Fundamentals and Implementation*. Springer Nature Switzerland. https://doi.org/10.1007/978-3-031-27230-1

Weimer-Jehle, W., Buchgeister, J., Hauser, W., Kosow, H., Naegler, T., Poganietz, W.-R., Pregger, T., Prehofer, S., von Recklinghausen, A., Schippl, J., & Vögele, S. (2016). Context scenarios and their usage for the construction of socio-technical energy scenarios. *Energy*, *111*, 956–970. https://doi.org/10.1016/j.energy.2016.05.073

Zumbrunn, L. (2023). Resilience through Foresight: Implications for the Public Sector. *Swiss Yearbook of Administrative Sciences*, *14*(1), 45–57. https://doi.org/10.5334/ssas.183

Beyond profits

An exploration of energy commoning practices in local energy communities

Hannah Charlotte Müller

Abstract: *The future of both societal and climate resilience is uncertain. Each faces growing pressures that are deeply interconnected. As climate crisis intensifies, its consequences extend far beyond environmental degradation. Rising temperatures and extreme weather events now coincide with growing inequalities and distrust in democratic institutions. Regarding climate crisis, the energy transition is a central undertaking for reaching climate neutrality amongst various sectors, i.e. industry, housing, and mobility. Within this extensive transformation the ways in which energy is consumed, produced, and distributed will undergo drastic change. In context of growing instability, distrust, and inequality there is a need for viable pathways to adapt and change the existing energy system while making it more resilient, equitable, and inclusive. Empowering citizens and fostering their participation in the energy transition can not only advance the transformation but also strengthen democratic values and a sense of efficacy amongst individuals and communities. The concept of energy commoning offers a lens to explore the transformative capacities of collective energy initiatives. Energy commoning refers to practice-related activities and values along the line of production, distribution, and consumption of renewable energy. To gain a deeper understanding of the concept, this study examines energy communities as sites of energy commoning. By exploring the practices associated with commoning within these communities, the discussion gains both practical grounding and valuable insights into how energy commoning can contribute to more equitable and socially sustainable futures.*

1. From Eroding Confidence to Collective Action

Democracies around the world appear to be under pressure as trust in representative institutions declines (Valgarðsson et al., 2025, 18–20). In Germany, recent empirical studies underscore a troubling erosion of societal confidence in the capacity of the government to respond effectively to pressing challenges. Social cohesion and trust in democratic values appear increasingly fragile. The *Mitte-Studie*, published in 2023, describes a population under strain from overlapping crises—such as the COVID-19 pandemic, the Russian invasion of Ukraine, inflation, and climate change—where 42% of the respondents report heightened insecurity and more than half express a retreat toward nationalistic and authoritarian orientations, often accompanied by declining trust and weakened support regarding democratic institutions (Zick, Küpper & Mokros, 2023, 227–30). Moreover, studies have shown that while support for climate protection in Europe and Germany remains high, public confidence in the ability to address climate crisis has dropped significantly (Frick et al., 2025, 4–6).

This growing disconnect between persistent environmental concern and limited trust in the collective ability to take adequate action is particularly evident in the energy transition. The transformation of energy sector faces not only substantial technological and infrastructural challenges, but also social and political hurdles that cannot be overcome by investment in technology alone (Cloke et al., 2017, 263). Top-down measures and profit-driven decision-making harbor the risk of aggravating frustration and undermining the urgency and inclusivity required for rapid transformation. Rather than allowing trust to erode further, there is an urgent need for viable alternative pathways that empower, motivate climate action, and rebuild trust (Apajalahti & Kungl, 2022, 222–3). Those pathways evidently need to address questions of exclusion and inequality. The burdens and responsibilities in context of climate crisis are distributed highly unequally (Chancel et al., 2023). While the global north is not only responsible for a disproportionately large share of global CO_2 emissions it also tends to have greater capacity to shape energy systems and exploit natural resources than the global south. In addition, the consequences of climate change, like flooding and desertification, have a greater impact on the global south (Deivanayagam et al., 2023). Similarly, energy poverty persists as a critical issue, on global as well as regional and local scales. Lower-income communities often face higher energy costs, limited access to clean technologies, and greater vulnerability to price shocks and infrastructural deficits (Belleflamme, 2018; Chancel et al., 2023). Subsequently, questions of social justice and equitable participation are increasingly recognized as central aspects of a successful energy transition. However, many mainstream approaches to energy transition remain centered on market-based mechanisms or technological innovation; they risk reinforcing existing disparities unless explicitly designed to address them (Cloke et al., 2017, 263–4). No single technology or policy can integrate environmental, social, and economic objectives across all societal groups and system domains. Instead, the complexity and interconnectedness of transformative efforts demands approaches that are dynamic, participatory, and context-sensitive (Sovacool, 2021). There is a consensus across disciplines within the scientific community that the energy transition does not only entail the restructuring of the energy system through technological adaptation and policy changes; it requires multifaceted and decentralized strategies (Bernstein & Hoffmann, 2019; McCauley, et al., 2019; Oliver et al., 2023). Consequently, alternative approaches that move beyond conventional economic paradigms and top-down policies, emphasizing sufficiency, equity, and human wellbeing need to be examined (Vogel & Hickel, 2023, 766).

One promising example of such an approach is the emergence of energy communities, which offer new pathways for more inclusive and participatory energy systems. By providing a form of decentralized and horizontal organization they have the capacity to democratize energy production, distribution, and consumption (Broska et al., 2022). They enable collective action and citizen-led renewable energy systems that allow for the production and provision of energy not as a commodity but as a common resource. The framing of energy as a common resource, that should be accessible and serve the common good has close connections to the concept of energy commons. Unlike market-based models that treat energy as a commodity, the energy commons perspective reimagines energy as a collectively governed resource, foregrounding relational, social, and ecological dimensions over profit maximization (De Angelis, 2017; De Angelis & Harvie, 2014). Beyond considering energy as a common resource, energy communities are also valued for their ability to "[...] increase awareness, knowledge, and intention to adopt low-carbon technologies and other sustainable measures" (Broska et al., 2022, 2). Within this context, the concept of energy commoning can offer a valuable lens for exploring socially and culturally embedded practices performed by energy communities (Brandtner et al., 2023). Energy commoning, understood as a dynamic, ongoing process of collectively managing shared resources, highlights the relational and practical dimension of energy (Bollier, 2021). It draws attention to how communities organize, negotiate, and sustain collective action, embedding energy transitions within local cultures, values, and everyday practices (Kaandorp et al., 2024). This focus on relationality and practice stands in contrast to purely economic or technocratic approaches, offering a richer, more holistic understanding of what a just and effective energy transition might entail. Moreover, energy commoning extends beyond shared resources and goods, such as means of energy production, distribution infrastructure, and renewable energy itself, that are often referred to as energy commons. The concept of commoning highlights the social connections, cultural practices, and relationships within energy communities, while also embracing diverse ways of knowing, performing, and imagining energy (Cloke et al., 2017, 264). By understanding energy commoning as a transformative practice, it can challenge the status quo and create community-centered alternatives. The collective engagement in commoning practices within energy communities can foster trust and cohesion and empower democratic participation (De Angelis, 2017; Holloway, 2010).

This text aims to explore energy commoning within local energy communities as a promising pathway for local energy transition. By investigating how collective practices shape values, governance, and social relations, it responds to the urgent need to move beyond narrow technological fixes and top-down approaches. The following analysis contributes to the practical understanding of energy commoning, grounding it in real-world cases, focusing on the research question: How do local energy communities engage in energy commoning, and how do these practices influence their shared values and activities? To answer this, the article first lays out the conceptual foundations of energy commons, emphasizing commoning as a dynamic, practice-oriented lens that captures the diverse ways communities collectively manage energy. It then synthesizes theoretical and empirical research from case studies to map the field and identify key themes. Building on these insights, the article proposes an analytical framework to further examine energy commoning and its potential in the energy transition. Ultimately, this work aims to explore how energy commoning can empower citizens, foster social cohesion, and rebuild trust contributing to a more inclusive, democratic, and resilient energy transition capable of addressing effects of both climate and societal crises.

2. From resource-based Commons to relational commoning

This section introduces the evolving concept of energy commons and presents energy commoning as a dynamic lens for exploring energy communities. The notion of energy commons that are neither governed by the market nor controlled top-down by the state can be traced back to Ostrom's (1990/2005) work on common-pool resources (CPR). Her contribution marked a significant development in commons theory addressing the tragedy of the commons and privatization paradigms (Ostrom, 1990/2005). Garrett Hardin's concept of the "tragedy of the commons" describes a world in which individuals, inevitably acting in their own self-interest, exploit shared resources without contributing to their maintenance, ultimately undermining collective outcomes (Hardin, 1968, 1243–8). This view of human behavior and shared resources reinforces the assumption that commons are inherently vulnerable to overuse and mismanagement, thereby requiring oversight and regulation by either a centralized state authority or private entities to ensure their sustainability. Ostrom (1990/2005) opposes this top-down approach by providing empirical evidence from around the world showing that communities can and do successfully self-govern shared resources. However, both Hardin and Ostrom's foundational works conceptualized commons primarily as tangible, often finite resources—such as fisheries, forests, or irrigation systems. This resource-based view, while influential, is limiting: it overlooks the intangible and non-depletable dimensions of commons, such as social relationships, collective processes, and shared knowledge, which are central to the practice of commoning (Brandtner et al., 2023, 920). Ostrom's later work began to address these dimensions, notably with the concept of "knowledge commons" (Hess & Ostrom, 2007, 66–8); however, her frameworks remained anchored in the governance of defined systems.

A broader shift in commons research since the 1990s—sometimes called the "New Commons" (Hess, 2008)—has moved the field beyond natural resources, incorporating digital, urban, and collaborative commons as well as their social and cultural embeddedness. More recent scholars such as De Angelis (2017) have called for a deeper shift—from managing resources to enacting alternative social relations—which signifies a "social turn", emphasizing collective action, cultural embeddedness, and the relational constitution of commons (Bollier & Helfrich, 2012; De Angelis & Harvie, 2014; Linebaugh, 2008). Yet, as Bauwens et al. (2024) note, literature on social or relational commons remains fragmented, and definitions often remain fuzzy. Bollier

(2021, 351) highlights that "[...] a commons consists not just of a resource, but of a community that manages a resource by devising its own rules, traditions, and values [...]". However, despite this recognition, he continues to anchor the commons in the realm of resources. In contrast, De Angelis and Harvie (2014) argue for a more radical approach: seeing the commons not as a resource, but as a site of social practice and contestation, where alternative value systems are enacted. This approach shifts the focus from the materiality of the commons to the social relations, practices, and contestations that constitute commoning. They emphasize that commoning is not merely a means of managing resources but is inherently transformative, capable of generating new forms of social organization, cooperation, and value creation (Bollier, 2021, 351–2; De Angelis & Harvie, 2014). This shift away from static definitions of the commons toward an understanding rooted in commoning—emphasizing practices, relationships, and processes—offers a compelling lens for exploring various fields (Euler, 2018, 15).

2.1 Energy Commoning: Definitions and Analytical Value

The field of energy commons exemplifies these theoretical developments. While the energy transition is often framed in terms of technological deployment, market incentives, and regulatory design, such approaches risk neglecting the social and relational practices that are integral to fostering transition and engaging communities (Bauwens et al., 2024, 9–10; Sovacool, 2014, 25). This gap is especially consequential for energy commons, where the viability and transformative potential of community-led initiatives depend on precisely these social dynamics (Caffentzis & Federici, 2014, i102).

Energy commons are frequently linked to the idea of energy democracy (Atutxa et al., 2024; Feldpausch-Parker et al., 2021; Nadesa et al., 2023). According to Burke and Stephens (2017, 37), energy democratization involves three interconnected aims: resisting the dominance of fossil fuel-driven energy agendas, reclaiming social and public control over renewable energy sources, and restructuring energy systems to promote democratic participation and environmental sustainability. Together, these goals position energy democracy as a transformative process that challenges existing power structures while advancing more equitable and ecologically responsible forms of energy governance that are closely tied to the idea of commoning. Especially regarding renewable energy sources like sunshine and wind the commons concept is positioned as a means to oppose the extraction and enclosure of natural resources by centralized market actors " [...] reconceptualizing energy as a commons rather than as a commodity, owned and managed by communities deploying systems of rules for energy conversion and use." (Burke, 2021, 209). Regarding energy democracy, commoning is particularly significant when considering the intersection of energy, wealth, and justice. By focusing on the practices and relationships that constitute commoning, scholars and practitioners can better understand how collective energy initiatives might address, rather than reproduce, existing inequalities in access, participation, and value creation (De Angelis & Harvie, 2014). In doing so, energy commoning becomes not only a technical or organizational alternative but a potential vehicle for advancing social justice and mitigating the deep-seated inequities through democratic and collective action.

Yet, the practical reality is complex. State involvement—especially in grid infrastructure and regulation—remains significant, and many energy communities operate within hybrid models that blend market, state, and collective logics (Burke & Stephens, 2017, 39). Following Ostrom (2005) the commons should be neither state-led nor controlled by private organizations. This raises the question: Is it meaningful to speak of energy commons when collective organization is partial, or when communities are embedded in larger networks and legal frameworks? Szulecki (2018, 35–6) suggests shifting focus from whether energy, its modes of production, distribution and management qualify as commons to how communities navigate and reshape these structures through collective action. In a similar vein, Brandtner, Douglas, and Kornberger (2023, 921) propose the notion of relational commons as they promote a "[...] theory of meaningful social interaction, not a theory of property or natural resources [...]" highlighting relational and social phenomena as fundamental to the commons.

Drawing on De Angelis's (2017) notion of boundary commoning, Holloway's (2010) idea of "cracks in capitalism," and Euler's (2018) call to shift from goods-based to practice-based definitions, in the following, I conceptualize energy commoning as an analytic and empirical lens for studying relational, social, and informational commons. Energy commoning thus refers to the ongoing, collective social practices through which communities engage with, reshape, and co-produce energy systems (Kaandorp et al., 2024). It is less about full ownership or ideal-typical governance, and more about the relational, informational, and procedural dimensions of collective action. This broad definition enables the inclusion of investment-driven cooperatives, regionally networked communities, and hybrid models, provided they are grounded in collective practices and shared governance. Local energy communities are likewise defined broadly and not limited to a type of organization or size constraints: they may be geographically rooted but can also operate at regional scales or as part of wider networks, provided their activities are collectively organized and they engage in the production, distribution, or management of renewable energy (Atutxa et al., 2020).

Despite growing interest and ongoing research in energy commons and communities, there is often little differentiation between tangible, intangible, goods-based and social commons. This conceptual fuzziness is understandable, given the interconnected nature of energy systems, but it risks obscuring the social practices, relationships, and knowledge flows that constitute energy commons and shape communities. Especially when linking energy commons and energy communities, the existence of commoning is often simply assumed without critical examination of the degree, forms, or implications of these practices. This article addresses this gap by adopting a practice-oriented lens: rather than debating whether an initiative is *truly* a commons, it investigates how communities navigate state and market constraints, co-produce energy systems, and enact commoning through everyday relationships, governance, and knowledge-sharing. By foregrounding the procedural, relational, and knowledge-based dimensions of energy commoning, this approach offers a more nuanced and inclusive framework for understanding the transformative potential of collective energy initiatives. Furthermore, the lens of commoning also foregrounds forms of value creation that are often overlooked in conventional economic frameworks—such as trust, solidarity, social inclusion, and environmental care—thus enabling a richer understanding of the transformative capacities of collective energy initiatives.

3. Methodology

The following analysis aims to explore energy commoning by not only engaging with the concept on a theoretical level but also by examining case studies that relate energy communities to energy commons and commoning. For this reason, an integrative literature review is conducted to systematically draw on existing theoretical and empirical work, not only to summarize key findings but to distill central themes and conceptual insights by identifying patterns and connections, thereby synthesizing the findings in a comprehensive framework (Snyder, 2019, 335–8). While this study adopts a practice-oriented lens to understand energy commoning, it draws primarily on academic literature that documents and analyzes practical cases. This approach was chosen for several reasons. First, the field of energy commoning is still emerging and much of the available knowledge is captured in published case studies and empirical analyses grounded in research projects. Second, academic publications often provide rich descriptions of community practices alongside critical reflection informed by both practical perspectives and theoretical foundation. However, it must be acknowledged that such accounts may carry theoretical biases or interpretations shaped by authors' frameworks. The analysis therefore is conducted cautiously, drawing from a diverse range of publications. Finally, given constraints related to time, resources and access existing literature represents an efficient way to map current knowledge and various representation of commoning practices in energy communities. Regarding the extent of research, it should be noted that this is an explorative review. It does not capture the full scope of research on energy commons and commoning. Instead, it offers a focused analysis that highlights and integrates key issues related to energy commoning and energy communities.

3.1 Sample selection

As illustrated in Figure 1, relevant academic and grey literature was identified using the Scopus database, chosen for its broad coverage of publications. The search included all English-language publications available as of May 2025, with no limitations on the starting date, thereby broadening the scope of the relevant literature.

Based on the research question the search was narrowed down to "energy commons" and "energy commoning" and restricted to potentially relevant subject areas—social sciences (SOCI), energy (ENER), environmental science (ENVI), earth and planetary sciences (EART), arts and humanities (ARTS) and business and management (BUSI)—as well as curated document types—article (ar), book chapter (ch) and book (bk).[1]

---

1 The initial search query was formulated as follows: TITLE-ABS-KEY("energy commons" OR "energy commoning") AND (LIMIT-TO (SUBJAREA,"SOCI") OR LIMIT-TO (SUBJAREA,"ENER") OR LIMIT-TO (SUBJAREA,"ENVI") OR LIMIT-TO (SUBJAREA,"EART") OR LIMIT-TO (SUBJAREA,"ARTS") OR LIMIT-TO (SUBJAREA,"BUSI") OR LIMIT-TO (SUBJAREA,"ECON") OR LIMIT-TO (SUBJAREA,"AGRI") OR LIMIT-TO (SUBJAREA,"HEAL")) AND (LIMIT-TO (DOCTYPE,"ar") OR LIMIT-TO (DOCTYPE,"ch") OR LIMIT-TO (DOCTYPE,"bk"))

Figure 1: Sample selection

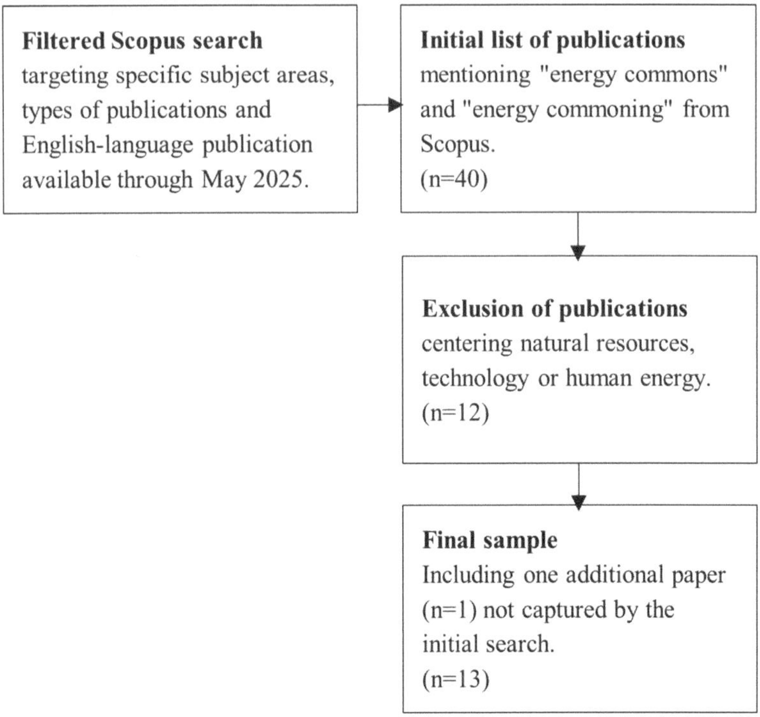

Source: Own illustration

Figure one illustrates the sample selection process, starting at the first step—a filtered Scopus search by subject areas, types of publications, English language publication, and availability through May 2025. The initial list contained 40 publications each mentioning "energy commons" and "energy commoning". In the next step an exclusion of publications followed, centering natural resources, technology, or human energy. This resulted in a sample of 12 publications. The final sample contained 13 papers—one more paper that was not captured by the initial search.

The initial literature search produced 40 entries for further screening. The relevance of each paper was assessed, selecting only those that engaged explicitly with energy commons or energy commoning, either through theoretical analysis or empirical examination. Particular attention was given to studies situated within the context of energy sharing, collective energy governance or energy communities. Papers were excluded if they used the term commons in a broader or unrelated sense, for example, referencing fossil fuels (e.g., oil and gas) as common-pool resources or human energy (e.g., motivational, physical, or emotional energy) as a collective resource. In addition, publications primarily focused on the technological integration of energy systems, or the digital and IT dimensions of energy production and management were also excluded, as they fell outside the conceptual scope of this review. The literature search was complemented by manually adding relevant papers identified through previous work.[2] Ultimately, a total of 13 publications (n=13) were included in the final sample for the full-text thematic analysis. For a structured overview of the papers included see Table 2.

3.2 Thematic analysis

Core themes and key dimensions of energy commoning were identified using a deductive thematic analysis approach, drawing on established frameworks in qualitative research (Ahmed et al., 2025; Braun & Clarke, 2006; Fereday & Muir-Cochrane, 2006). As a result of scoping coding a coding guide was developed based on concepts and categories found in the selected literature (see Table 1). This thematic coding guide provided a structure for examining underlying patterns, tensions, and interconnections within the sample. The deductive guide provided the foundational structure for the subsequent thematic analysis, while also allowing space for inductive insights to emerge during the coding process (Braun & Clarke, 2006). This blended approach, using deductively derived themes while remaining open to inductive findings, ensured both theoretical grounding and responsiveness to additional insights (Fereday & Muir-Cochrane, 2006). The dimensions, themes and codes sketched out in the thematic coding guide not only enabled a systematic exploration of underlying practices of energy commoning but also served as a fundamental base for the development of the analytical framework.

---

2 After careful consideration, one supplementary article was selected based on its direct thematic relevance. While supplementing systematic searches with targeted additions can introduce potential bias, this step was taken transparently and is supported by the article's clear relevance and contribution to thematic completeness.

Table 1: Thematic coding guide

Key dimension	Themes	Codes
Relational	Collective governance	e.g. democratic decision-making processes, polycentricity
	Participation	e.g. financial investment, community action
	Collective engagement	e.g. trust, care
Social	In-/Exclusion	e.g. financial power, housing stock
	(In-)Justice	e.g. social cohesion, spatial inequalities
	Socio-economical sustainability	e.g. support for the local economy, consumption behavior
Informational	Types of knowledge	e.g. community values, operational knowledge
	Knowledge exchange and informal learning	e.g. information sharing, active communication
	Transparency and data collection	e.g. horizontal privacy, awareness campaigns

4. Results

The review focused on how the examined contributions conceptualize, frame, and evaluate energy commoning in local energy communities. While not all papers explicitly used the term energy commoning, each selected study was included based on its substantive engagement with the concept, whether through exploring how communities and practices shape the constitution of energy commons, or by highlighting the transformative potential of reimagining energy systems beyond commodity logics, emphasizing democratization of the energy system and social justice. Regarding the number of publications over time, a slight upward trend from 2024 on is notable, though given the total number of publications reviewed (n=13) this incline can only be understood as a first indication and needs to be examined more broadly.

Figure 2: Number of publications on energy commons and commoning research over time 2015-May 2025.

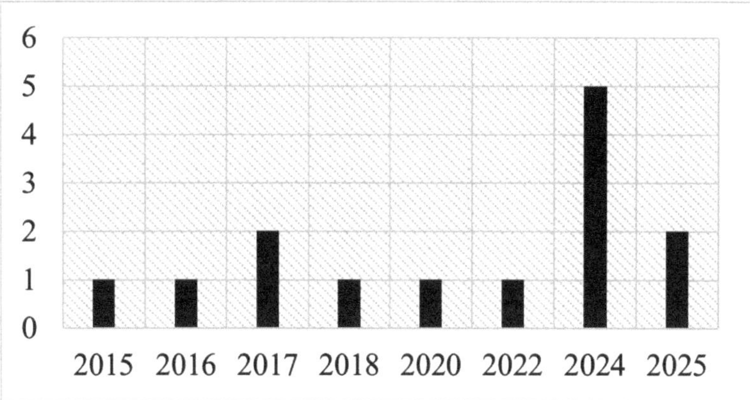

Source: Own illustration

The reviewed publications originate from a wide range of journals, reflecting diverse disciplinary perspectives, including energy studies (e.g. Yang et al., 2021), social sciences (e.g. Campbell, 2024), geography (Hastie et al., 2025), law (e.g. Hoops, 2025), and technology (e.g. Giotitsas et al., 2015). While most contributions are from peer-reviewed journals, one reviewed work is part of an edited book (Cervas & Giancatarino, 2017). In terms of methodological approaches, empirical case studies constitute the largest share of the sample, representing over 60 percent of all studies reviewed (see Table 2). This indicates a strong emphasis on real-world, context-specific inquiry within the field. The prominence of case studies is consistent with broader trends in commons research, as noted in previous reviews (Bauwens et al., 2024; van Laerhoven et al., 2020). Case studies offer detailed insights into localized practices and dynamics, underscoring the importance of understanding how commons operate within diverse and often complex social-ecological systems. Though not all the publications can be classified as case studies, they are all at least partially empirical and reference specific spatial contexts. The spatial references concentrate in western Europe but the articles reviewed also include examples from the US, Chile, Nepal and South Korea (see Table 2).

Table 2: List of analyzed articles

Author	Approach	Spatial reference
Yang, S., Chen, W., & Kim, H. (2021)	Comparative case study	Seoul, South Korea
Kaandorp, C., Moreno Pessoa, I. T., Pesch, U., van de Giesen, N., & Abraham, E. (2024).	Single case study	Amsterdam, Netherlands
Hastie, H., Dawney, L., & Butler, C. (2025)	Qualitative study	Multiple UK cities, UK
Giotitsas, C., Pazaitis, A., & Kostakis, V. (2015)	Conceptual study	Kythnos, Greece & Huatacondo, Chile
Atutxa, E., Zubero, I., & Calvo-Sotomayor, I. (2024)	Comparative empirical study	Various initiatives, Spain
Hoops, B. (2025)	Comparative empirical study	Various initiatives, Germany
Acosta, C., Ortega, M., Bunsen, T., Koirala, B., & Ghorbani, A. (2018).	Single case study	Haarlem, Netherlands
Lee, J., Byrne, J., & Seo, J. (2023)	Case study	Delaware, USA & Seoul, South Korea
Atutxa, E., Zubero, I., & Calvo-Sotomayor, I. (2020)	Comparative empirical study	Rubí, Barcelona & Basque Country, Spain
Campbell, B. (2024)	Single case study	Chitwan District, Nepal
Cervas, S., & Giancatarino, A. (2017)	Case study	California & Philadelphia, USA
Islar, M., & Busch, H. (2016)	Comparative case study	Samsø, Denmark & Feldheim, Germany
Melville, E., Christie, I., Burningham, K., Way, C., & Hampshire, P. (2017)	Single case study	Multiple neighborhoods, UK

Regarding the conceptualization of the commons, the sample reflects the diversity of commons and commoning in academic literature. Approximately half of the reviewed publications align with a goods-based commons concept. The authors refer to means of energy production (Yang et al., 2021), energy infrastructures (Giotitsas et al., 2015), energy cooperatives (Acosta et al., 2018; Hoops, 2025; Melville et al., 2017), or locally produced renewable energy (Islar

& Busch, 2016) as commons. However, it is essential to note that the publications identified as aligning with a goods-based conception of the commons, to varying degrees, extend beyond merely framing the commons as shared resources. For example, Islar & Busch (2017, 315) describe how common good in the context of energy is "[...] structured around 'socially-related' commons such as locally produced energy, the local economy and internet access.". In the same vein, Melville et al. (2017, 14) highlight the potential small-scale commons approaches "[...] to motivate more sustainable energy consumption practices, whilst providing social benefits of a greater sense of belonging, agency and social connection [...]". The reviewed publications explicitly going beyond the goods-based concept highlight practices of commoning that encompass values of care (Campbell, 2024; Hastie et al., 2025), democratic participation (Cervas & Giancatarino, 2017) and community building (Atutxa et al., 2024; Lee et al., 2023) as well as collective governance (Atutxa et al., 2020; Kaandorp et al., 2024).

4.1 Exploring dimensions of energy commoning

During the thematic analysis, publications with a clear reference to commoning or those exploring the social and relational aspects of energy commons offered relevant insights into the relational, social, and informational dimensions of the commons. These findings provided the initial foundation for the thematic analysis. In addition, the publications grounded in a goods-based conception contributed valuable insights and revealed meaningful thematic intersections that enriched the analysis.

Energy commoning is widely understood not as a fixed structure, but as an evolving set of social practices, relationships, and governance processes. It entails collective ownership, participatory decision-making, and shared responsibility in managing energy systems. Practices include peer-to-peer microgrid operations (Giotitsas et al., 2015), democratic decision-making processes (Cervas & Giancatarino, 2017), time-donation or resistance funds (Atutxa et al., 2024) and community-driven warmth provisioning (Hastie et al., 2025). Commoning emphasizes cooperation, trust, and decentralization, contrasting them with market logics and centralized energy infrastructures. It is embedded in cultural, social, and material contexts, as seen in Nepal's biogas systems (Campbell, 2024) or the local contexts of community energy projects in Germany and Denmark (Islar & Busch, 2016).

4.2 Relational dimension

The relational dimension of commoning focuses on how energy is governed, how actors interact with one another, and how collective agency is exercised. Several studies underscore the centrality of participatory governance in shaping these relationships. Atutxa et al. (2024), in their comparative study of Spanish energy commons, show how sociocratic models are employed to build consent-based, transparent governance, navigating inequality and ensuring all members are heard in decision-making processes. In their prior research on the scalability of energy communities Atutxa et al. (2020) identify loss of participation as a consequence of growth in communities. This implies that the size of communities plays a significant role in shaping the active engagement and participation of their members. The empirical findings of the study suggest that as the single communities grow "[n]etworks are created on the basis of joint action and mutual trust and knowledge" to enable energy commons to expand and grow (Atutxa et al., 2020, 12). In Amsterdam, Kaandorp et al. (2024) illustrate how relational energy commoning is enacted through intermediaries like *Platform 02025*, which connects citizens, professionals, and state actors to challenge the centralized and technocratic nature of the urban heat transition. Commoning practices in this case include free advisory services, peer exchange events, and lobbying, all aimed at reconfiguring the governance structure of energy systems to increase local influence and procedural justice.

Melville et al. (2017) highlight the interconnectedness of energy commons and accountability. Their UK-based study of a community demand-response trial aimed to explore how community accountability for individual energy consumption shapes everyday energy practices. The interviews conducted showed that despite privacy concerns and time restrains the participants welcomed the idea to take responsibility on a local level as it "[...] appealed to their sense of community, desire to connect with others, compassion and recognition of different people's needs and circumstances, and the desire to work together with others in mutually supportive relationships" (Melville et al., 2017, 19).

Regarding diverse forms of collective organization, Hoops (2024) identifies five types of energy commons among German cooperatives, revealing a wide spectrum from participatory self-management to investment-oriented models with passive membership. This "empirical reality of disbursed dividends and the normative ideal of an Energy Commons without any financial purpose [...]" (Hoops, 2025, 23) contrasts commoning practices and more conventional, market-oriented energy governance. The case of investment-oriented initiatives demonstrates that acts of commoning, such as shared ownership, collective decision-making, or localized governance, can still emerge within frameworks that are partially embedded in market logics. Rather than a strict binary, the boundary between commoning and mainstream energy provision appears porous, with practices potentially drifting toward or away from commons-based principles over time. This highlights both the conceptual flexibility of commoning and its analytical usefulness in capturing hybrid forms of energy governance that operate at the intersection of economic profits, civic engagement, and institutional normalization.

4.3 Social dimension

The social dimension of energy commoning concerns itself with questions of equity, inclusion, mutual support, and everyday routines. Campbell's (2024) ethnographic work in Nepal offers a vivid account of layered commoning in a rural biogas initiative, where collective practices—such as shared access to pastures and reciprocal herding—were foundational to the biogas system. Here, energy commoning was embedded in broader patterns of everyday life and cultural meaning, rather than being limited to technical or financial arrangements. When political leadership disrupted access to communal land, it destabilized the energy system, demonstrating the fragility of the commons under shifting governance regimes. This illustrates how commons and commoning can propose a means to overcome inequalities and pluralize wealth production and value creation but also highlights their ongoing vulnerability to structural power and economic inequalities, as such initiatives can still be overtaken or undermined by broader political or economic shifts.

Hastie et al. (2025) push this analysis further into the urban context by exploring "warm spaces" in the UK during the energy crisis of 2022–2023. These spaces, often hosted in libraries or community centers, provided not only physical warmth but also social connection, food, and access to care, functions which reframe energy provision as a shared, caring infrastructure. Though not formal commons, these spaces enacted commoning through relational, needs-based provisioning and anti-stigmatizing design. Within the warm spaces different "[...] hubs offering communal digital and computing access, community spaces providing parent and child groups, skills-based activities and board games" emerged (Hastie et al., 2025, 2). The study highlights how everyday practices of care, especially in times of crisis, can temporarily realign local energy systems toward social solidarity and inclusion.

Other studies foreground the relevance of commoning practices for economic inclusion. Acosta et al. (2018), in their case of the *DE Ramplaan* solar cooperative in the Netherlands, emphasize the importance of flexible design, mutual trust, and phase-based development in making the project accessible and socially robust. Similarly, Cervas and Giancatarino (2017) document how energy democracy movements in California and Philadelphia mobilize resources for solar investment in low-income and renter communities, using tools like Green Zones and Energy Investment Districts to institutionalize energy equity.

Social inequalities—including wealth disparities and energy poverty—are particularly pronounced within the social dimension of energy commoning. Factors like financial resources, place of residence, or proximity to infrastructure can limit the ability of marginalized groups to access clean energy solutions or participate in community initiatives. Entrance fees that restrict memberships, for example, can be exclusive (Atutxa et al. 2024; Hoops 2025). To overcome this restriction, some communities offer alternatives like "resistance funds based on mutual support and solidarity [or] the option to donate time instead of money [...]" (Atutxa et al., 2024, 20).

Spatial disparities also play a crucial role in determining the capacities of individuals and communities to partake in energy commoning. In the mini-PV case studies of Seoul (Yang et al., 2021), high-density housing was perceived as an obstacle preventing the inhabitants from using PV-systems to locally and collectively produce renewable energy in their living environment. They were able to overcome this difficulty. Leadership from apartment office managers, combined with the creative use of shared resources (e.g., collective repair funds), facilitated collective ownership of decentralized solar systems. In Spain, Atutxa et al. (2024, 24) found out that communities are facing "[...] spatial and material limits" which will force them to decline new members when there is no more space to increase their energy production further. Furthermore, spatial inequalities like the distribution of heating infrastructures, the quality of housing development, or segregation patterns can limit access to and the potential of energy commoning in local contexts (Kaandorp et al., 2024).

4.4 Informational dimension

Informational commoning refers to the process by which knowledge is created, shared, and utilized to empower collective action and decision-making. Many energy commons rely on informal learning, peer exchange, and networks shaped by situated knowledge rather than top-down information pipelines. In Amsterdam, Kaandorp et al. (2024) show how civic platforms function as knowledge intermediaries, enabling distributed learning about heating alternatives and rights. In addition, a number of regular networking and knowledge-sharing events were recorded and partially attended by the researchers, like the monthly "energy breakfast" (Kaandorp et al., 2024, 3).

Melville et al. (2017) add nuance by showing the limits of information sharing in a UK-based community demand-response pilot. While collective incentives were welcomed, participants resisted mutual monitoring or publicizing household-level data due to fears of surveillance and social pressure. This highlights the fine line between transparency and coercion in informational commoning, as well as the need for trust-sensitive design when energy data is involved.

Lee, Byrne and Seo (2023) place knowledge production at the heart of their conceptual model of energy democracy. They argue that energy transitions require not just technological diffusion but the cultivation of what they term an interactive set of "[...] motivating, operational, and organizing principles" (Lee et al., 2023, 60); each rooted in shared values, democratic structure, and local context that are closely tied to knowledge and empower communities to imagine and realize sustainable and just futures. Informational commoning thus becomes a cornerstone of civic capacity, enabling communities to articulate alternatives and navigate complex transitions.

In their Californian case study, Cervas and Giancatarino (2017) highlight how campaigns fostered community engagement and broader public outreach. A similar dynamic can be observed in Feldheim, Germany. Islar and Busch (2016) describe how Feldheim's ambitious renewable energy project gained significance over time, particularly through external attention and interest. As a response, the village established the *Neue Energien Forum,* an information center for renewable energy, reflecting a shift toward broader public engagement and knowledge sharing.

The informational dimension of energy commoning also addresses inequality. Access to knowledge, technical expertise, energy literacy and the availability of information about renewable energy options is often unequally distributed along the lines of wealth and education (Sovacool et al., 2019). This can reinforce existing divides, as those with greater resources are better able to navigate complex systems, access subsidies, or adopt new technologies. Effective commoning thus depends on creating inclusive learning environments and transparent communication strategies that empower all community members, regardless of socioeconomic status (Hastie et al., 2025).

4.5 Towards an energy commoning framework

Concluding this iterative review process, beginning with a deductive thematic coding guide and evolving through close engagement with both empirical and conceptual literature, I developed a framework that structures and presents the key insights gained. Rather than merely summarizing findings, this framework is designed to operationalize the diverse dimensions of energy commoning for future research and practice. The initial coding guide served as a starting point, focusing on relational, social, and informational aspects; however, ongoing analysis revealed the necessity to adapt and broaden these categories in response to the complexities encountered within energy commoning practices. This approach aligns with methodologies in related fields, where frameworks are dynamically shaped by integrating theoretical synthesis with empirical evidence to identify context-sensitive, practice-oriented dimensions (Bauwens et al., 2024). In developing the analytical framework, special attention has been paid to how each dimension interacts with the structural realities of wealth inequality, exclusion and trust in the energy transition. In the following section, each dimension is presented and briefly described. The framework provides general themes, key aspects and guiding questions for each dimension. This format is chosen to make the framework applicable to empirical research settings, as it, for example, can serve as a starting point for developing interview guides. It allows for both broad exploration and more targeted research designs depending on the context.

Table 3: Analytical Framework regarding the Relational Dimension of Commoning

Themes	Key Aspects	Guiding Questions
Collective Governance	Modes of governance (e.g., sociocracy, energy democracy); integration into broader networks, size/scope of the organization	How are decisions made? How do members relate to each other? Is the community networked?
Participation & Engagement	Active participation, empowerment, mobilization, shared responsibility	Is active participation expected or required? What roles do members take on?
Community Practices	Community events, informal communication, member integration	How do members interact regularly? How are new members integrated?

The relational dimension focuses on the modes of collective governance, participation, and the enactment of agency within energy communities. The literature consistently highlights that the success and durability of energy commons depends not only on formal rules or ownership structures but on the quality of relationships, trust, and mutual engagement among participants. This dimension was adapted from the initial coding guide to place greater emphasis on the diversity of governance models (e.g., sociocracy, polycentricity), the fluidity of participation (ranging from active to passive forms), and the importance of informal community practices such as peer exchange, regular events, and the integration of new members. These aspects reflect the theoretical shift from resource-based to practice-oriented understandings of the commons, where the focus lies on how collective agency is enacted and negotiated in everyday settings. When analyzing collective governance and participation, it is essential to consider how economic and social status influences who can participate and whose voices are heard in decision-making processes. In addition, the size and scope of a community can drastically impact how members interact and relate to one another and the community as a whole.

Table 4: Analytical framework regarding the Social Dimension of Commoning

Themes	Key Aspects	Guiding Questions
Inclusion & Accessibility	Time donations, financial contributions, entry barriers, fee waivers	What mechanisms ensure inclusivity? What may exclude participation or can reinforce existing inequalities?
Equality & Justice	Social/spatial inequalities, fairness in benefit distribution, internal tensions	How are benefits shared? Are different needs and experiences considered?
Everyday Practices	Routine tasks in energy production and maintenance; local or circular economic activities	What daily tasks are involved in operating the system? What routines shape participation?

The social dimension addresses issues of inclusion, equity, and the reproduction of everyday life within energy commoning. While the initial coding focused on exclusion, justice, and socio-economic sustainability, the literature review underscored the need to broaden this dimension to capture the multiple ways in which energy commons intersect with social inequalities, access barriers, and local livelihoods. The studies reviewed highlight that commoning is not only about distributing benefits, but also about creating mechanisms for participation (e.g., solidarity funds, time donations), negotiating internal tensions and embedding energy practices in the routines and values of local communities. This dimension is therefore shaped by both distributive and procedural justice concerns, aligning with theoretical arguments that stress the socially embedded and transformative potential of commoning. Value creation and wealth within energy commons are plural and extend well beyond economic considerations, encompassing intangible outcomes such as community cohesion, mutual support, and the advancement of social justice. The framework addresses social commoning as it shapes both individual and collective capacities for change.

Table 5: Analytical framework regarding the Informational Dimension of Commoning

Themes	**Key Aspects**	**Guiding Questions**
Knowledge Generation	Situated knowledge, know-how, 'learning by doing,' development of shared norms and goals	How is knowledge developed and maintained? How are shared values shaped?
Knowledge Sharing & Learning	Peer learning, informal training, collective troubleshooting, learning events	How is knowledge exchanged in daily practice? Who has access to key knowledge?
Transparency & Communication	Internal communication, openness of decision-making, external communication, data handling	How is information shared within and outside of the community? How transparent are processes?

The informational dimension explores how knowledge is generated, shared, and mobilized to empower collective action in energy commons. The initial coding guide focused on types of knowledge, knowledge exchange, and transparency. However, the literature review revealed additional nuances, such as the role of informal learning, peer-to-peer networks, and the tensions between transparency and privacy. This dimension was thus refined to include not only the mechanisms of knowledge production and dissemination but also the cultivation of shared values, the design of inclusive learning environments, and the management of information flows within and beyond the community. Theoretical work on the commons emphasizes that informational commoning is crucial in building civic capacity and enabling communities to articulate and pursue alternative energy futures.

In summary, the analytical framework presented here is the result of a combination of deductive coding and inductive adaptation, shaped by the interplay between theoretical perspectives and empirical findings. By foregrounding the relational, social, and informational dimensions, the framework offers a comprehensive and flexible tool for analyzing the dynamic processes of energy commoning and for understanding how these processes are shaped by, and in turn shape, broader questions of justice, inclusion, and sustainability in the context of energy transitions.

5. Concluding remarks

In this contribution, energy commoning has been assessed as a promising approach to energy transition. One that transcends profit-driven logics and centers added values such as social cohesion, trust, and community empowerment as integral outcomes of restructuring energy systems Against the backdrop of intensifying climate crises, rising inequalities, and eroding trust in democratic institutions, this research explored energy commoning as a promising pathway for fostering societal and climate resilience. Within the context of energy transition the concept of energy commoning served as a dynamic and practice-oriented lens for analyzing collective action within local energy communities. Building on an integrative literature review, this contribution has synthesized key themes across relational, social, and informational dimensions, resulting in the development of an analytical framework to guide future empirical and theoretical research in this field. The analysis demonstrates that energy commoning is not a fixed structure or set of rules, but an evolving constellation of practices, relationships, and governance processes embedded in diverse local contexts. The analysis demonstrates how energy commoning is not merely an alternative model for resource management, but a dynamic set of practices deeply embedded in local contexts, practices that have the potential to reimagine how energy systems are governed, experienced, and shared.

By examining local energy communities through a practice-oriented lens, this study has moved beyond narrow technological fixes or top-down policy approaches. Instead, it reveals how collective action, rooted in relational ties, social inclusion, and knowledge sharing, can generate new forms of agency and belonging. The multidimensional analytical framework developed here captures these complexities by foregrounding three interrelated dimensions: relational (how governance structures foster participation and trust), social (how inclusion, equity, and everyday routines shape access), and informational (how knowledge is produced, shared and mobilized). These dimensions are not static categories but reflect ongoing negotiation processes within communities as they respond to shifting challenges and opportunities.

The findings underscore that successful energy commoning depends on more than formal ownership or infrastructure; it is sustained by mutual trust, participatory decision-making, flexible organizational models, and mechanisms for overcoming exclusion. Yet persistent barriers remain: economic disparities can limit participation; spatial inequalities affect access; informational divides risk reinforcing existing power imbalances. As such, while energy commoning offers significant promise for building more equitable and resilient systems at the community level, its transformative potential will depend on addressing these structural challenges. The concept of energy commoning is frequently linked to the democratization of energy systems. However, the review produced little results regarding the capacity of energy commoning in facing political uncertainty and fostering trust in democratic institutions. There appears to be a tension—which require further investigation—between the transformative potential and radical change of energy commoning on the one hand, and, on the other, the need to collaborate with local administrations and build functional networks that bridge state, market, and civil society.

It is important to acknowledge several limitations inherent to this review. Regarding the relatively small sample (n=13) as well as the broad and cross-disciplinary field of commons and commoning, the review does not capture the full diversity of energy commoning practices. Additionally, nuances and debates within the literature on energy commons may not be fully addressed. Furthermore, the landscape of energy commoning is rapidly evolving, with new initiatives, policies, and crises (such as energy price shocks or climate events) continually reshaping the field. As such, the findings and framework presented here should be seen as provisional and subject to ongoing revision. Moreover, the framework has not yet been applied to new empirical material or a specific case study. It is intended to guide future research and support the analysis of energy commons in diverse contexts. Further development and the practical application and evaluation of the framework are necessary to improve and validate the proposed dimensions, themes and guiding questions.

Looking forward, future research is necessary to gain a better understanding of the transformative potential of energy commoning. For this purpose, the proposed analytical framework should be applied and tested across diverse contexts to assess its robustness and refine its dimensions. Comparative studies could illuminate how different governance models, policy environments, and cultural settings shape energy commoning practices in local contexts and over time, while also clarifying how these practices intersect with broader patterns of trust, social cohesion, and inequality. Greater attention is needed to how energy commoning can address barriers to participation for marginalized groups and foster genuine inclusion and equity, rather than inadvertently reproducing existing divides. Further investigation into the role of policy, institutional frameworks, and hybrid governance models will be essential to understanding the enabling and constraining factors that shape energy commoning on the ground. Transdisciplinary and participatory approaches, involving practitioners and community members, will enrich theoretical development and ensure that future research remains grounded in lived realities.

Ultimately, this article argues that empowering citizens through participatory forms of collective action, such as those embodied in energy commoning, is essential for advancing just transitions capable of addressing both climate change and deepening social divides. By operationalizing key themes across relational, social, and informational domains—and remaining attentive to issues like exclusion or trust—the proposed framework supports both critical scholarship and practical experimentation toward more inclusive democratic futures. In doing so, it responds directly to the urgent need for viable pathways that make our energy systems not only greener but fairer—and ultimately more resilient in the face of interconnected societal challenges and climate crisis.

References

Acosta, C., Ortega, M., Bunsen, T., Koirala, B., & Ghorbani, A. (2018). Facilitating Energy Transition through Energy Commons: An Application of Socio-Ecological Systems Framework for Integrated Community Energy Systems. *Sustainability*, *10*(2), 366. https://doi.org/10.3390/su10020366

Ahmed, S. K., Mohammed, R. A., Nashwan, A. J., Ibrahim, R. H., Abdalla, A. Q., M. Ameen, B. M., & Khdhir, R. M. (2025). Using thematic analysis in qualitative research. *Journal of Medicine, Surgery, and Public Health*, *6*, 100198. https://doi.org/10.1016/j.glmedi.2025.100198

Apajalahti, E.-L., & Kungl, G. (2022). Path dependence and path break-out in the electricity sector. *Environmental Innovation and Societal Transitions*, *43*, 220–236. https://doi.org/10.1016/j.eist.2022.03.010

Atutxa, E., Zubero, I., & Calvo-Sotomayor, I. (2020). Scalability of Low Carbon Energy Communities in Spain: An Empiric Approach from the Renewed Commons Paradigm. *Energies*, *13*(19), 5045. https://doi.org/10.3390/en13195045

Atutxa, E., Zubero, I., & Calvo-Sotomayor, I. (2024). Gobernar los Comunes de la Energía europeos: normas y condiciones. *Convergencia Revista De Ciencias Sociales*, *31*, 1. https://doi.org/10.29101/crcs.v31i0.21201

Bauwens, T., Wade, R., & Burke, M. (2024). The energy commons: A systematic review, paradoxes, and ways forward. *Energy Research & Social Science, 118*, 103776. https://doi.org/10.1016/j.erss.2024.103776

Belleflamme, E. (2018). *The role of justice and equity in energy transition: Concepts, theories and empirical findings.*

Bernstein, S., & Hoffmann, M. (2019). Climate politics, metaphors and the fractal carbon trap. *Nature Climate Change*, 9(12), 919–925. https://doi.org/10.1038/s41558-019-0618-2

Bollier, D. (2021). Commoning as Transformative Social Paradigm. In J. G. Speth & K. Courrier (Eds.), *The new systems reader: Alternatives to a failed economy* (pp. 348–361). Routledge.

Bollier, D., & Helfrich, S. (Eds.). (2012). *The wealth of the commons: A world beyond market and state*. Levellers Press.

Brandtner, C., Douglas, G., & Kornberger, M. (2023). Where Relational Commons Take Place: The City and its Social Infrastructure as Sites of Commoning. *Journal of Business Ethics, 184*(4), 917–932. https://doi.org/10.1007/s10551-023-05361-9

Braun, V., & Clarke, V. (2006). Using thematic analysis in psychology. *Qualitative Research in Psychology, 3*(2), 77–101. https://doi.org/10.1191/1478088706qp063oa

Broska, L. H., Vögele, S., Shamon, H., & Wittenberg, I. (2022). On the Future(s) of Energy Communities in the German Energy Transition: A Derivation of Transformation Pathways. *Sustainability, 14*(6), 3169. https://doi.org/10.3390/su14063169

Burke, M. (2021). Energy commons and alternatives to enclosures of sunshine and wind. In A. M. Feldpausch-Parker, D. Endres, T. R. Peterson, & S. L. Gomez (Eds.), *Routledge Handbook of Energy Democracy* (pp. 200–214). Routledge. https://doi.org/10.4324/9780429402302-21

Burke, M., & Stephens, J. C. (2017). Energy democracy: Goals and policy instruments for sociotechnical transitions. *Energy Research & Social Science, 33*, 35–48. https://doi.org/10.1016/j.erss.2017.09.024

Caffentzis, G., & Federici, S. (2014). Commons against and beyond capitalism. *Community Development Journal*, 49(suppl 1), i92-i105. https://doi.org/10.1093/cdj/bsu006

Campbell, B. (2024). Bringing Commoning into View. *Social Analysis*, 68(2), 99–118. https://doi.org/10.3167/sa.2024.680206

Cervas, S., & Giancatarino, A. (2017). Energy Democracy Through Local Energy Equity. In D. Fairchild & A. Weinrub (Eds.), *Energy Democracy: Advancing Eq-*

uity in Clean Energy Solutions. Island Press. https://ebookcentral.proquest.com/lib/kxp/detail.action?docID=5508345

Chancel, L., Bothe, P., & Voituriez, T. (2023). *Climate Inequality Report 2023.* World Inequality Lab Study 2023/1.

Cloke, J., Mohr, A., & Brown, E. (2017). Imagining renewable energy: Towards a Social Energy Systems approach to community renewable energy projects in the Global South. *Energy Research & Social Science, 31,* 263–272. https://doi.org/10.1016/j.erss.2017.06.023

De Angelis, M. (2017). *Omnia sunt communia: On the commons and the transformation to postcapitalism. In common.* Zed Books Ltd.

De Angelis, M., & Harvie, D. (2014). The Commons. In M. Parker, G. Cheney, V. Fournier, & C. Land (Eds.), *The Routledge Companion to Alternative Organizations* (pp. 280–294). Routledge.

Deivanayagam, T. A., English, S., Hickel, J., Bonifacio, J., Guinto, R. R., Hill, K. X., Huq, M., Issa, R., Mulindwa, H., Nagginda, H. P., Morais Sato, P. de, Selvarajah, S., Sharma, C., & Devakumar, D. (2023). Envisioning environmental equity: Climate change, health, and racial justice. *Lancet (London, England),* 402(10395), 64–78. https://doi.org/10.1016/S0140-6736(23)00919-4

Euler, J. (2018). Conceptualizing the Commons: Moving Beyond the Goods-based Definition by Introducing the Social Practices of Commoning as Vital Determinant. *Ecological Economics, 143,* 10–16. https://doi.org/10.1016/j.ecolecon.2017.06.020

Feldpausch-Parker, A. M., Endres, D., Peterson, T. R., & Gomez, S. L. (Eds.). (2021). *Routledge Handbook of Energy Democracy.* Routledge.

Fereday, J., & Muir-Cochrane, E. (2006). Demonstrating Rigor Using Thematic Analysis: A Hybrid Approach of Inductive and Deductive Coding and Theme Development. *International Journal of Qualitative Methods, 5*(1).

Frick, V., Fülling, J., Harms, C., Grothmann, T., & Marken, G. (2025). *Umweltbewusstsein in Deutschland 2024: Kurzbericht zur Bevölkerungsumfrage.*

Giotitsas, C., Pazaitis, A., & Kostakis, V. (2015). A peer-to-peer approach to energy production. *Technology in Society,* 42, 28–38. https://doi.org/10.1016/j.techsoc.2015.02.002

Hardin, G. (1968). The tragedy of the commons. *Science (New York, N.Y.), 162*(3859), 1243–1248. https://doi.org/10.1126/science.162.3859.1243

Hastie, H., Dawney, L., & Butler, C. (2025). Warm spaces as commoning: Rethinking energy poverty beyond the private doctrine. *Geo: Geography and Environment, 12*(1), Article e70001. https://doi.org/10.1002/geo2.70001

Hess, C. (July 2008). *Mapping the New Commons.* University of Gloucestershire. 2th Biennial Conference of the International Association for the Study of the Commons, Cheltenham, England. https://doi.org/10.2139/ssrn.1356835

Hess, C., & Ostrom, E. (2007). *Understanding knowledge as a commons: From theory to practice*. MIT Press.

Holloway, J. (2010). *Crack Capitalism*. Pluto Press. https://doi.org/10.2307/j.ctt183p362

Hoops, B. (2025). Two Tales of the Energy Commons Through the Lens of Complexity. *Global Jurist, 25*(1), 1–34. https://doi.org/10.1515/gj-2024-0010

Islar, M., & Busch, H. (2016). "We are not in this to save the polar bears!" – the link between community renewable energy development and ecological citizenship. *Innovation: The European Journal of Social Science Research, 29*(3), 303–319. https://doi.org/10.1080/13511610.2016.1188684

Kaandorp, C., Moreno Pessoa, I. T., Pesch, U., van de Giesen, N., & Abraham, E. (2024). 'Commoning practices' for energy justice? Perspectives on the heat transition in the city of Amsterdam. *Energy Research & Social Science, 108*, 103369. https://doi.org/10.1016/j.erss.2023.103369

Lee, J., Byrne, J., & Seo, J. (2023). Re-imagining energy-society relations: An interactive framework for social movement-based energy-society transformation. In M. Nadesa, M. J. Pasqualetti, & J. Keahey (Eds.), *Energy Democracies for Sustainable Futures* (pp. 59–71). Elsevier. https://doi.org/10.1016/B978-0-12-822796-1.00007-3

Linebaugh, P. (2008). The Magna Carta Manifesto: Liberties and Commons for All.

McCauley, D., Ramasar, V., Heffron, R. J., Sovacool, B. K., Mebratu, D., & Mundaca, L. (2019). Energy justice in the transition to low carbon energy systems: Exploring key themes in interdisciplinary research. *Applied Energy, 233–234*, 916–921. https://doi.org/10.1016/j.apenergy.2018.10.005

Melville, E., Christie, I., Burningham, K., Way, C., & Hampshire, P. (2017). The electric commons: A qualitative study of community accountability. *Energy Policy, 106*, 12–21. https://doi.org/10.1016/j.enpol.2017.03.035

Nadesa, M., Pasqualetti, M. J., & Keahey, J. (Eds.). (2023). *Energy Democracies for Sustainable Futures*. Elsevier.

Oliver, T. H., Bazaanah, P., Da Costa, J., Deka, N., Dornelles, A. Z., Greenwell, M. P., Nagarajan, M., Narasimhan, K., Obuobie, E., Osei, M. A., & Gilbert, N. (2023). Empowering citizen-led adaptation to systemic climate

change risks. *Nature Climate Change*, *13*(7), 671–678. https://doi.org/10.1038/s41558-023-01712-6
Ostrom, E. (2005). *Governing the commons: The evolution of institutions for collective action* (17. print). *Political economy of institutions and decisions*. Cambridge Univ. Press. https://doi.org/10.1017/CBO9780511807763 (Original work published 1990)
Snyder, H. (2019). Literature review as a research methodology: An overview and guidelines. *Journal of Business Research*, *104*, 333–339. https://doi.org/10.1016/j.jbusres.2019.07.039
Sovacool, B. K. (2014). What are we doing here? Analyzing fifteen years of energy scholarship and proposing a social science research agenda. *Energy Research & Social Science*, *1*, 1–29. https://doi.org/10.1016/j.erss.2014.02.003
Sovacool, B. K. (2021). Who are the victims of low-carbon transitions? Towards a political ecology of climate change mitigation. *Energy Research & Social Science*, *73*, 101916. https://doi.org/10.1016/j.erss.2021.101916
Sovacool, B. K., Martiskainen, M., Hook, A., & Baker, L. (2019). Decarbonization and its discontents: a critical energy justice perspective on four low-carbon transitions. *Climatic Change*, *155*(4), 581–619. https://doi.org/10.1007/s10584-019-02521-7
Szulecki, K. (2018). Conceptualizing energy democracy. *Environmental Politics*, 27(1), 21–41. https://doi.org/10.1080/09644016.2017.1387294
Valgarðsson, V., Jennings, W., Stoker, G., Bunting, H., Devine, D., McKay, L., & Klassen, A. (2025). A Crisis of Political Trust? Global Trends in Institutional Trust from 1958 to 2019. *British Journal of Political Science*, *55*. https://doi.org/10.1017/S0007123424000498
van Laerhoven, F., Schoon, M., & Villamayor-Tomas, S. (2020). Celebrating the 30th Anniversary of Ostrom's Governing the Commons: Traditions and Trends in the Study of the Commons, Revisited. *International Journal of the Commons*, *14*(1), 208–224. https://doi.org/10.5334/ijc.1030
Vogel, J., & Hickel, J. (2023). Is green growth happening? An empirical analysis of achieved versus Paris-compliant CO2-GDP decoupling in high-income countries. *The Lancet. Planetary Health*, 7(9), e759-e769. https://doi.org/10.1016/S2542-5196(23)00174-2
Yang, S., Chen, W., & Kim, H. (2021). Building Energy Commons: Three Mini-PV Installation Cases in Apartment Complexes in Seoul. *Energies*, *14*(1), 249. https://doi.org/10.3390/en14010249

Zick, A., Küpper, B., & Mokros, N. (Eds.). (2023). *Die distanzierte Mitte: Rechtsextreme und demokratiegefährdende Einstellungen in Deutschland 2022/23*. Friedrich-Ebert-Stiftung.

List of Contributors

Stefan Gärtner (Prof. Dr.) is managing director of the Institute for Work and Technology at Westfälische Hochschule Gelsenkirchen. There, he is responsible for the research focus Spatial Capital. His academic work concentrates on urban and regional economies as well as on forms of urban production. He completed both his studies and his doctorate at Technische Universität Dortmund. https://orcid.org/0009-0006-3982-1916

Judith Terstriep (Dr. rer. pol.) is Head of the Research Department 'Innovation, Space & Culture' at the Institute for Work and Technology at Westfälische Hochschule Gelsenkirchen and a lecturer at Ruhr-Universität Bochum. She has extensive experience in innovation research. Her primary research interests focus on the interplay of innovation, social relations, and knowledge from the perspectives of innovation studies, management, and spatial theory, contributing to just transitions and societal change. https://orcid.org/0000-0002-1579-0469 Stefan Gärtner's and Judith Terstriep's introduction was co-authored by Benedikt Pühmeyer (https://orcid.org/0009-0002-3391-8726) and Inga Seiffert (https://orcid.org/0009-0003-3027-6411) who are research assistants at their respective research departments.

Marlen Reinschke is pursuing her doctorate in Philosophy through a binational Cotutelle de thèse at the Université libre de Bruxelles and the Europa-Universität Viadrina Frankfurt/Oder. She is a doctoral fellow of the Heinrich Böll Foundation. Her research interests include social and cultural philosophies, philosophical anthropologies, and critical theories. In her dissertation project, she examines Bruno Latour's ecologically repositioned ontology and his conception of *compositionism* as a practice of immanent critique. https://orcid.org/0009-0001-3546-4134

Philipp Schepelmann (Dr-Ing.), born in 1966, is Senior Researcher at the Wuppertal Institute for Climate, Environment, and Energy. He is associated professor at the Institute for political science at Wuppertal University. https://orcid.org/0000-0002-1776-7035

Christian Hein (M.Sc.), born in 1994, is a project manager for research and development at ENTEGA AG and e-netz Südhessen AG. Since 2023, he has been pursuing a doctorate in sustainability sciences (Dr. rer. sust.) at Darmstadt University of Applied Sciences on sustainability assessment and technology design using the example of overhead line-based road freight transport systems. He leads or has lead BMWE (formerly BMWK)-funded joint projects such as PAMAd, ELISA, CIRCULUS, and MobiGrid. His research focuses on electric road systems (eHighway), dynamic and stationary charging, grid-friendly flexibilities in the distribution grid, energy storage and the circular economy. His publications have appeared in EW Magazin, Netzpraxis, and Klima und Recht, among others (one article was listed as recommended reading by the Federal Council in 2023/2024). https://orcid.org/0009-0006-2536-0725

Michelle Alfers (M.Sc.) is a PhD student at the Chair of Macroeconomics at Ruhr-University Bochum. Her research focuses on the links between human needs, well-being and sustainable behavior, and explores their role in advancing a social-ecological transition. https://orcid.org/0000-0001-9184-9656

Elias-Johannes Schmitt, born in 1993, is a PhD student at the Chair of Macroeconomics at Ruhr-University Bochum, he worked as research assistant in the research projects ELEGANCY and CLARISA. In his doctoral research, he applies system-dynamic methods to modeling climate policy issues. https://orcid.org/0000-0003-4922-717X

Marvin Fendt (M.A. Social Work, M.A. Education) is pursuing his doctorate at the Department of Psychology at Ludwig-Maximilians-University Munich. In his research, he focuses on pedagogic interventions against misinformation and media education. https://orcid.org/0000-0002-3144-2851 Co-authors for his contribution are Fabian Reinwarth (https://orcid.org/0009-0003-2400-9771) and Peter Adriaan Edelsbrunner (https://orcid.org/0000-0001-9102-1090).

Carlotta Terhorst (M.Sc.), born in 1993, is a doctoral candidate at Johannes Kepler University in Linz, Austria. Her research focuses on the socio-ecological transformation and distributional dimensions of climate policy. https://orcid.org/0009-0006-8002-2366

Hannah Charlotte Müller, born in 1995, is a researcher in the Department of Environmental Sciences at FernUniversität in Hagen. With a master's degree in "Urban Culture, Society, and Space" from the University of Duisburg-Essen and a focus on critical urbanism, her research focuses on the sociocultural dynamics, participation, and empowerment within (urban) transformation processes—especially regarding the energy transition. https://orcid.org/0009-0007-0145-1865